In a Time of Trouble

IN A TIME OF TROUBLE

Law and Liberty in South Africa's State of Emergency

STEPHEN ELLMANN

CLARENDON PRESS . OXFORD

This book has been printed digitally and produced in a standard specification in order to ensure its continuing availability

OXFORD
UNIVERSITY PRESS

Great Clarendon Street, Oxford OX2 6DP

Oxford University Press is a department of the University of Oxford.
It furthers the University's objective of excellence in research, scholarship,
and education by publishing worldwide in

Oxford New York

Auckland Bangkok Buenos Aires Cape Town Chennai
Dar es Salaam Delhi Hong Kong Istanbul Karachi Kolkata
Kuala Lumpur Madrid Melbourne Mexico City Mumbai Nairobi
São Paulo Shanghai Taipei Tokyo Toronto

Oxford is a registered trade mark of Oxford University Press
in the UK and in certain other countries

Published in the United States
by Oxford University Press Inc., New York

Reprinted 2004

ISBN 0-19-825666-3

Cover illustration: May Day, Khotso House, 1985. Paul Weinberg, Southlight.

Remembering my parents

Richard Ellmann

Mary Joan Donahue Ellmann

Preface

No American who seeks to know South Africa is likely to be unaffected by the experience, for South Africa inescapably reminds its American observers of home. South African white rule reminds us of white rule here, not only in the heyday of the South's *de jure* segregation but also in the *de facto* patterns of power and poverty that remain in North and South. Visitors to South Africa, however, find not only oppression but also dedicated struggle against it. This book is an effort to describe one arena of this struggle: the efforts of some lawyers and judges to temper the outrages of apartheid through the use of the law.

Perhaps readers will not be surprised that what I found resembled, and reaffirmed, lessons I had learned in the United States. Before coming to Columbia I had the privilege, and the pleasure, of clerking in Atlanta, Georgia, for the Honorable Elbert Parr Tuttle of the United States Court of Appeals for the Eleventh Circuit, a judge whose courageous decisions have played a significant part in the battle against segregation and injustice in America's southern states. There are courageous and humane South African judges as well, though their role, as this book will reflect, is more constrained. From Atlanta I went to Montgomery, Alabama, where I practised law at the Southern Poverty Law Center. There, in civil rights cases of many sorts, I learnt a style of practice which was, in its way, quite traditional. We were, I would say, self-consciously professional rather than political, devoting our best lawyerly efforts to the wholly untraditional cases we took. I realize now that in South Africa I have come to know a group of lawyers who are pursuing a somewhat similar course, under much more difficult, and more morally chastening, circumstances. I have been moved by what I've seen, and this book is in a sense my explanation of the difficulty, and the value, of these lawyers' work.

Many people have helped me to become acquainted with South African law. I have had the pleasure of learning about this field while teaching on it with a series of South African lawyers who have been both instructive and patient: Dikgang Moseneke, Felicia Kentridge, Sydney Kentridge, Arthur Chaskalson, T. Lewis Skweyiya, and George Bizos. Arthur convinced me that I needed to visit South Africa in order to begin to understand it, and he and his wife Lorraine Chaskalson were inordinately hospitable in the course of the two visits I have now made to South Africa. In South Africa a great many people were very generous with their time and thoughts; some I will mention for other help in a moment but I am particularly grateful to Johann van der Westhuizen, Geoff Budlender, and Etienne Mureinik for all their assistance.

A number of people have read this manuscript, or parts of it, in earlier drafts and have helped to correct its errors (those that remain are my responsibility).

Some of them I have already referred to, but I also thank—among others—Rick Abel, Bob Amdur, George Bermann, Vince Blasi, Edwin Cameron, Martin Chanock, Marvin Chirelstein, Steve Cohen, Lori Damrosch, John Dugard, Hal Edgar, Gail Gerhart (who also provided me with very helpful news-clipping files), Kent Greenawalt, Lou Henkin, Karen Johnson, Tom Karis, John Leubsdorf, Jerry Lynch, Gilbert Marcus, Anthony Mathews, Eben Moglen, Henry Monaghan, Richard Neumann, Mark Osiel, Dick Pierce, Rick Pildes, Peter Strauss, Lucie White, and Mike Young. This book reflects what I have learnt from these and other people in ways too numerous to detail, but I will occasionally refer to specific debts in its footnotes.

Nadine Havenga translated virtually all of the Afrikaans materials which I use in this project. Without her diligent work on my many translation requests, I would have been unable to proceed with this project. Several Columbia law students have done valuable research for me (mostly in English), including Sara Corello, Jim Hennessey, Jon Klaaren, and Brad May. Lydia Levin and Ferial Heffajee of the Centre for Applied Legal Studies have also been very helpful, in the course of my research, as have Mark Bernstein, Phil Oxley, and others at the Columbia Law Library. My assistant Sally Otos has helped cope with the various burdens of the production of this manuscript, and Dr Murray Fisher prepared the index.

Columbia Law School and the Parker School have provided support for my work. I am grateful as well to the *New York University Review of Law and Social Change* for their editing of my article, 'Legal Text and Lawyers' Culture in South Africa', forthcoming in the Review; much of this article is now incorporated in Chapter 6 of this book, and I also thank them for permission to incorporate it here. Similarly I thank the *South African Journal on Human Rights* for permission to use here a revised version of 'Lawyers Against the Emergency', published in that journal, and the *Columbia Human Rights Law Review* for permission to incorporate brief passages from an article published there, 'A Constitution for All Seasons: Providing Against Emergencies in a Post-Apartheid Constitution.'

Nancy Rosenbloom, my wife, has discussed these ideas with me for years, edited my drafts, and given me much, much more besides.

Stephen Ellmann
New York, N.Y.
20 June 1990

Contents

Abbreviations

ABF Res. J.	*American Bar Foundation Research Journal*
Am. J. Int. L.	*American Journal of International Law*
Am. J. Leg. Hist.	*American Journal of Legal History*
Am. Soc. Int. L. Proc.	*American Society for International Legal Process*
Brit. JL and Soc.	*British Journal of Law and Society*
BULR	*Buffalo University Law Review*
Calif. L. Rev.	*California Law Review*
Cardozo L. Rev.	*Cardozo Law Review*
Case W. Res. L. Rev.	*Case Western Reserve Law Review*
Colum. HRLR	*Columbia Human Rights Law Review*
Colum. L. Rev.	*Columbia Law Review*
Duke LJ	*Duke Law Journal*
Harv. L. Rev.	*Harvard Law Review*
HRLJ	*Human Rights Law Journal*
HRQ	*Human Rights Quarterly*
Ind. LJ	*Indiana Law Journal*
Int. J. Soc. L.	*International Journal for the Sociology of Law*
J. Afr. Hist.	*Journal of African History*
J. So. Hist.	*Journal of Social History*
Law Q. Rev.	*Law Quarterly Review*
N.Ca. L. Rev.	*North Carolina Law Review*
NYU L. Rev.	*New York University Law Review*
NYU Rev. L. and Soc. Ch.	*New York University Review of Law and Social Change*
SAJHR	*South African Journal of Human Rights*
SALJ	*South African Law Journal*
Stan. J. Int. L.	*Stanford Journal Of International Law*
Stan. L. Rev.	*Stanford Law Review*
Tul. L. Rev.	*Tulane Law Review*
Tex. L. Rev.	*Texas Law Review*
U. Chi. L. Rev.	*University of Chicago Law Review*
UCLA L. Rev.	*University of California at Los Angeles Law Review*
U. Pa. L. Rev.	*University of Pennsylvania Law Review*
U. Pitt. L. Rev.	*University of Pittsburgh Law Review*
Va. L. Rev.	*Virginia Law Review*
Vand. L. Rev.	*Vanderbilt Law Review*
Wash. and Lee L. Rev.	*Washington and Lee Law Review*
Wash. ULQ	*Washington University Law University*
Wisc. L. Rev.	*Wisconsin Law Review*
Yale J. L. and Human.	*Yale Journal of Law and the Humanities*
Yale LJ	*Yale Law Journal*

Introduction

Can the rule of law preserve us from oppression? Or must the complex institutions of justice that we establish and nurture inevitably become mere bystanders, or even helpmates, to governments determined to rule by authoritarian or totalitarian means? Is the proud independence of judges only another vanity, to be blown away like gossamer by the winds of power? Or can legal institutions and traditions develop so deep an interweaving with principles of human rights that law's disciples will stand firm even when their neighbours and friends deny the force of these principles?

These questions echo through modern Western history, for courts have carried on the business of administering justice in the midst of some of the most unjust regimes we have yet experienced. Northern and Southern judges in the pre-Civil-War United States were called upon to enforce the laws of slavery; German judges continued to work while the Nazis used legal and extralegal means to pursue the Jews of Europe; Argentinian judges held office while the junta caused its opponents to disappear. So, too, South African judges have ascended the bench throughout the long decades of apartheid.

Like early astronomers trying to study the sun, those who seek to measure the value of the rule of law as a shield against such malign power risk being blinded by the sheer intensity of the injustice of the societies which they examine. Unlike those astronomers, moreover, we cannot rely primarily on data gathered during periods of eclipse—during those periods, that is, in which the potential confrontation between power and law is defused because government does not routinely resort to the instruments of oppression. Courts' loud assertions of concern for human rights during such calmer times, after all, may prove of little force when the pressure once again rises. We must look, therefore, directly into the light, and gauge the meaning of the rule of law at the worst of times.

This book undertakes that task by studying the lessons of South African law. In particular, it focuses on the response of South Africa's highest court, the Appellate Division of the Supreme Court, to the state of emergency under which the government sought to subdue anti-apartheid mobilization for almost five years, from 1985 to 1990. During the emergency the Appellate Division became the forum for an extended test, reflected in eighteen different decisions, of whether law could restrain state violations of human rights. This book examines how the Appellate Division fared in this test and why.

Answering these questions will help us to gauge and to explain the force of law as a restraint on injustice in South Africa. Doing so is important to an understanding of the South African legal system, and of that system's potential to serve as a support rather than an obstacle to the profound social changes needed in that country. This understanding in turn can help guide the shaping of a new South Africa, a process which seems, in 1990, at last to be under way.

Answering these questions for South Africa is also important to a broader understanding of the role of judges in an unjust society, of the extent to which those who preside in such a society's courts can hold and give voice to values opposed to those embraced in the councils of state. Similarly, our assessment of South African emergency law is important to an understanding of the role of courts in emergencies, a subject of sadly frequent significance not only in the new nations of the world but even in longer established countries such as the United States and the United Kingdom. These are questions of moral and sociological interest, but they are also of intensely practical significance: when we understand better what the rule of law has meant in South Africa, we can better assess the value and the wisdom of efforts by the victims of oppressive power, and their lawyers, and their sympathizers on the bench, to make use of the courts and the law to stand against injustice.

The Appellate Division in the emergency years provides a particularly vivid case-study of the value of the rule of law, for South Africa is at once a country of extreme injustice and of elaborate legality. South Africa lays claim to fidelity to Western legal ideals, and its lawyers and judges apply a law largely familiar to any lawyer of the Anglo-American world. Yet South Africa's modern, common-law courts confront truly massive violations of human rights, both those intrinsic to the long-standing injustice of apartheid and those generated by the special powers entailed in the state of emergency.

A state of emergency is no easy test of law's domain, for the idea that courts should employ the law to frustrate the plans of the government inevitably loses some of its lustre in times of real or perceived national emergency. Then the courts of a country are prone to become the country's courts—that is, to enlist or acquiesce in the state's battle against its enemies. There is nothing very surprising in this. Judges are citizens of their countries, and probably influential and established citizens as well; how could they not make common cause with their nation when they see it under threat?

But this quick suggestion of inevitability is misleading. Judges will make common cause with their country, we say, but what does that mean? We would hardly expect it to mean that courts of a democratic nation would simply declare the liberties of their citizens suspended *in toto* until the executive chooses to reinstate them. We don't expect this in part because we doubt that such steps are strictly necessary, even though total power undeniably has its uses. We also don't expect such a response from the courts because we think that the courts will continue to stand, however shakily, as guardians of the liberties of the country of which they are a part. So we are unsurprised by some invasions of human rights in times of emergency, but we assume that these invasions will be partial rather than total.

By now, however, we are adding expectations on to expectations. Surely it is possible to understand the behaviour of courts during emergencies more deeply than this set of assumptions permits us to. If we come to the study of a judicial system armed only with these broad and easy predictions, we cannot hope to understand why one decision does intrude on human rights while another does not. Nor can we hope to explain why a court at one point in an emergency might make one sort of decision, and at another point make decisions of quite a different cast.

It might have been thought that South Africa would shed little light on these problems. If the behaviour of the judiciaries of democratic states is hard to understand, the behaviour of South Africa's judiciary might be less puzzling, for South Africa is *not* a democracy. Instead, South Africa is a country ruled by a white minority who make up approximately one-seventh of the nation's total population. For more than forty years, in fact, South Africa has been governed by a single, white political party, which has had ample time to institutionalize its elaborate system of racial discrimination against a disfranchised black majority, and which has also had time to appoint every judge now on the bench. Moreover, South Africa has no Bill of Rights, no broad constitutional guarantees of human rights on the basis of which courts are empowered to strike down legislation. Given this background, we might assume that South Africa's judges would have little disposition to protect the rights of anti-apartheid protesters even in the best of times. And what could be more likely than that the white judges appointed by this white government—despite their protestations of fidelity to Western values—would accept the government's emergency assertion of special powers over a resurgent black opposition?

The reality is more complex. The conclusions South African experience suggests will not be cause for elation, but neither will they be cause for despair. The first step in developing these conclusions will be to demonstrate that South African law, despite forty years of apartheid and centuries of racial discrimination before that, does contain the doctrinal resources for significant judicial action on behalf of human rights. In this sense, South Africa is not an alien legal world, and South African experience bears on, and may be compared to, the experience of judiciaries in more just nations. To capture the ambiguous character of South African law will be the subject of the first two chapters of this book. Chapter 1 will discuss the constitutional framework of Parliamentary supremacy and the statutory edifice of internal security law which Parliament has erected in South Africa. Chapter 2 will study closely the doctrinal bases for human rights jurisprudence that survive none the less, and will argue in particular that the doctrines of statutory interpretation by which the South African courts essay to carry out the intention of Parliament actually reflect a distinct judicial reserve towards the legislature and give the judiciary considerable power to make the law while interpreting Parliament's acts.

Whether and why these doctrinal resources were mined during the state of emergency will be our next enquiry. In part, this will examine concrete and readily accessible data—the written judgments of the Appellate Division. Measuring the significance of these decisions, however, takes us on to more treacherous ground, for the cases' importance lies at least as much in the climate they contributed to as in the particular relief they granted or denied. Finally, explaining why the judges decided as they did is not an enterprise in which we can hope for complete certainty; we cannot read the minds of the judges. What we can do, however, is to set these decisions in the context of South African legal doctrine and legal culture, and so offer an explanation of these decisions that fits them into broader patterns of South African life.

Chapters 3 and 4 will examine the performance of the Appellate Division under the leadership of Chief Justice (and then Acting Chief Justice) Pieter Rabie. This is not an arbitrary focus. On the contrary, the decisions of the Rabie court form a group not only chronologically but also because they are the work of a small set of judges, chosen, presumably by Rabie himself, to serve on grossly disproportionate numbers of emergency cases. The Appellate Division during this period had an average of seventeen full or acting judges of appeal, but the court did not (and does not) sit *en banc*. Instead, five-judge panels decided each of the emergency cases. At least three of the five judges in every emergency case of this period were members of what deserves to be called the 'emergency team'. The team was composed of Rabie himself and four other like-minded judges, none of whom ever disagreed with one another on the result in any emergency case of this period. Five judges thus dominated a much larger court in the field of emergency law, not, it would seem, by force of intellect but by privilege of assignment. These assignments violated no law, but they tore at the ideal of judicial objectivity—an ideal South Africa has cherished.

Chapter 3 demonstrates the role of the emergency team and then turns to a study of the human rights claims that the Rabie court denied. These denials amount to a story of opportunities lost or forsaken. Under Rabie's leadership the Appellate Division rejected a series of legally well-founded challenges to emergency power, challenges for which doctrinal support in South African law could readily have been marshalled. No attack on the validity of an emergency regulation ever succeeded in South Africa's highest court (under Rabie or afterwards), and a cascade of decisions insisted on the validity of the state's emergency authority and shielded emergency power from close judicial supervision. Moreover, in the course of turning back these substantial claims the court repeatedly failed to articulate persuasive legal arguments, often relied instead on conclusory, even emotional, assertions, and on occasion simply ignored contrary argument. In addition, both in its results and in its own reasoning, the court revealed a marked disposition in favour of the executive. And on the rare occasions where judges outside the core group failed to concur in the majority's views, they did not sit again on emergency cases. Message and medium converged in these cases, to underline the sweeping, discretionary power which the state wielded under the state of emergency, and perhaps to feed into the pattern of endemic official lawlessness that characterized emergency-law enforcement during these years. Thousands of people may have suffered more as a result.

But this is not yet a complete picture. Even in the midst of this series of grim decisions there were other judgments which vindicated human rights rather than state power, and did so on the strength of doctrinal innovations that were hardly compelled. Chapter 4 turns from the rights denied by the Rabie court to those it upheld. The evidence—both from the few cases that were actually decided in favour of the victims of emergency authority, and from several other cases in which benign elements of South African legal doctrine were left relatively intact—indicates that even in the darkest period of the Rabie court's jurisprudence security concerns were not all-powerful. Though the broad reach of emergency power was not to be disturbed, particular aspects of the exercise of that power were not immune from scrutiny. In these respects, the Rabie decisions tell a story of boundaries being set.

These aspects of the Rabie court, as well as the grimmer and weightier features surveyed in Chapter 3, help us to understand this court's emergency perspective, and so to grasp the continuing significance of fidelity to law in the court's response to the emergency. Though the emergency team's domination of the panels in these cases itself tore at the fabric of legal norms, the judgments reflect a legal rather than lawless approach. The court's perspective included an executive-mindedness founded on its belief that South Africa faced a real emergency, its trust in the good faith of the officials dealing with this threat, and its sympathy for the difficulties faced by law enforcement officers. But its perspective also included attitudes which qualified its executive-mindedness: a determination to preserve a legal order in South Africa, a jealous guarding of the institutional role of the courts, and a genuine disapproval of abusive treatment by the state. As damaging as many of the court's decisions were to the protection of human rights through law in South Africa, therefore, those decisions reflect that the court held to the idea that law should set the bounds of state power. Perhaps this message too got through, and placed some drag, at least, on the security forces' movement towards wholly extralegal 'law enforcement'. If the court's modest legalistic message helped in some measure to keep South Africa from degenerating even further than it did towards rule by pure state terror, that was not a trivial accomplishment.

These two chapters, however, will tell us only about the Rabie court and in a sense only about the sentiments of the members of the emergency team. In Chapter 5 we will turn to an assessment of the decisions of the Appellate Division since Rabie ACJ retired in January 1989 and Chief Justice Michael Corbett took office. With Corbett's appointment, the cascade of decisions bluntly rejecting human rights claims came to an end, and the court began to render some decisions which were plainly meant to circumscribe the very powers which scarcely one or two years earlier the court had no less plainly meant to leave largely unfettered. For the first time the judgments of the court expressed intense and explicit concern about the impact of emergency power on fundamental rights. They demonstrated as well a willingness to make new and innovative law in order to protect such rights. And they reflected a new insistence on confining the powers of the state and a correspondingly diminished attention to the exigencies, as seen from the state's perspective, of emergency law enforcement.

None of this is to say, however, that the Corbett court has mounted a radical challenge to the core of emergency authority. Instead, analysis of the two cases in which the Corbett court has not granted relief suggests that the court has no inclination to challenge the fundamental executive assertion of an emergency. The court also has not rejected the generous grants of power to the State President to make regulations, and to lower officials to act under those regulations, which the Rabie era countenanced. Moreover, the court's human rights concerns may be more acute in some cases, in particular detention cases, than in other areas of emergency authority. Despite its willingness to innovate, finally, the Corbett court appears reluctant to alter too visibly or too quickly the work of the Rabie court.

Even with these important qualifications, however, the Corbett decisions attest to the continuing, or renewed, force of law as a constraint on state power in South Africa. Two immediate causes for the quickening of the court's human rights concerns under Chief Justice Corbett are apparent. The first is that the emergency team is no longer in place. The decisions of the Corbett court are, much more than those of its predecessor, actually decisions of the whole court, delivered by panels on which almost every member of the court has sat at least twice. This observation underlines the importance of the panel choices of the Rabie era, and the extent to which they undermined South African law's aspirations to fair and neutral process. But the same observation suggests that if the panels had not been chosen so systematically the Appellate Division might well have given a better account of itself during the Rabie years.

We must not speculate too quickly about what the court might have done, however, because of a second consideration: what the court has done under Corbett it has done in a South Africa that is different from the South Africa in which the Rabie court worked. South Africa's political changes during Chief Justice Corbett's tenure have been sudden and dramatic, as the National Party has moved to escape its endless confrontation with South Africa's black majority by adopting a policy of negotiation rather than mere subjugation. No doubt the courts have taken note of these developments. Thus we might say that when we look at the Corbett decisions we are no longer looking directly at oppressive power but are instead in a period of eclipse, in which any conclusions we draw must be guarded.

To understand the significance of the signs of fidelity to law that both the Rabie and Corbett courts reveal, we must place these decisions in a larger context. This is the focus of Chapter 6, which will trace the roots of these decisions in more fundamental features of South African law and culture. I will argue, first, that the Rabie decisions were not worse than they were—as they could have been—because of a long-standing acceptance among South Africa's ruling white population of the value of adherence to law. This acceptance has several overlapping sources. Law is a useful governmental tool, in South Africa as elsewhere, and has been put to much use there in the service of apartheid as well as of other governmental objectives. Law is also a potentially legitimizing tool, which South African whites may hope and believe enhances the state's standing in the eyes of foreign observers, South African blacks, and the white population itself. But adherence to law is not merely a matter of sophisticated calculation of self-interest. It is also a long-standing cultural tradition among South African whites.

These factors combine to make South African law a real constraint on government and courts alike. A tradition of adherence to law is not, however, a guarantee against lawless oppression—Nazi Germany proves that notion false. In South Africa, too, the grip of the law on white sentiment is hardly absolute, for adherence to law is far from the only principle which South African whites hold dear. But the force of this constraint may well have grown since the zenith of apartheid in the 1950s and 1960s, as the fires of Afrikaner nationalism, which might once have militated against the acceptance of law that threatened to interfere with Afrikaner authority, have now partially faded away. That the value of adherence to law made itself felt to the extent that it did, even in decisions dominated by the special segment of the Appellate Division that constituted the emergency team, is thus a measure of the considerable force of this value in the balance of sentiments in South Africa as apartheid appears to be grinding to its close—and an example of the potential salience of legal values in some, though not all, oppressive regimes.

The superior performance of the Corbett court, I will suggest, is the fruit of another tradition, long a part of South African legal culture but largely denied a voice in the Rabie emergency decisions. This tradition is a tradition of concern for human rights. This has not been the dominant concern in South African legal culture, but it has long been a salient element of that culture and it too seems to have gathered force in recent years. Several features of the structure of legal institutions in South Africa have encouraged lawyers to take up this concern, or at least have protected them when they did so. Anti-apartheid lawyers in South Africa have often been people of exceptional prestige. Moreover, the most prestigious portion of South Africa's divided bar, the advocates' profession, has long held to institutional structures and ideals that tend to encourage independence of mind on the part of advocates. A similar tradition of judicial independence, overlapping and expanding on that of advocates, also provides moral space for judges concerned for human rights. Finally, the cause of human rights in South Africa has been helped by the characteristics of human rights advocacy, for in South Africa—unlike the antebellum United States in its fugitive slave cases—courtroom advocacy has largely been couched in the dominant jurisprudence of the day and presented to judges in a decorous, familiar style which cushions against the danger of polarizing potentially sympathetic judges.

The upshot of the analysis in Chapter 6 is a confirmation of an old lesson: that law can restrain power, even deeply unjust and autocratic power. The emergency decisions of the Appellate Division do not display a concern for maintenance of a legal order, and later for protection of human rights, by happenstance; instead, these features of the court's decisions reflect elements of South African legal culture that the oppression of apartheid did not extinguish.

In addition, South African experience helps to clarify the conditions under which law can have this restraining force, not only in South Africa but in other countries as well. A society's adherence to law turns out to be important, and from this perspective society's use of law can be welcomed even when its roots are quite unedifying. Indeed, South African experience suggests how difficult it may be for a society to use law without also, in some measure, coming to value it.

Yet a general adherence to law does not ensure that law will be heeded in times of crisis. Widely felt political passions may trump or distort adherence to law, and South African events suggest the value of both political and legal responses to this danger. The political struggle against apartheid has continued for decades, during which the institutional and ideological supports for this system slowly unravelled; surely no strategy for protecting human rights can be complete without unremitting political struggle as well (and even then success cannot be guaranteed). At the same time, features of the legal system are important. The traditions of independence of lawyers and judges may well have shielded the South African courts from the full force of white passions. What South Africa did not do also points to the importance of law as a check on passion, for the failure to use the law to impose explicit constraints on the selection of Appellate Division panels opened the way for the emergency team. In a society facing this danger, more law can be part of the answer.

The law's endorsement of human rights is also important, but words alone are not enough. Instead, South Africa's experience reminds us that lawyers and judges can play a significant role in protecting such ideals. This is a role lawyers frequently claim they fill, and it is reassuring to find that these claims can have reality. But it is also important to understand *when* lawyers will act this way. While a full grasp of lawyers' contribution to liberty will emerge only as the result of broad comparative study, South Africa points to an intriguing, seemingly paradoxical, answer: that nurturing an élitist, individualist legal profession can be a way to secure broad, and egalitarian, liberty. Jurisprudence can also matter to the law's impact on human rights. Success in advocacy, as South Africa reflects, may depend on whether arguments for human rights can be and are put to judges in easily digestible form, or only in terms connoting doctrinal and personal outrage. South Africa suggests, then, that incremental jurisprudence, élitist legal institutions, and forthright, even radical, politics are not always alien to each other. On the contrary, they can be valuable companions in the struggle against oppression.

The analysis in Chapter 6, however, is incomplete. It tells us that the law can provide some shelter against state oppression, and identifies features of legal institutions, and strategies of lawyering, that can help law play this role. But this analysis does not yet address the intensely practical and intensely important question of whether pursuing human rights in the courts of profoundly oppressive states is a valuable strategy in light not only of its possible benefits but also of its potential costs. I turn to this question in Chapter 7, focusing not on the often discussed question of whether judges should resign—although my argument ultimately speaks to this issue—but rather on the question of whether lawyers opposed to apartheid, and their counterparts in other states, are wise to pursue emergency litigation as a method of struggle.

This is a question in part of lawyers' professional and moral responsibility, and in part of complex calculation of the consequences of the practice of emergency law. I will argue that lawyers opposed to apartheid cannot decide to pursue emergency cases, or any others, simply because would-be clients ask them to do so. Instead, they must inescapably shoulder at least some responsibility for choosing, on political and moral grounds, what cases they believe are worth bringing. But an assessment of emergency litigation points in favour of choosing to bring such cases. Even under the Rabie court, and all the more so under the Corbett court, emergency lawyers have been able to help their clients, modestly but genuinely, and through those efforts to provide some assistance to the broader communities and movements of which their clients have been part. These victories are not momentous but neither are they negligible. By contrast, the possible costs of this litigation, costs measured in terms of interfering with the progress of political challenge to apartheid, do not seem great. It is unlikely that lawyers' efforts have blunted the spirit of popular political mobilization and unlikely as well—despite the state's hopes for such a result—that emergency-law work lent a significant veneer of legitimacy to South African life in the eyes of most of its potential observers.

Moreover, the long-term political effects of emergency litigation, and anti-apartheid legal work generally, may be profoundly valuable. This is so even though such work may contribute to the legitimacy of the courts. To the extent that the courts are making genuine efforts to judge fairly and with attention to human rights, it is no loss, but rather a gain, if emergency litigation demonstrates this fact to the people of South Africa, for legal protection of human rights will remain important in a new South Africa. The litigation that has been brought over the years of the emergency may also have contributed to a new South Africa by maintaining a steady pressure on the judges of South Africa's highest courts to be or become the kind of judges a free country needs. We can already see the signs that the courts may be able to play a greater role in the months and years to come than they have in the past—

but this would have been less likely had they been held to a lesser standard until now.

Thus I maintain, in the end, that the enterprise of seeking human rights protection in the courts in South Africa has been well founded. Other strategies would have been possible, of more confrontational or Gandhian cast, but I will argue that lawyers had good reason to doubt that these alternatives would in fact be more productive. In general, therefore, lawyers were right to bring these cases; liberal judges were right to remain on the bench to hear them; and academic commentators were right to analyse sharply the many disappointments that the court's decisions have presented. I strongly suspect that the calculus this book performs for South Africa, moreover, will hold broadly true in many other countries as well. This is what the courageous struggles of human rights lawyers around the world suggest that they have concluded; this study of South African emergency law helps us to know why they are right.

1

South African Internal Security Law: Constitutional Framework and Statutory Designs

The sleep of reason brings forth monsters.[1]

It is quite possible to design a legal system—or at any rate a system calling itself 'legal'—which essentially brooks no opposition whatsoever. In Nazi Germany the penal code provided for the punishment of anyone who:

> commits a crime which has been declared punishable by the law or which deserves punishment according to the principles of a penal statute and according to the sound feeling of the people. If no penal statute can directly be applied to such crime, the crime is punished according to that statute whose basic idea is best fitted for it.[2]

The lawyers who represented those pursued under such laws were admonished that:

> Defence counsel is now closer to the State and to the community. He is part of the community of legal caretakers and has jettisoned his earlier role as partial advocate of the accused's interests. He who does not identify himself clearly and inwardly with this role, will never robe as a German lawyer, nor will he be ever allowed to enter the defence bench.[3]

The system of apartheid offers all too many echoes of Nazism, but South African law is not Nazi law. To take the measure of South African law, however, we must begin with its most chilling features: the constitutional framework which gives South Africa's Parliament, for which most South Africans cannot vote, virtually unchecked authority to work its will, and the statutes through which Parliament has exercised this prerogative. Not

[1] F. de Goya, *Los Caprichos* (1799), pl. 43 ('El sueño de la razón produce monstros').

[2] F. Neumann, *The Rule of Law: Political Theory and the Legal System in Modern Society* (Leamington Spa: Berg, 1986), 294 (quoting 'section 2 of the German Penal Code, valid since the law of 28th July, 1935').

[3] Quoted by H. Ostendorf, 'Strafverteidigung im "Dritten Reich"', 3 *Strafverteidiger* 120, 124 (1983), quoted and transl. in L. Fernandez, 'The Law, Lawyers and the Courts in Nazi Germany', 1 *SAJHR* 124, 131 (1985). For disturbingly similar formulations from modern Cuba and Bulgaria, see C. Fried, 'The Lawyer as Friend', 85 *Yale LJ* 1060, 1060–1 n. 1 (1976).

enjoys has been a dizzying array of laws, many of them devoted to specifying the elements of apartheid's stunningly inegalitarian segregation of South African life,[4] but others—our focus here—addressed to the manifold internal security tasks which the preservation of apartheid has demanded. These security laws not only authorize the declaration of states of emergency but also establish sweeping, and dangerous, state power even outside of periods of emergency. When we understand this complex of laws, we will be ready to ask in Chapter 2 how, despite the lack of constitutional checks and the presence of authoritarian statutes, South African courts retain significant zones of authority to regulate the power of the state.

A. Parliamentary Supremacy and the Constricted Field of Judicial Review of Legislation

The beginning of wisdom in this regard is to recognize that any limits on South African state power do not derive from constitutionally enshrined, judicially enforceable, human rights guarantees. South African constitutional law has embraced the doctrine of parliamentary supremacy with a vengeance. As long ago as the 1890s a constitutional crisis in the South African Republic, a short-lived nation dominated by Afrikaners, prompted the Republic's president, Paul Kruger, to denounce judicial review on the ground that '[t]he testing right is a principle of the Devil'.[5] To him, judicial intrusion on the legislature's sovereignty was divinely barred because '[t]he voice of the People is the voice of God'.[6] Despite these fierce words, however, nineteenth-century Afrikaners were of two minds about judicial review,[7] and the ascendance of the doctrine of parliamentary supremacy is also a heritage of British rule. After the National Party's electoral victory in 1948 brought Afrikaners into power in South Africa, Afrikaner lawyers and jurists sharply challenged the role of many

[4] For a detailed, though already somewhat dated, description of these laws, see J. Dugard, *Human Rights and the South African Legal Order* (Princeton, NJ: Princeton University Press, 1978), 24.

[5] Kruger's statement is quoted ibid. 24.

[6] T. Moodie, *The Rise of Afrikanerdom: Power, Apartheid, and the Afrikaner Civil Religion* (Berkeley: University of Calif. Press, 1975), 30: quoting, and explicating, Kruger's position.

[7] The South African Law Commission has recently asserted that '[t]he idea of unbridled parliamentary sovereignty is foreign to our common law. The 1854 Constitution of the Orange Free State is a much more faithful reflection of the philosophy of our common law than the Transvaal Constitution of 1858.' South African Law Commission, *Working Paper 25, Project 58: Group and Human Rights* (Pretoria, n.d., ?1989), 181 (emphasis omitted). In the Orange Free State constitution a number of human rights were guaranteed, and the Commission believes that judicial review of constitutional issues was provided for by statute. Ibid. 214–15. Whether the Commission's reappraisal of the true philosophy of South Africa's common law is accurate is open to doubt. See M. Chanock. 'A Post-Calvinist Catechism? Reading the South African Bill of Rights Debate' (unpubl., 1990), 11–12.

British doctrines in South African law.[8] But the principle of parliamentary supremacy was not rejected.

On the contrary, it became increasingly popular with the National Party. In good part the appeal of this principle stemmed from the government's reaction to temporarily successful efforts by the Appellate Division in the 1950s to exercise a power of judicial review of parliamentary action.[9] In two dramatic decisions, the court blocked the Nationalist-dominated Parliament's attempt to remove 'Coloured' voters in the Cape province from the common electoral roll and give them separate representation in Parliament, without mustering the two-thirds vote of both Houses of Parliament then required by the constitution for this segregation of the franchise.[10] At the time, Erwin Griswold praised these efforts as having 'provided two great landmarks in the field of constitutional law, and in judicial history, which will strengthen constitutions and the traditions of the bench in many other places'.[11] In South Africa, however, what followed was the expansion and packing of the Appellate Division,[12] and a final decision in which the court, with only one judge dissenting, permitted the government to work its will.[13]

The result of the embrace of parliamentary supremacy is that the present constitution of South Africa declares that 'no court of law shall be competent to inquire into or pronounce upon the validity of an Act of Parliament'.[14] There is, however, one qualification to this prohibition: the courts are in most cases 'competent to inquire into and pronounce upon the question as to whether the provisions of this Act were complied with in connection with any law' adopted under it.[15] Among 'the provisions of this Act' are a range of

[8] See Ch. 6, text at nn. 147–52; C. Forsyth, *In Danger for Their Talents: A Study of the Appellate Division of the Supreme Court of South Africa from 1950–80* (Cape Town: Juta, 1985), 220–4; E. Cameron, 'Legal Chauvinism, Executive-Mindedness and Justice—L. C. Steyn's Impact on South African Law', 99 *SALJ* 38, 50–1 (1982).

[9] See Dugard, *Human Rights* (cit. n. 4), at 28–34.

[10] *Harris and Others* v. *Minister of the Interior and Another*, 1952 (2) SA 428 (A); *Minister of the Interior and Another* v. *Harris and Others*, 1952 (4) SA 769 (A).

[11] E. Griswold, 'The Demise of the High Court of Parliament in South Africa', 66 *Harv. L. Rev.* 864, 872 (1953).

[12] The Appellate Division was expanded from 6 to 11 members, and Parliament provided by statute that constitutional tests of legislation would be heard before all 11 judges. Most of the senior members of the court appear to have resented the new appointees. One, Oliver Schreiner, 'was unhappy about the appointment of the five newcomers ..., not only because in the case of some of them he was worried about their having broken faith with their brethren, or been so foolish or egotistical as to think they had been promoted on merit, but also because he doubted their capacity and willingness to do the work of the court': E. Kahn, 'Oliver Denys Schreiner: A South African', in E. Kahn, ed., *Fiat Justitia: Essays in Memory of Oliver Deneys Schreiner* 1, 39 (Cape Town: Juta, 1983); for the attitude of Schreiner's colleagues, see ibid. 40–2.

[13] *Collins* v. *Minister of the Interior and Another*, 1957 (1) SA 552 (A). The lone dissent was by Schreiner JA, an eminent judge who was to be passed over for the position of Chief Justice and has been called 'the greatest Chief Justice South Africa did not have'. Kahn, *Fiat Justitia* (cit. n. 12), at 1.

[14] Republic of South Africa Constitution Act 110 of 1983, s. 34(3).

[15] Ibid., s. 34(2)(*a*).

procedural limits on Parliament's activity, and these the courts can enforce.[16]

It is tempting to try to read into this language a general power of substantive review as well. It might be argued, for example, that 'the provisions of this Act' implicitly establish requirements of just treatment of all citizens. One might find support for an implication along these lines in section 30 of the Act, which grants the legislature 'full power to make laws for the peace, order and good government of the Republic'.[17] One might look as well to the explicit declarations of the constitutions preamble, which articulates such 'national goals' as '[t]o respect and to protect the human dignity, life, liberty and property of all in our midst'.[18]

As we will see in Chapter 2, South African law *does* permit courts to imply the presence of unwritten statutory requirements—even requirements which violate the 'ordinary, literal, grammatical meaning' of the law—so long as these are justified in light of the courts' perception of the intention of Parliament.[19] But the greater the departure from the apparent meaning of the statutory text, the more difficult the implication will be to justify—and this would be a dramatic reinterpretation indeed. Certainly the fine language of the preamble will be of only modest assistance, for 'it is trite law that statements and declarations in preambles have very little constitutional significance'.[20] Moreover, the very history of acceptance of parliamentary sovereignty will weigh against interpreting ambiguous language to reshape the constitutional order.[21] In short, text and history combine to make it difficult to expect the courts to lay claim to a general 'testing right' under the present constitution, and so far they have not done so. In this sense, therefore, it must be said that 'judicial control over parliamentary enactments remains very restricted indeed'.[22]

[16] For example, laws dealing with 'general affairs' must be considered by all three of the racially segregated houses of Parliament, which represent whites, Coloureds, and Indians respectively, while laws dealing with the 'own affairs' of just one of these groups are handled only by the particular house in which that group is represented. Republic of South Africa Constitution Act 110 of 1983, ss. 30, 31. Similarly, certain portions of the constitution itself can be amended only with the approval of all three houses: ibid., s. 99. See G. Carpenter, *Introduction to South African Constitutional Law* (Durban: Butterworths, 1987), 359–60.

[17] Republic of South Africa Constitution Act 110 of 1983, s. 30. Johann van der Vyver assesses the import of this section in 'Judicial Review Under the New Constitution', 103 *SALJ* 236, 238 (1986).

[18] Republic of South Africa Constitution Act 110 of 1983, Preamble.

[19] *S.* v. *Tieties*, 1990 (2) SA 461 (A), at 463C–464F.

[20] Carpenter, *Introduction* (cit. n. 16), 357.

[21] See van der Vyver, 'Judicial Review' (cit. n. 17), 238.

[22] Carpenter, *Introduction* (cit. n. 16), 360. David Dyzenhaus has sketched the authority of Dworkinian judges in terms that suggest that such judges could—and actual judges of 'a bold Appellate Division' might—hold South African internal security statutes unconstitutional even in the absence of a textual authorization for such decisions. See Dyzenhaus, 'The Disappearance of Law?', 107 *SALJ* 227, 250 (1990). For now, however, this doctrinal stretch is only a hope rather than a reality.

B. South African Internal Security Statutes

The litany of South African statutes in this field is much too long for recitation here.[23] It is important, however, to have a sense of these laws. When we have sketched the profusion of statutory invasions of human rights, a profusion achieved primarily since the Nationalists took power, we will better understand the task which has confronted those judges who might wish to exercise their authority *in favorem libertatis*. We will be able to ask, in particular, how any non-statutory principles of liberty could survive such a legislative onslaught, the question to which we will turn in Chapter 2. Let us therefore sketch the features of this legal apparatus, as it stood during the emergency years.[23a]

The most conventional of South Africa's unconventional security laws may be those which permit detention and interrogation without trial. Perhaps the most notorious is section 29 of the Internal Security Act,[24] the modern formulation of a power first granted in the 1960s during the era when the government sought, seemingly with success, to crush organized black opposition to apartheid.[25] Section 29 permits detainees to be held in solitary confinement, virtually incommunicado, until 'the Commissioner [of police] orders [the detainee's] release when satisfied that the said person has satisfactorily replied to all questions at the interrogation or that no useful purpose will be served by his further detention in terms of the provisions of this section'.[26] This power is extraordinary, but not unique. Other provisions of the same Act allow the state to detain and interrogate trial witnesses until the trial is over, or for up to six months even if no one is ever charged in the case in question,[27] to make people charged with certain offences ineligible for bail,[28] and to use preventive detention of potentially unlimited duration[29]—and even this list is not exhaustive.

Arrest, detention, and interrogation, however, are only a part of the array of weapons by which the government restricts individuals' lives. South African statutes also permit the state to 'ban' organizations, gatherings, and even individuals. Banned organizations, as one might expect, become illegal; the government has wielded this power against such organizations as the African

[23] For comprehensive and valuable discussions, to which I am indebted, see A. Mathews, *Freedom, State Security and the Rule of Law: Dilemmas of the Apartheid Society* (Cape Town: Juta, 1986); Dugard, *Human Rights* (cit. n. 4), 107–202.

[23a] As this book was going to press, in June 1991, South Africa adopted major amendments to the Internal Security Act 74 of 1982, amendments which substantially cut back on many of the ferocious provisions of this Act.

[24] Internal Security Act 74 of 1982, s. 29.

[25] For an examination of the first incarnation of this authority in the 1960s, see A. Mathews and R. Albino, 'The Permanence of the Temporary: An Examination of the 90- and 180-Day Detention Laws', 83 *SALJ* 16 (1966).

[26] Internal Security Act 74 of 1982, s. 29(1)(i).

[27] Ibid., s. 31. [28] Ibid., s. 30. [29] Ibid., s. 28.

National Congress and the Pan Africanist Congress.[30] In addition, individuals who were members or supporters of such an organization prior to its banning can be included on what is known as the 'consolidated list', and subjected to severe restrictions which prevent them 'from being active or influential in the public life of the society'.[31]

Similarly, banned gatherings cannot legally take place. South African law permits the Minister of Law and Order to ban any gathering, or any type of gathering, at any place, at any time, and for any duration.[32] Nor has such power gone unused. All outdoor gatherings except sporting events were banned in South Africa from March 1977 through March 1991, unless permission for a particular gathering was obtained.[33] Magistrates, too, have a power to prohibit gatherings; any magistrate can, for example, prohibit 'every gathering in his district or [a] particular gathering or any gathering of a particular nature, class or kind' for up to forty-eight hours.[34]

The banning of an individual does not extinguish that person's life, but it can entail constraints so harsh that they amount 'to a civil death, and to a large extent a personal and social death, for the victim of the banning order'.[35] Anthony Mathews's catalogue of the 'typical' banning restraints imposed on the noted anti-apartheid cleric, Beyers Naudé, includes such features as

> a prohibition on attending any gathering of two or more persons; as a legal consequence of the ban on attending gatherings, a prohibition on the publication or dissemination of any speech or writing at any time made by him; confinement to the magisterial district of Johannesburg; a prohibition on entering areas designated for blacks, coloureds or Indians; a prohibition on entering the premises ... of various organizations, including broadly political organizations; ... a prohibition on taking part in the work of various organizations, including broadly political organizations; a prohibition on communicating with any other banned person; and, finally, an obligation to report to the police once a week.[36]

The targets of the state's wrath can also be prosecuted for a host of substantive offences, defined in stunningly broad statutory language. Sometimes, moreover, the state's task is further eased through statutory shifts in

[30] Section 4 of the Internal Security Act 74 of 1982 grants the power to declare an organization unlawful.

[31] Mathews, *Freedom* (cit. n. 23), 115. Mathews describes the procedures for and consequences of listing in detail, ibid. 110–15. Statutory authority for the listing of individuals connected with unlawful organizations appears in Internal Security Act 74 of 1982, ss. 4, 14(10), and 16.

[32] Internal Security Act 74 of 1982, s. 46(3). See Mathews, *Freedom* (cit. n. 23), 141.

[33] Ibid. 141 n. 377. The ban on outdoor political gatherings was allowed to expire on 31 Mar. 1991. See Human Rights Commission, *Human Rights Update, March 1991, 18.*

[34] Internal Security Act 74 of 1982, s. 46(1)(i). See Mathews, *Freedom* (cit. n. 23), 139–41. Magistrates are judicial officers below the Supreme Court, the court of general jurisdiction in South Africa. See Ch. 6, text at nn. 324–5, for a discussion of the institutional relationship between the judges of the Supreme Court and the magistrates.

[35] Mathews, *Freedom* (cit. n. 23), 125.

[36] Ibid. 124–5.

the burden of proof on elements of these offences.[37] It is, for example, a crime punishable by up to ten years in prison to 'advocate, advise, defend or encourage the achievement of any of the objects of [an] unlawful organization or objects similar to the objects of such organization'.[38] Ten years is likewise the potential penalty for anyone 'who advocates, advises, defends or encourages the achievement in the Republic of any of the objects of communism',[39] and 'communism' is defined to include:

> any doctrine, ideology or scheme ... which is based on, has developed from or is related to the tenets of Karl Marx, Friedrich Engels, Vladimir Lenin or Mao Tse-Tung, or of any other recognized theorist in connection with or exponent of those tenets, and which aims at the establishment of any form of socialism or collective ownership.[40]

In similar vein, it is 'subversion', punishable by up to twenty years' imprisonment, to seek 'any constitutional, political, industrial, social or economic aim or change in the Republic' by any of a variety of methods, including such means as 'crippl[ing], prejudic[ing], or interrupt[ing] ... any industry or undertaking ... or the production, supply or distribution of commodities or foodstuffs' or 'imped[ing] or endanger[ing] ... the free movement of any traffic'.[41] Even purely civil disobedience is heavily punished, for any person guilty of an offence 'proved to have been committed by way of protest against any law' may be sentenced to three years' punishment.[42] 'The effect is to convert a vast array

[37] For an eloquent attack on these and other statutory boosts to the prosecution, see S. Kentridge, 'The Pathology of a Legal System: Criminal Justice in South Africa', 128 *U. Pa. L. Rev.* 603 (1980). Although the Internal Security Act 74 of 1982 restored much of the traditional allocation of the burden of proof that earlier Nationalist laws had undermined, see J. Dugard, 'A Triumph for Executive Power: An Examination of the Rabie Report and the Internal Security Act 74 of 1982', 99 *SALJ* 589, 591–2 (1982), even this Act contains a long section of available presumptions in the state's favour. Internal Security Act 74 of 1982, s. 69. See nn. 41, 43 below.

[38] Internal Security Act 74 of 1982, ss. 13(1)(*a*)(v), 56(1)(*a*)(i).

[39] Ibid., s. 55.

[40] Ibid., s. 1 (definition of 'communism'). Amazingly enough, the original definition of communism, as enacted in 1950, was even more sweeping. Under that definition, as interpreted by South Africa's highest court, communism embraced 'any doctrine or scheme ... which aims at bringing about any political, industrial, social or economic change within the Union by the promotion of disturbance or disorder, [or] by unlawful acts or omissions'. Suppression of Communism Act 44 of 1950, s. 1(1)(ii)(*b*); *see R.* v. *Sisulu*, 1953 (3) SA 276 (A).

[41] Internal Security Act 74 of 1982, ss. 54(1)(*b*), 54(2)(*b*) and (*f*), 54(2)(*i*). A presumption makes proof of guilt easier: if it is proved in a prosecution for subversion 'that the accused has committed any act alleged in the charge, and if such act resulted or was likely to have resulted in the achievement of any of the objects specified [in the statute, such as the goal of bringing about constitutional change] ... it shall be presumed, unless the contrary is proved, that the accused has committed that act with intent to achieve such object'. Ibid., s. 69(6).

[42] Internal Security Act 74 of 1982, s. 58. This is another case in which the original statute enacted by the National Party was even harsher. That statute also provided for a potential sentence of 'whipping not exceeding ten strokes'. John Dugard writes that '[t]his Act succeeded in terminating the A.N.C. defiance campaign', a programme of civil disobedience initiated in the early 1950s. Dugard, *Human Rights* (cit. n. 4), 175.

of minor and technical offenses into major crimes if the accused had the requisite political motive.'[43]

There are, in addition, a range of restrictions on free speech and on a free press—besides the various laws already mentioned which so narrow the range of permissible speech and political activity. For example, statutes constrain what may be reported about the prisons, the police, and the military.[44] Another statute, the Protection of Information Act 84 of 1982, in the judgment of Anthony Mathews, 'punish[es] the unauthorised disclosure of virtually the whole range of official government information'.[45] In a different vein, broadly worded prohibitions against fomenting hostility between the races are on the statute-books; whatever the merits of such statutes in the abstract, in practice '[m]ost or all of the reported cases in South Africa refer to promotion of hostility against the white group'.[46] Meanwhile, publications other than newspapers—along with 'objects, films and public entertainments'—are subject to censorship for 'undesirability', moral or political.[47]

All of these provisions apply *all* the time. These laws are in some sense part of the 'ordinary law' of South Africa. The power to declare and govern in a state of emergency is a separate, additional authority, available under the Public Safety Act whenever the State President is of the 'opinion', in light of events anywhere in the country, that 'it appears that ... the ordinary law of the land is inadequate to enable the Government to ensure the safety of the public, or to maintain public order'.[48] In these circumstances, the State President has discretion to declare a state of emergency, lasting up to a year and renewable at the end of that period, and to promulgate emergency regulations. The scope of these regulations is very broadly defined, for the State President can

> make such regulations as appear to him to be necessary or expedient for providing for the safety of the public, or the maintenance of public order and for making adequate provision for terminating such emergency or for dealing with any circumstances which in his opinion have arisen or are likely to arise as a result of such emergency.[49]

Both the proclamation of a state of emergency and the promulgation of emergency regulations are shielded from judicial review by a 1986 addition to this Act. This amendment inserted what is known in South Africa as an

[43] Mathews, *Freedom* (cit. n. 23), 53. Prosecutions under this section are also supported by a burden-shifting presumption. Internal Security Act 74 of 1982, s. 69(8).

[44] See Dugard, *Human Rights* (cit. n. 4), 182–3; Mathews, *Freedom* (cit. n. 23), 150–60.

[45] Mathews, *Freedom* (cit. n. 23), 161.

[46] Ibid. 61.

[47] See Publications Act 42 of 1974, s. 47(2); Dugard, *Human Rights* (cit. n. 4), 195–6.

[48] Public Safety Act 3 of 1953, s. 2(1)(*c*).

[49] Ibid., s. 3(1)(*a*). As originally enacted, the Act provided that emergency regulations lost 'force and effect' if not subsequently approved by Parliament. By virtue of a 1986 amendment, however, regulations now lose their force and effect only *if* Parliament resolves to annul them. See Public Safety Act 3 of 1953, s. 6(*a*), as amended by Public Safety Amendment Act 67 of 1986, s. 2(*c*).

'ouster clause'. These clauses are common in South African security legislation.[50] Their apparent effect, as the name suggests, is to oust the courts' jurisdiction to review actions taken by the state. The Public Safety Act's ouster clause provides that '[n]o interdict or other process shall issue for the staying or setting aside of [any such proclamation or regulations, or certain other actions under the statute] ... and no court shall be competent to inquire into or give judgment on the validity of any such proclamation, notice or regulation'.[51] Whether the actual effect of this language is, or should be, the same as its apparent import is a question we will examine closely below; for now, it is important simply to add this provision to the catalogue of statutory restrictions on human rights.

The National Party secured the adoption of the Public Safety Act in 1953 'in order to put an end to a passive resistance campaign promoted by the African National Congress against discriminatory legislation'.[52] The threat alone—along with other laws—stopped that campaign, and the government actually employed its new authority for the first time only in 1960, after the Sharpeville massacre of sixty-seven black demonstrators by government troops.[53] That emergency lasted only 156 days, during which 11,503 people were detained.[54] The end of the emergency did not mark the end of draconian security measures, but it led to a change of tactics. Thereafter the government sought to avoid the international stigma, and attendant economic costs, entailed in emergency rule, and for this reason greatly elaborated the array of 'ordinary' statutory invasions of rights described above.[55] Using these extraordinary, ordinary powers, the white government maintained its domination of the black majority for the next twenty years.

While the National Party stayed on top, however, it did not succeed in simply maintaining the 1960s' *status quo*. Black opposition regrouped, catalysed by the black consciousness movement led by Steven Biko, and emerged emphatically in the Soweto uprising which began in 1976.[56] Again the government wielded its immense power under ordinary security legislation to suppress

[50] See e.g. Internal Security Act 74 of 1982, ss. 28(7) (ouster of jurisdiction to review regulations covering preventive detention); 29(6) (ouster of jurisdiction to review actions taken under provision for detention for interrogation, and of power to order the release of anyone so detained); 31(7) (ouster of jurisdiction over various aspects of detention of trial witnesses).

[51] Public Safety Act 3 of 1953, s. 5B.

[52] Dugard, *Human Rights* (cit. n. 4), 110.

[53] See ibid.; G. Gerhart, *Black Power in South Africa: The Evolution of an Ideology* (Berkeley: University of Calif. Press, 1978), 236–56 (desribing the Sharpeville shootings and the government repression that followed).

[54] Dugard, *Human Rights* (cit. n. 4), 110. Dugard notes that after the end of the national state of emergency, the government declared a separate state of emergency, based on different statutory authority, in the black 'homeland' called the Transkei. Applying almost exclusively to blacks, this state of emergency remained in effect for at least the next sixteen years, becoming, in Dugard's words, 'one of the forgotten facts of modern South African history' (ibid. 111).

[55] Ibid. 112.

[56] For a history of the black consciousness movement, see Gerhart, *Black Power* (cit. n. 53), 257–99.

its opposition by banning organizations, gaoling activists, and worse.[57] Yet again the victory was only temporary.[58] In 1983 South Africa adopted its present constitution, in which so-called 'Coloureds' and Indians were granted the franchise and their own houses of Parliament—though the system was carefully structured to preserve a white veto.[59] This putative reform of white domination was greeted with outrage by Africans, for whom the pretence of improvement underlined the fact of their continued disfranchisement. Popular opposition once again took shape, led by the United Democratic Front.

Perceiving itself again on the edge of a precipice, the government imposed a state of emergency in part of South Africa on 21 July 1985. Initially the government may have hoped that it would be able to dispense quickly with the embarrassing necessity of emergency rule, and less than a year after it was imposed, on 7 March 1986, the government lifted this state of emergency.[60] Meanwhile, the government proposed legislation to give it the authority to declare unrest areas, which essentially would be local states of emergency by another name.[61] Before Parliament passed this new legislation, however, the government decided to resort to full emergency power after all. Just three months after lifting the partial state of emergency, on 12 June 1986, State President P. W. Botha declared another state of emergency, this one applying nation-wide. A year later he renewed it, and a year after that, and a year after that.[62]

Not long afterwards, P. W. Botha left office, to be replaced as State President by F. W. de Klerk. De Klerk soon began his Gorbachevian moves to recast the South African political system. In the field of emergency power, he started in February 1990 by cutting back on the scope of emergency authority, in

[57] See Gerhart, *Black Power* (cit. n. 53), 312–16; A. Sparks, *The Mind of South Africa* (New York: Knopf, 1990), 301–3. The uprising began with a march by black school students, protesting against 'a government edict that half of all classes in black schools be taught in Afrikaans': ibid. 302. When 'police opened fire with live ammunition', they triggered a furious reaction in which violence ultimately 'spread to 160 different communities': ibid.

[58] See T. Karis, 'Revolution in the Making: Black Politics in South Africa', *Foreign Affairs*, 378, 384–9 (Winter 1983–4).

[59] The President's Council, the body empowered to resolve disputes between the three houses of Parliament, Republic of South Africa Constitution Act 110 of 1983, s. 32(1), contains 20 members selected by the whites' house—all of whom must be white—compared to a total of 15 selected by the two houses representing Coloured and Indian voters. Ibid., ss. 70(1), 71(1)(*b*). In addition, the State President selects 25 members, 10 of whom are nominated by the opposition parties in the various houses. Ibid., ss. 70(1), 70(2)(*a*). Meanwhile, the State President is chosen by an electoral college in which, again, the members designated by the white house of Parliament have an absolute majority. Ibid., s. 7(1)(*b*). The result is that the National Party, as the majority party in the white house of Parliament, has always been able to assure itself a majority on the President's Council. See generally H. Rudolph, 'Constitutional Law', *Annual Survey of South African Law 1983* 1, 5–7 (Cape Town: Juta, 1985).

[60] 'Human Rights Index', 2 *SAJHR* 252 (1986).

[61] Public Safety Amendment Act 67 of 1986, s. 4; see Public Safety Act 3 of 1953, as amended, s. 5A.

[62] See 'Human Rights Index', 5 *SAJHR* 261 (1989).

ways which I will sketch in a moment.[63] A few months later, in June 1990, he lifted the state of emergency completely except in one province, Natal.[64] Then, in October 1990, de Klerk ended the state of emergency in Natal,[65] although the 'independent homeland' of Bophuthatswana has retained its own, separate, state of emergency.[66] These are far-reaching changes, although they should not obscure the reality that the sweeping 'ordinary' security legislation is still in place. Moreover, in a distressing turn of events, the government has now declared what amount to mini-states of emergency, 'unrest areas', in a sizeable number of South African black areas, where violence between blacks has been intense. In these areas, as the government envisaged in 1986, it now wields quasi-emergency authority under a different name.[67]

All but one of the Appellate Division's emergency decisions examined in this book, however, were delivered before de Klerk began to cut back on emergency powers in February 1990, and the one exception dealt with events from long before then.[68] When we look at these decisions, therefore, we will not be looking primarily at the rippling effects of the new spirit of negotiation and change, but instead at the courts' response to emergency power when it was at its zenith. It is in such times as these, when the state asserts the most acute need and claims the most sweeping powers, that human rights are in greatest jeopardy, and the courts most sorely tested. To take the measure of the judiciary's performance in this period, and to draw guidance from that examination for other emergencies yet to come, we need to look briefly now at the kinds of powers which the government claimed for itself as elements of emergency rule.

In essence, the emergency regulations established a second internal security regime, covering the same sorts of fields as the ordinary laws described above but asserting even more complete power for the state. Thus, at the heyday of emergency power, emergency regulations greatly expanded the power to arrest and detain without trial. Under the regulations

> A member of a security force may, without warrant of arrest, arrest ... any person whose detention is, in the opinion of such member, necessary for the safety of the public or the maintenance of public order or for the termination of the state of emergency, and may, under a written order

[63] For a summary of the relevant changes, see text at nn. 84–9 below.

[64] See Proc. R. 96, *Government Gazette* 12523 (8 June 1990) (declaring state of emergency in Natal, and promulgating emergency regulations); Proc. R. 97, *Government Gazette* 12524 (8 June 1990) (promulgating 'security emergency regulations'); Proc. R. 98, *Government Gazette* 12525 (8 June 1990) (promulgating 'prison emergency regulations').

[65] Proc. R. 186, *Government Gazette* 12802 (18 Oct. 1990).

[66] See Human Rights Commission, 3 *Human Rights Update* (No. 9) 1 (Oct. 1990).

[67] See Notice R. 2062, *Government Gazette* 12722 (24 Aug. 1990) (declaring unrest areas and making regulations for those areas). The government's powers in unrest areas under these regulations are strikingly similar to many of those it formerly wielded under the states of emergency.

[68] The exception is *During NO* v. *Boesak and Another*, 1990 (3) SA 661 (A), argued on 20 Mar. 1990 and decided on 23 May of the same year. This case grew out of the banning of a Mandela birthday celebration in July 1988.

> signed by any member of a security force, detain ... any such person in custody in a prison.[69]

Such a detention cannot exceed thirty days, unless it is extended by the Minister of Law and Order. That official in turn

> may, without notice to any person and without hearing any person, by notice signed by him and addressed to the head of a prison, order that a person arrested and detained [under the section just quoted] ... be further detained, and in that prison, for the period mentioned in the notice or for as long as these regulations remain in force.[70]

Some 32,500 people were detained at one point or another as a result; an estimated 30 per cent were less than 18 years of age, and some were as young as 12.[71] While they were held, they were subject to interrogation[72] and reports of torture have been widespread, but another regulation provided that

> No person, other than the Minister or a person acting by virtue of his office in the service of the State ...
> (*a*) shall have access to a person detained in terms of this regulation except with the consent of and subject to such conditions as may be determined by the Minister or a person authorized thereto by him; or
> (*b*) shall be entitled to any official information relating to such person, or to any other information of whatever nature obtained from or in respect of such person.[73]

In addition, even after they were released detainees could be, and were, subjected to onerous restrictions like those of conventional banning orders.[74]

Other emergency provisions focused on organizations or activities rather than individuals. Emergency notices virtually banned a range of political organizations, including the United Democratic Front, and sought to shut down the political activity of the largest black union organization, the Congress of South African Trade Unions.[75] To cement the state's control still further,

[69] Public Safety Act, 1953: Security Emergency Regulations, Proc. R. 97, *Government Gazette* 11340 (10 June 1988), s. 3(1).

[70] Ibid., s. 3(3).

[71] N. Haysom, 'States of Emergency in a Post-Apartheid South Africa', 21 *Colum. HRLR* 139, 149 (1989).

[72] Public Safety Act, 1953: Security Emergency Regulations, Proc. R. 97, *Government Gazette* 11340 (10 June 1988), s. 3(6).

[73] Ibid., s. 3(7).

[74] Ibid., s. 3(8). People who had *not* been detained could also be subjected to such orders. Ibid., s. 8.

[75] See Notice No. 334, *Government Gazette* 11157 (24 Feb. 1988) (prohibiting 17 organizations, including the United Democratic Front, from 'carrying on or performing any activities or acts whatsoever'). 'Thirty-two anti-apartheid organizations' in all were so banned. Human Rights Commission, South African Council of Churches and Southern African Catholic Bishops' Conference, *Human Rights and Repression in South Africa: The Apartheid Machine Grinds On* (1989), 21. For the restriction on the Congress of South African Trade Unions (Cosatu), see Notice No. 335, *Government Gazette* 11157, s. 1 (prohibiting Cosatu from a wide range of opposition activities).

the regulations also provided that gatherings could be prohibited, areas closed off, and people even prohibited from wearing particular sorts of clothing.[76]

Still other provisions extensively controlled the press. It became illegal, for example, to photograph, without prior official permission, 'any unrest or security action or ... any incident occurring in the course thereof'.[77] Most information on security actions and on various forms of opposition activity could not be published or broadcast.[78] A host of 'subversive statements' could not be published, broadcast, written, or spoken.[79] Periodicals could be silenced altogether for periods of three to six months, and certain publications in fact suffered such penalties.[80]

In addition, the regulations sought to oust the courts from review of much of what was done in the name of the emergency. A broad immunity protected those who wielded emergency power from criminal or civil liability so long as they had acted in good faith.[81] Perhaps even more importantly, the regulations provided that 'No interdict or other process shall issue for the staying or setting aside of any orde[r], rule, or notice made or issued under [any of the emergency regulations] ... or any condition determined thereunder ...'.[82] Nicholas Haysom has concluded that:

> the emergency regime was primarily directed at severing forms of supervision over police conduct, undermining already attenuated structures of accountability, and allowing the security forces whatever additional latitude necessary to pacify the townships. The regulations were aimed at two things: an attack on legal accountability in the form of supervision by the courts, and an attempt to remove restraints imposed upon them by media scrutiny (i.e., by accountability to a broader international public). The aim of terminating any form of accountability is the most dominant and pervasive feature of the regulations.[83]

The February 1990 revisions of the emergency regulations eased the rigours of this regime in several important respects.[84] A number of these changes improved the lot of detainees: detentions without trial were limited to six months; detainees acquired a right of access to their lawyers and a somewhat qualified right of access to doctors not attached to the prisons; and a system

[76] Ibid., ss. 10(1)(*c*), 10(1)(*a*)(ii), 9(1)(*c*)(ii).

[77] Public Safety Act, 1953: Media Emergency Regulations, Proc. R. 99, *Government Gazette* 11342 (10 June 1988), s. 4.

[78] Ibid., s. 3.

[79] Ibid., ss. 1 (definition of 'subversive statement'), 5.

[80] Ibid., ss. 6, 7; see Human Rights Commission, *Human Rights Update, 1988 Review* 14 (n.d., ?1989) (reporting closures of three newspapers, the *New Nation, Weekly Mail,* and *South*).

[81] Public Safety Act, 1953: Security Emergency Regulations, Proc. R. 97, *Government Gazette* 11340 (10 June 1988), s. 15(1).

[82] Ibid., s. 15(3).

[83] Haysom, 'States of Emergency' (cit. n. 71), 147.

[84] These changes are concisely outlined by Lydia Levin of the Centre for Applied Legal Studies at the University of the Witwatersrand, 'Memorandum: Changes to Public Safety and Internal Security Act Proclamations After the State President's Speech Opening Parliament 02 Feburary 1990' (1 Mar. 1990): unpubl. memorandum on file with the author).

of advisers was established, with the mission of visiting and monitoring the lawfulness of treatment of detainees.[85] Other changes were part of the opening up of political life in the country: most of the emergency media restrictions were lifted,[86] and thirty-three restricted organizations were freed of their restrictions.[87] These changes complemented the earth-shaking decisions to unban the African National Congress, South African Communist Party, and the Pan Africanist Congress—changes which involved the application of the *ordinary* security laws of the state.[88] Yet it deserves mention that even in the midst of these reforms, the state also added a provision to the emergency regulations providing that the Minister's affidavit (or a document 'purporting to be' such an affidavit!) claiming that he took particular steps for authorized purposes 'shall, on its mere production ... be accepted as conclusive proof of the facts stated therein'.[89] This provision is a useful reminder that the new emergency regime was not a complete submission to the rule of law, or even to the rule of ordinary South African security law. While these regulations are no longer in force, the unrest area regulations carry over a number of features of the emergency's 'undermining [of] already attenuated structures of accountability'.[90] For example, the unrest regulations too contain a provision for treating purported ministerial affidavits as conclusive, as well as immunities for good faith conduct and a broadly phrased ouster clause.[91]

Finally, no survey of South African internal security measures can be complete without mention of those activities which, though clearly directed at the preservation of the state's security, do not have the sanction of law. These activities cover a wide range. Some of them are essentially part of the ordinary security law enforcement system, but a covert part; here we should place, above all, the recurrent reports of torture and sometimes inexplicable deaths in detention. Others lack even this degree of connection with legal boundaries. There have been repeated signs of police involvement in encouraging black vigilante attacks on black communities and leaders. There have also been notably professional bombings of the buildings in which activist groups have their offices. And there have been murders. In the past few months, remarkable evidence has come to light confirming what had long

[85] Security Amendment Emergency Regulations 1990, Proc. R. 18, *Government Gazette* 12287 (3 Feb. 1990), ss. 1, 2.

[86] The media regulations themselves were withdrawn in Withdrawal of Proclamation in Terms of the Public Safety Act 1953, Proc. R. 19, *Government Gazette* 12287 (3 Feb. 1990). Certain media restrictions, however, were inserted in the security regulations by the Security Amendment Emergency Regulations 1990, *Government Gazette* 12287 (3 Feb. 1990), ss. 3, 5.

[87] Public Safety Act, 1953—Order Under the Security Emergency Regulations, 1989, Notice R. 233, *Government Gazette* 12287 (3 Feb. 1990).

[88] Thirty-one other organizations were also legalized, bans on eight publications were removed, and it became lawful to publish the words of 225 people. Levin, 'Memorandum' (cit. n. 84), 4–6 (describing effects of Notices R. 229–32, *Government Gazette* 12287 (3 Feb. 1990)).

[89] Security Amendment Emergency Regulations 1990, Proc. R. 18, *Government Gazette* 12287 (3 Feb. 1990), s. 7.

[90] Haysom, 'States of Emergency' (cit. n. 71), 147.

[91] See Notice R. 2062, *Government Gazette* 12722 (24 Aug. 1990), ss. 11, 12(1), 12(3).

been suspected—that these murders are not just inspired by the climate of apartheid but are the direct work of agents of the South African government.[92]

These crimes form a backdrop for our study of emergency law, though our concern is not directly with them but rather with the courts' definition of the reach and limits of the law. Between 1986 and 1990, the state used its emergency powers, and the apparatus of the ordinary law as well, to seek once again to suppress black opposition. Tens of thousands of emergency detentions, the bannings of organizations, and thousands of criminal prosecutions under ordinary security laws[93] did in fact stifle much of the anti-apartheid movement—though never all of it. But the state's marshalling of legal powers did not go unresisted in the courts. Despite the doctrine of parliamentary supremacy, and despite the daunting array of bluntly worded statutory assertions of state power, lawyers brought a host of legal challenges to various aspects of the emergency system. Before we study the Appellate Division's response to these cases, however, we need to understand how such challenges could plausibly have been brought. In other words, we need to examine the doctrinal sources in South African law which made it possible for the victims of emergency power, despite all of the government's legislative activity, to invoke the aid of the courts in limiting the state's authority.

[92] For an overview of some of these events, see Human Rights Commission, *Information Manual M-1: Anatomy of Repression* (Dec. 1989), 8–9; Lawyers' Committee for Civil Rights Under Law, Southern Africa Project, *South Africa's Death Squads* (20 Sept. 1990). In the face of popular pressure, State President de Klerk designated a judge of the Supreme Court, Judge Harms, to serve as a one-person commission of inquiry into such crimes inside South Africa (similar crimes *outside* South Africa were not placed within the commission's purview): ibid. 16–17. Judge Harms's report sharply criticized a government agency suspected of responsibility, the Orwellian 'Civil Cooperation Bureau', but failed to find grounds for prosecution in all but two of over 70 unsolved murders which had been identified for the commission's consideration. See D. Ottaway, 'South African Judicial Inquiry Fails to Find Blame in Activists' Murders', *Washington Post* (14 Nov. 1990), A21, col. 1.

[93] According to a South African human rights monitoring group, 5,239 people faced trial on political charges in the period 1986–9. Probably very few of these charges were for violation of emergency regulations; in 1989 in particular only 9 out of the 534 convictions in such cases were for violating these regulations. Human Rights Commission, *Political Imprisonment in South Africa (Special Report SR-6)* (1990), 5–6. Of these 5,239 accused, only 1,172 (less than one quarter) were convicted. Human Rights Commission, *Human Rights Update: Review of 1989* 8 (Mar. 1990). The state's failure to secure more convictions may well have been one of the reasons that it found the emergency power to detain without trial so attractive.

2

Hurley's Case and the Doctrinal Basis for Human Rights Jurisprudence in South Africa

> The jurist has at his command a full rack of instruments of torture, called the rules of interpretation, enabling him to force the silent law into speech ...[1]

South African courts cannot test the substantive constitutionality of the Internal Security Act or the Public Safety Act or any other legislation passed by Parliament. Yet they are not powerless in the face of state instrusions into human rights, even when the state's defence of its actions rests on invoking one of the congeries of statutory provisions that authorize such intrusions. In fact South African law provides the courts with a range of grounds on which to limit such intrusions, even while acknowledging the principles of parliamentary supremacy. The most fundamental of these grounds is the power of statutory interpretation. Even a supreme parliament's laws must be applied in the courts, and to apply them the courts must interpret them. In this chapter I will look closely at the rules of statutory interpretation which the courts employ. I will argue that South African statutes in the fields of race and internal security do reflect an underlying intention to abridge human rights, but that the rules of interpretation embody a historic judicial reserve towards the actions of Parliament and not only permit but in some respects encourage judicial decisions in favour of human rights. Finally, at the end of the chapter, I will briefly take up the network of restrictions on the conduct of those who administer and enforce Parliament's laws, restrictions which such interpretive strategies have helped the courts to establish.

Our study of South African rules of interpretation will demonstrate that these rules provide the courts with quite powerful instruments for giving benign meanings to the seemingly grim intentions underlying South African legislation. That the rules of interpretation can have this effect is not because the notion of legislative intention is fictional. On the contrary, in South Africa (and elsewhere) it would be fictional wholly to deny the reality of such

[1] G. Radbruch, *Einfuehring in die Rechtswissenschaft* (9th rev. edn. by Konrad Zweigert, 1952), trans. and repr. H. Hart and A. Sacks, 'The Legal Process: Basic Problems in the Making and Application of Law' (Cambridge, Mass, tentative edn. 1958; unpubl.), 1409.

intentions. Nor do the rules have this potential simply because of the 'indeterminacy' of legal rules in general, although the manipulability of legal rules *is* a feature of South African legal interpretation.

Rather, many of these rules reflect, or can express, what two leading South African legal scholars, H. R. Hahlo and Ellison Kahn, have suggested may be 'an unconscious judicial antipathy to legislation in general, a wish for law to develop through the courts'.[2] The sources of this position will become more vivid when we look closely at South African legal culture in Chapter 6. As that discussion will suggest, South African courts have a longstanding, though by no means unqualified, tradition of concern for human rights, and an intertwined tradition of judicial independence. In turn, these sentiments probably stem in good part from South Africa's British legal heritage, and in particular from the historic efforts of British judges to keep their distance from, and maintain a check upon, the juggernaut of an unqualifiedly supreme Parliament. Although statutory law began its rise to ascendency in Britain in the nineteenth century, that period—a period when British law's influence over the developing corpus of South African law was great—was also a time when the image of judicial independence was accepted and celebrated.[3] It was also a period when the British courts were notably grudging in their statutory interpretation.[4]

Thus it does not seem coincidental that many of the doctrines in use in South Africa bear a striking resemblance to interpretive ideas now in fashion in the United States as elements of a conservative restraint on legislative power. Rather, this convergence reflects that these interpretive techniques are not so much intrinsically conservative as they are anti-legislative. In South Africa the law's fondness for literalism, its refusal to consider the bulk of legislative history, and its array of canons of interpretation all may contribute to a mode of interpretation that can generate liberal results far from the illiberal contemplation of Parliament's legislators—just as these tools can generate conservative results distant from the liberal objectives of American lawmakers. While vigilant legislators can take steps to correct these judicial deviations from their intentions, moreover, corrective measures can be costly in terms of time and public reaction, and even if legislators are prepared to bear these costs, the newly amended legislation will be subject in its turn to the same critical judicial interpretation.

Despite the availability of such tools, much of South African statutory interpretation has been far from vigilant in defence of human rights. These methods of interpretation do not compel courts to restrict legislative endeavours, and a reserved approach to legislation cannot automatically be equated with an unreserved approach to human rights. My point, rather, is that South

[2] H. Hahlo and E. Kahn, *The South African Legal System and Its Background* (Cape Town: Juta, 1968), 186.

[3] See M. Shapiro, *Courts: A Comparative and Political Analysis* (Chicago: University of Chicago Press, 1981), 107–8.

[4] See text at nn. 39–43 below.

African law does provide the tools for a rights-protective jurisprudence—and that South African courts, as we will see, do on occasion use those tools in just this way.

A. *Hurley* and the Character of Legislative Intention in South Africa

Both the importance of statutory interpretation and the availability of doctrines restricting governmental action are illustrated by a central Appellate Division decision of the 1980s, *Minister of Law and Order and Others* v. *Hurley and Another.*[5] *Hurley* was a challenge to a detention on the strength of section 29 of the Internal Security Act. This statute, as we have seen, was a fearsome tool indeed for the state, for it allowed indefinite, incommunicado detention and interrogation.[6] But while the statute was beyond legal attack, those who administered it were not—unless the statute made them so. Before we investigate the standards by which the conduct of those who enforce section 29 would be judged, therefore, let us examine whether it could be judged at all. This question was a very serious one in *Hurley*, because section 29, like many South African internal security laws, contained an ouster clause. This one declared that: 'No court of law shall have jurisdiction to pronounce upon the validity of any action taken in terms of this section, or to order the release of any person detained in terms of the provisions of this section.'[7] At first blush it is difficult to see how, in the face of this statute, the courts could claim any power to review detentions premised on this statute.

But there is at least one way out—if the courts want to take it. The escape is to reason that the ouster clause excludes the courts' jurisdiction only over action taken 'in terms of' this section. And when is an action taken 'in terms of' a statute? The answer would be that an action *purportedly* taken in terms of the statute in question, but actually based on a misapplication or misunderstanding or misuse of the statute, is not an action 'in terms of' the statute. As a result, the only government conduct immunized from review by the ouster clauses would be conduct that was validly undertaken in terms of the relevant statute. There was authority for this line of reasoning,[8] but prior to

[5] *Minister of Law and Order and Others* v. *Hurley and Another*, 1986 (3) SA 549 (A).

[6] See Ch. 1, text at nn. 24–6 above. June 1991 amendments to this statute significantly abridged this authority.

[7] Internal Security Act 74 of 1982, s. 29(6).

[8] See *Schermbrucker* v. *Klindt NO*, 1965 (4) SA 606 (A). *Schermbrucker* was a harsh decision handed down in the period of fear and repression following Sharpeville. The case held that a person detained for interrogation under a statute providing for detention without trial could not be brought to court to testify on allegations that he had been tortured. (For further discussion of this aspect of the case, see Ch. 4, text at nn. 30–59 below.) Three of the five judges, however, also expressed or concurred in the view that the ouster clause which appeared in the statute did not effectively divest the courts of jurisdiction to order the release of someone who had been unlawfully detained. See 1965 (4) SA at 623F–G (judgment of Trollip AJA, with whom Steyn CJ concurred); ibid. 613–14 (dissenting judgment of Rumpff JA).

Hurley it may not have been widely accepted.[9] In *Hurley*, however, this line of reasoning was authoritatively confirmed by the Appellate Division, South Africa's highest court.[10]

This ruling seems quite out of place with what we have seen of South African jurisprudence so far. Parliament is the supreme lawmaker, after all, and Parliament has acted. Moreover, the most popular South African formulation of the interpretive task of the courts affirms that it is the courts' duty to ascertain the intention of the lawmaker.[11] It is simply implausible to maintain that Parliament enacted an ouster clause with the *intention* to oust review only of those actions which were free of legal defect—the cases in which such review would be least intrusive on the activities of the security forces—and to permit such review in all other instances. In a country in which Parliament has so unmistakably and repeatedly intended to abrogate human rights protections for many or most of its people, fidelity to actual legislative intention logically should hamstring judicial efforts to protect such rights.

It might, of course, be argued that 'legislative intention' of the sort to which I have just alluded simply does not exist. If that were so, then of course the ostensible South African concern with discerning the intention of the legislature would be entirely vain, but equally there would be no basis for charging that courts endorsing benign statutory interpretations were in any way departing from what the legislature had in mind. It would remain important, though, to determine what elements of the rules of statutory interpretation tended to support such benign interpretations, and so the analysis to which I will turn shortly would still need to be carried out. If legislative intention is a reality, however, to close our eyes to it would mean that we missed a significant aspect of the legal reality of South Africa, and so we need to consider briefly the argument for the non-existence of intention.

Actually, the argument is not quite for the non-existence of intention. Rather, it might be claimed that Parliament always, or almost always, has no intentions as a body, *except* the intention of a majority of its members to pass the statute in question. 'Because legislatures comprise many members,' the argument would go, 'they do not have "intents" or "designs", hidden yet discoverable. Each member may or may not have a design. The body as a whole, however, has only outcomes.'[12] Legislation may be so weighted with

[9] See C. Plasket, 'Developments in Administrative Law in Regard to the Discretion of Arresting and Detaining Members', in N. Haysom and L. Mangan (eds.), *Emergency Law: Papers presented at a Workshop, Johannesburg, April 1987* (Johannesburg: Centre for Applied Legal Studies, University of the Witwatersrand, 1987), 17.

[10] The Appellate Division of the Supreme Court is the court of last resort in South Africa. The various provincial and local divisions of the Supreme Court constitute the court of general jurisdiction. Below the Supreme Court are the magistrates, who exercise limited, but still substantial, jurisdiction.

[11] See L. du Plessis, *The Interpretation of Statutes* (Durban: Butterworths, 1986), 35–6.

[12] F. Easterbrook, 'Statutes' Domains', 50 *U. Chi. L. Rev.* 533, 547 (1983). Richard Pildes has found similar imagery in recent opinions of the US Supreme Court. See Note, 'Intent, Clear Statements, and the Common Law: Statutory Interpretation in the Supreme Court', 95 *Harv. L. Rev.* 892, 900 (1982).

unprincipled compromises between opposing groups that the idea that it has any broad overarching purpose becomes quite fictional.[13] Or it may be that legislative choices are so influenced by whoever controls the order in which various options are presented for consideration that the legislators will wind up 'choosing' an option which actually is not the one which enjoys the greatest support among them.[14]

This radical scepticism is hard to square with the intuitive sense that legislation over time does tend to reflect dominant sentiments in a legislature.[15] There may be periods when that intuition is stronger or weaker, but who could look at, say, the race laws enacted by the South African Parliament during the heyday of apartheid and not sense that they expressed general sentiments about the relations between the races as well as specific agreement on particular words of statutory text? In principle, moreover, people who are capable of agreeing on a text are also capable of sharing an understanding of the text's meaning, and people who agree that a text should become law are capable of agreeing that an understanding of that text should become law as well.[16]

Such shared intention should be decidedly easier to achieve in South Africa than in, for example, the United States. We may grant that extensive agreement can become difficult to secure when legislation is, as in the United States, the product of dispute in a bicameral legislature by no means tightly controlled by one political party, and between that legislature and a president who need not be a member of the political party which enjoys a majority in Congress. In South Africa, however, the National Party has controlled both Parliament and the executive continuously since 1948, and has fashioned an allocation of power between the branches that seems designed to give effect to that party's will rather than to impose on its lawmaking efforts the constraints of a genuine separation of powers.[17] A South African political scientist has observed that

[13] See Easterbrook, 'Statutes' Domains' (cit. n. 12), 540–1.

[14] Ibid. 547. This, Judge Easterbrook argues, is a lesson of public choice theory. More generally, he contends, '[a]lthough legislators have individual lists of desires, priorities, and preferences, it turns out to be difficult, sometimes impossible, to aggregate these lists into a coherent collective choice'.

[15] It is also in tension with the social scientific findings of stability, rather than random unpredictability, in legislative behaviour. See D. Farber and P. Frickey, 'Legislative Intent and Public Choice', 74 *Va. L. Rev.* 423, 429–30 (1988).

[16] Richard Posner offers a different argument to a similar conclusion. He writes that '[i]nstitutions act purposively, therefore they have purpose. A document can manifest a single purpose even though those who drafted and approved it had a variety of private motives and expectations'. R. Posner, 'Legal Formalism, Legal Realism, and the Interpretation of Statutes and the Constitution', 37 *Case W. Res. L. Rev.* 179, 196 (1986).

[17] Although South Africa has had a bicameral or even tricameral legislature during most of the Nationalists' tenure in office, the multiple houses have generally posed only modest barriers to the National Party's legislative plans. When the Senate, the upper house of the bicameral structure, did prove to be an obstacle in the 1950s, the government responded with legislation which packed the Senate to the government's liking. J. Dugard, *Human Rights and the South African Legal Order* (Princeton, NJ: Princeton University Press, 1978), 31. The Senate's powers to block legislation were also restricted. G. Carpenter, *Introduction to South African Constitutional Law* (Durban: Butterworths, 1987), 253, and ultimately, in 1981, the Senate was abolished.

Nationalist members of Parliament are '[o]nly very rarely ... allowed to speak and vote in Parliament in a way that deviates from the party line. For any member hoping to gain promotion the conformity pressures are enormous'.[18] It seems all too likely, therefore, that South African legislation—especially legislation on such central issues as the structure of apartheid and its internal security defences—does express shared sentiments of the legislators.

If I am right that legislative intention does exist, and that the intentions underlying South African race and security legislation have been profoundly unjust, then statutory interpretation that seeks to limit the intrusions on human rights under these statutes *must* avoid being driven by these intentions. One way might be to adopt the position of Ronald Dworkin, who affirms the relevance of legislative intention but transmutes its meaning within his framework of 'law as integrity'. For Dworkin, the legislative intention to which courts should look does not consist of some common denominator of the opinions of the legislators but rather of that characterization of the legislation's purpose which puts that statute, and the rest of the institutional history of the community, in the best possible light.[19] On this account statutes, far from being 'negotiated compromises that carry no more or deeper meaning than the text of the statute declares', stem 'from the community's present commitment to a background scheme of political morality'.[20] The South African scholar Etienne Mureinik has employed such reasoning to press for legal interpretation that would hold Parliament to the humane principles that logically ought to, even if they factually do not, underlie Parliament's legislation.[21]

Ibid. 243. In the 1983 constitution, the legislature became tricameral, and thus the possibility for conflict between the separate houses again arose, but the significance of this possibility is much diminished by the structural assurance that effective control remains in the hands of the whites. See Ch. 1, text at n. 59, and n. 59.

Similarly, there has never been in South Africa the structural division between the legislative and executive branches that is so important to US politics and legislation. Until South Africa became a republic in 1961, the head of state was the English king or queen; the new republic's constitution 'merely substituted a symbolic State President for a constitutional monarch without changing the executive in essence in any way'. G. Carpenter, *Introduction*, 223. Parliament elected the State President. Ibid. Real leadership, meanwhile, resided above all in the Prime Minister, who was 'the leader of the majority party in Parliament': ibid. 226, 233. In the 1983 constitution, 'the roles of the former State President and Prime Minister have merged into one', ibid. at 293, under the title of State President. While this and other changes have made the State President's office a potent one, the State President is not directly elected by the people, but instead is chosen by an electoral college which Parliament selects. Republic of South Africa Constitution Act 110 of 1983, s. 7. Unsurprisingly, the majority party in the white house of Parliament can, and does, determine the outcome of this election.

[18] H. Giliomee, *Afrikaner Politics: How the System Works*, in H. Adam and H. Giliomee, *Ethnic Power Mobilized: Can South Africa Change?* (New Haven: Yale, 1979), 196, 201. Later Giliomee observes that 'in recent years. ... the party has increasingly usurped the functions of Parliament as the link between the electorate and the executive. ... Parliament still functions according to established procedure, but the debates have little influence on the course of legislation'. Ibid. 206.

[19] See R. Dworkin, *Law's Empire* (London: Fontana, 1986), 313–16.

[20] Ibid. 346.

[21] See e.g. E. Mureinik, 'Security and Integrity', *Acta Juridica*, 197 (1987); id., 'Fundamental

This is a difficult enterprise in Dworkinian terms because the South African institutional history is so deeply flawed that it may not be possible to give a benign account of it that even loosely fits the facts, as Dworkin maintains such interpretation must. 'The best interpretation may be a deeply skeptical one: that no competent account of the institution can fail to show it as thoroughly and pervasively unjust, and that it should therefore be abandoned.'[22] In this spirit, another South African interpreter of Dworkin, Raymond Wacks, has argued that the institutional history of South African law, which he equates to the institutional history of South African whites, requires judges faithful to their role to decide cases against human rights claims.[23]

No doubt South African legislators would assert to themselves and to the world, however, that they act out of good intentions and with the best interests of all South Africa's people at heart, and it may be that the lineaments of a benign institutional history can be traced in such sentiments.[24] Perhaps quite important aspects of a country's law can be cleansed through such a process of interpretation; Dworkin himself thinks it is 'not so obvious' that the Fugitive Slave Act was a part of *antebellum* United States law, properly interpreted.[25] Whatever the promise of this line of interpretation, in any case, it does not deny that South African legislators actually do hold the sort of grim subjective intentions which I have identified as the seeming obstacle to a liberal jurisprudence in that country. Moreover, while it is possible to discern intimations of a jurisprudence of integrity in South Africa, the conventional statements of the rules of South African statutory interpretation run on different lines—and it is to these that we need to turn.

B. The Interpretation of Intention

What these rules teach us is that 'the complex legal concept of the *intention* of the Act' is not the same as 'the *ambitions* of the government'.[26] The rules by which South African statutory interpretation divines or constructs 'intention' turn out to leave considerable room for judicial construction that departs dramatically from the legislators' wishes. This is not to say that the

Rights and Delegated Legislation', 1 *SAJHR* 111, 118–20 (1985). David Dyzenhaus, another South African scholar, is working on similar lines. See D. Dyzenhaus, 'The Disappearance of Law?' 107 *SALJ* 227 (1990).

[22] Dworkin, *Law's Empire* (cit. n. 19), 203.

[23] R. Wacks, 'Judges and Injustice', 101 *SALJ* 266, 272–8 (1984); see J. Dugard, 'Should Judges Resign?—A Reply to Professor Wacks', 101 *SALJ*. 286, 288 and n. 9 (1984).

[24] See Mureinik, 'Security' (cit. n. 21), 202.

[25] Dworkin, *Law's Empire* (cit. n. 19), 219, 438 n. 27. Dworkin has elsewhere argued that '[t]he general structure of the American Constitution presupposed a conception of individual freedom antagonistic to slavery', as well as other principles inconsistent with the Fugitive Slave Act. R. Dworkin, 'The Law of the Slave-Catchers', *TLS* 1437 (5 Dec. 1975).

[26] The quoted language is Lawrence Baxter's: 'A Judicial Declaration of Martial Law', 3 *SAJHR* 317, 320 (1987).

set of South African interpretive rules provides the courts with the greatest possible leeway to protect human rights; it may well be that some other set of rules would fit that task even better. Nor do I mean to argue here that the courts have vigorously availed themselves of the opportunities these rules present. On the contrary, their record has over the years been decidedly mixed, and this book will study a period in which South Africa's highest court seemed to stretch to avoid the opportunities or even invitations offered by these legal rules. My point here is only this: that these rules present opportunities, some indirect and awkward and some manifest and direct, for constraining legislative power. Three broad features of these rules combine to create this space for judicial manœuvre.

1. Literalism

The first of these is the continuing salience of interpretation focused on the literal language of the statute. The hold of literalism is on the decline, as we will see shortly, but its grip has not completely relaxed. South Africa inherited the English judicial fondness for this style of interpretation,[27] and as recently as 1968 Hahlo and Kahn observed that it was 'said to be the fundamental principle' that 'where the wording is clear its interpretation requires no more than the application of ordinary grammatical rules'.[28]

This rule, to be sure, was long subject to the exception expressed in what is sometimes called the 'Golden Rule':[29]

> that when to give the plain words of the statute their ordinary meaning would lead to absurdity so glaring that it could never have been contemplated by the legislature, or where it would lead to a result contrary to the intention of the legislature, as shown by the context or by such other considerations as the Court is justified in taking into account, the Court may depart from the ordinary effect of the words to the extent necessary to remove the absurdity and to give effect to the true intention of the legislature.[30]

But this exception has rarely been applied.[31] Indeed, the Appellate Division reiterated in 1990, in a case that *did* apply this proposition, that courts should do so only when they must: 'where this is necessary to give effect to what

[27] L. Baxter, *Administrative Law* (Cape Town: Juta, 1984), 313.

[28] Hahlo and Kahn, *SA Legal System* (cit. n. 2), 180.

[29] See *Caledonian Railway Co.* v. *North British Railway Co.*, 6 App. Cas. 114, at 131 (judgment of Lord Blackburn).

[30] *Venter* v. *Rex*, 1907 TS 910, at 914–15 (judgment of Innes CJ). For a quite similar, recent formulation, see *University of Cape Town* v. *Cape Bar Council and Another*, 1986 (4) SA 903 (A) at 913I.

[31] See Hahlo and Kahn, *SA Legal System* (cit. n. 2), 182; du Plessis, *Interpretation* (cit. n. 11), 109. For instances of the courts' resistance to claims of absurdity, see *Shenker* v. *The Master and Another*, 1936 AD 136 (A), at 142–3 (judgment of de Villiers JA); *Savage* v. *Commissioner for Inland Revenue*, 1951 (4) SA 400 (A), at 408G–410B (judgment of Centlivres CJ).

can with certainty be said to be the true intention of the Legislature'.[32] For, in the words of South Africa's present chief justice, 'it is dangerous to speculate on the intention of the Legislature ... and the Court should be cautious about thus departing from the literal meaning of the words of a statute'.[33]

It might have been thought that the acknowledged principle of fidelity to legislative intention would dictate a departure from plain meaning. Perhaps such erosion was inevitable, but it was not immediate, as the Chief Justice's words reflect. Instead, what the legislature intended could be equated with the plain meaning of the enacted words.[34] Lourens du Plessis, writing in 1986, comments that literalism and intentionalism have 'to a large degree intermarried',[35] and observes that: 'Most South African jurists will claim that the theory of literalism, in its crude and unmodified form, has to an extent become exploded in our law. However, under the cloak of intentionalism it is still alive and kicking.'[36] Let us consider, therefore, how literalism can operate as a protection of human rights.

That a plain-meaning rule can constrain the legislature may seem paradoxical, since the most obvious effect of such a rule is to constrain the courts. But contemporary American advocates of more textualist interpretation do convey an anti-legislative thrust as well. Thus Justice Scalia of the United States Supreme Court, suggesting that subjective legislative intention perhaps should not have become the focus of statutory interpretation, has argued that to depart from the text in favour of unenacted intentions is to move from a government of laws to a government of men. Moreover, he urges, reliance on legislative intention to determine the meaning of statutory language brings the legislature into the sphere of interpreting its own laws, a function Scalia suggests is the constitutional prerogative of those executive and judicial officials whose task it is to apply the law.[37] What the legislature wants to do, this reasoning suggests, it must *do*, and courts will not come to the legislature's aid if it has failed in or shrunk from its task. As another conservative American jurist has written in a related context, '[u]ntil the legislature supplies the fix or authorizes someone else to do so, there is no reason for judges to rush in'.[38]

[32] *S.* v. *Tieties*, 1990 (2) SA 461 (A), at 464A.

[33] *Summit Industrial Corp.* v. *Claimants Against the Fund Comprising the Proceeds of the Sale of the MV Jade Transporter*, 1987 (2) SA 583 (A), at 596J–597A (judgment of Corbett JA—as he then was).

[34] Du Plessis, *Interpretation* (cit. n. 11), 32 and n. 17.

[35] Ibid. 35.

[36] Ibid. 31.

[37] So Justice (then Judge) Antonin Scalia reasoned in an unpubl. address delivered in 1985 and 1986, 'Speech on Use of Legislative History', quoted in Farber and Frickey, 'Legislative Intent' (cit. n. 15), 454. This view is not unique to Scalia. For other expressions of a similar perspective, see W. Eskridge, 'The New Textualism', 37 *UCLA L. Rev.* 621, 647–8 and n. 101 (1990).

[38] Easterbrook, 'Statutes' Domains', (cit. n. 12), 550. Easterbrook is defending his proposed rule that 'statutes are inapplicable unless they either plainly supply a rule of decision or delegate the power to create such a rule'. Ibid. 549. Judge Posner, himself no liberal, criticizes Easterbrook's proposal, and comments that it 'might well reduce the effective power of the legislative branch'. Posner, 'Legal Formalism' (cit. n. 16), 198. Richard Pildes, perceiving a similar agenda, has linked

Literalism is an effective expression of such sentiments, for there are ample grounds for expecting that a literalist interpretation of statutes *will* undercut the effectiveness of legislation. First, it is impossible for legislators to spell out every detail of their intentions in words. The world is simply too complex for such extravagant elaboration. Indeed, it is hardly reasonable to expect legislators even to call to their own minds, much less write out, each of the results which they would agree—if asked—were within their statute's contemplation.

The American scholars Henry Hart and Albert Sacks, in their influential materials on the legal process, offer a striking example of this point, involving a British statute which forbade people to 'personate any person entitled to vote' at an election.[39] A British case held that this statute did not make it illegal to pretend to be a voter who, unbeknownst to the election officials, was dead, because such a person was no longer 'entitled to vote'.[40] If this was a hard case, then, as Hart and Sacks demonstrate, there were others as well.[41] Did each have to be addressed? No legislator could expect to achieve his or her purposes smoothly in the teeth of such highly, and narrowly, literalist judicial interpretation.[42] Those legislators who have to try will, we can predict, produce statutes notable for their prolixity—and that is what South African statutes are.[43]

Second, it is difficult and sometimes impossible for words read out of context to express dependably even those intentions that legislators do attempt to state with specificity. If language *can* convey meaning without regard to

the American resurgence of 'literalist doctrines of interpretation in the clear-statement model' to 'a vision of laissez-faire individualism as the embodiment of a "natural order"'. Note, 'Intent' (cit. n. 12), 911–12. (As I argue below, however, the anti-legislative quality of literalism can have conservative or liberal results. Judge Easterbrook himself has made a somewhat similar point. See 'Constitutional Law Conference', 59 *Law Week* 2272, 2282 (6 Nov. 1990) (reporting address by Judge Easterbrook).)

[39] Hart and Sacks, 'The Legal Process' (cit. n. 1), 1149–58.

[40] *Whiteley* v. *Chappell*, 4 LR–QB 147 (1868), in Hart and Sacks, 'The Legal Process' (cit. n. 1), 1149–50.

[41] For instance, the 'impersonation of another person who was enrolled as a voter but who has already voted'. Hart and Sacks, 'The Legal Process' (cit. n. 1), 1151.

[42] Hart and Sacks suggest that British courts' statutory readings so frequently disappointed the expectations of those affected by the statutes that 20th-century English social legislation sought to avoid 'the mercies of the courts' by restricting judicial review. Ibid. 1164. In a sense, it may not be correct to describe the vice of such interpretation as its literalism. Instead, the flaw of *Whiteley* v. *Chappell* may be the court's unduly narrow notion of what the literal text could mean. (I am grateful to Peter Strauss for this point.) Insistence on the supposedly evident meanings of a text and inattention to alternative possible meanings, however, are interpretive moves that fit well together, and so I would suggest that a 'narrow literalism' is a characteristic form of 'literalism'.

[43] See du Plessis, *Interpretation* (cit. n. 11), 3. A similar assessment of British judicial practice and legislative response was offered a century ago by Lieber, who saw judicial literalism as the cause of the 'tautology and endless repetition' in British statutes. F. Lieber, *Legal and Political Hermeneutics* (1880), quoted in Hart and Sacks, 'The Legal Process' (cit. n. 1), 1147. Lieber attributes the judges' interpretive stinginess to the 'British spirit of civil liberty'. Ibid.

context,[44] we cannot decide whether we are bound by such an acontextual meaning without asking such questions as whether the lawmakers intended us to read their words acontextually or whether acontextual readings promote a just legal system—and these questions are contextual questions![45] In any case, it is clear that context very frequently shapes the meaning of otherwise ambiguous or misleading words. A statute forbidding anyone to be near a bank after sundown may be a discouragement of bank robbery or it may protect people from drowning in rivers.[46] We know which meaning the legislators intended only when we look to the context. The more contextual data the reader ignores, and the more the reader imagines the interpretive task as acontextual, the more likely it will be that meaning will be lost.

Third, if judges bring to their putatively acontextual readings a set of conscious or unconscious preconceptions, then their misreadings will systematically tilt in the direction of those beliefs. To apply such preconceptions is, to be sure, to engage in contextual interpretation, but the rubric of fidelity to plain meaning does not make such latent contextual interpretation impossible. On the contrary, such impure acontextualism is most seductive when it is unconscious, when the judge's preconceptions insinuate themselves into his or her notions of what is plain without ever being so highlighted as to be subject to critical examination.[47] Clarity, like beauty, is in the eye of the beholder.[48]

Fourth, it is very unlikely that the legislature will be able to correct each judicial misapprehension of what its enacted statutes mean—whether the source of the misapprehension is a misplaced literalism or some other poorly calibrated interpretive tool. Important errors can be attended to, and South Africa's Parliament has on more than one occasion done so.[49] It may well be

[44] This is a disputed issue. Frederick Schauer has argued that 'meaning can be "acontextual" in the sense that that meaning draws on no other context besides those understandings shared among virtually all speakers of English', 'Formalism', 97 *Yale LJ* 509, 528 (1988). By contrast, Stanley Fish maintains that '[o]ne cannot understand an utterance without *at the same time* hearing or reading it as the utterance of someone with more or less specific concerns, interests, and desires, someone with an intention': 'Working on the Chain Gang: Interpretation in the Law and in Literary Criticism', in W. Mitchell (ed.), *The Politics of Interpretation* (1983), 271, 283. If so, then we might ask whether readers can discover or will inevitably invent this context, but we would not be able to imagine an 'acontextual' reading. In a similar vein, Richard Posner denies that any text can be understood merely from its words—and illustrates this by analysing the interpretation of the US constitution's requirement that the president be at least 35 years of age: 'Legal Formalism' (cit. n. 16), 187–8, 190–1.

[45] Indeed, Schauer's article, 'Formalism' (cit. n. 44), can be read as the formulation of precisely such a contextual basis for reliance on acontextual meaning. His argument that law can and perhaps should rely on rules meant to be read acontextually would indeed provide us with grounds for interpreting particular legal provisions as calling for acontextual reading.

[46] This example is Dworkin's: *Law's Empire* (cit. n. 19), 351.

[47] Cass Sunstein makes a similar point: 'Interpreting Statutes in the Regulatory State', 103 *Harv. L. Rev.* 405, 423, n. 65 (1989).

[48] See Dworkin, *Law's Empire* (cit. n. 19), 350–4.

[49] e.g. du Plessis describes Parliament's correction of the courts' assertion of a power to suspend sentences for certain drug offences: *Interpretation* (cit. n. 11), 38. For another example, see n. 55 below.

relatively easier for a legislature to keep the interpretation of its statutes on track if that legislature is as fully under one party's control, and as fully aligned with the executive branch, as South Africa's has been.[50] But correcting these errors may be politically costly (a point to which we will return later).[51]

Correction is also costly in most prosaic ways, for every national legislature has limited time, incomplete knowledge, and many responsibilities.[52] One of these limitations is on the legislators' grasp of the interpretive principles which will govern the reading of their laws. It is far from clear in the United States that legislators actually write their statutes with the rules of judicial interpretation in mind.[53] One American scholar says of assumptions that United States legislators are aware of the canons of interpretation and the other aspects of the legal background against which they act that '[e]veryone knows that these assumptions have virtually no basis in reality'.[54] While the National Party has had less need to compromise than American political parties, and so more room to select language that is precise and unambiguous, even South African legislators may not be close students of the rules of interpretation or of the other details of their legal environment. And the corrective legislation will itself be subject to interpretation, which may be no more in line with the legislators' intentions than the previous judicial response was.[55] Judicial errors of statutory interpretation are always correctable, but they will not always be corrected.

The result is that statutory lawmaking becomes a less valuable tool for working the legislators' will. In the United States, interpretation that has this effect may today coincide with a conservative political agenda. In South Africa, such interference with Parliament's statutory designs is potentially a liberal step, both because courts pursuing plain meaning will inevitably miss some part of what Parliament intends, and because courts so disposed might impute more benign 'plain meaning' than Parliament intended. Courts disposed differently, to be sure, may make statutes even more malign than they were designed to be, and I do not want to suggest that literalism is by itself a

[50] See Farber and Frickey, 'Legislative Intent' (cit. n. 15), 458, n. 130.

[51] See text at nn. 135–7 below.

[52] On the constraints under which legislators operate, see Easterbrook, 'Statutes' Domains' (cit. n. 12), 548–9; Farber and Frickey, 'Legislative Intent' (cit. n. 12), 458–9; Posner, 'Legal Formalism' (cit. n. 16), 198.

[53] See R. Posner, 'Statutory Interpretation—in the Classroom and in the Courtroom' 50 *U. Chi. L. Rev.* 800, 806 (1983).

[54] Eskridge, 'New Textualism' (cit. n. 37), 679; see ibid. 679–80 and n. 229.

[55] Thus, in *Ndabeni* v. *Minister of Law and Order*, 1984 (3) SA 500 (D & CLD) (Didcott J.), a leading liberal judge in South Africa described the legislature's response to an earlier decision which had limited the reach of the statutory prohibition on performing acts calculated to further the achievement of any of the objects of an unlawful organization. After setting out the amendment passed by the legislature, Didcott J. commented that '[t]he aim, one supposes, was to enlarge the meaning of the section beyond the limits set by the ... [earlier] decision. Whether this was accomplished, and if so to what extent it was managed, are questions I shall not explore.' Ibid. 507.

necessarily or strongly liberal mode of interpretation. It can, however, be of value.

A classic example of the potential liberal effect of literalist interpretation is the case of *Dadoo, Ltd. and Others* v. *Krugersdorp Municipal Council*.[56] *Dadoo* dealt with the effect of statutes which prohibited Asiatics and coloured persons from owning or acquiring property, statutes which Dadoo (an Indian) had circumvented by forming Dadoo, Ltd. and acquiring property through it. The lower court emphasized that in interpreting statutes courts 'must not confine ourselves to the particular words of a particular section, but we must take into consideration the whole Act so as to arrive at what exactly the legislature intended to prohibit'.[57] Doing so, the trial court concluded that this statute expressed the legislature's policy 'to prevent coloured persons from obtaining control over Transvaal land', and found Dadoo's scheme illegal as a breach of that policy. But the Appellate Division overturned this judgment. Denying that the statute embodied so broad a policy, one of the appellate judges declared:

> I can find no reason for imputing to it [the legislature] any intention other than that which is to be deduced from the words it has used ..., and it appears to me that to extend the restriction contained in that statute beyond its plain meaning would be in effect to legislate rather than to declare what the law is.[58]

2. Circumscribed Contextualism

Despite the continued emphasis on the importance of the literal meaning of statutes, South African law *has* increasingly embraced the principle that statutes must be interpreted in rather than out of context. In fact it is now, as South Africa's highest court recently put it, 'a well-known rule of construction that words used in a statute should be read in the light of their context'.[59] Even words that are clear and unambiguous on their face 'may require to be read in the light of their context ... in order to arrive at the true intention of the Legislature'.[60] These statements are not directly inconsistent with a predominant literalism, since a judge disposed to follow the 'plain meaning' of a statute may deny that the particular language in question *does* require such a

[56] *Dadoo, Ltd. and Others* v. *Krugersdorp Municipal Council*, 1920 AD 530.

[57] Ibid. 533 (judgment of Wessels J. in the lower court).

[58] Ibid. 555–6 (judgment of Solomon JA). The Appellate Division's reasoning was also shaped by a rule of construction, itself bearing little relation to the apparent subjective intentions of the legislature in this case, that '[i]t is a wholesome rule of our law which requires a strict construction to be placed upon statutory provisions which interfere with elementary rights'. Ibid. 552 (judgment of Innes CJ); see ibid. 555 (judgment of Solomon JA).

[59] *University of Cape Town* v. *Cape Bar Council and Another*, 1986 (4) SA 903 (A) at 914A.

[60] *S.* v. *Radebe*, 1988 (1) SA 772 (A), at 778F; see *University of Cape Town* v. *Cape Bar Council and Another*, 1986 (4) SA 903 (A) at 914D. The seminal judgment legitimizing contextual interpretation is the dissent of Schreiner JA in *Jaga* v. *Dönges NO and Another*, 1950 (4) SA 653 (A), at 662G–664H.

contextual reading,[61] or may offer an interpretation of the context that is shaped by his or her understanding of the plain meaning.[62] But a willingness to take context into account does open the door to an understanding of legislative intention more accurate than that fostered by literalism, and so can encourage the implementation of imperfectly expressed legislative ambitions to invade human rights.

Indeed, some of the most egregious decisions of South Africa's courts have been notably contextual in their approach. In *Moller* v. *Keimoes School Committee and Another*,[63] a unanimous Appellate Division upheld the exclusion of mixed-race children from a public school, on the ground that the children of a white father and a mixed-race mother were not, as the statute specified, of European extraction. While some of the justices asserted that the meaning of 'European extraction' was plain, at least in South African usage,[64] the well-known opinion of Chief Justice de Villiers declared that 'in construing a vague expression in a statute, like that of "European parentage or extraction or descent", the Court should endeavour to ascertain its popular sense and place itself as far as possible in the position of the authors of the enactment'.[65] After reviewing the history of white 'prepossessions, or, as many might term them, ... prejudices',[66] the chief justice concluded that it was 'certainly inconceivable that ... [the average legislator] would be a consenting party to an Act by which European parents could be compelled to send their children to a school which children of mixed origin can also be compelled to attend'.[67] In giving such weight to a context of racist prejudice, Chief Justice de Villiers uncannily echoed the notorious contextual approach of Chief Justice Taney in the *Dred Scott* case in the United States—though de Villiers, unlike Taney, was not pushing a highly controversial agenda on his white fellow-citizens.[68]

[61] This option would be quite consistent with the guidance of Schreiner JA in *Jaga* v. *Dönges NO and Another*, 1950 (4) SA 653 (A). Schreiner suggested that there was no difference of substance between an approach which resorted to the context only if the language was not plain, and an approach which looked to the context in every case, ibid. 664B, and he treated each as an accepted form of contextual interpretation, ibid. 662H–663A. For a critique of Schreiner's seeming acceptance of these two methods of interpretation as equivalent, see du Plessis, *Interpretation* (cit. n. 11), 107–8.

[62] See e.g. *Dadoo, Ltd. and Others* v. *Krugersdorp Municipal Council*, 1920 AD 530, 549–50 (judgment of Innes CJ). The judgment of Centlivres CJ in *Jaga* v. *Dönges, NO and Another*, 1950 (4) SA 653 (A), at 659E–660E has something of this flavour as well.

[63] *Moller* v. *Keimoes School Committee and Another*, 1911 AD 635.

[64] See ibid. 653–4 (judgment of de Villiers JP); ibid. 655 (judgment of Kotzé JP).

[65] Ibid. 643 (judgment of Lord de Villiers CJ).

[66] Ibid.

[67] Ibid. 642.

[68] The resemblance between these cases' arguments is striking, as Judge Higginbotham has noted: 'Racism in American and South African Courts: Similarities and Differences', 65 *NYU L. Rev.* 479, 507–8 n. 81 (1990). De Villiers CJ defended his reading of the school segregation statute on the grounds that: 'As a matter of public history we know that the first civilized legislators in South Africa came from Holland and regarded the aboriginal natives of the country as belonging to an inferior race, whom the Dutch, as Europeans, were entitled to rule over, and whom they refused to admit to social or political equality ... . These prepossessions, or as many might term them, these prejudices, have never died out, and are not less deeply rooted

Two other justices also made contextual arguments. One invoked the venerable 'mischief rule' of statutory construction, which permits a court to interpret a statute in light of the mischief against which it was directed,[69] and decided that 'there seems little doubt that what the Act was intended to remedy was the possibility of white and coloured children associating in the schools'.[70] And yet another found that compelling integrated education 'would, in the present state of our Society, disorganize the whole system and render it practically impossible for the educational authority to perform its statutory duties'.[71] As these various judgments and other cases as well reflect, an accurate rendition of the South African context could be far from beneficial to human rights.[72]

But South African contextualism is far from an automatic expression of the grim intentions of its Parliament, for two central reasons. First, South African contextualism is constrained by limits on the kinds of contextual material which the courts may consult. Of these, perhaps the most important for our purposes is that courts in South Africa are denied one crucial source of potentially damning contextual evidence: the bulk of the legislative history to which American courts commonly resort. Like their counterparts in Great Britain, courts in South Africa will not look at legislative debates.[73] Only in

at the present day among the Europeans in South Africa, whether of Dutch or English or French descent. We may not from a philosophical or humanitarian point of view be able to approve this prevalent sentiment, but we cannot, as judges, who are called upon to construe an Act of Parliament, ignore the reasons which must have induced the legislature to adopt the policy of separate education for European and non-European children.' *Moller* v. *Keimoes School Committee and Another*, 1911 AD 635, at 643–4 (judgment of Lord de Villiers CJ). Just over half a century earlier, in *Dred Scott*, Chief Justice Taney had argued that blacks could not be citizens of the United States on similar grounds: 'It is difficult at this day to realize the state of public opinion in relation to that unfortunate race [black people], which prevailed in the civilized and enlightened portions of the world at the time of the Declaration of Independence, and when the Constitution of the United States was framed and adopted. But the public history of every European nation displays it in a manner too plain to be mistaken. They had for more than a century before been regarded as beings of an inferior order, and altogether unfit to associate with the white race, either in social or political relations; and so far inferior, that they had no rights which the white man was bound to respect; and that the negro might justly and lawfully be reduced to slavery for his benefit.' *Scott* v. *Sanford*, 60 US (19 How.) 393, 407 (1857).

[69] This is the rule of *Heydon's Case*, 30 Co. 7a, 76 Eng. Rep. 637 (Exchequer 1584).

[70] *Moller* v. *Keimoes School Committee and Another*, 1911 AD 635, 648 (judgment of Innes J.). Innes J. turned to this point only after urging that the language of the statute was clear, or clear enough, to justify the same result. Ibid. 645, 647.

[71] Ibid. 651–62 (judgment of Laurence J.).

[72] Another important, and damaging, decision that shows at least a contextual flavour is *Minister of the Interior* v. *Lockhat and Others*, 1961 (2) SA 587 (A). This case found that the Group Areas Act, by which the National Party sought to increase and systematize the segregation of South African cities, not only authorized segregation but also, impliedly, authorized inferior treatment of one racial group, Indians, as compared to another, whites. The Appellate Division reasoned that: 'The Group Areas Act represents a colossal social experiment and a long term policy. It necessarily involves the movement out of Group Areas of numbers of people throughout the country. Parliament must have envisaged that compulsory population shifts of persons occupying certain areas would inevitably cause disruption and, within the foreseeable future, substantial inequalities.' Ibid. 602D–E.

[73] Du Plessis, *Interpretation* (cit. n. 11), 134.

1985 did the Appellate Division even go so far as to look at the reports of commissions of inquiry that precede the adoption of legislation,

> when construing the words of a statute which are not clear and unambiguous ... in order to ascertain the mischief aimed at, provided that there is a clear connection between, on the one hand, the subject-matter of the enquiry and recommendations of the report and, on the other hand, the statutory provisions in question.[74]

In a similar vein, courts which seek to shed light on legislative intent by looking to the circumstances under which the legislature acted are not to hear evidence; what they consider must be material of which they can take judicial notice, 'so notorious as not to be the subject of reasonable dispute'.[75]

Opposition to the use of legislative history is not necessarily political, and when it is political it is not necessarily rooted in liberal rather than conservative convictions. In the United States today, several conservative justices of the Supreme Court have made their reluctance to resort to legislative history clear.[76] The effect of this stance may be to block the efforts of those who control much of the making of legislative history—such as the Democratic, perhaps liberal, committee heads. But the impact of a disregard of legislative history is itself a matter of context, and in South Africa the effect of such

[74] *Westinghouse Brake & Equipment (Pty) Ltd.* v. *Bilger Engineering (Pty) Ltd.*, 1986 (2) SA 555 (A), at 562J–563A. A lower court case subsequently suggested that such commission reports could be considered in construing even language on its face free of ambiguity, *S.* v. *Nel*, 1987 (4) SA 276, 292B (O), overruled in part, on other grounds, 1989 (4) SA 845 (A)—but, as a South African critic points out, this same case declined to consider the Act's short and long titles as an aid to interpretation in the absence of a problem of ambiguity! Ibid. 288; see G. Devenish, 'An Ambivalent Approach to Contextual Interpretation', 105 *SALJ* 199 (1988). For a precursor to the *Westinghouse Brake* rule, permitting reference to the events leading to the passage of a 'constitutional Act' (that is, an Act establishing part of the constitution of a country), see *Harris and Others* v. *Minister of the Interior and Another*, 1952 (2) SA 428 (A) at 456H–457C.

[75] See du Plessis, *Interpretation* (cit. n. 11), 133. The quoted language is from *United Democratic Front* v. *State President*, 1987 (3) SA 296 (N), at 306–7, overruled on other grounds in *Staatspresident en Andore* v. *United Democratic Front en 'n Ander*, 1988 (4) SA 830 (A). (Acting Chief Justice Rabie did not question the correctness of the views of the lower court on this point, although he did seem to feel that the evidence at issue in this case might have been admissible. He may have meant that this evidence would have helped to justify, rather than to interpret, the regulations. Ibid. 843D–F.) Of course, what is notorious to one judge may be sheer speculation to another. For a state-of-emergency case asserting that courts could take judicial notice that 'for many a month this domestic turbulence has been accompanied and intensified by a mounting political, psychological, socio-economic and terror onslaught upon the Republic of South Africa from beyond its borders', see *Bloem and Another* v. *State President and Others*, 1986 (4) SA 1064 (O), at 1067H, 1068B.

[76] e.g. Justice Kennedy, joined by Chief Justice Rehnquist and Justice O'Connor, recently argued against 'rummag[ing] through unauthoritative materials to consult the spirit of the legislation' where the statutory language is plain and its results are not 'patently absurd'. *Public Citizen* v. *US Dept. of Justice*, 105 L.Ed. 2d 377, 403–4 (1989) (opinion of Kennedy J., concurring in the judgment). (The majority, however, 'explicitly reject[ed]' this limitation on the use of legislative history: ibid. 391 n. 9 (majority opinion of Brennan J.).) Justice Scalia has expressed a view very similar to Justice Kennedy's, see *Immigration and Naturalization Service* v. *Cardoza-Fonseca*, 480 US 421, 452 (1987) (Scalia J., concurring in the judgment).

judicial blinkering may be to shield the courts from cogent evidence of the malign intentions underlying pieces of legislation.

This statement, to be sure, assumes that what legislators say in the course of passing legislation does offer genuine guidance about their intentions. That is a controversial position, of course, and not automatically or always correct.[77] A government which can rely confidently on the votes of its supporters—as South Africa's can[78]—might prefer to speak in code, knowing that the faithful will interpret or acquiesce. In such circumstances the parliamentary debates might clothe the ruthless provisions of proposed laws with gentler language, and courts unable to invoke legislative history will be unable to read the resultant statutes in light of these protestations. (The courts will also be unable to consider *sincere* statements of benign intentions, where those are offered.)[79] But what the parliamentary leaders say will at least represent what the ruling party wishes to have heard. As Hahlo and Kahn observe, 'with a system of responsible Government, where the Cabinet's wishes are given expression to by the majority of the lower House at least, surely the speeches of the Minister piloting the Bill are expressive of the House's intention'.[80] If those in the majority are confident of their control of the process, and if they are unashamed of their enterprise, their actual intentions may then come through quite clearly. Wherever this is the case, the impact of the exclusion of legislative history is to blunt the courts' awareness of the legislature's intention to interfere with human rights.

Contextual interpretation can become a force for human rights decisions in South Africa in a second way as well: the task of determining what the context means provides the opportunity for an interpretation that characterizes the background as supporting rather than undermining human rights claims. After all, the determination of purpose from context calls for the exercise of judgement. Contexts 'do not announce themselves',[81] and although ignoring context can lead to misunderstanding, the sheer multiplication of data involved in looking to context can also complicate, and even confuse, the task of

[77] For a discussion and criticism of the attack on legislative history mounted by Justice Anonin Scalia, see Farber and Frickey, 'Legislative Intent' (cit. n. 15), 437–52. They maintain that '[l]egislative history is, after all, merely evidence of intent. That it may not be perfectly reliable evidence is no reason to exclude it from consideration entirely. ... Thus, although legislative history should not be the starting point nor the end of the interpretive process, it is a legitimate part of it.' Ibid. 448.

[78] See text at nn. 17–18 above, and accompanying notes.

[79] For a distressing example of judicial inattention to what appears to be a relatively benign legislative history, see G. Budlender, 'On Citizenship and Residence Rights: Taking Words Seriously', 5 *SAJHR* 37, 56–8 (1989).

[80] Hahlo and Kahn, *SA Legal System* (cit. n. 1), 185. (The reference to the 'lower House' reflects the bicameral Parliament which South Africa had when Hahlo and Kahn wrote.) Hahlo and Kahn recite the reasons for denying that legislative history sheds light on legislative intent, but find some of them 'not very impressive', and conclude that '[t]he criticisms go rather to the weight to be given to this material than the legitimacy of using it'. Ibid. at 184, 185.

[81] Fish, 'Chain Gang' (cit. n. 44), 277. Fish is speaking of 'similarities' between cases, but his point seems equally applicable to 'contexts' of all sorts.

interpretation. Meanings might be still less plain, and courts still more empowered, if the accepted sources of contextual information were expanded to include legislative history—though not if, as is clearly possible in South Africa, the new information proved all too clear in its implications.[82] Even a circumscribed inquiry into context, however, calls for interpretation of considerably more than just the statute's text. Just as courts could bring their predispositions to bear in the reading of plain words, so, and all the more so, they can bring these leanings to the understanding of context.[83]

Notable examples exist of contextual readings which have discerned benign, or at least less malign, legislative purposes in language that could easily have been read quite differently. In *R.* v. *Detody*,[84] for instance, the Appellate Division construed a statute requiring '[a]ny native' to carry a pass at night, and defining 'native' to include 'every person belonging to any of the aboriginal races or tribes', as actually not requiring African women to carry passes. Two of the majority justices had no hesitation in considering 'person' an ambiguous word,[85] whose meaning they resolved by looking to such contextual factors as prior legislation and the mischief against which the law appeared to be directed.[86] John Dugard, a leading liberal critic of South African jurisprudence, has commented that 'it is difficult not to sympathize with the findings of the Transvaal Provincial Division and the dissenting judges of appeal that the words of the statute were sufficiently clear to preclude any departure from their literal meaning'.[87]

Such interpretive freedom can readily be criticized for enabling courts to depart from the actual intention of the legislature. In the caustic words of Justice Kennedy of the United States Supreme Court, '[t]he problem with spirits

[82] Even where legislative histories do not speak with special clarity, including legislative history in the materials which courts consult for statutory interpretation might limit rather than expand judicial freedom, despite expanding the range of data that courts could interpret. As William Eskridge writes, 'it is mildly counterintuitive that an approach asking a court to consider materials generated by the legislative process [that is, legislative history], in addition to statutory text (also generated by the legislative process), canons of construction (generated by the judicial process), and statutory precedents (also generated by the judicial process), leaves the court with *more* discretion than an approach that just considers the latter three sources'. Eskridge, 'New Textualism' (cit. n. 37), 674–5.

[83] Etienne Mureinik has commented that '[m]uch in the case law that masquerades as literalism is a disguised value coherence .... It is equally true that much of what is superficially purposive can be justified on value-coherent grounds. And that is true especially because the identification of the purpose of a statute is itself frequently determined, though often unconsciously, by value considerations.' Mureinik, 'Administrative Law in South Africa', 103 *SALJ* 615, 625 (1986).

[84] *R.* v. *Detody*, 1926 AD 198.

[85] Ibid. 202 (judgment of Innes CJ); 212 (judgment of Solomon JA). The third justice in the majority only went so far as to say that 'the mere use of the words "every person" is ... not conclusive': 222 (judgment of de Villiers JA).

[86] See e.g. ibid. 203–11 (judgment of Innes CJ).

[87] Dugard, *Human Rights* (cit. n. 17), 311. Much more recently, the Appellate Division contributed to the demise of the pass laws in a decision which relied in part on earlier legislation (and thus was engaged in a limited form of contextual interpretation) to find a 'necessary implication' of protected residence rights for certain blacks. *Komani NO* v. *Bantu Affairs Administration Board, Peninsula Area*, 1980 (4) SA 448 (A), at 472.

[of legislation] is that they tend to reflect less the views of the world whence they come than the views of those who seek their advice'.[88] But this very feature may well commend itself to judges who believe that the legislature's own views are flawed, who hold the 'unconscious judicial antipathy to legislation in general' which Hahlo and Kahn suspected underlay the South African courts' 'unyielding resistance' to the use of legislative history.[89]

This attitude need not amount to a denial of legislative supremacy, if the reach of that supremacy is carefully delimited. Yet it is a considerable distance from the perspective urged by Judge Posner in the United States, that courts 'are part of an organization, an enterprise—the enterprise of governing the United States', and share a responsibility with 'their superiors', the legislature, 'for helping to make the enterprise succeed'.[90] It also has a different flavour than the recommendations by Hart and Sacks that courts should approach statutory interpretation with a '[r]espect [for] the position of the legislature as the chief policy-determining agency of the society', and should '[b]e mindful of the dependence of the legislature upon the good faith and good sense of the agencies of authoritative interpretation'.[91]

In some societies, such perspectives as these may well be incumbent on the courts. In South Africa, however, antipathy towards legislative lawmaking has a strong, and just, foundation, in revulsion against the pattern of South African statutory invasions of human rights. As we will see in a moment, moreover, the potential to give effect to this revulsion in benign construction of the statutory context (and in benign literalism as well) is further enhanced by the availability of a range of interpretive presumptions with which South African courts can cabin legislative meanings.

3. Canons of Interpretation

To understand the role of canons of interpretation, or presumptions, in South African law, we must first consider the function of these rules in law in general. When courts decide, consciously or unconsciously, that language is not plain,

[88] *Public Citizen* v. *US Dept. of Justice*, 105 L.Ed. 2d 377, 404 (1989) (Kennedy J., concurring in the judgment).

[89] Hahlo and Kahn, *SA Legal System* (cit. n. 2), 186. If Hahlo and Kahn are right in their diagnosis of the source of South African courts' rejection of legislative history, then a judiciary less hostile to legislative lawmaking might be expected to make more use of legislative history. Justice Kennedy, on the other hand, might well contend that the use of legislative history lends itself to covert judicial resistance to legislative will and therefore that a true respect for legislative prerogatives counsels against resort to legislative history. That the same concern might be used to support both use and non-use of legislative history should not surprise us; as I have already suggested (see text at nn. 76–7 above), the likely impact of reference to legislative history depends on the context in which this reference is used. Indeed, the same can fairly be said of most, if not all, of the tools of statutory interpretation.

[90] Posner, 'Legal Formalism' (cit. n. 16), 189–90.

[91] Hart and Sacks, 'The Legal Process' (cit. n. 1), 1410–11. For an overview of Hart and Sacks's vision, see W. Eskridge and P. Frickey, 'Legislation Scholarship and Pedagogy in the Post-Legal Process Era', 48 *U. Pitt. L. Rev.* 691, 694–8 (1987).

they must turn elsewhere for direction in their task of statutory interpretation. When they also decide, consciously or unconsciously, that the aspects of statutes' context which they are prepared to examine fail to create clarity, then they are likely to resort to interpretive canons or presumptions, which explain, or purport to constrain, what legislative language means. The use of interpretive rules is thus a corollary of a judicial perception, or assertion, of the opacity of legislative language; as we have already seen, moreover, that judicial attitude may reflect not only genuine confusion but also an institutional or even political reluctance to credit the legislature with meaning what it says. More bluntly, resort to the canons may not be a response to any linguistic problem at all, but rather the enforcement of a rule, or sentiment, of substantive law.[92]

In the circumstances, one function of the canons might be to impose order on what could otherwise be chaos. It is very much a matter of dispute, however, whether the canons do impose order. If it turns out, on examination, that for every canon pointing one way there is an equal and opposite one pointing the other way, then the true function of the canons may not be to 'impose' anything but rather to provide a vehicle for expressing, or dressing up, the decisions judges choose for altogether distinct reasons.[93] If this view is correct, then we can move at once to an examination of the rules available for use by South African judges, and we can expect to find that those rules permit decisions favouring human rights—as well as decisions of quite opposite tenor.

I am inclined to believe, though, that the guiding function of canons of construction can be greater than this 'realist' critique suggests. After all, even if the set of canons is perfectly balanced, a state of affairs that seems intuitively unlikely, the use of those canons may not be. To the extent that a canon attains customary acceptance in a given type of case (say, for instance, the rule of lenity in interpretation of criminal statutes) it becomes harder for a

[92] I am grateful to Richard Pildes for calling my attention to this point.

[93] For the classic American expression of this view, including a table of 28 pairs of opposing maxims of interpretation, see K. Llewellyn, 'Remarks on the Theory of Appellate Decision and the Rules or Canons about how Statutes are to be Construed', 3 *Vand. L. Rev.* 395, 399–406 (1950). Hahlo and Kahn appear to share this perspective. Hahlo and Kahn, *SA Legal System* (cit. n. 2), 212. It is not necessarily a mark against the canons that they may be mutually contradictory. Hart and Sacks offer a defence of the canons, which they say *should* be 'susceptible of being invoked for opposing conclusions' because their function is not to specify the statute's meaning but to show the range of possible meanings from which, on other grounds, the interpreter chooses. Hart and Sacks, 'The Legal Process' (cit. n. 1), 1221. So, also, Eskridge and Frickey comment that '[p]erhaps the best defense of the canons is to posit that they are just a checklist of things to think about when approaching a statute': W. Eskridge and P. Frickey, *Cases and Materials on Legislation: Statutes and the Creation of Public Policy* (1988), 694. These perspectives would point to the importance of the presence of relatively liberal rules among South Africa's various presumptions, either because these rules would make liberal decisions linguistically supportable or because they would prompt judges to consider the desirability of a liberal decision.

judge to ignore.[94] I do not suggest that in these circumstances the canons *compel* judges to render particular decisions, but I do suggest that they can become a force in the judges' thinking. If so, their function will not be limited merely to providing a basis for 'order' in the law; they will be capable as well of guiding judges in one direction rather than another.

I will argue in this section that South African canons of interpretation unquestionably enable judges to make decisions favouring human rights. The support these canons provide for such decisions can be direct, as in the various presumptions which explicitly urge benign readings of statutes, or indirect, as in the presumption that statutes are not presumed to alter the common law (which is much more solicitous of human rights than many of South Africa's statutes). The existence of this body of presumptions attests again to the reserve with which the South African judiciary has greeted the work of Parliament, and to the long-standing presence of somewhat liberal principles within the judiciary and the common law. The relative vigour of liberal presumptions in South African law suggests that they exercise a modest, and potentially liberal, guiding function as well.

In any event, if resort to the canons is a corollary of a belief, perhaps a willed belief, in the opacity of legislative meaning, it should not surprise us that South African courts make extensive use of these interpretive aids. Indeed, as the resurgent conservative literalists in the United States have challenged the prevalence of thoroughgoing contextual interpretation, they have also resuscitated certain canons of interpretation, several of which tend markedly to limit the courts' ability to read statutes expansively.[95] In South Africa, the courts' gingerly attitude towards legislation has been more of a constant than in the United States. Always concerned with the plain meaning of language, and never prepared to undertake a full contextual study of legislation's background, the courts have steadily relied on interpretive canons. These cover a wide range, from the broad guide-lines of literalism and contextualism to more detailed guide-lines such as *eiusdem generis* or *expressio unius* and rules on such issues as the use of statutory titles and of the contemporaneous administrative interpretation of a statute.

Here, however, I want to focus on what Hahlo and Kahn call '[t]he so-called

[94] In a similar vein, Cass Sunstein has denied that Llewellyn's interpretive canons were wholly indeterminate. He suggests that 'some of the canons actually influenced judicial behavior insofar as they reflected background norms that helped to give meaning to statutory words or to resolve hard cases': 'Interpreting Statutes' (cit. n. 47), 452. See also du Plessis, *Interpretation* (cit. n. 11), 48.

[95] e.g. '[*i*]*nclusio unius* arguments have grown like weeds in a vacant lot during the last two Terms of the [Supreme] Court': Eskridge, 'New Textualism' (cit. n. 37), 621, 664 (1990). Eskridge also observes that '[o]ftentimes, procedural canons [rules of thumb for allocating decisionmaking authority] reflect policies whereby the courts defer to other decisionmakers, and the new textualism has enthusiastically embraced these canons'. Ibid. 664. The new textualists have also enforced 'with exceptional vigour' canons of federalism, which often operate to limit the power of the national government. Ibid. 665–6. See also ibid. 675–6 (on Justice Scalia's choice of some canons over others).

presumptions of legislative intent'.[96] They observe that the courts assert that these presumptions are to be used only where the other rules of construction do not resolve statutory ambiguity. 'In fact,' Hahlo and Kahn comment, 'many instances can be found where the presumptions were applied to get at the meaning of the legislature where prima facie the wording was unambiguous.'[97] Du Plessis agrees with this observation (and endorses the view that interpretation should '*both begin and end* with the ... presumptions'), though he believes that the case-law in South Africa does not conclusively settle the question of the presumptions' role.[98] For those courts that embrace this broad view of their role, it would seem that the presumptions could be invoked to show that a statute *is* ambiguous (and therefore that contextual rather than literalist interpretation should apply), or even to show that a statute is *not* ambiguous, but rather has a 'plain' meaning once it is read in light of these rules. Even courts that foreswear so free a use of presumptions may in practice make equally great use of them, if they find that the other guide-lines for interpretation leave the statute's meaning ambiguous—a finding that must inevitably be possible in a great many cases. In short, in South Africa the presumptions are potent tools in the judicial response to statutes.

The content of these rules is therefore a matter of considerable importance. The South African rules, as we will see, do not all lend themselves to use in favour of human rights, but many of them do. In fact, the array of presumptions available to the South African courts includes certain decidedly, even remarkably, liberal rules; the compilation of interpretive rules by the South African scholar Lourens du Plessis suggests that rules with a 'statist' colouring may be distinctly less numerous.[99] American readers may be surprised to learn that South African law contains a presumption 'that the lawmaker intends equal and impartial treatment for all'.[100] Similarly, 'an interpretation which avoids harshness and injustice will, if possible, be adopted'.[101] Moreover, 'where a statute is reasonably capable of more than one meaning, a court will give it the meaning which least interferes with the liberty of the individual'.[102] Even

[96] Hahlo and Kahn, *SA Legal System* (cit. n. 2), 202.

[97] Ibid. 202 and n. 51.

[98] Du Plessis, *Interpretation* (cit. n. 11), 52, 53.

[99] Among the broad presumptions identified by du Plessis, only two seem particularly helpful to arguments against human rights claims. One is the innocuous-sounding presumption that statutes promote the public interest, as to which see text at n. 124 below. The other is the rule that '[a]n enactment does not bind the state': du Plessis, *Interpretation* (cit. n. 11), 76. The significance of this latter rule in the field of apartheid and internal security legislation seems rather diminished by the fact that, if the legislation were not applicable, then the markedly more benign common law would be. See text at nn. 109–11 below. In any event, the sorts of cases listed by du Plessis in which this presumption has been at issue have been far removed from race and internal security law: see *Interpretation* 79–80.

[100] Hahlo and Kahn, *SA Legal System* (cit. n. 2), 208; *R.* v. *Abdurahman*, 1950 (3) SA 136 (A).

[101] *Tshwete* v. *Minister of Home Affairs*, 1988 (4) SA 586 (A), at 612G (dissenting judgment of Nestadt JA). Such an interpretation may not be 'possible', however, unless the words can reasonably be read this way. See du Plessis, *Interpretation* (cit. n. 11), 95–6.

[102] *Tshwete* v. *Minister of Home Affairs*, 1988 (4) SA 586 (A), at 612F (dissenting judgment of Nestadt JA). See Hahlo and Kahn *SA Legal System* (cit. n. 2), 208; du Plessis, *Interpretation* (cit. n. 11), 85–6.

this protection may be augmented in certain cases, for South African courts appear to recognize the existence of 'fundamental' common-law rights, and the legislature will not be taken to have authorized government officials to abolish these rights through 'subordinate legislation', such as administrative regulations, unless it has used 'the clearest language'.[103]

Perhaps the most illuminating of these rules is the principle that statutes are presumed not to alter the common law (or, for that matter, pre-existing statutory law). In the words of a venerable case, which du Plessis described in 1986 as '[a] classical and accurate *dictum*':

> It is a well-known canon of construction that we cannot infer that a statute intends to alter the common law. The statute must either explicitly say that it is the intention of the legislature to alter the common law, or the inference from the Ordinance must be such that we can come to no other conclusion than that the legislature did have such an intention.[104]

This rule is a close cousin of the maxim that statutes in derogation of the common law are to be strictly construed. This maxim, once popular in the United States, appears to have faded from prominence there as the courts evolved away from their role as exponents of *laissez-faire* liberty as a constraint on the modern state.[105] In 1936 Justice (later Chief Justice) Harlan Fiske Stone caustically criticized the grudging interpretation of statutes, and argued that:

> A generation ago no feature of our law administration tended quite so much to discredit law and lawyers in the lay mind. A narrow literalism often defeated the purpose of remedial legislation, while a seeming contest went on with the apparent purpose of ascertaining whether the legislature would ultimately secure a desired reform or the courts would succeed in resisting it.[106]

'Happily,' he continued, 'the abrasive effect of the never-ending judicial labor of making a workable system of our law, so largely composed of statutes, is bringing about a more liberal attitude on the part of the courts.'[107]

Yet a cautious attitude toward statutes in seeming derogation of the common law has remained an acknowledged element of South African law throughout the twentieth century.[108] That it has done so is quite remarkable,

[103] *Mandela* v. *Minister of Prisons*, 1983 (1) SA 938 (A), at 959. See Mureinik, 'Fundamental Rights' (cit. n. 21), 111; du Plessis, *Interpretation* (cit. n. 11), 86.

[104] *Casserley* v. *Stubbs*, 1916 TPD 310, at 312. See du Plessis, in *Interpretation* (cit. n. 11), 69.

[105] See Sunstein, 'Interpreting Statutes' (cit. n. 47), 408–10, 444, and n. 136. Sunstein points out that ideas reminiscent of *laissez-faire* thinking are now enjoying a revival. The more narrowly statutes are read, as American 'new textualists' might, the more of life will be subject only to the common law. For an illustrative instance, see Easterbrook, 'Statutes' Domains' (cit. n. 12), 544 (advocating restriction of 'the domain of the statute', with 'the parties (and court) remitted to whatever other sources of law might be applicable').

[106] H. Stone, 'The Common Law in the United States', 50 *Harv. L. Rev.* 4, 14–15 (1936).

[107] Ibid. 15.

[108] It has, however, been qualified. See e.g. *Gordon NO* v. *Standard Merchant Bank Ltd.*, 1983 (3) SA 68 (A), at 91G–H (Judgment of Corbett JA).

for South African common law is in many respects decidedly supportive of human rights, and South African statutory law has patently been directed at undercutting such rights. Given the vivid inconsistencies between South African common and statutory law, it might have been thought that fidelity to legislative intention entailed abandoning the notion that the legislature meant to alter the common-law regime only where it made that design unambiguously clear. The survival of the presumption to the contrary indicates that this transformation did not happen. Even in the absence of this doctrinal shift, it might have been expected that the more benign rules of the common law would change over time to resemble those of the statutes. Yet this plausible response also has not taken place.

Certainly the benign rules of the common law have survived despite extensive legislative invasion. Thus it remains possible to say, after decades of the elaboration of a security apparatus that makes ready use of detention without trial or hearing, that in the absence of contrary law every person detained is entitled to be heard on his detention. This right derives from one of the core principles of 'natural justice', common-law protections closely akin to the rights secured in the United States by the constitutional guarantees of 'due process of law'.[109] Here the principle in play is expressed in the maxim *audi alteram partem*, whose command to hear the other side has proved to be capable of supple and wide-ranging meaning.[110] Similarly, a host of South African statutes deliberately subject blacks to discriminatory treatment, yet 'it is the duty of the Courts to hold the scales evenly between the different classes of the community and to declare invalid any practice which, in the absence of the authority of an Act of Parliament, results in partial and unequal treatment to a substantial degree between different sections of the community.'[111]

Courts might affirm the significance of the common law, yet undercut its independence of legislative control by modifying the common law itself in areas where legislative action seemed to point the way even though it did not directly apply. A notable instance of this approach is *R.* v. *Pitje*.[112] There the Appellate Division upheld the contempt conviction of Godfrey Pitje, a black articled clerk in the law firm of Nelson Mandela and Oliver Tambo,[113] who had objected to being required to sit at a separate table designated for non-

[109] See Baxter, *Administrative Law* (cit. n. 27), 536.

[110] Ibid. 541–2.

[111] *R.* v. *Abdurahman*, 1950 (3) SA 136 (A), at 145. This formulation could be seen as simply another version of the presumption that the legislator does not intend to enact discriminatory laws, discussed above. But Hahlo and Kahn comment that 'the courts are equally prepared to declare invalid as contrary to natural justice, judicial and quasi-judicial decisions of the executive and of administrative bodies ... which offend against the rule requiring impartial and equal treatment': *SA Legal System* (cit. n. 2), 58.

[112] *R.* v. *Pitje*, 1960 (4) SA 709 (A). For a close and impassioned analysis of this case, see Higginbotham, 'Racism' (cit. n. 68), 503–14.

[113] The partners of the firm, Mandela and Tambo, subsequently have worked on a larger stage. Pitje himself is now one of the senior black lawyers in South Africa. (One serves as an 'articled clerk' as part of qualifying for practice as an attorney.)

European practitioners.[114] Such segregation could have been effected under a particularly repellent statute, the Reservation of Separate Amenities Act, a law which permitted separate and *unequal* segregation.[115] The Appellate Division assumed, however, that the magistrate had not acted under this statute. Still, Chief Justice Steyn wrote for the court, 'the fact that such action could have been taken [under the statute] is not entirely irrelevant. It shows that the distinction drawn by the provision of separate tables in this magistrate's court, is of a nature sanctioned by the legislature, and makes it more difficult to attack the validity of the magistrate's order on the ground of unreasonableness.'[116]

Pitje reflects a judicial stance towards statutes of which, abstractly, Justice Stone would surely have approved. This reasoning would in the course of time gradually narrow the space in which common-law rules inconsistent with statutory policies held sway. Hart and Sacks appear to encourage such thinking,[117] and it might well be appropriate for courts which saw themselves as engaged in a joint enterprise of governing with the legislature. That image, however, does not seem to capture the South African courts' stance. Writing of the judgment in *Pitje*, Edwin Cameron declared that 'Steyn CJ was here breaching a judicial dike which has elsewhere held with remarkable firmness against the tide of statutory segregation and discrimination.' To Cameron, 'the unacceptability of the argument by inference from statute' was clear,[118] and du Plessis confirms that 'very little room is left for the application of analogical interpretation'.[119] Statutes are supreme in the spheres to which they apply, but elsewhere the common-law rules remain the law, and provide the gel within which the statutes are suspended.

By this point it may not be surprising to learn that '[i]t is a well recognized rule in the interpretation of statutes ... "that the curtailment of the powers of a Court of law is, in the absence of an express or clear implication to the contrary, not to be presumed"', as the *Hurley* court put the point in the course of concluding that the ouster clause before it did not divest it of jurisdiction.[120] But the court's use of this presumption in *Hurley* was hardly foreordained. The presumption, after all, predated the case, yet it had been 'widely believed that

[114] *R.* v. *Pitje*, 1960 (4) SA 709 (A), at 710.

[115] See Reservation of Separate Amenities Act 49 of 1953, s. 3; *R.* v. *Pitje*, 1960 (4) SA 709 (A), at 710.

[116] Ibid.

[117] They suggest that even where restrictive statutory language does not reach the facts of a particular case, 'it may nevertheless be proper for the court to rely upon the policy expressed in the statute in formulating, upon its own responsibility, a parallel ground of decision in the case at bar'. Hart and Sacks, 'The Legal Process' (cit. n. 1), 1224; see 1406. They also propose, however, that a court should not 'understand a legislature as directing a departure from a generally prevailing principle or policy of the law unless it does so clearly' (p. 1413).

[118] E. Cameron, 'Legal Chauvinism, Executive-Mindedness and Justice: L. C. Steyn's Impact on South African Law', 99 *SALJ* 38, 70 (1982).

[119] Du Plessis, *Interpretation* (cit. n. 11), 156.

[120] *Minister of Law and Order and Others* v. *Hurley and Another*, 1986 (3) SA 568 (A), at 584A. See Hahlo and Kahn, *SA Legal System* (cit. n. 2), 205–6; du Plessis, *Interpretation* (cit. n. 11), 73–7.

ouster clauses ... precluded the courts from examining the validity of security legislation arrests'.[121] There were, in fact, a number of precedents, of both old and fairly recent vintage, suggesting that ouster clauses in general did significantly constrict the courts' jurisdiction.[122]

One reason for hesitation about the outcome of *Hurley* may have been the existence of another canon of construction prescribing the courts' interpretation of security legislation. For at least in this field the rule of strict construction in favour of liberty has been deprived of much of its potential force. *Rossouw* v. *Sachs*, another of the decisions of the grim 1960s, rejected this principle in favour of another:

> I accordingly conclude that in interpreting [the law] this Court should accord preference neither to the 'strict construction' in favour of the individual ... nor to the 'strained construction' in favour of the Executive referred to by Lord Atkin in *Liversidge*'s case ... but that it should determine the meaning of the section upon an examinaton of its wording in the light of the circumstances whereunder it was enacted and of its general policy and object.[123]

In reaching this decision the court took account of the canon of South African statutory interpretation perhaps most hostile to human rights claims: that 'an enactment promotes [the] public interest', potentially even at the expense of individuals' interests.[124] The court also showed acute—all too acute—sensitivity to the internal security context of this statute.[125]

For the court to reject a 'strict construction' in favour of the rights of the citizen was a major rejection indeed. In *Rossouw* v. *Sachs* itself the court found that Parliament had established a system of nearly incommunicado detention in order to induce detainees to speak,[126] and, in light of the new canon of

[121] Plasket, 'Developments' (cit. n. 9), 17. See also du Plessis, *Interpretation* (cit. n. 11), 75–6.

[122] A number of these cases are discussed in Ch. 3 in connection with an emergency case in which the question of ouster was addressed again—and in quite different fashion from *Hurley*—by the Appellate Division. See Ch. 3, text at nn. 220–4 and nn. 220, 224 below.

[123] *Rossouw* v. *Sachs*, 1964 (2) SA 551 (A), at 563–4. As has frequently been noted, the judgment in *Rossouw* v. *Sachs* traces its decision to the British wartime case of *Liversidge* v. *Anderson and Another*, (1941) 3 All ER 338 (HL). Ironically, it is Lord Atkin's dissent in *Liversidge* rather than the majority position that has stood the test of time in Britain. See R. Heuston, '*Liversidge* v. *Anderson in Retrospect*', 86 *Law Q. Rev.* 33, 67–68 (1970). Lord Scarman has bluntly declared that, '[t]he ghost of *Liversidge* v. *Anderson* ... need no longer haunt the law': *Internal Revenue Commissioners* v. *Rossminster Ltd.*, [1980] AC 952, 1025 (judgment of Lord Scarman); see 1011 (judgment of Lord Diplock).

If the application of *Rossouw* v. *Sachs*'s canon of construction results in the discovery of a clear meaning for the statute, then that meaning must be given effect. If, however, the statute remains ambiguous, then that ambiguity must apparently be resolved 'in a way which least interferes with the rights of the individual'. *State President and Others* v. *Tsenoli; Kerchhoff and Another* v. *Minister of Law and Order and Others*, 1986 (4) SA 1150 (A) at 1175.

[124] See *Rossouw* v. *Sachs*, 1964 (2) SA 551 (A) at 563F; du Plessis (cit. n. 11), 64–7.

[125] *Rossouw* v. *Sachs*, 1964 (2) SA 551 (A) at 563C–E. David Dyzenhaus finds the roots of this decision in the court's undue sensitivity to Parliament's 'actual intention' instead of to the normative principles which, he argues, judges should interpret legislation to satisfy. See Dyzenhaus, 'Disappearance' (cit. n. 21), at 237–41.

[126] *Rossouw* v. *Sachs*, 1964 (2) SA 551, at 561B (A).

construction, concluded that Parliament did not intend 'that detainees should as of right be permitted to relieve the tedium of their detention with reading matter or writing materials', even though for 'intellectuals', this deprivation might 'approximate to ... "psychological compulsion"'.[127] In *Schermbrucker*'s case this same stance informed the court's refusal to assert the power to order a detainee brought to court to testify concerning allegations that he was being subjected to torture, despite the absence of an explicit prohibition of such orders in the statute.[128] But the *Hurley* court made no mention of *Rossouw*'s rule in deciding that its jurisdiction had not been ousted. Nor did it mention the contrary suggestions in any of the earlier cases that such clauses did limit the courts' jurisdiction.

It deserves emphasis how thoroughly this result departed from the evident intention underlying this ouster clause. The effect of this decision is, in fact, to make the ouster clause wholly nugatory[129]—itself a violation of yet another canon of interpretation, which holds that '[n]o enactment contains ... purposeless provisions'.[130] It did so on the basis of a choice of interpretive canons which Parliament could hardly have anticipated. Perhaps most remarkably, the judgment of the court was written by Chief Justice Rabie, who had himself chaired a governmental commission which had recommended the adoption of section 29 on the lines eventually enacted.[131] The Rabie Commission did propose certain changes in the system of detention embodied in section 29, but it retained, largely intact, the ouster clause of the pre-existing legislation,[132]

[127] *Rossouw* v. *Sachs*, 1964 (2) SA 551 (A), at 565.

[128] *Schermbrucker* v. *Klindt NO*, 1965 (4) SA 606 (A), at 617–18.

[129] Rabie is obviously concerned to avoid the conclusion that his interpretation renders the statute, as the state contended, 'ineffective and redundant'. *Minister of Law and Order and Others* v. *Hurley and Another*, 1986 (3) SA 568 (A), at 586G. He argues that the clause is not redundant because the court, though authorized to determine whether there were reasonable grounds for the arrest (a point which I will discuss below, see text at nn. 140–5), is 'precluded by [the ouster clause] from going further and considering whether, if there were such grounds, [the officer concerned] should nevertheless not have held the belief that he did, or not have arrested the person concerned'. Ibid. 586H. If the statute, absent the ouster clause, would have made arrests unlawful when a court made such findings, then Rabie's argument would mean that there were some violations of the statute that remained immune from judicial review by virtue of the ouster clause. But this is not the reading of the statute that the rest of Rabie's judgment suggests. Rabie argues (ibid. 578) that the statute requires reasonable grounds for arrest. He does not suggest, however, that arrests undertaken by authorized officers who do have reasonable grounds might none the less be unlawful on the ground of, say, unwisdom. In fact, the issues Rabie here says are excluded from the court's ambit by the ouster clause do not seem to bear on the lawfulness of arrests under this statute at all. The upshot of this argument is that Rabie's position on the ouster clause *does* render the clause redundant, at least so far as any legal requirements he identifies elsewhere in his judgment are concerned.

[130] Du Plessis, *Interpretation* (cit. n. 11), 61, 62.

[131] See J. Dugard, 'A Triumph for Executive Power: An Examination of the Rabie Report and the Internal Security Act 74 of 1982', 99 *SALJ* 589, 603 (1982).

[132] Terrorism Act 83 of 1967, s. 6(5), provided that 'No court of law shall pronounce upon the validity of any action taken under this section, or order the release of any detainee.' Dugard reports that s. 29 of the Internal Security Act 74 of 1982 're-enact[s] s. 6 of the Terrorism Act, subject to the modifications recommended by the Rabie Commission'. Dugard, 'Triumph' (cit. n. 131), 603. Section 29(6), as adopted, provides that '[n]o court of law shall *have jurisdiction to* pronounce upon the validity of any action taken *in terms of* this section, or *to* order the

and was understood by critics at the time to recommend 'the continued exclusion of judicial supervision'.[133] Thus Rabie in effect appears to have construed his own legislation contrary to his own original intent—a result reflecting the potential of South African interpretive presumptions but surely also the sentiments of the other judges who sat on the *Hurley* case.

I have argued that South African rules of interpretation permit, and even encourage, the courts to render decisions in statutory cases that are favourable to human rights. I have also suggested that such decisions are unlikely to reflect accurately the intentions guiding Parliament's legislation. This interpretive capacity gives the courts a significant potential check on Parliament, despite the principle of parliamentary supremacy. Even if members of Parliament wanted to correct each judicial misinterpretation, and even if, unlike their counterparts in the United States, South Africa's legislators were close students of the rules of interpretation,[134] they would have to come to grips with a system of interpretive rules which is, as I have tried to show, shot through with areas of judicial discretion. Will a court perceive a plain meaning? How will it reconstruct the context if it chooses to look at the context? And which presumptions will it apply, if any, and with what vigour? I do not suggest that these questions are completely unanswerable, but they are impossible to answer completely. And if they could be answered completely at any one time, the legislators would have no assurance that the courts' answers would not change, and then change again. *Hurley*'s case reflects that the use to which the courts will put the rules of construction may change in directions the legislature did not predict and may not welcome.[135]

These various difficulties do not mean that legislatures *cannot* work their will. The process may be difficult, however, and the steps necessary to squelch a determined judiciary are not without their own price. Parliament presumably could prescribe the rules of interpretation by statute, and abolish those rules it found too liberal—but that would involve tearing at the fabric of the law and so potentially disrupting legal relations in many other areas of South African life. The public relations price of enacting new legislation may be

release of any *person detained in terms of the provisions of this section*' (new material underlined). On their face, the additions do not seem to alter the substance of the section.

[133] J. Dugard (rapporteur), 'Detention for the Purpose of Interrogation', in J. Dugard (ed.), *Report on the Rabie Report: An Examination of Security Legislation in South Africa* (Johannesburg: Centre for Applied Legal Studies, University of the Witwatersrand, Occasional Paper 3, Mar. 1982), 18, 41.

[134] See text at nn. 53–4 above.

[135] If Parliament had the will, time, and knowledge required for the task of constant scrutiny of judicial interpretations, then it would follow that any benign statutory readings that Parliament did not overturn were actually intended, if not by the enacting Parliament then at least by the later Parliament that considered the amendment. There may well be cases where the courts' benign readings accurately capture Parliament's intentions; there are surely cases where the rules of interpretation enable the courts to depart from the realities of Parliament's intent.

greater than the cost of merely keeping the old legislation on the books would have been. Moreover, the requisite statutory language may have to be bald, even naked—for example, a fully effective ouster clause might have to deprive courts of jurisdiction to inquire into any action 'claimed, regardless of the good faith of the claim, to be taken in terms of these regulations'. As we will see later in this book, the legislature may be reluctant to exhibit such language to the various audiences of South African law: South African whites to whom the ideal of the rule of law, and the belief that they adhere to this ideal, are important; South African blacks, both those who now have some representation in Parliament and those who do not; and the watching world.[136] It may even be, when a court forces unbowdlerized language upon Parliament, that Parliament's political will may fail, or at least evolve, so that in the end Parliament may never take the steps available to it to achieve the goals whose attainment the courts have forestalled.[137]

We began this chapter by looking at the *Hurley* case, and we can now understand how the court was able to eviscerate the ouster clause in that case while still claiming fidelity to the principle of parliamentary supremacy. Once the barrier of the ouster clause is removed, however, the power of the courts can dramatically increase. Statutes, after all, are not self-executing. People must act under them in order to give them effect, and the courts are empowered—ouster clauses aside—to review the lawfulness of the conduct of those who administer the laws.

The review of administrative action (like the interpretation of ouster clauses purporting to bar such review) falls in the domain of administrative law, a field whose importance in South Africa is especially great because it must do so

[136] For an example of the awkwardness of accomplishing repellent ends with sanitized language, consider the South African statutes establishing the so-called independent homelands of Transkei, Ciskei, Bophuthatswana, and Venda. These statutes, obviously meant to establish black states as part of the grand design of apartheid of rendering South Africa a nation with a white polity, shrank from the actual use of racial designations. As a result, it is possible to read the 'plain language' of these statutes as depriving South African *whites* of their nationality along with South African blacks. For such a reading, see S. Ellmann, 'Who are the Citizens of South Africa and Transkei?', 4 *SAJHR* 76 (1988).

[137] The most striking recent example of the impact of courtroom victories on legislative policy is probably the abolition of the influx control laws, including the pass laws. These hated laws, responsible for astonishing amounts of human suffering among South Africa's blacks, could not, of course, be held invalid in court. But it was possible for lawyers to prevail on courts to hold that certain aspects of the administration of these laws were invalid, and so to show that thousands or tens of thousands of blacks were entitled to urban residence rights that the state had previously denied them. See e.g. *Komani NO* v. *Bantu Affairs Administration Board, Peninsula Area*, 1980 (4) SA 448 (A); *Rikhoto* v. *East Rand Administration Board and Another*, 1983 (4) SA 278 (W), appeal dismissed sub nom. *Oos-Randse Administrasieraad en 'n Ander* v. *Rikhoto*, 1983 (4) SA 595 (A). One response for the state would of course have been to revoke these rights by new legislation (and indeed this approach was initiated). As it happened, however, a range of political forces crystallized on this issue, and the result was that the pass laws were not reinforced but instead abolished. The story is not over, for the struggle over blacks' right to live in urban areas continues, but a phase of the struggle had been concluded and I would say that subsequent events have broadly confirmed the popular victory embodied in the abolition of the pass laws.

much of the work which in the United States is the focus of constitutional protections. If, for example, a statute empowers 'subordinate legislators' such as executive officials to make regulations in order to carry out its commands, the courts not only can interpret the meaning of those regulations but can also strike them down altogether if, in the courts' judgment, the regulations are not authorized by the statutes on which they purport to rest. Parliament is supreme, but those to whom Parliament delegates only subordinate legislative authority are not. So, in particular, regulations which create partial and unequal treatment of the races are subject to being struck down unless the courts deem them to have been authorized by Parliament.[138] If, similarly, a statute empowers administrative officials to take adverse action against people—to build a road across their property, say, or to detain them in a prison—South African law requires compliance with the principles of natural justice, including the bedrock requirements of notice and a hearing embodied in the maxim *audi alteram partem* discussed above.[139]

So, too, if a statute authorizes an official to act on specified grounds, the courts will be able to review whether those grounds were present. This brings us back to *Hurley* once again. Section 29 permits detentions without trial when an officer of or above the rank of lieutenant-colonel has 'reason to believe' that the person to be detained has committed or intended to commit certain offences, or is withholding from the police information bearing on such offences.[140] Did this mean that the officer had to have demonstrable, and reasonable, grounds for this belief, grounds whose existence and weight a court could review? Or did it only mean that the officer had to *think* there was reason for the belief, in which case judicial review would be at an end when it was established that the officer had actually applied his or her mind to the matter and genuinely—even if unreasonably—held this opinion?

The question of whether the officer had the former authority, an 'objective discretion', or the latter, a 'subjective discretion', was a question of statutory interpretation. Counsel for the state maintained that while 'there must in fact exist grounds which cause [the officer] to have the required belief ... [t]he Legislature's intention is ... that the officer concerned should be the sole judge of these matters'.[141] Readers of this chapter will not be surprised at the thought that the courts had the authority to resolve this question either way.

The Appellate Division rejected the state's characterization of the statute. Writing for the court, Chief Justice Rabie argued that, in light of the very serious consequences of action under this statute for the individual arrested, it was 'inconceivable that the Legislature could have intended that a belief based on grounds which cannot pass the test of reasonableness would be sufficient to provide justification for such arrest and detention'.[142] Incon-

[138] See text at n. 111 above.
[139] See text at n. 109–10 above.
[140] Internal Security Act 74 of 1982, s. 29(1).
[141] *Minister of Law and Order and Others* v. *Hurley and Another*, 1986 (3) SA 568 (A), at 577.
[142] Ibid. 578C–D.

ceivable, that is, unless the statute provided to the contrary. Hence this far-reaching judicial sentiment came with a severe qualification. The state's position would have meant, in effect, that the expression 'if he has reason to', used in this section of the statute, and the expression 'if in his opinion there is reason to', used in the detention provision of the preceding section,[143] were identical in meaning, and that both made the officer 'the sole judge of these matters'.[144] Chief Justice Rabie seized on the distinction in the language of these two sections, construing the words in *Hurley* as describing an objective standard, while emphasizing that the other section conferred a subjective authority.

Hurley was a victory for human rights. The Appellate Division concluded that, under the objective standard it had ascertained, the detainee was entitled to his freedom. In addition, of course, it established the objective standard itself, a result that was by no means a foregone conclusion.[145] But while the case was a victory, in retrospect it was a rather Pyrrhic one, for Chief Justice Rabie's judgment clearly signalled the language the state should use if it wished to confer on its arresting officers a subjective rather than objective discretion. A court more convinced that it was inconceivable, or at least deeply improper, for Parliament to authorize detentions 'based on grounds which cannot pass the test of reasonableness' might have read both of the statutes discussed in *Hurley* as conferring an objective discretion, but this was not the course *Hurley* took. The case is thus emblematic at once of the potential of South African law and of the courts' failure to realize that potential fully. We must now turn to the decisions under the state of emergency itself, to assess the extent to which the courts' response to this political and juridical crisis took advantage of the liberal resources of the South African law.

143 Internal Security Act 74 of 1982, s. 28(1)(*a*).

144 *Minister of Law and Order and Others* v. *Hurley and Another*, 1986 (3) SA 568 (A), at 577B–E.

145 In his judgment for the Appellate Division, Rabie CJ took the opportunity to disagree with the statement of the court below that this interpretation of the statute was supported by 'abundant authority'. *Minister of Law and Order and Others* v. *Hurley and Another*, 1986 (3) SA 568 (A), at 580A.

3

The Rabie Court and the Judicial Protection of the State of Emergency

The play's the thing, wherein I'll catch the conscience of the King.[1]

A. The Rabie Era

The principal focus of this chapter and the next will be on the Appellate Division's handling of state of emergency cases during the years in which the court was headed by Chief Justice, then Acting Chief Justice, Pieter J. Rabie. The state of emergency outlasted Chief Justice Rabie's tenure in office, and the Appellate Division has continued to make emergency law decisions since he left the court. We will look at those post-Rabie decisions, but we will begin by focusing on the Rabie court. We will do so because a study of the emergency cases of 'the Rabie court' is a study of a court of a particular character, and not simply of an arbitrary period of time.

Two factors make this court distinctive. One is the pattern of the court's decisions, a pattern of repeated, though not absolutely constant, rejection of human rights claims. Elucidating the features of this pattern will be the principal task of this chapter, and of the next. The other distinctive feature, however, calls for our attention first. This feature is the assignment of judges to the panels which heard the emergency cases. The Appellate Division sits in panels, normally of three or five judges, rather than as a full bench of approximately seventeen.[2] The selection of the judges for the panels, therefore, potentially can shape the outcome of the decisions of the court. During the Rabie era, the selection process placed the final say on emergency law in the hands of just five judges, who never disagreed with each other on the result in any case. The pre-eminence of these five judges, and the voicelessness of many of their colleagues, violated no written rule of South African law. It did, however, fly in the face of the norms of judicial objectivity that South African law holds dear. When we ask why the court's decisions did not make more vigorous use

[1] *Hamlet*, II, ii. 641.

[2] Supreme Court Act 59 of 1959, s. 12. The size of the Appellate Division is not fixed by statute, see ibid., s. 3(1). From January 1986 to May 1990, the average size of the court, including the chief justice and acting judges of appeal, was 17. M. Kidd, 'Internal Security and Specialist Judges: A Study of the Composition of the Appellate Division Bench in Internal Security Cases from 1986 to the Present', 6 *SAJHR* 417, 419 (1990).

of the resources of South African law to vindicate the human rights claims of the victims of emergency powers, our first answer will have to be that this departure from neutrality in the selection of judges distorted the voice of the Appellate Division.

Before examining the panels we need to examine the process of their selection. No statute specifies this process. Apparently, however, it is the Chief Justice who does the selecting. Thus Christopher Forsyth, in his study of the Appellate Division from 1950 to 1980, writes without qualification that '[t]he task of allocating which judges are to hear which appeals, [i.e.] drawing up the roll, falls to the Chief Justice'.[3] Forsyth cites two sources for the paragraph which begins with this observation (a paragraph that goes on to describe the process of consideration of cases by the judges on a panel): a personal communication from Chief Justice Rabie himself, and an anonymous source listed as 'Smith'.[4] Michael Kidd, similarly, states that 'the Chief Justice is responsible for allocating judges to cases',[5] although Nicholas Haysom and Clive Plasket, incisive critics of the Rabie court's decisions, go only so far as to say that 'Rabie ACJ must, we assume, bear some responsibility for the composition of the courts which hear security related matters.'[6]

Prior to the state of emergency, the power to select panels had not been a source of great controversy. When the Appellate Division consisted of only five or six judges, this power was much less significant, and Forsyth reports that where members of the court who were not on a panel were not comfortable with the view their colleagues were taking, 'the practice was to call a meeting of the whole court to ensure that the court's view prevailed rather than some unrepresentative sample of the court's view'.[7] When the Nationalists resorted to court-packing in 1955,[8] the potential impact of panel composition became more significant. There was in fact disturbing evidence of politically based allocation of cases at the trial court level. But as late as 1985 Forsyth found that 'there appears to be little substance to this charge as far as the Appellate Division is concerned. Leading counsel much experienced in such trials have never felt that Benches were picked in order to ensure that they received an

[3] C. Forsyth, *In Danger for their Talents: A Study of the Appellate Division of the Supreme Court of South Africa from 1950–80* (Cape Town: Juta, 1985), 46. If the chief justice is temporarily absent, an acting chief justice would be designated and would make these selections. See ibid. 22.

[4] Ibid. 46 n. 144, xxxi. Elsewhere, Forsyth cites personal communications from Rabie, F. L. H. Rumpff (Rabie's predecessor as chief justice), and, again, 'Smith' on particular criteria 'used by Chief Justices in drawing up the roll'. Ibid. 49 nn. 153, 155, 156, and 50 n. 157.

[5] Kidd, 'Internal Security' (cit. n. 2), 418.

[6] N. Haysom and C. Plasket, 'The War Against Law: Judicial Activism and the Appellate Division', 4 *SAJHR* 303, 310 (1988). See also E. Cameron, G. Marcus, and D. Van Zyl Smit, 'The Administration of Justice, Law Reform and Jurisprudence', in *Annual Survey of South African Law 1988* (Cape Town: Juta, 1989), 500, 516–17.

[7] Forsyth, *In Danger* (cit. n. 3), 47.

[8] See Ch. 1, text at nn. 12–13 above.

unsympathetic hearing when they represented a politically unpopular litigant.'[9] During the emergency, however, this was to change.

Chief Justice Rabie headed the Appellate Division, and thus apparently wielded the authority to draw up the roll, for six and a half years, from 15 June 1982, when he was appointed chief justice, to 31 January 1989, when he retired. Pieter Rabie, the son of an attorney, was originally a classicist.[10] In 1943 he received a doctorate in classics from the University of Michigan, and he then began teaching in that field at the leading Afrikaner university, the University of Stellenbosch.[11] He did not serve in the armed forces during the Second World War; perhaps he, like many (though by no means all) Afrikaners of that day, looked on South Africa's entry into the Second World War as yet another instance of submission to the will of the British, against whom Afrikaners had fought a bitter war of their own at the turn of the century.[12]

Rabie turned to law while at Stellenbosch, and was admitted to the Pretoria bar in 1948. This was, as Adrienne van Blerk observes, a propitious moment for a young Afrikaner to enter the practice of law,[13] for the National Party, the voice of Afrikaner nationalism, that year won an electoral victory which gave it a grip on South African life that it has not yet relinquished. Because Pretoria is 'the administrative capital of South Africa', members of its bar may be well positioned to come to government attention and, in particular, to the attention of officials involved in the process of selecting advocates for appointment to the bench;[14] though only 17 per cent of South Africa's advocates are members of the Pretoria bar, by 1980 almost 50 per cent of the Appellate Division came from it.[15] The Pretoria bar 'is also one of the most conservative in South Africa'.[16]

In due course, in 1962, Rabie became a senior counsel. One of his most notable cases during these years, a case which may have reflected government confidence in him, was his successful defence of South Africa's governance of South-West Africa (Namibia) before the International Court of Justice in 1965.[17] The following year he was appointed to the Transvaal Provincial Division of the Supreme Court.[18] In 1971 he went to the Appellate Division.[19] Beginning

[9] Forsyth, *In Danger* (cit. n. 3), 50.

[10] See 'Appelregter P. J. Rabie', *De Jure* (No. 1) 1, 1 (1978); A. van Blerk, 'New Chief Justice—the Honourable Justice P. J. Rabie DVD', *De Rebus* 348, 348 (Aug. 1982) (Afrikaans title 'Nuwe hoofregter—Sy Edele Regter P. J. Rabie DVD'; tr. by Nadine Havenga).

[11] Ibid. 348.

[12] For an account of Afrikaner responses to the 2nd World War, see D. Harrison, *The White Tribe of Africa* (London: Ariel, 1985), 117–36.

[13] Van Blerk, 'New Chief Justice' (cit. n. 10), 348.

[14] Forsyth, *In Danger* (cit. n. 3), 41.

[15] Ibid. 41–2. Forsyth includes long-time Pretoria civil servants in this group, although they would presumably not have been members of the bar during their work as civil servants.

[16] Ibid. 42.

[17] See Van Blerk, 'New Chief Justice' (cit. n. 10), 348; J. Dugard, *Human Rights and the South African Legal Order* (Princeton, NJ: Princeton University Press, 1978), 116.

[18] Van Blerk, 'New Chief Justice' (cit. n. 10), 348.

[19] Ibid.

in 1976, he also worked as the chairman of the South African Law Commission.[20] More controversially, he chaired a Commission of Inquiry into Security Legislation, whose 1982 report became the basis for the Internal Security Act of 1982.[21] The Commission asserted in its report that 'in its view it could not venture onto the political terrain', but this disavowal of politics did not deprive the report of political import.[22] The Commission did recommend certain reforms in the security laws.[23] In parliamentary debate, as John Dugard reports,

> The new Minister of Law and Order ... expressed his satisfaction 'that a judicial commission has established the principle beyond all doubt once and for all that the people responsible for national security "must be the sole judges of what the national security requires", as was stated in the English decision in *The Zamora* case.'[24]

Later in 1982, Rabie became chief justice. For the next four and a half years, from 1982 to 1987, Rabie's title was 'Chief Justice'. When Rabie reached the mandatory retirement age of 70 in January 1987, however, he was appointed as 'Acting Chief Justice' for two more years. The government's decision to offer him this 'acting' position was novel, though not completely unprecedented; in an effort to preclude the appointment of the liberal Oliver Schreiner as chief justice, the government had made a similar offer in 1956 to then Chief Justice Centlivres.[25] Centlivres, however, declined the offer, and Rabie's decision to accept this appointment made him the only acting chief justice to serve in the absence of an actual chief justice in the history of South Africa as an independent nation.[26] The appointment was controversial among lawyers and apparently the public.[27] As Edwin Cameron has trenchantly commented, 'this extraordinary appointment has never been explained'. Since there were other judges who could have become chief justice when Rabie reached retirement age—

[20] Van Blerk, 'New Chief Justice' (cit. n. 10), 349.

[21] See J. Dugard, 'A Triumph for Executive Power—An Examination of the Rabie Report and the Internal Security Act 74 of 1982', 99 *SALJ* 589, 602–3 (1982).

[22] The quoted language is a translation from the report's Afrikaans, in A. Mathews, 'Why Rabie Couldn't Wash Hands of Politics', *Rand Daily Mail*, 29 Mar. 1982, at 11.

[23] For a discussion of the Commission's recommendations, see Dugard, 'Triumph' (cit. n. 21), at 591–601. While acknowledging some 'welcome' improvements, ibid. 592, Dugard strongly criticized the 'failure of the Act [the Internal Security Act of 1982] to provide effective safeguards for the detainee held for the purpose of interrogation'. Ibid. 604.

[24] Dugard, 'Triumph' (cit. n. 21), 603, citing *House of Assembly Debates*, cols. 986–7 (16 Feb. 1982). Dugard also notes that the Commission's Report itself cited this statement from *The Zamora* with approval. Ibid. 591; see *The Zamora*, [1916] 2 AC 77, 107.

[25] Forsyth, *In Danger* (cit. n. 3), 26.

[26] See E. Cameron, 'Nude Monarchy: The Case of South Africa's Judges', 3 *SAJHR* 338, 344 (1987). On various occasions a member of the Appellate Division has temporarily stood in as acting chief justice while the chief justice was for one reason or another not available. While Rabie was acting chief justice, however, there was no chief justice at all.

[27] See E. Cameron, G. Marcus, and D. van Zyl Smit, 'The Administration of Justice, Law Reform and Jurisprudence', in *Annual Survey of South African Law 1987* (Cape Town: Juta, 1988), 482, 493. Cameron's own sharp criticism, 'Nude Monarchy' (cit. n. 26), 343–6, was important to this controversy.

one of them, Michael Corbett, *did* become chief justice when Rabie finally retired as acting chief justice—it is impossible not to wonder what the government felt required Rabie to continue in office as long as he did.[28]

What we *know* is what happened. The first of the nation-wide states of emergency of the 1980s had been declared in June of 1986, and all but one of the dozen emergency cases that the Rabie court considered were argued and decided after Rabie's appointment as acting chief justice.[29] In all of these, and in the other internal security cases of these years, it was apparently Rabie who normally selected the judges who sat. The pattern of his choices gradually became evident, and became as well the subject of criticism. Haysom and Plasket compiled the panels for twelve internal security decisions over a two-year period (roughly 1986–8) and found: 'Rabie ACJ has sat in all but one of the cases, and Hefer JA, a relatively junior judge of appeal, has sat in nine cases. No other judge can compare with this record. For example, Smalberger, Corbett, Van Heerden, Hoexter and Botha JJA, have sat in only a handful of matters.'[30] Moreover, the judges listed as having sat in only a handful of cases are not a random list. They include some of the most senior members of the court, such as Corbett (now the chief justice) and Botha, and some of the most liberal.[31] More recently, Kidd had tabulated the panels for every reported

[28] Ibid. 344–6.

[29] Only one emergency case was decided by the Rabie court prior to Rabie's becoming the acting chief justice. This was *State President and Others* v. *Tsenoli; Kerchhoff and Another* v. *Minister of Law and Order and Others*, 1986 (4) SA 1150 (A), argued on 10 Sept. 1986 and decided three days later.

[30] Haysom and Plasket, 'War Against Law' (cit. n. 6), 310.

[31] Chief Justice Corbett's concern for human rights is evident in the opening address which he gave at the 1979 First International Conference on Human Rights in South Africa: 'Human Rights: The Road Ahead', 96 *SALJ* 192 (1979). A speech which he gave after his appointment as chief justice has a similar tenor. M. Corbett, 'Speech to Johannesburg Bar', *Consultus*, 73, 75, 78 (Oct. 1989). I sketch Corbett CJ's views in more detail in Ch. 5. Van Heerden JA's thinking is reflected in his dissenting judgments in two emergency cases, *Staatspresident en Andere* v. *Release Mandela Campaign en Andere*, 1988 (4) SA 903 (A) and *Staatspresident en Andere* v. *United Democratic Front en 'n Ander*, 1988 (4) SA 830 (A), and in a security-related case arising in South-West Africa (Namibia), *Cabinet for the Territory of South West Africa* v. *Chikane and Another*, 1989 (1) SA 349 (A). Hoexter JA was the lone dissenter in another emergency case, *Omar and Others* v. *Minister of Law and Order and Others; Fani and Others* v. *Minister of Law and Order and Others; State President and Others* v. *Bill*, 1987 (3) SA 859 (A), and the author of the judgment in a post-Rabie emergency case which modestly but genuinely circumscribed emergency authority, *Visagie* v. *State President and Others*, 1989 (3) SA 859 (A). Botha JA is the author of the widely criticized judgment in *S.* v. *Safatsa and Others*, 1989 (1) SA 868 (A) (the 'Sharpeville Six' case), declaring that South African law permits a conviction for murder based on a shared common purpose even where the accused's acts do not contribute 'causally' to the death. Ibid. 894E. He is also the author of a dissenting judgment in the case of *S.* v. *Toms; S.* v. *Bruce*, 1990 (2) SA 802 (A), in which he argued that the statutory sentence for draft resistance is a mandatory sentence which courts cannot shorten or suspend. In that case, however, Botha JA also wrote that he considered this statutory 'reduc[tion of] a sentencing court to a mere rubber stamp, to be wholly repugnant'. Ibid. 831A–B. In a number of other cases, moreover, Botha JA has held in favour of human rights claims. This was true, for example, of such internal security law cases, decided during Rabie's tenure as Chief Justice, as *Minister of Law and Order and Others* v. *Hurley and Another*, 1986 (3) SA 549 (A); and *Kabinet van die Tussentydse Regering vir Suidwes-Afrika en 'n Ander* v. *Katofa*, 1987 (1) 695 (A), at 744D (concurring in judgment of Trengrove JA). It is also true of two internal security cases on which Botha JA has sat since Rabie's

internal security case from 1986 to May 1990, and has found very similar patterns.[32] In particular, he notes that Rabie and four other judges, Joubert, Viljoen, Hefer, and Vivier JJA, all sat on disproportionately large numbers of Rabie-era internal security cases, while Corbett, Hoexter, Botha, Smalberger, and others sat on disproportionately few.[33]

These analyses, however, do not distinguish between emergency cases and other internal security cases, and so do not identify the particularly striking patterns of the emergency panels. During Rabie's era, there were twelve such cases, eleven reported and one unreported.[34] Table 1 shows the number of

resignation: *S.* v. *Tshoba and Others*, 1989 (3) SA 393 (A) (overturning convictions for terrorism); and *Minister of Law and Order* v. *Matshoba*, 1990 (1) SA 280 (A) (ordering the release of an emergency detainee because he was not held at the prison specified in the detention order). Smalberger JA is the author of judgments favouring human rights claims in such cases as *S.* v. *Toms*; *S.* v. *Bruce* (holding that the statutory sentence for draft resistance is not a mandatory sentence); *S.* v. *Tieties*, 1990 (2) SA 461 (A) (narrowing the state's authority to convert a trial in a lower court into a preparatory examination, despite broad statutory language); and a post-Rabie emergency case, *Minister of Law and Order, KwaNdebele, and Others* v. *Mathebe and Another*, 1990 (1) SA 114 (A) (holding that 'homeland' police have no authority to make emergency arrests in South Africa proper). For a tentative characterization of the other members of the Appellate Division as of Mar. 1990, see Ch. 5 n. 95 below.

[32] The category 'internal security' is not self-defining. Kidd follows the categorization by the editors of the *South African Law Reports*, see 'Internal Security' (cit. n. 2), 417–18, and so his survey includes all reported cases 'involving either the emergency regulations promulgated in terms of the Public Safety Act 3 of 1953 or the Internal Security Act 74 of 1982' (ibid. 418), as well as two detention cases from South-West Africa (now Namibia). There are certainly other cases besides these that bear on 'internal security' and the anti-apartheid struggle, such as prosecutions for treason and for politically motivated killings.

[33] Ibid. 419, 422 (table A).

[34] Beginning with the earliest, the reported cases were: *State President and Others* v. *Tsenoli*; *Kerchhoff and Another* v. *Minister of Law and Order and Others*, 1986 (4) SA 1150 (A) (hereafter cited as *Tsenoli*); *Omar and Others* v. *Minister of Law and Order and Others*; *Fani and Others* v. *Minister of Law and Order and Others*; *State President and Others* v. *Bill*, 1987 (3) SA 859 (A) (hereafter cited as *Omar*); *Minister of Law and Order and Another* v. *Dempsey*, 1988 (3) SA 19 (A) (hereafter cited as *Dempsey*); *Nkwentsha* v. *Minister of Law and Order and Another*, 1988 (3) SA 99 (A) (hereafter cited as *Nkwentsha*); *Ngqumba en 'n Ander* v. *Staatspresident en Andere*; *Damons NO en Andere* v. *Staatspresident en Andere*; *Jooste* v. *Staatspresident en Andere*, 1988 (4) SA 224 (A) (hereafter cited as *Ngqumba*); *Staatspresident en Andere* v. *United Democratic Front en 'n Ander*, 1988 (4) SA 830 (A) (hereafter cited as *United Democratic Front*); *Staatspresident en Andere* v. *Release Mandela Campaign en Andere*, 1988 (4) SA 903 (A) (hereafter cited as *Release Mandela Campaign*); *Apleni* v. *Minister of Law and Order and Others*; *Lamani* v. *Minister of Law and Order and Others*, 1989 (1) SA 195 (A) (hereafter cited as *Apleni*); *Minister of Law and Order and Another* v. *Swart*, 1989 (1) SA 295 (A) (decided 29 Sept. 1988) (hereafter cited as *Swart*); *Van der Westhuizen NO* v. *United Democratic Front*, 1989 (2) SA 242 (A) (decided 30 Nov. 1988) (hereafter cited as *Van der Westhuizen*); and *Minister of Law and Order and Another* v. *Parker*, 1989 (2) SA 633 (A) (argued 1 Nov. 1988; decided 24 Feb. 1989) (hereafter cited as *Parker*). I include *Parker* despite its having been decided after Rabie's retirement on 31 Jan. 1989; it was argued, and its panel selected, during his tenure. (Some of these cases, or portions of them, are in Afrikaans; in discussing and quoting them I rely on translations prepared by Nadine Havenga from the typed or reported judgments.)

Not all Appellate Division decisions are reported, but Kidd writes that '[a]ll Appellate Division cases during this period, which were judged by the editors of the *Law Reports* to be "Internal Security" matters have, according to the editors, been reported'. 'Internal Security' (cit. n. 2), 418. Internal security cases include emergency cases, and so one would expect every emergency case to be reported. In fact, however, one was omitted. This case is *Minister of Law*

TABLE 1. *Availability and actual cases of members of the Rabie court*

Judge	Cases on which he sat	Cases on which he could have sat
Rabie	10	12
Hefer	10	12
Viljoen	8	12
Joubert	8	12
Vivier	8	11
EM Grosskopf	4	12
Van Heerden	3	12
Steyn	3	11
Boshoff	1	6
Corbett	1	12
Eksteen	1	4
Hoexter	1	12
Jansen	1	6
Nestadt	1	12
Botha	0	12
Smalberger	0	12
Nicholas	0	12
Kumleben	0	8
Milne	0	7
Jacobs	0	3
Trengrove	0	1
Galgut	0	1

these cases on which each full or acting member of the court sat, and the number of cases for which he was available to sit.[35] In fact, even these data do not fully reflect the extent to which the court's emergency jurisprudence

and Order and Others v. *Bishop of the Roman Catholic Church of the Diocese of Port Elizabeth*, Case No. No. 165/87 (Appellate Division, 29 Sept. 1988) (hereafter cited as *Bishop of the RC Church*). Since *Bishop of the RC Church* does not appear to be widely known even in South Africa, it may be useful to provide a brief account of it. The case dealt with the legality of the emergency detention of a Father Graham Cornelius. The lower court had ruled in Cornelius's favour, *Bishop of the RC Church of the Diocese of Port Elizabeth and Another* v. *Minister of Law and Order and Others*, Case No. 1101/86 (EPD 11 Aug. 1986) (Kroon J), but the state appealed and prevailed before the Appellate Division. Rabie ACJ wrote the judgment in the case, and the four other members of the panel, Joubert, Hefer, Vivier, and Steyn JJA, concurred. I know of no other emergency judgments from this era. It is possible, however, that the Appellate Division may have denied leave to appeal in one or more emergency cases during this period; such decisions are not made by announced panels of the court and normally would not be accompanied by written opinions. Hence they would not affect the figures for the dominance of particular judges in the make-up of emergency panels, as reported in the text.

[35] I determined the number of cases on which each judge served from the cases' listing of their panel members. Kidd's tabulation of all internal security cases, however, was very helpful as a complete list of the judges who could have served on any of these cases, and of the number

was under the control of just five members of the court. These five judges were Rabie himself, Hefer, Viljoen, Joubert, and Vivier. The fact is that, in every one of the twelve emergency cases, at least three of the five judges on the panel were from the emergency team, and the members of this team never disagreed with each other on the result in any of these cases.[36] The data deserve to be set out in full; Table 2 does so.

The presence of these judges is so overwhelming that it seems appropriate to call them the 'emergency team'.[37] In giving them this label, I mean to recall a phenomenon of the 1950s, when the senior members of the Appellate Division responded to the National Party's dramatic expansion of the court by viewing themselves as the 'first team', and endeavouring to limit the influence of the 'second team'.[38] The first team then, however, apparently saw its role as one of ensuring quality of decision-making rather than determining outcomes.[39] It is hard to characterize the emergency team's role under Chief Justice Rabie as comparably neutral, and its influence was immense. In fact, their votes were enough to determine the result in every case—no mean feat in such potentially controversial cases, and in an era when overt disagreements

of cases for which each judge was available. Kidd, 'Internal Security' (cit. n. 2), 422 (table A). I supplemented Kidd's information on availability with data on the periods of service of judges, prepared by my research assistant Bradford May from the lists of judges in the vols. of the *South African Law Reports*. My figures on emergency cases differ from Kidd's only in that I include the unreported *Bishop of the Roman Catholic Church* case. I should note that Kidd and I both count Jacobs JA as unavailable for two cases, *Dempsey* and *Ngqumba*, which were argued before his retirement on 15 Feb. 1988 but not decided until after he had left the court. Since a judge who reached retirement age in the midst of deliberations might be able to continue on as an acting judge, it is possible that Jacobs JA should be treated as available for these cases; this same possibility might require small adjustments elsewhere in my (and, I believe, Kidd's) figures.

[36] The closest approach to disagreement among the members of the emergency team took place in *United Democratic Front*, in which Rabie ACJ wrote a judgment in which Hefer and Vivier JJA both concurred. Hefer JA, however, also wrote a judgment in which only Vivier JA concurred. In addition, Grosskopf JA gave a brief judgment in which he agreed generally with both Rabie and Hefer, but developed one argument of his own, and Hefer and Vivier, but not Rabie, concurred in this judgment as well. The only dissent, however, came from Van Heerden JA—not a member of the emergency team.

[37] These same judges, as Kidd found (see 'Internal Security' (cit. n. 2), 419), sat in disproportionate numbers of all internal security cases, including but not limited to emergency cases, and so they might be called the 'internal security team' instead. For two reasons, however, the label 'emergency team' seems more appropriate. First, these years *were* the years of the emergency, and it seems plausible to suggest that it was this feature, rather than the continued enforcement of long-standing internal security provisions, that made this period special. Second, although the members of the emergency team did play a very prominent role in non-emergency internal security cases during this period, they were not quite as dominant in these cases as they were in the emergency ones. Of the 11 non-emergency cases tabulated by Kidd, emergency team members made up a majority in only 6. If we exclude cases decided in 1986, however, when emergency anxieties might not yet have reached their peak, the members of the emergency team made up a majority in 6 of the 7 remaining cases.

[38] Forsyth, *In Danger* (cit. n. 3), 21–3.

[39] Ibid. 23; E. Kahn, 'Oliver Deneys Schreiner: A South African', in E. Kahn (ed.), *Fiat Iustitia: Essays in Memory of Oliver Deneys Schreiner* (Cape Town: Juta, 1983) 1, 41–2.

TABLE 2. *Judges in the twelve emergency cases*

Case	Number and names of judges from the emergency team on the five-judge panel
Tsenoli	3: Rabie, Joubert, Viljoen
Omar	3: Rabie, Joubert, Viljoen
Nkwentsha	3: Rabie, Hefer, Vivier
Dempsey	4: Rabie, Joubert, Viljoen, Hefer
Ngqumba	5: Rabie, Joubert, Viljoen, Hefer, Vivier
Release Mandela Campaign	3: Rabie, Hefer, Vivier
United Democratic Front	3: Rabie, Hefer, Vivier
Apleni	4: Rabie, Viljoen, Hefer, Vivier
Swart	4: Joubert, Viljoen, Hefer, Vivier
Bishop of the RC Church	4: Rabie, Joubert, Hefer, Vivier
Van der Westhuizen	4: Rabie, Joubert, Viljoen, Hefer
Parker	4: Joubert, Viljoen, Hefer, Vivier

within the Appellate Division were on the increase.[40] Moreover, when judges from outside the team dissented from emergency decisions—and even in one case where the judge did not dissent but rather concurred in the result on quite different grounds—they never sat on another emergency case during Rabie's tenure in office.[41] The members of the team also wrote the sole, or principal, judgments of the court in all of these cases. Rabie himself wrote the sole, or principal, judgment in six of the cases, in every instance denying relief to those challenging the government's actions.[42] In these respects,

[40] Starting in 1968, if not earlier, the level of dissents and separate concurrences in Appellate Division cases declined, until in 1980 there were absolutely no expressed disagreements, even as to rationale, in roughly 98% of all decisions. Forsyth, *In Danger* (cit. n. 3), 53. 'The year 1988 evidenced a dramatic change in that pattern', however, with the rate of dissent or separate concurrences rising to 19 out of 90 reported decisions (approximately 21%). Cameron, Marcus, and Van Zyl Smit, 'Administration' (cit. n. 6), 541–2. But the rate of disagreement in the emergency cases, despite the presence of the emergency team, was greater than that: in 3 cases out of 12 there were dissents, and in another there was a separate concurrence. (There was also a separate concurrence in one of the cases with a dissent.) Thus in 4 of the 12 emergency cases, or 33%, the Appellate Division was not of one mind.

[41] These judges were Hoexter JA, who dissented in *Omar*, 1987 (3) SA 859 (A); Nestadt JA, who concurred with the majority's result, but on other grounds, in *Dempsey*, 1988 (3) SA 19 (A); and Van Heerden JA, who dissented in *United Democratic Front*, 1988 (4) SA 830 (A), and *Release Mandela Campaign*, 1988 (4) SA 903 (A) (cases which were both argued on 21 Mar. 1988 and then both decided on 13 Sept. 1988).

[42] In chronological order, these were *Tsenoli*, 1986 (4) SA 1150 (A); *Omar*, 1987 (3) SA 859 (A); *Ngqumba*, 1988 (4) SA 224 (A); *United Democratic Front*, 1988 (4) SA 830 (A); *Release Mandela Campaign*, 1988 (4) SA 903 (A); *Bishop of the RC Church*, Case No. 165/87 (Appellate Division 29 Sept. 1988). Hefer JA was the next most active, writing the judgment for the court in an important case decided in favour of the government, *Dempsey*, 1988 (3) SA 19 (A); an extended concurrence in *United Democratic Front*; the judgment for the court, again in favour of the government, in *Van der Westhuizen*, 1989 (2) SA 242 (A); and the judgment for the court in a case which *did* grant relief to a detainee, *Swart*, 1989 (1) SA 295 (A). Vivier JA wrote for

especially, Rabie's tenure marks an era;[43] as we will see in Chapter 5, the dominance of the emergency team did not survive Rabie's retirement.[44]

What accounts for the existence of the emergency team? Chance can hardly explain this pattern, for the chance of random selection producing these results is in the order of 1 in 244,000,000.[45] Nor can such details of judges' availability as their 'long leaves' provide an explanation.[46] Nor does seniority account for what we have found. Forsyth wrote in 1985 that there was 'some evidence that when a political case [arises]—e.g. one dealing with security matters or one in which a government plan was challenged in a controversial way—the Chief Justice and a selection of senior judges would be chosen to hear the case'.[47] Rabie, to be sure, was the chief justice, and two other members of the team, Joubert and Viljoen, *were* senior members of the court. But Hefer JA did not become a full member of the court until the last quarter of 1984, and Vivier JA did not become a full member of the court until the beginning of 1987—after the state of emergency began. Such judges as Corbett (now the

the court in two cases, both of which granted relief to detainees, *Nkwentsha*, 1988 (3) SA 99 (A), and *Apleni*, 1989 (1) SA 195 (A). Joubert JA wrote only once, at the very end of this period, in an arrest case which worked what appears to be a quite modest variation on already established principles, *Parker*, 1989 (2) SA 633 (A). Viljoen JA never wrote an emergency judgment, though he sat on 8 of these cases.

[43] Rabie may also have helped to shape the Appellate Division in another way as well. As chief justice, he may have been able to influence the government's decisions about appointments of other members of the court, particularly if his relationship with the government was good (as his appointment as acting chief justice suggests it was). For evidence of consultation between the chief justices and the government on appointments, see Forsyth, *In Danger* (cit. n. 3), 34–5. During Rabie's tenure, 10 of the present members of the Appellate Division received their appointments. These were Justices Eksteen, E. M. Grosskopf, Hefer, Kumleben, Milne, Nestadt, Smalberger, M. T. Steyn, Van Heerden, and Vivier. It appears, moreover, that only one of these judges, Van Heerden JA, had been an acting judge of appeal—often a prelude to appointment as a full member of the court—before Rabie became chief justice.

[44] See Ch. 5, text at nn. 94–103.

[45] If we conservatively assume a court of 14 judges, we can calculate the chance that a randomly selected panel of 5 judges would include at least 3 people from a particular 'team' of 5 members of the court. There appear to be 406 possible panels that would have at least 3 team members on them, and 2002 possible panels in all. (For the methodology underlying these calculations, see S. Ross, *A First Course in Probability* (New York: Macmillan, 3rd edn., 1988), 6–7. Hence the chance of selecting a panel with at least 3 team members would be 406/2002, or approximately 1 in 5. This is not tremendously improbable. But the chance of selecting such a panel in each of 12 cases in a row (assuming that all judges are equally available in each case) is then 1/5 (approximately) to the twelfth power, or approximately 1 in 244,140,625. (I appreciate the assistance of Bernard Black on this point; responsibility for the calculations, however, is solely mine.)

[46] 'Long leaves' are not taken into account in Table 1. Kidd, however, comments that 'it would appear, from looking at judges' involvement in other cases during the period in question, that only Hoexter and Botha JJA could have been affected'. 'Internal Security' (cit. n. 2), 418. Availability might also be affected if certain judges, for whatever reason, worked more slowly than others. Since not all Appellate Division cases in this period were reported, it would be difficult to compute the total productivity of each judge. It is possible to observe, however, that under Corbett CJ the burden of emergency jurisprudence has been distributed much more evenly, despite whatever productivity problems there might be. See Ch. 5, text at nn. 94–103.

[47] Forsyth, *In Danger* (cit. n. 3), 50. Forsyth cites a personal communication from the then-recently retired Chief Justice Rumpff as authority for this statement. Ibid. 50, n. 157.

chief justice), Botha, Hoexter, and van Heerden were more senior than either Hefer or Vivier, while E. M. Grosskopf and Smalberger were more senior than Vivier (and Nestadt and Vivier became full members in the same quarter).[48]

We are left with the inference that the members of the emergency team were chosen to bring some special quality to the decision-making process. That quality might be technical, neutral expertise; as Kidd suggests, the members of the emergency team might have been 'specialists' in security law in the same way that other judges were specialists in tax or patent law.[49] As Kidd points out, however, security law is not a terribly technical field.[50] Moreover, *no one* could have been an expert in emergency law prior to 1986, for there had been no emergency cases at all since the 1960s. In addition, if Forsyth's account of panel selection prior to the emergency is correct, the court's past response to politically charged cases had been to select senior panels. This practice would not have fostered the growth of a group of security experts other than the most senior judges—and the emergency team's composition cannot be explained as merely a function of seniority.

Why then were the members of the emergency team selected as specialists in emergency and internal security law? The unanimity of these judges' positions, and the exclusion of dissenting voices, help confirm the answer that surely jumped to readers' minds at once: the members of the emergency team were selected for the 'soundness' of their judgment on these issues. This is not to suggest that they were asked how they would vote on any case before they were assigned to it; I very much doubt that any such vetting took place. The views of these judges would have been evident, however, not only from the growing record of their decisions but also from their past work and from the countless interactions that must take place between members of a court. Nor is it to insist that the selection of these judges was *consciously* political. Chief Justice Rabie may have perceived the test for selection as one of judgment rather than ideology. But judgment on the clash of emergency exigency and human liberty cannot help but have an ideological component, and the selection of this small group of judges to create the Appellate Division's emergency jurisprudence inescapably, even if unconsciously, reflected ideology as well—Rabie's own views and those of the judges whom he chose to join him. The sound judgment of the members of the team was a judgment that weighed security against rights and repeatedly found security the weightier concern.

[48] This information is based on the lists of judges in the vols. of the *South African Law Reports*. I thank Bradford May for his work in compiling the data.

[49] Kidd, 'Internal Security' (cit. n. 2), 419. As Kidd's discussion reflects, if other judges were specializing in other areas (he mentions Corbett JA and Nicholas AJA as examples of tax specialists), then in addition to their supposed lack of security expertise these other specialists would also have been likely to have less time available for undertaking cases outside their specialties. Ibid. 421. I know of no evidence that specialist judges work *only* within their specialties, however, and so presumably workload differences could have been made up in many areas, and did not have to find expression in the field of emergency law or internal security. See ibid. 421.

[50] Ibid. 420.

This pattern of panel selection did not violate any express limit on the chief justice's authority, but it did undercut values that are important to South African law's image of itself. In 1983, only two years before the beginning of emergency rule, a government-appointed Commission of Inquiry into the Structure and Functioning of the Courts had addressed a related matter. The chairman of this Commission, G. G. Hoexter, is now a member of the Appellate Division; during the Rabie years, he sat on only one emergency case, in which he dissented.[51] In 1984, the Hoexter Commission responded to allegations of political assignment of security cases at the trial level by writing that:

> Confidence in the law is a fragile plant. Any noticeable tendency for only certain judges to be assigned to preside at criminal trials involving the security of the state would run counter to the proud tradition of our administration of justice; it would debase the judicial office; and inevitably breed suspicion and disquiet.[52]

The sheer existence of the emergency team belies the hope that judges' decisions might somehow be free of political preconceptions. That hope has real force in South African legal thinking (and elsewhere).[53] Indeed, Rabie's successor as chief justice, Michael Corbett, said in 1979 that 'experience has shown that good, well-qualified judges are generally impervious to extraneous influences and bring to bear on the problems before them a professional objectivity which transcends personal predilections'.[54] One need not share Corbett's assessment in order to understand that South Africans might well value what the Dean of the Rand Afrikaans University Law Faculty has called 'clinically sober judgments in the best South African judicial tradition',[55] on the ground that these approach as closely as possible to the ideal of objectivity. When some members of the country's highest court are effectively disfran-

[51] This case was *Omar*, 1987 (3) SA 859 (A).

[52] Commission of Inquiry into the Structure and Functioning of the Courts, 1 *Fifth and Final Report*, RP 78/1983, Part II, paragraph 1.3.8.4, pp. 64–5 (n.d., ?1984). The Commission had before it a submission by Professor John Dugard, contending that 'in the Transvaal there was a noticeable tendency for only a relatively small group of judges from the full complement of judges to preside in criminal trials involving State security'. Ibid. 63. The Commission asked the Judge President of the Transvaal Provincial Division for his comments, but he offered none. As a result the Commission considered itself 'not in a position to go into the matter thoroughly', though it averred that Professor Dugard's evidence did not 'sustain as the only or even the likeliest inference that in those particular trials discretion had been exercised improperly or even injudiciously in the assignment of the trial judges concerned'. Ibid. 64. Then the Commission went on to offer the comments quoted in the text. Cameron, Marcus, and Van Zyl Smit, 'Administration' (cit. n. 6), 516, point out that these comments 'are equally applicable to the assignment of appellate judges'.

[53] See J. Dugard, 'The Judicial Process, Positivism and Civil Liberty', 88 *SALJ* 181, 187 (1971).

[54] Corbett, 'Human Rights' (cit. n. 31), 199.

[55] J. Van Der Walt, 'N. P. van Wyk Louw: A Few Consequences for Legal Thought', 1986 *TSAR* 257, 278 (Afrikaans title, 'N. P. van Wyk Louw: Enkele Konsekwensies vir die regsdenke'; tr. by Nadine Havenga). Van Der Walt uses this phrase to describe the majority and dissenting judgments of the Appellate Division in *S.* v. *Marwane*, 1982 (3) SA 717 (A).

chised, however, while others are given amplified voice, the tacit message is that even the discipline of the judicial tradition is not enough to produce proper judging. Such panel selection thus in effect embraces the political character of judging, and simultaneously excludes some political voices within the court—to say nothing of the unrepresented black population of the nation.

We can also call this period an era because its decisions, the decisions of the emergency team, reflect a consistent approach to emergency issues. Indeed, when we paint with a broad brush it is painfully easy to characterize the Rabie court's overall performance. Every challenge to an emergency regulation which made its way to the Appellate Division was rejected.[56] Government powers to arrest were buttressed.[57] The rights of detainees were undermined.[58] The power to ban meetings was supported.[59] Subordinate officials were held entitled to expand sharply the scope of subversive statements whose utterance was prohibited.[60] 'Undue delegation' arguments, asserting that the State President had unlawfully delegated too much or too arbitrary power to subordinate officials, were rejected.[61] In this gloomy landscape, the only points of light are

[56] *Tsenoli*, 1986 (4) SA 1150 (A) (upholding regulations providing for arrest and detention without trial); *Omar*, 1987 (3) SA 859 (A) (upholding regulations denying detainees a right to a hearing and a right of access to counsel); *Ngqumba*, 1988 (4) SA 224 (A) (again upholding the regulations providing for denying detainees a right to a hearing and a right of access to counsel); *Ngqumba*, 1988 (4) SA 224 (A) (again upholding the regulations providing for arrest and detention without trial); *United Democratic Front*, 1988 (4) SA 830 (A) (upholding emergency media regulations); *Release Mandela Campaign*, 1988 (4) SA 903 (A) (applying *United Democratic Front*).

[57] Besides the cases rejecting attacks on the emergency arrest regulations (see n. 56), see *Dempsey*, 1988 (3) SA 19 (A) (limiting the grounds for challenge of an emergency arrest, and placing part of the burden of proof on the challenger); *Ngqumba*, 1988 (4) SA 224 (A) (rejecting a range of challenges to the validity of arrests and subsequent detentions, though also acknowledging one requirement for validity—that the arrestee must be told the cause of his arrest as soon after his arrest as is practicable—which would later be applied in a detainee's favour in *Swart*, 1989 (1) SA 295 (A)); *Bishop of the RC Church*, Case No. 165/87 (Appellate Division 29 Sept. 1988) (upholding the validity of an emergency arrest, in good part on the basis of *Dempsey* and *Ngqumba*). See also *Parker*, 1989 (2) SA 633 (A) (finding the requirement that the arrestee be told the cause of his arrest satisfied without an explicit statement of the cause, in light of the circumstances of the arrest).

[58] See *Omar*, 1987 (3) SA 859 (A) (upholding regulations denying detainees a right to a hearing and a right of access to counsel).

[59] In *Van der Westhuizen NO* v. *United Democratic Front*, 1989 (2) SA 242 (A), the Appellate Division interpreted an emergency regulation authorizing the Commissioner and Divisional Commissioners of Police to prohibit gatherings as conferring on them a power that was *not* objectively justiciable).

[60] *Release Mandela Campaign*, 1988 (4) SA 903 (A) (upholding validity of a notice issued by the Commissioner of Police, the effect of which was to make it a subversive statement to encourage any of an extremely wide range of actions meant to protest against detentions without trial).

[61] See *Tsenoli*, 1986 (4) SA 1150 (A), at 1182 (rejecting claim that regulations failed to provide sufficient guidance to arresting officers on criteria for arrest); *United Democratic Front*, 1988 (4) SA 830 (A), at 843–6 (rejecting claim that regulations granted Commissioner of Police excessive authority to add to the regulations' listing of proscribed 'subversive statements').

a few decisions setting outer limits on the arrest power and seeking to respond to powerful allegations of mistreatment of detainees.[62]

This is roughly what one might expect of an independent judiciary in the midst of emergency: that it would largely vindicate the demands of state security, yet not altogether forget the claims of the victims of the security apparatus. It is also roughly what one might expect from a judiciary consciously seeking to support the exercise of state power while lending it a legitimizing gloss. That these decisions were the work of the emergency team does not enable us to choose either of these broad and beguilingly easy generalizations, for we do not yet know how to characterize these judges' understanding of their own responsibilities. My purpose in this chapter and the next will be to look more closely at the decisions of the Rabie court, in an effort to uncover the judicial attitudes that informed these cases and that, I suggest, will help us subsequently to explain more thoughtfully why this court, or any court in an emergency, goes as far as it does, and why it goes no further. We will look carefully, therefore, at several of the Rabie court's decisions, not in order to analyse them for their own sake—although they richly, or rather grimly, reward such analysis—but to gather the data from which we may catch the conscience of the court.

Our inquiry will produce results both chilling and reassuring. In this chapter, we will look more closely at some of the most important claims the court has denied. These cases suggest four conclusions. First, the challenges which the Appellate Division rejected have included, as the previous chapter would lead us to expect, claims that were far from frivolous. Each of these decisions must therefore be regarded as one in which the court *chose* to rule as it did. Second, the Appellate Division was repeatedly unable to develop legally persuasive rationales for the results it embraced. The court simply does not succeed in grounding its decisions in existing South African law. It responds to this inability in various unsatisfactory ways: by using existing doctrine without confronting its potential rigour; by announcing its conclusions on the basis of strikingly abrupt explanations; by ignoring opposing arguments; and (particularly in Hefer JA's case) by recasting the law, sometimes dramatically—though even these innovations do not escape the logical problems in which the court finds itself ensnared. Third, when we look at the particular claims that were denied, we will see that the court's decisions betoken a judicial willingness to accept the risk of invasion of human rights in order to maintain the efficacy of the emergency system. Fourth, and finally, the composition of the court's panels emphatically reflects the centrality of the emergency team.

[62] See *Nkwentsha*, 1988 (3) SA 99 (A) (emergency detainee can be brought to court to testify concerning lawfulness of his arrest); *Apleni*, 1989 (1) SA 195 (A) (devising procedural steps by which to help protect detainees from alleged police abuse); *Swart*, 1989 (1) SA 295 (A) (holding that emergency detention is invalid if the emergency arrest was invalid by reason of failure to inform the arrestee of the reasons for his detention in timely fashion).

Though the Appellate Division firmly set its face against systemic challenges to the emergency, in Chapter 4 we will consider the evidence that it still did not abandon all attention to human rights. Some of this evidence will come from cases which actually upheld human rights claims; some, however, will emerge from a further appraisal of the very cases in which the court denied such claims. We will find that the court usually was careful to preserve the institutional role of the judiciary against the emergency's momentum towards extra-legal power. Similarly, we will learn that although the court's decisions risked invasion of human rights, the court's willingness to take these risks may have been founded in part in trust in the government rather than in indifference to the rights at stake. On occasion, when the court encountered what it recognized as instances of actual abuse of governmental power, it was capable of responding creatively and vigorously. Even in decisions that rejected human rights claims, we will see that the court's reasoning repeatedly displays both a reluctance to dislodge existing legal doctrine more than is necessary and an angry ambivalence towards the task of shielding the emergency from the inroads of human rights advocates. With these findings in mind, Chapter 5 will look at the decidedly different performance of the Appellate Division under its present chief justice, and seek to explain the complex and cross-cutting patterns which the cases present.

B. The Rights Denied

If we are to judge the judges of the Appellate Division, we must look carefully at the claims which they adjudicated. It will not do simply to assume that the Appellate Division had considerable interpretive leeway in reading the statutory provisions and the regulations of the emergency. To demonstrate that the court rejected legally substantial, rather than merely colourable, claims, we must look at those claims themselves against the background of South African law. To show that the court developed and even stretched the law to deny these claims, we must look at whether the court responded to them with persuasive arguments or with its own merely colourable doctrinal devices. To prove that the court was prepared to risk invasion of human rights if the preservation of emergency authority entailed such risk, we must consider what the judgments tell us about the courts' weighing of these concerns. Finally, to see the role of the emergency team we must look both at the judgments in which the emergency team joined and at the fate of non-members who sat on emergency (or closely related) cases and failed to join in those judgments. Let us conduct this examination with three of the critical cases by which the Rabie Appellate Division loosened the limits on emergency powers: *Dempsey*,[63]

[63] *Dempsey*, 1988 (3) SA 19 (A), reversing *Dempsey* v. *Minister of Law and Order and Others*, 1986 (4) SA 530 (C).

which made it easier for the state to defend emergency arrests in court; *Omar*,[64] which cut back on the rights of those in detention; and *United Democratic Front*,[65] which ruled that a challenge to an emergency regulation could not be heard because of an ouster clause.

1. Dempsey

In *Dempsey* the acting regional superior of the Dominican Order of South Africa (Dempsey) sought the release of one of the nuns of her Order, Sister Harkin, who had been arrested and detained on the basis of the emergency regulations. In one sense, the issues on appeal were relatively confined, for Dempsey did not challenge the validity of the regulations, but only sought to show that under those regulations the arrest of Sister Harkin was unjustified. From another perspective, however, the case was very important indeed, for it laid out much of the framework within which all emergency arrests would be judged, and did so in a fashion profoundly unsympathetic to challenges to those arrests. As we shall see, the court's route to this result involved not only striking, and notably ill-founded, judicial creativity but also entailed the overriding of the more liberal views of at least two members of the Appellate Division (not on the emergency team), who were not made part of the panel in *Dempsey*.

The regulation under which Sister Harkin was arrested authorized any member of a 'Force'[66] to arrest without warrant 'any person whose detention is, in the opinion of such member, necessary for the maintenance of public order or the safety of the public or that person himself, or for the termination of the state of emergency ...'.[67] Because this regulation made the 'opinion' of the officer the touchstone for arrest, it was apparent from *Hurley*—decided just weeks before this regulation was promulgated—that courts would not be empowered to test whether there were reasonable, objective grounds for the officer's opinion.[68] In the words of the *Dempsey* court, '[i]t is ... obvious that the question of the necessity for detention has in terms of reg 3(1) been left for decision to members of the Forces and to no one else. ... It is trite that it is not the function of the Court in such a case to enquire into the correctness of the opinion.'[68a]

What was not obvious as a matter of legal doctrine, however, was whether the subjective standard embodied in the regulations would turn out to be a rigorous or a relaxed one. The ingredients for developing a taut standard were at hand. First, it was well established that the *onus* (the burden of proof) in a

[64] *Omar*, 1987 (3) SA 859 (A).
[65] *United Democratic Front*, 1988 (4) SA 830 (A).
[66] 'Force' was defined to encompass the South African Police, Railways Police Force, Defence Force, and Prisons Service. Reg. 1(ii), Proc. R. 109, *Government Gazette* 10280 (12 June 1986).
[67] Reg. 3(1), Proc. R. 109, *Government Gazette*, 10280 (12 June 1986).
[68] See Ch. 2, text at nn. 140–5.
[68a] Dempsey, 1988(3) SA at 34B–D.

case challenging an arrest lay on the party defending the arrest. Second, the fact that only subjective review could be carried out did not mean that *no* review could be carried out. On the contrary, South African law already provided a range of criteria on which even subjective discretion could be tested. As *Dempsey* itself put it, '[t]he validity of the arrest may ... be challenged on any of the well-known grounds on which the performance of his functions by a statutory functionary endowed with discretionary powers may be challenged'.[69]

Some of these grounds are straightforward and of little practical value. It is well settled that if the public officer acts '*mala fide* or from ulterior and improper motives' then relief may be granted.[70] Moreover, to prove bad faith Dempsey would have been entitled to seek to prove that the officer's decision to arrest was unreasonable—not because he had to have a reasonable opinion but because *grossly* unreasonable conduct could indicate bad faith.[71] But the cases in which such bad faith can be proved against the contrary testimony inevitably presented by the officer in question will surely be rare ones.

Public officials must, however, do more than act in good faith. They must act on the right questions: they must 'apply their minds'. The well-known *Northwest Townships* case, cited approvingly by *Dempsey* itself, recognizes an array of failures to apply one's mind, including 'capriciousness, a failure, on the part of the person enjoined to make the decision, to appreciate the nature and limits of the discretion to be exercised, a failure to direct his thoughts to the relevant data or the relevant principles, reliance on irrelevant considerations, an arbitrary approach, and an application of wrong principles'.[72]

These diverse and ambiguous requirements offered the potential for quite stringent scrutiny of putatively subjective decisions, and lawyers[73] and some courts[74] began trying to realize that potential. The lower court decision in *Dempsey* was an important example of this thinking. Mr Justice Marais held that even if Sister Harkin's conduct provided the arresting officer with grounds

[69] *Dempsey*, 1988 (3) SA at 35B. The court observes (at 35C) that '[t]he grounds on which this may be done are listed in cases such as *Shidiack* v. *Union Government (Minister of the Interior)* 1912 AD 642 at 651–2 and *Northwest Townships (Pty) Ltd.* v. *Administrator, Transvaal, and Another*, 1975 (4) SA 1 (T) at 8.' Aspects of both of these cases are discussed in the text at nn. 70–2 below.

[70] *Shidiack* v. *Union Government (Minister of the Interior)*, 1912 AD 642, at 642.

[71] *Northwest Townships (Pty) Ltd.* v. *Administrator, Transvaal and Another*, 1975 (4) SA 1 (T), at 8F (full bench) (hereafter cited as *Northwest Townships*).

[72] Ibid. 8G.

[73] A workshop of human rights lawyers in 1987 'was of the opinion that civil rights lawyers should concentrate on establishing higher standards of reasonableness required of an official exercising a discretion even where it is subjectively framed and as set out, for example, in the *Northwestern* [sic] *Townships* case ...'. N. Haysom and L. Mangan (eds.), *Emergency Law: Papers Presented at a Workshop—Johannesburg, April 1987* (Johannesburg: Centre for Applied Legal Studies, University of the Witwatersrand, 1987), 13.

[74] See *Radebe* v. *Minister of Law and Order and Another*, 1987 (1) SA 586 (W) at 595G (arresting officer, if acting *bona fide*, must have 'done so upon a misconception of his powers'); *Jaffer and Another* v. *Minister of Law and Order and Others*, 1986 (4) SA 1027 (C) (arrester failed to have any opinion on the need for detention lasting more than 3 days).

for arrest, the officer had to determine not merely that she was subject to arrest but that she was due to be arrested under the emergency regulations. One difference between arrest under the ordinary law of the land and arrest under the emergency regulations is that only those arrested under the emergency regulations are normally subject to detention without trial, and accordingly the officer ordering the arrest was required to

> weigh, not only whether the arrest was called for, but also whether the ensuing detention under the emergency regulations was called for. That necessarily entailed considering whether or not Sister Harkin, being at liberty after the day's events were over [as she would have become if arrested under ordinary law, assuming she was released on bail or on her own recognizance], posed any potential threat to the maintenance of public order or the safety of the public or the termination of the state of emergency. That he failed to consider. So fundamental an omission, in my view, prevents his opinion from qualifying as the kind of opinion which he was required to hold before he became entitled to exercise powers of arrest and detention in terms of reg 3(1).[75]

This argument would have given some teeth to the general 'apply the mind' doctrine in emergency-arrest cases. Given the array of internal security laws, not to mention the general criminal law, which the South African authorities could use instead of emergency powers, detainees might have been able to point to a variety of alternatives which officers had to consider on pain of invalidating an emergency arrest. Moreover, it might have been possible to maintain that some alternatives were so manifestly satisfactory that the officer could not have concluded that an emergency arrest was necessary if he had properly considered the alternatives.[76] The upshot of this logic might have been a significant limitation on the power to make emergency arrests. Indeed, one could imagine an 'apply the mind' doctrine so rigorous that the limits on 'subjective' discretion would become essentially indistinguishable from those applicable to 'objective' discretion.

In studyng the Appellate Division's response to this case, and to this prospect, it is important for us to see both what it did and what it did not do. There were two issues: whether the 'apply the mind' requirement would apply to arrests, and which party would have the *onus* on this requirement if it applied at all. The most thoroughgoing rejection of this line of argument would have been to deny that the 'apply the mind' doctrine could be employed in this context, but this the Appellate Division did not do.[77] The court *did* give this requirement a less demanding cast than the lower court had seemed to have in mind, and than *Northwest Townships* suggested. According to the judgment

[75] *Dempsey* v. *Minister of Law and Order and Another*, 1986 (4) SA 530 (C) at 542.

[76] For an examination of the limits which such reasoning could place on the power to arrest, see C. Plasket, 'Clipping Dempsey's Wings: The Consideration of Alternatives to Regulation 3(1) of the Emergency Regulations', 3 *SAJHR* 76 (1987).

[77] *Dempsey*, 1988 (3) SA 19 (A) at 35B–C.

of Hefer JA, 'it is primarily his [the official's] task to decide what is relevant and what is not, and, also, to determine the weight to be attached to each relevant factor'.[78] Hence the officer's decision could not be overturned 'merely because a factor which the Court considers relevant was not taken into account, or because insufficient or undue weight was, according to the Court's objective assessment, accorded to a relevant factor'.[79]

This characterization of the doctrine certainly limited its force. In part, Hefer JA's obiter dictum (for such it was) may have departed from pre-existing South African law on the 'apply the mind' rule, not by declaring the officer's discretion to decide how much weight to give to relevant factors (this discretion was generally recognized) but by asserting that the officer had a comparable discretion to decide what is and is not relevant at all.[80] At the least, Hefer JA was staking out a position on a controversial question, without any express acknowledgement that the point was even controversial, and without citing any authority actually supporting his position.[81] It is striking to compare *Dempsey* on this issue with another Appellate Division decision, handed down eleven days later by a panel which included none of the members of the emergency team. In this commercial case, *Johannesburg Stock Exchange* v. *Witwatersrand Nigel Ltd.*, Corbett JA writes for the court and states clearly that a failure to apply the mind can be shown by demonstrating that the official in question 'took into account irrelevant considerations or ignored relevant ones'.[82] Apparently the Appellate Division was of two minds on this question and those who took the narrower view decided the emergency case. Corbett himself sat on the first of the Rabie emergency cases, *Tsenoli*, and no others.

[78] Ibid. 35E.

[79] Ibid. 35E–F.

[80] Standard doctrine left it largely up to the official making the decision to decide how much weight to give to the factors he or she was considering but, according to Lawrence Baxter, author of one of the leading treatises on South African administrative law, required the decisionmaker at least 'to take the relevant considerations *into account*': *Administrative Law* (Cape Town: Juta, 1984), 505 (emphasis in the original). Baxter notes decisions contrary to his position, but he considers them 'contrary to the weight of modern authority' (ibid. 503 n. 128). Another leading administrative-law scholar, Marinus Wiechers, agrees that this duty to take all relevant points into account should be the law, *Administrative Law*, trans. G. Carpenter (Durban: Butterworths, 1985), 297, though he seems at least somewhat doubtful that this *is* what the law requires (see ibid. 293–4). For a case supporting such doubts, see *Administrateur van Suidwes-Afrika en 'n Ander* v. *Pieters*, 1973 (1) SA 850 (A) at 859 (asserting that a decision reviewable only on subjective grounds would not be invalid if it rested on both valid and invalid bases).

[81] Hefer JA cites only one case in support of his view that it is 'primarily' up to the decision-maker to decide what factors are relevant, unless the statute under which the functionary acts resolves this matter. The cited portion of this case, *Johannesburg City Council* v. *The Administrator, Transvaal, and Mayofis*, 1971 (1) SA 87 (A) at 99A, declares only that 'the weight to be attached to any particular factor relevant to the enquiry was primarily a matter for the decision of the Board'. This statement on its face does not suggest that it was equally up to the Board, or other decisionmaker, to decide whether factors were relevant at all, nor did the *Johannesburg City Council* court decide the case on the basis that the officials involved had wholly ignored a relevant factor.

[82] *Johannesburg Stock Exchange and Another* v. *Witwatersrand Nigel Ltd. and Another*, 1988 (3) SA 132 (A) at 152C–D.

While the difference in judicial mood which these two formulations capture may be very great, it must be said that Hefer JA's statement of the standard need not, in theory, greatly alter the content of the 'apply the mind' standard. After all, if a decisionmaker can satisfy the duty to take a factor into account by considering it but giving it minimal weight, the ultimate decision is likely to be identical to the one that would have been reached had the decisionmaker ignored the factor altogether. The court appeared still to acknowledge that the arresting officer's failure to consider aspects of the matter at hand which the court deemed relevant could bear on whether, under all the circumstances, he had properly applied his mind.[83] At least for the purposes of this case, moreover, the court did not dispute the relevance of considering the availability of arrest under the ordinary law of the land, and the likely character of Sister Harkin's future behaviour.[84] Hefer JA's characterization of the 'apply the mind' requirement thus did not foreclose a decision in favour of Sister Harkin. It was left for a later case to give a definitively narrow cast to this doctrine.[85]

The critical doctrinal move in *Dempsey* was on the second issue, the question of *onus*. Here the court engaged in a familiar judicial manœuvre: it allocated this *onus* in a way that disfavoured the party alleging a failure to apply the mind. The challenge to the arrest in the lower court had been decided on affidavits alone, and the lower court's decision had thus rested on inference from the absence of any indication in the arresting officer's affidavit that he had considered the required questions. The Appellate Division, however, concluded that on a proper allocation of the burden of proof the lower court's inference could not be sustained.[86] As we will see, the question of *onus* was one on which the Appellate Division had divided, without reaching a conclusive resolution, in an earlier case. Those judges who had expressed a more liberal view in that earlier case, however, were not on the panel in *Dempsey*, and in their absence the court was able to reach a decision that was by no means dictated by existing doctrine. Rather, this decision rested on distinctly unpersuasive grounds.

The general question of the *onus* of proof of justification of a warrantless arrest was not a new one. In fact, it had been addressed only the previous year in the *Hurley* case, which on this point, as on others, had decided in favour of the rights of the detainee. Moreover, the court's opinion in *Hurley* had suggested that on this issue there was considerable precedent for its decision, which was that the *onus* to justify a warrantless arrest lies on the arresting officer.[87] Speaking for the court, Rabie CJ went on to

[83] *Dempsey*, 1988 (3) SA at 35F. [84] Ibid. 40F.

[85] See text at nn. 114–21 below (discussing *Ngqumba*).

[86] *Dempsey*, 1988 (3) SA at 41H. One member of the court concurred in the result only, and would have reached this result without regard to burden of proof, on the ground that it was unnecessary for the arresting officer to consider the matters on which the lower court had focused: ibid. 42G–J (judgment of Nestadt JA). As noted below, see text at n. 97, Nestadt JA never sat on another emergency case while Rabie headed the Appellate Division.

[87] *Minister of Law and Order and Others* v. *Hurley and Another*, 1986 (3) SA 568 (A) at 586–9 (A).

> add that I consider it to be good policy that the law should be as there stated. An arrest constitutes an interference with the liberty of the individual concerned, and it therefore seems to be fair and just to require that the person who arrested or caused the arrest of another person should bear the *onus* of proving that his action was justified in law.[88]

In *Dempsey* the Appellate Division did not reject *Hurley*. It 'accept[ed], of course, that the *onus* to justify an arrest is on the party who alleges that it was lawfully made and, since an arrest can only be justified on the basis of statutory authority, that the *onus* can only be discharged by showing that it was made within the ambit of the relevant statute'.[89] But the court argued that the extent of that burden was specified by the statutory authority at issue here: regulation 3(1) of the emergency regulations. That regulation required only that the arresting officer hold the subjective opinion that the arrest was necessary for one of the broad purposes specified in the regulation itself. What if he held the opinion, but for reasons that amounted to a failure to apply his mind? The court answered: '[I]f it is alleged that the opinion was *improperly* formed, it is for the party who makes the allegation to prove it.'[90]

This ruling was hardly compelled. Another panel of the Appellate Division had wrestled with similar issues, without resolving them, in *Katofa*'s case, decided in 1986.[91] *Katofa* was a challenge to a detention in South-West Africa (now Namibia) under a proclamation permitting the Administrator General to issue a warrant for arrest of anyone whom he was 'satisfied' was involved in violence or intimidation—a subjective discretion not unlike that at issue in *Dempsey*. Every member of the *Katofa* court agreed, or assumed, that when the detention was challenged the Administrator General bore the *onus* of justifying the arrest. Everyone also agreed that the Administrator General had to show that he in fact was 'satisfied', that is, that he did actually hold the opinion that the detainee was someone involved in violence.

Two members of the *Katofa* panel (Trengove JA, joined by Botha JA) took the view that the Administrator General had to demonstrate not only that he held the opinion, but that he had arrived at it through a proper application of his mind.[92] Trengove JA says that to do so the Administrator General would have had to show that he was aware of the limits on his powers to arrest. Moreover, according to Trengove JA, where (as here) the Administrator General chose not to disclose the reasons or facts underlying his being 'satisfied' that the person in question fell within those powers, he ran the risk of failing to discharge his *onus*. These requirements are potentially strict ones, although it is also possible that Trengove JA would have permitted them to be satisfied

[88] Ibid. 589E–F.

[89] *Dempsey*, 1988 (3) SA at 38B.

[90] Ibid. 38G.

[91] *Kabinet van die Tussentydse Regering vir Suidwes-Afrika en 'n Ander* v. *Katofa*, 1987 (1) SA 695 (A) (hereafter cited as *Katofa*).

[92] Ibid. 739–43 (judgment of Trengove JA, with whom Botha JA concurred).

very summarily.[93] In any event, this view was obviously quite distant from the position Hefer JA adopts in *Dempsey*.

Rabie CJ, joined by one other judge, took a narrower view in *Katofa* than Trengove JA had advocated—but even their view was not necessarily as strict as the position Hefer JA articulated in his *Dempsey* judgment, with which Rabie concurred. Rabie argued that when an arrest is challenged, and the challenge does not assert claims of bad faith or failure to apply the mind or similar shortcomings in the Administrator General's exercise of his discretion, he need only aver that he held the opinion in question.[94] (Unlike Hefer JA, Rabie CJ did not assert that, if such a challenge to the Administrator General's exercise of his discretion *was* made, the challenger would bear the *onus* of showing an improper exercise of discretion rather than the Administrator General bearing the *onus* of proving that his exercise of discretion was proper.)[95] *Katofa* did not resolve the issue of what the state had to prove in order to meet a challenge that had not raised bad faith or similar challenges, however, because the fifth judge on the panel, van Heerden JA, announced that he considered it 'expedient' not to offer an opinion on it.[96] The practical extent of the state's *onus* therefore remained unsettled until *Dempsey*.

The panel that decided *Dempsey*, however, was remarkably different from the panel that heard *Katofa*. The *Dempsey* panel included neither of the justices from *Katofa* who had urged that a relatively heavier *onus* be placed on the arresting official. One of these, Trengove JA, had retired, but the other, Botha JA, never sat on a state-of-emergency case during Rabie's tenure as chief justice. Van Heerden JA was also absent from this panel, although he did sit on three emergency cases during this era. Chief Justice Rabie himself, however, sat on the second case as he had on the first. Joining him on the *Dempsey* panel were three of the four other members of what I have called the 'emergency team'.[97] The remaining member of the panel was Nestadt JA, who concurred in the result but on quite different grounds from those advanced for the court by Hefer JA. Nestadt JA never sat on another emergency case while Rabie was chief (or acting chief) justice.

Hefer JA's judgment for four members of this court resolved the question of *onus* in part on the ground that it would be too burdensome and too intrusive to require the arresting officer to demonstrate that he had avoided each of the possible ways of failing to apply his mind in response to a mere general averment that the detention was unlawful.[98] The court put considerable

[93] *Kabinet van die Tussentydse Regering vir Suidwes-Afrika en 'n Ander* v. *Katofa*, 1987 (1) SA at 743–4 (judgment of Trengove JA). For a discussion of Trengove JA's ambiguous indication that this test could be met very easily, see E. Mureinik, 'Security and Integrity', 1987 *Acta Juridica* 197, 215–16.

[94] *Katofa*, 1987 (1) SA at 735 (judgment of Rabie CJ, with whom Jansen JA concurred).

[95] Dempsey's counsel made this point in heads of argument. *Dempsey*, 1988 (3) SA at 29G–H (argument of counsel).

[96] *Katofa*, 1987 (1) SA at 744 (judgment of van Heerden JA).

[97] These were Hefer JA, Viljoen JA, and Joubert JA.

[98] *Dempsey*, 1988 (3) SA at 37I–38A.

emphasis on its view that the pleadings in *Dempsey* itself failed to apprise the arresting officer that the question of his applying his mind was at issue.[99] But this argument is surely overdrawn as a general matter, for it would have been possible to ease the arresting officer's difficulty by requiring the party challenging the arrest to plead the basis for his position while placing on the arrester the burden of proving the facts thus placed in issue.[100] Another potential response to this problem might have been to outline the fundamental points the arrester had to prove in order to make out a prima-facie case that he had properly exercised his discretion; indeed, Trengove's judgment in *Katofa* could be taken to suggest just such requirements.[101]

The court argued, in any event, that the 'more fundamental reason'[102] for its subdivision of the burden of proof was that regulation 3(1) prescribed only one limit on the power of arrest, namely, that the officer hold the requisite subjective opinion. This, and this alone, was a 'jurisdictional fact' on whose presence the lawfulness of arrest turned. To be sure, if it were shown that the officer had formed that opinion in some improper fashion, such as by failing to apply his mind, then the arrest would not be valid, but proper formation of the opinion was not a jurisdictional fact.[103] Hence in each arrest case, as Hefer JA says, there are 'two separate and distinct issues, each having its own *onus*'.[104] The arresting officer must prove that he actually held the opinion in question; the arrested person must prove that the officer formed that opinion improperly.

Hefer JA offers little foundation for this 'more fundamental' rationale in terms of precedent or broad principle. In fact, he cites *no* arrest case in which

[99] Ibid. 41. *Bishop of the RC Church*, No. 165/87 (Appellate Division, 29 Sept. 1988), another arrest case, follows *Dempsey* in pointing to the failure of the detainee's pleadings to raise the issue of the arresting officer's applying his mind. Typed judgment at 19–20.

[100] Christopher Forsyth makes a similar point: 'The Sleep of Reason: Security Cases before the Appellate Division', 105 *SALJ* 679, 694 n. 67 (1988). As it happens, Dempsey's papers did include affidavits alleging that Sister Harkin's arrest could not have been the result of the officer's properly applying his mind. These allegations led one member of the court, Nestadt JA, to conclude that 'on a benevolent interpretation' Dempsey's allegations were sufficient to raise this issue: *Dempsey*, at 42E. (Nestadt JA concurred in the result, but on different grounds than the majority. See n. 86 above.) The majority felt the pleadings basically pointed in a different direction, and emphasized the need for specific pleading on such points as these (ibid. 40–1). This issue could, of course, have been assessed within the context of a rule placing the burden of proof on the arrester to meet any well-pleaded objections. In the mean time, *Dempsey*'s discussion of the need for specific pleading raised the grim possibility that an explicit, but unspecific, pleading of improper exercise of discretion on the part of the arresting officer not only would not sustain the arrestee's *onus* but would not even suffice to entitle the arrested person to an evidentiary hearing. For a discussion of the difficulties faced by detainees seeking to have oral evidence heard in their cases, see K. Satchwell, 'Referral to Oral Evidence', in Haysom and Mangan (eds.), *Emergency Law*, (cit. n. 73), 94, 123–5.

[101] *Katofa*, 1987 (1) SA at 743–4 (judgment of Trengove JA).

[102] *Dempsey*, 1988 (3) SA at 38A.

[103] Ibid. 38D–G. For an incisive analysis of Hefer JA's use of the 'jurisdictional fact' concept, see E. Mureinik, 'Pursuing Principle: The Appellate Division and Review under the State of Emergency', 5 *SAJHR* 60, 67–9 (1989).

[104] *Dempsey*, 1988 (3) SA at 38G–H.

such a slicing of the *onus* had been carried out. He does offer what amounts to a policy justification, namely that this allocation of the burden of proof 'will bring applications of the present kind in line with other applications for the review of the decisions of statutory functionaries, except that the [state] will first have to prove that the required opinion was actually formed'.[105] It is difficult to know whether Hefer JA's point is that arrests are actually not very different from other governmental actions, and so should be subject to similar legal regulation, or whether he means to say that, despite the differences between arrests and other government conduct, similarity of legal doctrine is so important that it should be sought even in significantly dissimilar fields. On either reading, the argument is unappealing.

Nor is it persuasive in terms of technical legal reasoning. Consider two possible explanations of the fact that what Hefer JA called the 'well-known grounds' (such as the 'apply the mind' requirement) 'on which the performance of his functions by a statutory functionary endowed with discretionary powers may be challenged' actually do have legal force.[106] Either these grounds are part of the arrest regulation itself (an implied part, since they certainly are not express), or they are independent common-law requirements.[107] If they are part of the regulation, then they would be encompassed within Hefer JA's observation that '[a]ny statutory function can ... only be validly performed within the limits prescribed by the statute itself'.[108] Compliance with these rules would also be a jurisdictional fact, if this compliance is 'prescribed as a precondition to the performance of the function'.[109] Since the regulation does not even mention these requirements, however, but only—on our assumption—implies them, it is not easy to tell whether it impliedly makes them preconditions or not. To be blunt, the regulation is ambiguous on this point. In that case the South African rules of statutory construction calling for resolution of ambiguities in favour of the liberty of the subject are obviously relevant, and would point towards treating these requirements as preconditions since that would make it easier for arrested people to challenge the lawfulness of their arrests.[110]

Suppose, instead, that these grounds are not impliedly incorporated in the

[105] Ibid. 38J–39A. Hefer JA also observes that this rule is in line with the allocation of the burden of proof in cases of 'so-called negligent performance of an act authorised by statute' (ibid. 39B).

[106] Ibid. 35B.

[107] It is not important now for us to choose between these explanations. We will have occasion to explore this choice in discussing the *United Democratic Front* case, see text at nn. 217–74 below.

[108] *Dempsey*, 1988 (3) SA at 38C.

[109] Ibid.

[110] Mureinik provides another argument to the same conclusion. He writes that 'if the only fact essential to the jurisdiction of the official is the bare existence of his opinion, understood as an empty husk independent of how it has been reached, then the official is acting within his jurisdiction—within his powers—even when he is abusing his discretion. What, then, entitles the court to interfere with his decision? Hefer JA's judgment strikes, therefore, at the ultimate justification for review for abuse of discretion ...'. 'Pursuing Principle' (cit. n. 103), 68–9.

regulation, but instead are independently applicable rules of the common law. If these non-statutory rules are still binding, as *Dempsey* says they are, it is presumably because they are elements of the common law which have not been overturned by any legislative enactments and so retain their validity. But in that case it seems mistaken to say, as the court does, that 'an arrest can only be justified on the basis of statutory authority'.[111] If both statutory and common-law rules apply to the arrest decision, and apply independently of each other, then proof that the statutory requirements are satisfied simply would not amount to proof that the relevant legal requirements for a valid arrest have been met.

By now it is evident that *Dempsey* displays each of the features with which we are concerned. First, *Dempsey*'s legal position was far from frivolous. Second, the court rejects this position by abridging the legal principle that the *onus* in an arrest case is on the party defending the arrest. This is an act of judicial creativity, and, as we have seen, one with a decidedly weak doctrinal foundation. Third, the case vividly displays a judicial decision to value the interests of emergency-law enforcement over the rights of those arrested under emergency authority. The impact of the case, after all, required no powers of prophecy to gauge. By imposing the *onus* on the detainee on every opinion issue except whether the officer actually held the opinion in question—on which the officer's testimony to his own subjective state of mind would obviously be particularly hard to dispute—the court made it harder for detainees to challenge their arrests. By the same token, the court made it harder for detainees to win relief even in those cases in which the arresting officers really had failed to apply their minds. The court did not shut the door to these cases altogether, for a detainee might succeed in carrying his *onus*, but it placed what should indeed be called the *risk* of non-persuasion on the targets of emergency power. (Indeed, even before this decision lawyers for detainees were finding that once the police offered reasons for their arrest decisions, 'the detainee had little chance of success in any application for release'.)[112] Fourth, the absence of the authors of the most liberal *Katofa* judgment, and the subsequent absence of the sole *Dempsey* dissenter, confirm the importance of the presence of the emergency team.

Two years later, after Rabie ACJ's retirement, considerations akin to some of these would lead the Appellate Division to reject *Dempsey*'s allocation of part of the *onus* in arrest cases to the arrested person.[113] For now, however, *Dempsey* was not a question mark but rather a stepping-stone for a court determined to forestall the prospect of serious impairment of emergency arrest powers. As Etienne Mureinik has written, 'in a judgment given a fortnight

[111] *Dempsey*, 1988 (3) SA at 38B.

[112] N. Haysom and S. Kahanovitz, 'Courts and the State of Emergency', in G. Moss and I. Obery (eds.), *South African Review 4* (Johannesburg: Ravan, 1987), 187, 194.

[113] *During NO* v. *Boesak*, 1990 (3) SA 861 (A). I discuss this decision below. See Ch. 5, text at nn. 53–9 and 80–93.

later, the court adopted so uncompromisingly hostile an approach to the kind of inquiry pioneered by Marais J [in the lower court in *Dempsey*] as to make it most unlikely that many more applications of the present kind will be brought in the foreseeable future'.[114] That case was *Ngqumba*,[115] decided by almost the same panel that had decided *Dempsey*.[116] *Ngqumba* rejects a range of challenges to emergency arrests and detentions, among them the 'apply the mind' argument. The *Ngqumba* court's treatment of the 'apply the mind' point is quite different from the *Dempsey* judgment, for here the court puts no weight on deficiencies of pleading, does not focus on the technical question of *onus*, and does not explicitly revisit Hefer JA's *Dempsey* challenge to the doctrinal principle that a decisionmaker must consider the relevant matters in order to have applied his or her mind.

Instead *Ngqumba* concentrates on the question of whether an officer's failure to tell the court which alternatives to emergency arrest he considered, and why he rejected these alternatives, justifies a finding that the officer failed to apply his mind. The court's answer appears to be that such a finding would only be justified if the detention otherwise appeared 'so drastic and unnecessary' that it demanded explanation.[117] (Roughly the same standard applies, the court says, to review of the Minister's post-arrest decision to extend an arrestee's detention.)[118]

These answers have the flavour of a decision about *onus*, but the court's discussion suggests that it has more than *onus* in mind. The Appellate Division does not seem to believe that the arresting officer must always actually consider these matters, though it stops short of declaring that officers are free as a matter of routine to fail even to consider the possibility of alternatives to arrest under the emergency regulations. Writing for the court, Rabie ACJ observes that the arresting officer will '*probably* ... as well as he is able to in the circumstances, consider whether a less drastic action will not be adequate'.[119] Moreover, he says, those who are empowered to make emergency arrests 'are not lawyers' and may not always know 'whether the situation which they want to counteract "can properly be dealt with under the ordinary laws of the land"'.[120] Rabie firmly declares that the fact that emergency powers are meant for times when the ordinary law of the land is inadequate 'does not entail that an emergency measure cannot be applied in instances where the ordinary laws of the land would also be applicable'.[121] Or, as Rabie put it six months later

[114] Mureinik, 'Pursuing Principle' (cit. n. 103), 69.

[115] *Ngqumba*, 1988 (4) SA 224 (A).

[116] The only difference was that Nestadt JA did not sit on *Ngqumba*. His place was taken by Vivier JA. The five judges who sat on *Ngqumba*, Rabie ACJ and Joubert, Viljoen, Hefer, and Vivier JJA, were the five members of the emergency team.

[117] Ibid. 252F–G.

[118] Ibid. 256E–F. The court in *Ngqumba* accepts that the Minister did apply his mind without even having an affidavit from the Minister saying so! Ibid. 254C–255J.

[119] Ibid. 252E.

[120] Ibid. 254A. ('Lawyers' may also be translated as 'jurists'.)

[121] Ibid. 254C. Dennis Davis and Hugh Corder maintain that '[t]his extraordinary statement

in *Bishop of the Roman Catholic Church*, 'it is incorrect to say that a detention is lawful only when there is "no viable alternative"'.[122]

No doubt a careful doctrinal argument could have been prepared to support these conclusions, but *Ngqumba* does not contain it. What it does convey is the strong sense that the court responds to the conflict between the exigencies of emergency-law enforcement and the rights of people not to be subjected to unjustified emergency detention with solicitude for the difficulties faced by the arresting officers. Against the background of *Ngqumba* and *Dempsey*, we should not be surprised that during Chief Justice Rabie's tenure (and afterwards as well) only one emergency arrest was ever held invalid by the Appellate Division.[123] Between July 1985 and June 1990 approximately 41,700 people were detained under emergency powers.[124] Some people were held without trial for 'periods totalling in excess of three years'.[125] Among the detainees were a sizeable number of children 17 years of age or less.[126] The Appellate Division's decisions helped to shield these detentions from effective scrutiny.

2. Omar

Omar takes up where *Dempsey* leaves off—in terms of subject-matter, that is, for actually *Omar* is the earlier of the two decisions. *Dempsey* tells us how readily the courts will find that an emergency arrest is justified; *Omar* tells us how circumscribed the rights of those detained following such arrests will be. To give us the measure of these rights, the *Omar* court must not only interpret the emergency regulations, but also address their validity. The court decides that the emergency regulations deny detainees the right to a hearing in connection with the Minister of Law and Order's decision to extend their detentions, and also that the regulations deny detainees a right of access to their lawyers. The court concludes that, so construed, the regulations are valid applications of the State President's statutory power to make emergency regulations.

Omar dealt a demoralizing blow to those who sought to protect detainees' rights; it was called a 'devastating decision',[127] which gave the state 'an

seems to go counter to the purpose of the legislature in enacting the Public Safety Act': 'A Long March: Administrative Law in the Appellate Division', 4 *SAJHR* 281, 291 (1988).

122 *Bishop of the RC Church*, No. 165/87 (Appellate Division, 29 Sept. 1988), typed judgment at 21.

123 *Swart*, 1989 (1) SA 295 (A).

124 Human Rights Commission, *Human Rights Update June 1990* (June 1990), 4. During the same period approximately 12,700 people were detained under the Internal Security Act or under the laws of the 'independent' homelands. Ibid.

125 Human Rights Commission, South African Council of Churches, and Southern African Catholic Bishops' Conference, *Human Rights and Repression in Southern Africa: The Apartheid Machine Grinds On* (May 1989), 21.

126 Human Rights Commission, *Children and Repression 1987–1989 (Special Report SR-4)* (Jan. 1990), 14–17.

127 Davis and Corder, 'Long March' (cit. n. 121), 286.

executive carte blanche'.[128] I will not analyse every aspect of these judgments in detail, but we will look at the two broad issues of the case, and our study will find ample evidence of the traits of the Appellate Division's emergency decisionmaking with which this chapter is concerned. Thus it will be apparent that the court's conclusions were once again not compelled by the constraints of legal doctrine—an assessment amply confirmed in any event by the fact that judges in the lower courts had been 'fairly even divided' on these issues.[129] Moreover, the court again fails in important respects to develop an adequate legal argument for the decision it embraces. *Omar*, as we will see, seeks to couch its conclusions in the language of existing doctrine rather than overtly developing the law as *Dempsey* did. But the court's application of this doctrine is marked by the indistinct, and undemanding, cast which it gives to principles limiting state power, by a tendency to offer abrupt conclusions supported by little argument, and by a striking indifference to contrary argument, particularly in the case of one substantial challenge articulated not only by counsel but also by the sole member of the court who dissented. Not surprisingly, the views which the court articulates also convey anew the court's great concern for the interests of emergency–law enforcement, and its willingness to accept sharp intrusions on normally available rights as the price for effective emergency rule. Finally, we will find in the role of the lone dissenter further confirmation of the dominance of the emergency team.[130]

(*a*) *The Denial of Hearings.*

Regulation 3 of the emergency regulations addressed the circumstances in which persons could be arrested and detained, as in *Dempsey*, and the circumstances under which their detention could be extended beyond an initial fourteen-day period. Regulation 3(3) specified that such extensions, which could last as long as the emergency itself (and then be renewed if the emergency was renewed), could be ordered by the Minister 'without notice to any person and without hearing any person'.[131] This regulation was issued on the authority of the Public Safety Act, which allows the State President to 'make such

[128] L. Baxter, 'A Judicial Declaration of Martial Law', 3 *SAJHR* 317, 318 (1987); see A. Mathews, '*Omar* v. The Oumas', 3 *SAJHR* 312, 315 n. 2 (1987).

[129] J. Dugard, '*Omar*: Support for Wacks's Ideas on the Judicial Process?', 3 *SAJHR* 295, 297 (1987).

[130] *Omar* has been the subject of intense scholarly criticism, which has informed my discussion here. See the articles by Dugard, Rabie, Mathews, Baxter, McQuoid-Mason, Davis, Van der Leeuw, and Van der Vyver in 'Focus on *Omar*', 3 *SAJHR* 295–337 (1987); Davis and Corder, 'Long March' (cit. n. 121), 286–8; Forsyth, 'Sleep of Reason' (cit. n. 100), 694–700.

[131] Reg. 3(3), as amended in Proc. R. 207, *Government Gazette* 10003 (31 Oct. 1985). (For the text of the 1988 version of this regulation, not materially different from the text promulgated in Proc. R. 207, see Ch. 1, text at n. 70.) The amendment added the words 'without notice to any person and without hearing any person', and gave them retroactive effect, presumably in response to a lower court decision that had held that the right to a hearing was implicit in the regulation as it previously had been drafted (without those words). See *Nkwinti* v. *Commissioner of Police and Others*, 1986 (2) SA 421 (E).

regulations as appear to him to be necessary or expedient' for dealing with the circumstances of the emergency.[132] The challenge to the denial of hearings therefore posed two interpretive tasks for the Appellate Division: to construe the regulation and then to construe the statute to determine whether the regulation, so construed, was authorized by the statute.

(*i*) *Interpreting the Regulation.* The right to a hearing in South African law is embodied in the maxim *audi alteram partem.*[133] This maxim's mandates are multifaceted. According to counsel for the detainees in *Omar,*

> [i]t varies with the circumstances. In its fullest extent, it may include the right to be apprised of the information and reasons underlying the impending decision; to disclosure of material documents; to a public hearing and, at that hearing, to appear in person with legal representation, and to examine and cross-examine witnesses ... The test is always one of fundamental fairness and for this reason the principles of natural justice are always flexible.[134]

As we shall see, the majority finds that the emergency regulation completely does away with this maxim. The court does not overtly alter existing doctrine to reach this conclusion, for it seems to adopt the standard doctrinal formula for determining whether legislation has abrogated *audi alteram partem* in whole or in part. But the court fails to produce a satisfactory explanation of its result in terms of that doctrine, and adopts an interpretation visibly coloured by attention to security concerns.

To be sure, it can hardly be denied that the regulation at issue here deprived the detainees of much of the protection of this maxim, since it permitted the Minister to extend their detention without notice to them and without hearing from them. Indeed, a casual reader of the words 'without notice and without hearing' might think that the operation of the maxim had been excluded so totally that detainees simply had no rights of due process whatsoever.

This conclusion, however, would apparently have represented a misreading of the regulation—a misreading, that is, in South African terms. In *Omar* it was not disputed by the state[135] that the detainee still retained the right to make representations to the Minister *after* the decision to extend his detention.[136] Acting Chief Justice Rabie, in his judgment for the Appellate

[132] Public Safety Act 3 of 1953, s. 3(1)(*a*). This provision is set out in Ch. 1 at n. 49.

[133] See Ch. 2, text at nn. 109–10.

[134] *Omar,* 1987 (3) SA at 863 (argument of counsel).

[135] *Omar,* 1987 (3) SA at 878G, 881D (arguments of counsel). (*Omar* actually was a decision in three separate appeals, and in one, *Omar* itself, counsel adopted the lower court's conclusions—which included a finding that the *audi* principle had been totally excluded—but did not specifically address the question of a right to make representations after the decision. See ibid. 869–71 (argument of W. G. Burger SC).)

[136] This point, as noted in text, was undisputed. Counsel for the detainees argued for a reading of reg. 3(3) that would have narrowed its meaning much further. According to this construction, the fact that the Minister could act 'without notice to any person' should have

Division, also acknowledged that 'it seems to me that [a detainee] would be entitled ... after his further detention has been ordered, [to] make representation to the Minister concerning such detention'.[137]

From this observation significant consequences might follow. If the detainees enjoy the right to make representations to the Minister after his decision because it is a part of *audi alteram partem* that has not been cut off by the regulation, other parts of *audi alteram partem* might also be preserved. The Minister might be obliged (at least if the detainee so requests) to furnish him with a statement of the reasons for the detention—for otherwise the detainee's post-decision representations could hardly be meaningful ones.[138] The Minister might also be obliged to consider any post-decision representations the detainee chooses to make, again because otherwise the right to make representations would be an empty one. So, in fact, the dissenting judge in *Omar* and certain lower court judgments held.[139] This reading would not have given the detainees all that they sought, but it would have reflected an effort to carve from a seemingly bleak regulation some residual area of human rights protection.

Rabie, however, does not take this view. He writes, instead, that 'reg 3(3) does away completely with the *audi alteram partem* rule',[140] and that

> when the Minister makes an order for a person's further detention in terms of reg 3(3), the order is a final one, and that there is thereafter no obligation on the Minister to inform the detainee of the grounds on which it was made and then, after considering such representations as

been construed to free the Minister of the duty to tell the detainee that an extension of his detention was being considered (or, later, had been ordered), but still to require him 'to inform detainees generally that they may make representations concerning the extension or otherwise of their detention and to afford the detainee an opportunity of making such representations': *Omar* at 874G (argument of counsel). Moreover, the Minister's power to act 'without hearing any person' could be similarly construed to free the Minister of the duty to hear oral representations but not of the duty to read written ones. (Ibid.) The Appellate Division concluded that in context it was clear that the regulation should not be given such an interpretation. (Ibid. 891.)

[137] Ibid. 900D–E.

[138] The Appellate Division itself had commented in interpreting another statute, one which authorized detentions and required the Minister to give the detainee notice of the 'reasons' for his detention, that 'the Legislature intended that the person on whom a notice has been served should have a fair opportunity of dealing with the reasons furnished by the Minister for his detention and of persuading the Minister that the issue of the [detention] order was unjustified. Merely to be informed of the statutory ground on which the Minister found against him would hardly give the person concerned a fair opportunity of making representations to the Minister ...'. *Nkondo and Others* v. *Minister of Law and Order and Another; Gumede and Others* v. *Minister of Law and Order and Another; Minister of Law and Order* v. *Gumede and Others*, 1986 (2) SA 734 (A) at 772I–773A.

[139] See *Omar*, 1987 (3) SA at 907F (Hoexter JA dissenting); *Momoniat* v. *Minister of Law and Order and Others; Naidoo and Others* v. *Minister of Law and Order and Others*, 1986 (2) SA 264 (W) at 276E–G (judgment of Goldstone J.) (hereafter cited as *Momoniat*); *Nqumba* [sic] *and Others* v. *State President and Others*, 1987 (1) SA 456 (E) at 481A–B, appeal dismissed on other grounds in *Ngqumba*, 1988 (4) SA 224 (A).

[140] *Omar*, 1987 (3) SA at 900H.

the detainee may wish to make in regard to such grounds, to reconsider the order previously made by him.[141]

Rabie's position has at least two flaws. First, it is difficult to explain why the detainee has a right to make representations after the Minister's detention, as Rabie agrees he does, except on the ground that in this respect *audi alteram partem* has not been completely extinguished. It may be that Rabie means to argue that the right to make after-the-fact representations derives from some other source than the *audi alteram partem* principle[142]—in which case the right to make representations might not carry with it any of the other protections implied by this principle. If this is Rabie's position, it is legally problematic, because it does not explain where this 'entitlement' comes from. Certainly this entitlement is not stated in the regulations; accordingly, it must rest on a common-law interpolation into, or supplement to, the regulations. But the most plausible, if not the only, source for such a common-law right would seem to be the *audi alteram partem* principle.[143]

Second, whether or not the Minister's decision is described as final it is also a decision which the Minister can alter at any time. As Hoexter JA points out in dissent, the Minister always retains the authority to change his mind. 'Since the ministerial order in terms of reg 3(3) is final only unless and until he changes his mind,' Hoexter argues, 'the application of the *audi alteram partem* rule during detention subsequent to the order is not excluded.'[144] Rabie does not actually mention that Hoexter has made this argument—not his only such omission, as we will see. His response, however, seems to be that the elimination of *audi alteram partem* before the extension is so thorough that he 'find[s] it difficult to accept that it was nevertheless the intention that the Minister would be obliged, after he had made an order,' to then give effect to the maxim.[145]

This response is problematic not because it is a mistaken reading of the State President's subjective intention (it may well be a *correct* reading of that), but because, as with Parliament, so here subjective intention presumably is not in itself dispositive. The interpretive task is to determine what the language used by the State President in the regulation accomplished, when that language is considered in accordance with the rules of interpretation (rules with which the State President is presumed to be familiar). As Hoexter JA emphasizes, one of those rules is that the operation of the *audi alteram partem* maxim can only be excluded explicitly, or by necessary implication.[146]

[141] Ibid.

[142] Counsel for the state in one of the *Omar* appeals seems to suggest such a view, see ibid. 881–2 (argument of counsel).

[143] Compare *Momoniat*, 1986 (2) SA at 275–6, a seminal case in which Goldstone J. seems clearly to derive detainees' right to make representations after the fact from this rule.

[144] *Omar*, 1987 (3) SA at 907D (dissenting judgment of Hoexter JA).

[145] The quoted language appears in *Omar* at 900F, but the sentence expresses my synthesis of the broader argument Rabie makes on this page.

[146] *Omar*, 1987 (3) SA at 906E (dissenting judgment of Hoexter JA).

As in our examination of *Dempsey*, so here it is important to see both what Rabie ACJ does and what he chooses not to do. Rabie ACJ might have challenged this rule, for example by arguing that the maxim can be excluded whenever the 'clear intention of Parliament negates and excludes' it.[147] But he does not do this. Indeed, he endorses the very principle that Hoexter uses, although in the context of the interpretation of statutes rather than of regulations.[148] Since Rabie ACJ never offers any argument, or even assertion, that the same principle is inapplicable to the interpretation of regulations, it might well be that he accepts its applicability in this context as well. Certainly, if he does not, he has failed to say so or to explain why.

Assuming that the requirement of express exclusion or necessary implication applies, and is construed strictly, it is not easily satisfied here. However 'clear' the State President's desire to abridge *audi alteram partem* after the extension order may have been, Rabie does not argue that this intention is expressly stated. Was it necessarily implied? The answer to that question might depend on an understanding of the reasons for the elimination of any right to notice or a hearing *before* the extension order, for if those reasons held true afterwards as well as before then exclusion might apply at both stages as well. One explanation for the pre-extension invasion of *audi alteram partem* is that it was a consequence of the need for expeditious decisionmaking. But if that explanation is correct, then it would not necessarily follow from this limitation on *audi alteram partem* that the State President intended also to abrogate the maxim after the decision, when time would no longer be at a premium.[149]

Rabie says that such time considerations cannot have been the State President's sole concern, and offers a broader rationale instead. He maintains that '[i]t is quite conceivable' that the express exclusion rested on a different rationale, the need to avoid disclosure of sensitive information, a rationale which would apply throughout detention.[150] This may well have been a concern of the State President's; his affidavit suggested as much. But the fact that the State President had this concern does not necessarily mean that he intended to eliminate the right of *audi alteram partem* at every stage as a result. Nor does Rabie quote any passage from the State President's affidavit that states that the State President *did* have at this intention.[151] Neither did precedent compel the court to infer so sweeping an intention. Only a year earlier, in the *Hurley* case, the Appellate Division had discounted the risk of revealing sensitive information in concluding that the statute at issue in that case should

[147] This formulation was in fact endorsed in such cases as *Publications Control Board* v. *Central News Agency Ltd.*, 1970 (3) SA 479 (A) at 489C–D, and *Winter and Others* v. *Administrator-in-Executive Committee and Another*, 1973 (1) SA 873 (A) at 889B–C.

[148] *Omar*, 1987 (3) SA at 893E–F.

[149] *Momoniat*, 1986 (2) SA at 276B–C.

[150] *Omar*, 1987 (3) SA at 901F.

[151] Omar's counsel at one point seemed to argue that this affidavit made such an intention 'apparent', *Omar*, 1987 (3) SA at 867B–C (argument of counsel). Evidently, however, it was *not* explicit—and such evidence of subjective intention might not have been admissible anyway.

be read to require the state to demonstrate a reasonable basis for arrests under it.[152] In *Omar* itself the court observed at another point that '[i]t may be ... that a hearing given to someone whose detention is being considered need not necessarily, or always, result in the disclosure of the source of information that ought not be disclosed'.[153] Yet although disclosure may not always be a danger, the court's position is that the regulation expresses an across-the-board elimination of the *audi* guarantees.

In short, it seems quite wrong to say that the State President's putative desire to eliminate the *audi alteram partem* rule altogether was necessarily—in the sense of inescapably—implicit in the words of the regulation. Plainly, therefore, *Omar* could have been decided in favour of the detainees' right to a hearing. What seems equally clear is that *Omar*'s contrary result is more apparent than its rationale. Whether the court was tacitly rejecting the 'necessary implication' standard or tacitly giving it a loose interpretation, the majority judgment fails to articulate a satisfactory less rigorous argument for its decision to endorse an interpretation which makes regulation 3(3), as Acting Chief Justice Rabie himself says, 'a very harsh provision'.[154] We are left with the sense that the court was loath to abridge what it took to be the State President's judgment that sweeping power was necessary for the emergency.

(ii) Interpreting the Statute. The next question is whether, so interpreted, the regulation is authorized by the Public Safety Act. The question before the court turned on the meaning of the statutory language empowering the State President to 'make such regulations as appear to him to be necessary or expedient' for the wide purposes related to dealing with the emergency. This is very broad language indeed. But it is not very specific: it does not declare, for example, that the State President has authority to override fundamental rights protected by the common law. The interpretive problem before the court, therefore, was in a sense whether to place more weight on the breadth of this language or on its non-specificity.

If *Omar*'s broad reading of this regulation stemmed from a desire not to confine the executive's emergency powers, we would hardly expect the court to hold that the regulation it had just interpreted was actually too broad to be valid—and the court does not do so. To affirm the regulations, however, the court has to resolve three questions. The first is whether the State President's power to make regulations is subject to any limits at all. If this power is limited, the next task is to determine what those limits are, and in particular to decide whether the statute authorizes the State President to make

[152] *Hurley*, 1986 (3) SA 568 (A) at 583D–H. Rabie argues in *Omar* that *Hurley* is not authority for requiring an emergency detainee to be informed of the reasons for the extension of his detention, *Omar*, 1987 (3) SA at 903–4. He is obviously right that *Hurley* deals with a different statutory scheme than the one at issue in *Omar*, but *Hurley*'s logic none the less seems to cast doubt on the logic Rabie employs in *Omar*.

[153] Ibid. 894E.

[154] Ibid. 900I.

regulations abrogating *audi alteram partem*. Finally, assuming the statute grants him this power, the third issue is whether the State President properly exercised this authority. As we will see, Rabie ACJ's resolution of these questions is to maintain that the courts do have the authority to review the State President's regulations, but to find, in the exercise of that authority, that the *audi* regulation is valid. In taking this course, Rabie ACJ rejects the most stark doctrinal assertion of executive power. But he also rejects lines of argument, with substantial support in South African law, that would have called into question the validity of this regulation. His grounds for doing so reflect a dismaying combination of rather indistinct application of the doctrines which he accepts and very distinct, and abrupt, rejection of arguments which seek to invoke those doctrines on behalf of detainees' *audi* rights.

The broadest interpretation which the court could have given to the State President's authority would have been to declare that he had been vested with the full legislative power that Parliament itself possessed. Normally, regulations issued under a statute are treated as 'subordinate legislation' and, unless the statute indicates otherwise, the subordinate legislators are subject to a variety of limits on their power, such as requirements that they exercise their authority only for purposes authorized by the empowering statute,[155] or that the subordinate laws they make not be so grossly unreasonable as to be oppressive or discriminatory to any group within the society.[156] But South African law has been understood to permit Parliament to delegate all of its power, including its prerogative to settle on purposes which it wishes to implement and to act oppressively or discriminatorily if it so chooses. Delegations approaching this totality are very much the exception and not the rule, but they are not forbidden.

There was precedent on which the Appellate Division could have relied for such a reading of the Public Safety Act, had it been of a mind to do so. In 1960 a lower court case had in fact declared that, subject to certain exceptions provided in the Act itself, 'the intention of the legislature was to confer upon the Governor-General,[157] with respect to any area in which a state of emergency had been proclaimed to exist, powers of legislation equal to those of Parliament'.[158] If the State President were vested with this plenary power, the regulations he promulgated would be subject to interpretation, as legislation is,

[155] See *Van Eck, NO and Van Rensburg, NO* v. *Etna Stores*, 1947 (2) SA 984 (A) at 996–7.

[156] See H. Hahlo and E. Kahn, *The South African Legal System and Its Background* (Cape Town: Juta, 1968), 53–60.

[157] Today what was the Governor-General's authority is wielded by the State President.

[158] *R.* v. *Maphumolo and Others*, 1960 (3) SA 793 (N) at 799B. The court did, however, appear to believe that these powers could not be used *mala fide*—a limitation that it seems unlikely could be applied to Parliament itself. See G. Carpenter, *Introduction to South African Constitutional Law* (Durban: Butterworths, 1987), 361. A decade earlier, the Appellate Division had unanimously declared that 'another statute gave the Governor-General Parliament' over all 'native areas': *R.* v. *Maharaj*, 1950 (3) SA 187 (A) at 194D. 'Subject to the provisions of [one section of the statute], ... powers of legislation, within the [native] area concerned, equal to those of Parliament'. *R.* v. *Maharaj*, 1950 (3) SA 187 (A) at 194D.

but most, if not all, of the normal grounds for review of subordinate legislation would be inapplicable.

The Appellate Division chose not to embrace this extraordinary, though not unprecedented, assertion of virtually unlimited executive authority. In *Omar* the court specifically denied 'that the exercise by the State President of the powers conferred upon him by the Act is immune from attack', and listed certain grounds for such challenge.[159] A year later, in the *United Democratic Front* case, the state decided at the last minute to press the plenary power argument upon the court.[160] The court addressed it at length, and affirmed that the State President's exercise of the power to make regulations is subject to the same review as any other exercise of a subjective discretion.[161]

Once the notion of plenary power is put to one side, the next interpretive question before the court is a familiar one, namely whether the Public Safety Act expressly or by necessary implication authorized a regulation which nullified *audi alteram partem*. Rabie ACJ's approach to this issue is somewhat indistinct. The statute's language, as we have seen, is very broad; it seems quite reasonable to say that the State President's authority to 'make such regulations as appear to him to be necessary or expedient' for emergency purposes does encompass regulations invading *audi alteram partem*. Rabie ACJ emphasizes the breadth of the State President's authority, but he does not in so many words declare that the statute 'expressly' authorizes this regulation.[162]

While this omission may be unintentional, it may instead reflect that Rabie was not prepared to assert that the broad, but unspecific, language of this provision would suffice. Whether specific language is required is not a point on which South African law appears to be completely clear. Etienne Mureinik, however, has carefully delineated the basis in South African law for concluding that broad, but unspecific, statutory language should not be taken to authorize subordinate legislation eliminating fundamental rights (such as the protection of *audi alteram partem*).[163] Mureinik points, in particular, to *Mandela* v. *Minister of Prisons*.[164] That case dealt with a statute whose language authorized, *inter alia*, the making of regulations as to 'the general government and management of prisons, the maintenance of good order and discipline therein, and the acts or omissions which shall be deemed to be offenses against discipline'.[165] This

[159] *Omar*, 1987 (3) SA at 892H. The court had also reviewed the validity of regulations in *Tsenoli*, 1986 (4) SA 1150 (A).

[160] The state did not raise this claim until it filled its 'additional heads of argument drawn up only a few days before the appeal was heard': *United Democratic Front*, 1988 (4) SA 830 (A) at 848F.

[161] Ibid. 851I.

[162] See *Omar*, 1987 (3) SA at 893E–H.

[163] E. Mureinik, 'Fundamental Rights and Delegated Legislation', 1 *SAJHR* 111 (1985). See also A. Rabie, 'Failure of the Brakes of Justice: *Omar* v. *Minister of Law and Order* 1987 (3) SA 859 (A)', 3 *SAJHR* 300, 308 (1977).

[164] *Mandela* v. *Minister of Prisons*, 1983 (1) SA 938 (A) (hereafter cited as *Mandela*). The appellant was Nelson Mandela.

[165] S. 94(1), Act 8 of 1959, quoted in *Mandela*, 1983 (1) SA at 959E.

language seems broad enough to encompass a rule making 'seeing one's lawyer' a breach of discipline. The Appellate Division observed, however, that '[a] power to abolish a fundamental right would require the *clearest* language .... Obviously, s[ection] 94 of Act 8 of 1959 does not expressly and by clear language confer the power to nullify the fundamental right of access to a legal adviser.'[166] This is strong interpretive medicine. Rabie hints at one point in *Omar* that he might not accept 'what has been said in the cases about the taking away of a fundamental right', but he goes no further than that,[167] and his failure to rely on the 'express' language of the statute may be attributable to this constraint.

In any event, Rabie chooses in *Omar* to invoke another portion of the Public Safety Act, which provides that a state of emergency can be declared only when the State President is of the opinion that 'the ordinary law of the land is inadequate to enable the Government to ensure the safety of the public, or to maintain public order'.[168] Rabie maintains that this provision 'indicates that Parliament contemplated that the need to ensure the safety of the public or to maintain public order might necessitate the taking of extraordinary measures which might make drastic inroads into the rights and privileges normally enjoyed by individuals'.[169] Though he offers little argument for this conclusion, he is surely right that this language embodies a parliamentary intention to authorize the State President to override the ordinary law of the land in some respects.[170] After all, what else would a state of emergency do? And Parliament's *subjective* intention may have gone just as far as Rabie suggests.[171]

But it was not foreordained, as a matter of doctrine, that the court should read this language to permit the State President to abrogate any and all of

[166] *Mandela*, 1983 (1) SA at 959H (emphasis added).

[167] *Omar*, 1987 (3) SA at 894J.

[168] S. 2(1), Public Safety Act 3 of 1953.

[169] *Omar* 1987 (3) SA at 892A; see ibid. 893G. Rabie also notes that the decision that a state of emergency should be declared is up to the State President alone. Ibid. 891I. The lower court judgment in *Omar* had also looked to certain other sections of the Public Safety Act—among them a reference to potential regulations providing for 'summary arrest and detention'—which it felt provided additional evidence of the 'very wide discretion' conferred by the Act. *Omar and Others* v. *Minister of Law and Order and Others*, 1986 (3) SA 306 (C) at 314B–G. Whatever the significance of these provisions (and this was a matter of debate in the lower court, see ibid. 320D–I (dissenting judgment of Friedman J.)), Rabie makes no mention of them.

[170] So Baxter appears to agree, in 'Judicial Declaration' (cit. n. 128), 319.

[171] It is particularly hard to deny that Parliament concurred in the State President's actions if we assume that Parliament approved the regulations at issue in *Omar* by resolution, as the Act then called for. (Prior to its 1986 amendment, ss. 3(5) and 3(6) of the Public Safety Act 3 of 1953 provided that all emergency regulations were to be 'laid on the Tables' in Parliament for 28 days, and would 'cease to be of force and effect' if Parliament then failed to approve them by resolution before it was prorogued. In June of 1986, this provision was amended so that regulations would remain in force *unless* Parliament annulled them.) Rabie does not invoke this provision, however, perhaps on the grounds that such resolutions did not constitute legislation directly validating the regulations so approved, and that Parliament's approval of regulations in 1986 would not demonstrate the meaning of the Public Safety Act originally enacted over 30 years earlier, see *More* v. *Minister of Co-operation and Development and Another*, 1986 (1) SA 102 (A) at 116F–H.

those specially valued protections of the common law falling in the category of 'fundamental rights'. Even with the addition of the sections Rabie points to, the statute still does not provide specific authority for the invasion of such important rights; indeed, the additional language adds very little to the specific reach of the State President's power.

Nor does this language compel the conclusion that such authority is necessarily implied by the statute. The fact that the ordinary law of the land was insufficient does not automatically demonstrate that it was left to a subordinate legislator to eliminate *any* provision of the ordinary law of the land. Many such provisions might still be retained, after all, and the ends of the emergency sufficiently protected.[172] If we invoke interpretive presumptions in favour of avoiding harshness and injustice or interference with liberty,[173] or even impute to Parliament a particular reluctance to overturn fundamental rights,[174] we might conclude that Parliament meant to authorize only invasion of less-than-fundamental rights.[175] Or, more modestly, we might argue that Parliament was willing to see fundamental rights abridged but not completely erased.[176] Or we might even agree that Parliament must have recognized that some fundamental rights might have to be overridden during an emergency, yet deny that Parliament meant to allow people to be held not only without a judicial trial but also without even an administrative hearing. The upshot of this analysis is that there existed a reasonable argument that the Public Safety Act did not authorize the State President to abrogate the fundamental right embodied in *audi alteram partem*—and that Rabie's doctrinal grounds for rejecting it remain somewhat cloudy.

Having found that the State President has very wide authority, Rabie ACJ must still consider whether he exercised his authority properly. Characteristically, Rabie does not foreswear the court's power to address this question. Instead he declares that: '[i]t need hardly be said that he [the State President] must apply his mind to whatever matter may be in issue, that he must act

[172] Clive Plasket sounds a similar note when he contends that 'the emergency regulations are intended to supplement, and not replace, the ordinary law of the land': 'Clipping Dempsey's Wings: The Consideration of Alternatives to Regulation 3(1) of the Emergency Regulations', 3 *SAJHR* 77, 80 (1987). See also Baxter, 'Judicial Declaration' (cit. n. 128), 319.

[173] See Ch. 2, text at nn. 101–2. In the lower court in *Omar*, the dissenter resisted the idea that Parliament had authorized the State President to abrogate *audi alteram partem* in part on the ground that '[o]ne's sense of justice is offended by any such suggestion': *Omar and Others* v. *Minister of Law and Order and Others*, 1986 (3) SA 306 (C) at 323I, quoting *Nkwinti* v. *Commissioner of Police and Others*, 1986 (2) SA 421 (E) at 438I–439A.

[174] Etienne Mureinik argues for such imputation of concern for fundamental rights to Parliament: 'Fundamental Rights' (cit. n. 163), 118–20.

[175] Graham Van der Leeuw offers a somewhat similar formulation, that Parliament 'did not contemplate that [the State President's] powers should include the negation of procedural fairness': 'The *Audi Alteram Partem* Rule and the Validity of Emergency Regulation 3(3)', 3 *SAJHR* 331, 333–4 (1987).

[176] In *Mandela* the Appellate Division had reasoned that the standard for an 'interference' with a fundamental right was less demanding than for an abolition of such a right. *Mandela*, 1983 (1) SA at 959–60.

bona fide and that he must exercise the powers conferred on him by s[ection] 3(1)(a) of the Act [the section authorizing emergency regulations] for the purposes mentioned in the section.'[177] He proceeds, however, to deal swiftly, and negatively, with a series of objections on these and similar grounds.[178] His discussion insistently reiterates the breadth of the State President's power, and tells us, with little elaboration that he can see a security rationale for eliminating *audi* protections,[179] and that even if security concerns do not always require eliminating hearings, the State President was free to decide that all hearings should be eliminated.[180]

Rabie ACJ's treatment of these claims is significant on two counts. First, the abruptness of his discussion is startling, and no doubt is part of what John Dugard had in mind when he wrote that the decision is '[w]ritten in the style of a judgment on the interpretation of a hire-purchase agreement or municipal bye-law rather than a law that has authorized the detention without trial of many thousands'.[181] Second, the security-consciousness embedded in these views is by now familiar, and suggests again the court's resistance to arguments which it saw as undermining the emergency system.

We have not looked in detail at the court's treatment of these claims, and we should not conclude too much from what we have seen so far. There are two more telling measures of the intensity of the review which the Rabie court was prepared to apply. One is that, in the emergency cases to come, every challenge to the validity of emergency regulations which the court addressed on the merits would be rejected. The second is the court's treatment of one of the objections raised in *Omar* itself against the other element of the emergency system at issue, the denial of detainees' right of access to counsel. Let us turn to this point now.

(*b*) *The Denial of Access to Counsel.*

The denial of a right of access to counsel was effected under regulation 3(10) of the emergency regulations, and rule 5(1), issued by the Minister of Justice in the exercise of his power 'to regulate the detention of persons in terms of' regulation 3.[182] Regulation 3(10) of the Emergency Regulations provided that

> [n]o person, other than the Minister or a person acting by virtue of his office in the service of the State—(*a*) shall have access to any person detained in terms of the provisions of this regulation, except with the consent of and subject to such conditions as may be determined by the Minister or the Commissioner of the South African Police.[183]

177 *Omar*, 1987 (3) SA at 892G–H.
178 Ibid. 892H–894F.
179 Ibid. 892H–893G.
180 Ibid. 894E–F.
181 Dugard, '*Omar*' (cit. n. 129), 297.
182 Reg. 3(9)(*a*), Proc. R. 121, *Government Gazette* 9877 (21 July 1985).
183 Reg. 3(10), Proc. R. 121, *Government Gazette* 9877 (21 July 1985).

The Minister of Justice, in turn, had issued rule 5(1), which specified that

> [no] person detained ... shall ... be visited by any person, except with the permission of the person in command of the prison in question, acting with the concurrence of the Commissioner of the South African Police or any person acting on his authority: Provided that if a legal representative desires to visit such a detainee, the permission of the Minister of Law and Order or the Commissioner of the South African Police shall be obtained for such a visit.[184]

Let us assume that these provisions were correctly interpreted to deny detainees a right of access to counsel, although there were arguments to the contrary.[185]

These provisions were valid only if, so interpreted, they were authorized by the Public Safety Act, and it is this issue on which we should focus. There were in fact several challenges to their validity.[186] For example, the court deferred to the State President's seeming judgment that nothing short of a denial of the right of access to lawyers would suffice to deal with the risk of interference with emergency-law enforcement through lawyer-client contacts.[187] Similarly, the court denied that the decision to grant the state the power to block such contacts was grossly unreasonable because it would interfere with lawyer-client meetings on matters completely unconnected to the emergency; the court found in rule 5(1) an implied requirement that lawyer-client meetings be refused only for purposes related to the emergency, rather than for any purposes whatsoever.[188] Whether or not these decisions were justified, *Omar* ultimately leaves no doubt of its profoundly dismissive stance towards challenges to emergency regulations. This attitude emerges from the court's treatment of another such challenge, one which was the basis for the dissenting judgment on this issue by one member of the court, Hoexter JA.

This argument concerned the denial of access to counsel to one particular subgroup of detainees, those who were detained—as regulation 3(1) then permitted—not for the maintenance of public order or the safety of the public

[184] Rule 5(1), quoted in *Omar*, 1987 (3) SA at 890F.

[185] Even if rule 5(1) did quite clearly deny detainees access to their lawyers, this rule was only valid if it was consistent with the regulations under which it was issued. Counsel for the detainee argued, as to reg. 3(10), that it affected the right of lawyers (and others) to have access to detainees, but not the right of detainees to have access to their lawyers, *Omar*, 1987 (3) SA at 894J–895A (argument of counsel)—and this argument is simply not mentioned by the court. It might also have been contended that contact between lawyer and client is not the 'access' which reg. 3(10) regulates. This argument becomes more plausible in light of the decision in *Nkwentsha*, to be discussed in Ch. 4, which declared that 'it cannot be said that when a witness is produced in Court and is then under the control of the presiding Judge, the latter or any person leading his evidence or cross-examining him would be having access to him in the sense in which that word is used in reg 3(10)': *Nkwentsha*, 1988 (3) SA 99 (A) at 115G–H.

[186] See *Omar*, 1987 (3) SA at 895–7.

[187] Ibid. 897C–G.

[188] Ibid. 896H–897C.

but for their own safety.[189] The dissenting justice, Hoexter JA, argued that there was 'no possible room' for a belief that denial of such persons' access to their lawyers might be necessary for their own safety, or for the sake of public order.[190] And he found nothing in the affidavits submitted to the court from the official responsible for the restrictions that 'suggest[ed] the remotest justification' for denying *these* detainees access to their laywers.[191]

To some readers this argument may seem rather odd. After all, one might well assume that most detainees are being held for purposes of public safety rather than for their own protection. Even if the regulation creates an invalid limitation on these detainees' rights, Hoexter himself concedes that with other detainees there might indeed be valid security reasons for denying them access to counsel.[192] But Hoexter points out that '[o]ne does not know and one cannot know' the basis for a person's detention.[193] One cannot know because the Appellate Division has ruled that the detainee is not entitled to be informed of the reasons for the Minister's extension of his detention![194] At least in theory, therefore, there could have been individuals who—unbeknownst to anyone except the detaining authorities—were being held solely for their own safety.[195]

In addition, as Hoexter JA says, 'the provisions of reg 3(10)(*a*) in no way differentiate categories of detainees [and so] those provisions must ... be seen as one and inseparable'.[196] South African law offered support for the proposition that where subordinate legislation fails to make such differentiation between the groups to whom it applies, it will be held invalid in all of its applications if it is found invalid in any.[197] Hence, Hoexter reasons, the entire denial of

[189] Reg. 3(1), Proc. R. 121, *Government Gazette* 9877 (21 July 1985).

[190] *Omar*, 1987 (3) SA at 909A (dissenting judgment of Hoexter JA).

[191] Ibid. 909C (dissenting judgment of Hoexter JA).

[192] Ibid. 908H (dissenting judgment of Hoexter JA).

[193] Ibid. 909H (dissenting judgment of Hoexter JA).

[194] Despite the court's refusal to require the Minister to inform the detainee of the reasons for the extension of his detention, the detainee would in theory have had access to *some* information bearing on these reasons. A detainee would, for example, have been entitled to be told the basis for his or her arrest as soon as reasonably practicable after the arrest, see *Ngqumba*, 1988 (4) SA 224 (A) at 268–9—but this information might not be the same as the basis for the Minister's subsequent extension of his or her detention. Similarly, a detainee could challenge the Minister's decision to extend his detention in court, on the ground that it reflected, say, a failure by the Minister to apply his mind. Faced with such a challenge the Minister might choose to attest to some or all of his reasons—although he could still refuse to do so, and might prevail in court none the less. Finally, one of the lawyers for the state appeared to suggest that many detainees know why they are detained and therefore do not need to be told, see *Omar*, 1987 (3) SA at 881I (argument of counsel). This argument counsel for the detainees called 'repugnant to any society predicated on civilized legal norms' and it was not repeated by the court. Ibid. 885E (argument of counsel). As a general proposition, it seems safe to assume that many, if not most, detainees did not succeed in being told the full reasons for their continued detention.

[195] One might wonder, however, why the detaining authorities would not normally tell such a person that this was their purpose.

[196] *Omar*, 1987 (3) SA at 909H (dissenting judgment of Hoexter JA).

[197] Cf. *Komani NO* v. *Bantu Affairs Administration Board, Peninsula Area*, 1980 (4) SA 448 (A) at 473 (commenting that '[*p*]*rima facie* there would appear to be no substance' to the argument

access falls.[198] This argument was not unassailable. In response to the dissent's extended discussion of the point, however, Rabie ACJ offered *no* direct response, nor *any* explicit mention.[199] But Hoexter JA never sat on another emergency case during Rabie's tenure as chief justice. Perhaps that exclusion expresses even more clearly than the judgment's silence the Rabie era's rejection of what it saw as interference with the emergency system.

Omar's result was that emergency detainees had neither the protection of the *audi alteram partem* maxim nor the right of access to their lawyers. Our study of *Omar* would not be complete, however, without a recognition of why these results, as well as the way in which they were reached, were seen as 'devastating'. This is not a subtle point. Each of these decisions was a denial of a valuable protection from South Africa's ordinary law, and *Omar* leaves us in no doubt about the vulnerability of the benign features of that ordinary law to the ravages of the State President's emergency lawmaking. Each, moreover, risked other injustices as a result.

The elimination of *audi* protections may have increased the risk of unjustified detentions, for it denied detainees any formal vehicle for persuading their captors that they should be released. Even full hearings, to be sure, might well have been unlikely to persuade state officials to release detainees (although when detainees' cases were reviewed in 1989, in the wake of the detainee hunger strikes, many were in fact released). Yet the availability of such hearings might have encouraged law enforcement officers toward less arbitrary decisionmaking. Perhaps such hearings could also have laid the groundwork for court proceedings. At the least, the opportunity for a hearing, or even for receipt of a statement of reasons for detention followed by the chance to submit representations to the Minister, might have eased the emotional strain of detention.

The denial of detainees' right of access to their lawyers also worsened the plight in which detainees were placed. This is not because many detainees were permanently blocked from seeing their lawyers; in practice, they were

that a regulation which the court had just found invalid as applied to certain people could be valid as applied to others). The exact scope of this principle may, however, have been open to dispute. See *Tsenoli*, 1986 (4) SA 1150 (A) at 1170J–1181C (argument of counsel).

[198] *Omar*, 1987 (3) SA at 909I (dissenting judgment of Hoexter JA).

[199] The state, however, apparently took note of it. The emergency regulations issued at the beginning of the 1986–7 and 1987–8 emergencies continued, like the 1985 regulations at issue in *Omar*, to authorize the detention of people for their own safety. See reg. 3(1), Proc. R. 109, *Government Gazette* 10280 (12 June 1986); reg. 3(1), Proc. R. 96, *Government Gazette* 10771 (11 June 1987). When *Omar* was decided on 26 June 1987, the 1987–8 regulations had already been issued, but the regulations issued the following June to govern the 1988–9 emergency no longer authorized detention of individuals for their own protection. Reg. 3(1), Security Emergency Regulations, Proc. R. 97, *Government Gazette* 11340 (10 June 1988). By this action, of course, the state rendered Hoexter's argument irrelevant. It would be distressing to think that the court's silence on the point reflected its hope that the issue would, as in fact it did, just 'go away'.

not. Because permission had to be obtained for such access, however, the system built in the risk of temporary interferences, which could result in significant delays even though permission would ultimately be granted.[200] It requires no special insight to suspect that the occasions of greatest difficulty in obtaining permission would include precisely those cases in which the gaolers had the most to hide—cases, say, of assault on detainees, whose bruises might disappear before their lawyers could win access to them. One would expect this pattern even if the Minister and Commissioner of Police were completely opposed to such abusive treatment, for they must inevitably rely heavily on subordinate officials for their information about particular cases.

These points are not startling. *Omar* expresses the Appellate Division's choice, a choice neither compelled by doctrine nor satisfactorily supported by argument, to see the Public Safety Act and its implementing regulations as conferring immense, largely unchecked discretion on the state authorities. Checks on power exist because unchecked power is so dangerous. In *Omar*, the Appellate Division affirms state authority fraught with such peril.

3. United Democratic Front

Though not the last of the Appellate Division's emergency decisions, *United Democratic Front* can rightly be considered the culmination, or better the nadir, of the Rabie era's work. In this case the Appellate Division for the first time undercut *Hurley*'s great contribution to South African jurisprudence, its authoritative imprimatur to the courts' evisceration of the ouster clauses by which the state sought to abridge their jurisdiction. *Hurley* had not resulted in the state's abandoning the effort to enact or promulgate such provisions, and each year's emergency regulations, as well as, by virtue of a 1986 amendment, the Public Safety Act itself, contained such clauses.[201] In *United Democratic Front*, for the first time, the Appellate Division gave effect to one of these clauses, when it found that the Public Safety Act's ouster clause precluded it from reviewing or invalidating emergency regulations which were challenged as being incomprehensibly vague and therefore invalid.

[200] In *Omar* itself the detainees' attorney secured permission only after three telexes to the authorities. Having first applied for permission as to some of the detainees on 8 Nov. 1985 (and subsequently as to others), he ultimately met with his clients on 18 and 19 Nov. *Omar and Others* v. *Minister of Law and Order and Others*, 1986 (3) SA 306 (C) at 317G. M. T. Steyn J. sets out at length the details of the authorities' egregious failures to respond, as well as refusal of access, in *Bloem and Another* v. *State President and Others*, 1986 (4) SA 1064 (O) at 1071–3. Nicholas Haysom and Steven Kahanovitz, writing before *Omar*, observed that '[w]hen courts ordered legal access to detainees, police and prison officials introduced and enforced administrative obstacles leading to delays of three to four weeks before a lawyer could visit a detainee.' 'Courts and the State of Emergency' (cit. n. 112), 197.

[201] See Public Safety Act 3 of 1953, s. 5B (added by Public Safety Amendment Act 67 of 1986, s. 4); reg. 15(3), Security Emergency Regulations, Proc. R. 97, *Government Gazette* 11340 (10 June 1988); reg. 12(3), Proc. R. 96, *Government Gazette* 10771 (11 June 1987); reg. 16(3), Proc. R. 109, *Government Gazette* 10280 (12 June 1986); reg. 11(2), Proc. R. 121, *Government Gazette* 9877 (21 July 1985).

The court's decision epitomizes the traits of this era. That is to say, first, the case could easily have been decided otherwise; in fact, a series of cases that had addressed the interpretation of this clause *had* decided it otherwise,[202] and there was ample doctrinal support for doing so. It is also to say that the court was unable to fashion a coherent rationale for its decision. Indeed, the two judgments in which the majority sought to shape such a rationale recapitulate the weaknesses we have seen in *Dempsey* and *Omar*. Rabie ACJ, reluctant as always to depart from the familiar contours of the law, finally does so but with almost no explanation, while Hefer JA, willing here as in *Dempsey* to recast the law, dramatically reshapes South African doctrine but ultimately finds himself reduced to assertion rather than argument too. The case also displays the court's pro-executive tilt, both because the only possible effect of leaving vague regulations on the books is an *in terrorem* one and because, as we will see in a moment, the court's very decision to rule on the ouster issue may be driven by its sense that otherwise it might have to rule against the state on the validity of an emergency regulation. Finally, the case once again points to the importance of the emergency team, though here even the team members are driven to the point of multiple, not entirely consonant, opinions to explain the result in which they concur—for the lone dissenter yet again is not a team member, and yet again ceases to sit on emergency cases after this decision.

It is appropriate to begin our analysis by looking at the claim which the court found itself without jurisdiction to review. The regulations at issue in *United Democratic Front* were contained in the 'media emergency regulations'.[203] One of the challenges to these regulations was that they were unlawfully vague,[204] and the lower court agreed that the regulations' definitions of 'unrest' and 'security action' were indeed unacceptably vague, and hence that these definitions, and the regulations incorporating them, were to that extent *ultra vires* and invalid. The defect in the definitions was that, rather than simply listing a series of events which would constitute unrest (or security action),

[202] See *Metal and Allied Workers Union and Another* v. *State President and Others*, 1986 (4) SA 358 (D) at 367B–368A; *Natal Newspapers (Pty) Ltd. and Others* v. *State President and Others*, 1986 (4) SA 1109 (N) at 1117I–1118H; *Nqumba* [sic] *and Others* v. *State President and Others*, 1987 (1) SA 456 (E) at 460A–462J, appeal dismissed on other grounds, *Ngqumba*, 1988 (4) SA 224 (A). Cf. *Bloem and Another* v. *State President and Others*, 1986 (4) SA 1064 (O) at 1079C–H.

[203] Proc. R. 224, *Government Gazette* 10541 (11 Dec. 1986).

[204] To say that a regulation is unlawfully vague is to say that, even after the court has endeavoured to construe it to cure the difficulty, the regulation does not 'convey to the persons affected by it with reasonable clarity what they may or may not do'. See *United Democratic Front and Another* v. *State President and Others*, 1987 (3) SA 296 (N) at 313G (the lower court judgment in *United Democratic Front* itself). If a regulation is so vague that it thus defies the courts' efforts to give it a reasonably clear meaning, then it 'cannot be carried into effect': see *United Democratic Front*, 1988 (4) SA 830 (A) at 856E–F (dissenting judgment of Van Heerden JA). If a regulation has a clear core of meaning, however, then South African law apparently would enforce that aspect of the regulation, even if its core meaning beyond this point remains doubtful. See *R.* v. *Marshall and Another*, 1951 (2) SA 326 (A) at 334H–335A.

each of them provided that any events which 'to a reasonable bystander would appear to be' among a set of listed events fell within the definitions.[205] The lower court concluded that the regulations' reliance on the perceptions of the 'reasonable bystander' was unacceptably vague because 'it is impossible for the persons affected by the regulation to know what experience, education, knowledge or other qualities they should attribute to a reasonable bystander whose reaction they are required to anticipate'.[206] Part of the problem, according to the court, was that South Africa was so diverse a nation that defining the 'reasonable' bystander was extremely difficult.[207]

We cannot tell how strong the court felt this claim was from what the majority judgments actually say about it, for the ouster relieved those in the majority of the necessity of expressing an opinion. We do know that the only dissenting judge, Van Heerden JA, agreed that the regulations were unacceptably vague, though for rather different reasons.[208] But we can begin to gauge the court's feelings from its handling of a vagueness challenge to a different regulation in another case, *Ngqumba*. There the court ruled on and rejected the claim,[209] and having done so decided that it was 'not necessary' to consider whether its jurisdiction to address the matter had been ousted by the same statutory provision at issue in *United Democratic Front*,[210] while at the same time hinting, at least, that it viewed the ouster issue as very substantial.[211] Moreover, this was not the first time that the court had declared that it was 'unnecessary' to consider the effect of this ouster clause while it was ruling in favour of the state on the merits, for the court had done so in *Omar* as well.[212] The inference that the court reached the ouster clause issue in *United Democratic Front* because its view of the strength of the vagueness claim made adjudication of the ouster clause's effect 'necessary' is surely invited.

The sense that the court's attention to the ouster clause is a function of its

[205] Reg. 1(1) (definitions of 'unrest' and 'security action'), Proc. R. 224, *Government Gazette* 10541 (11 Dec. 1986).

[206] *United Democratic Front and Another* v. *State President and Others*, 1987 (3) SA 296 (N) at 320; see ibid. 318–23.

[207] Ibid. 319–20.

[208] Unlike the lower court, Van Heerden JA maintained that the concept of a reasonable bystander was sufficiently clear. For Van Heerden the problem with the regulation was that incidents of possible unrest or security action might look very different to different reasonable observers, not because the observers differed from each other intrinsically but because their physical vantage points were not the same. The regulations were therefore defective because they did not in any way make clear whose perspective should be determinative. *United Democratic Front*, 1988 (4) SA 830 (A) at 860J–861B (dissenting judgment of Van Heerden JA).

[209] *Ngqumba*, 1988 (4) SA at 248E–249I.

[210] Ibid. 250C–D. The ouster clause in question in both of these cases, and also in *Omar*, was s. 5B of the Public Safety Act 3 of 1953.

[211] The court set out the state's ouster argument at some length, *Ngqumba* 1988 (4) SA at 249I–250C, and observed that it was rejecting the vagueness claim '[e]ven if it is accepted that a court has the jurisdiction' to address it. Ibid. 249B–C.

[212] *Omar*, 1987 (3) SA at 904C.

disquiet on the merits is strengthened by a consideration of the language of the ouster clause itself. This clause, section 5B of the Public Safety Act 3 of 1953, does not merely preclude a court from invalidating a regulation made under the Public Safety Act, though it does expressly preclude this. Instead, it also precludes a court from 'inquir[ing] into or giv[ing] judgment on the validity of any such ... regulation'.[213] Thus, according to the literal provisions of the statute, it was 'necessary' for Rabie to determine that section 5B did not apply before he could even consider the merits of the challenges to the regulations.[214] To give a judgment upholding the validity of a clause which the statute bars the court from investigating is in fact to violate the literal command of the statute. The court apparently preferred, however, to go on passing judgment on such regulations—until, perhaps, the point arrived at which such a judgment might have been against the state.[215]

To consider the arguments which Rabie ACJ and Hefer JA offer on the ouster clause, we need to recall the framework which *Hurley* provides for such an analysis. Section 5B provides in relevant part:

> **Validity of action by State President or Minister.**—No interdict or other process shall issue for the staying or setting aside of ... any regulation made under section 3 [of the Public Safety Act] ... and no court shall be competent to inquire into or give judgment on the validity of any such ... regulation.[216]

The media regulations at issue in *United Democratic Front* had been proclaimed by the State President, purportedly under section 3. But *Hurley* makes clear that the fact that the state claimed that these regulations had been made under section 3 was not conclusive. Instead, *Hurley* teaches, and *United Democratic Front* appears to agree, that the courts have the power to examine the regulations to determine whether they can be said to fall 'under' the statute,

[213] S. 5B, Public Safety Act 3 of 1953.

[214] Haysom and Plasket also note this aspect of the language of s. 5B: 'War against Law' (cit. n. 6), 328.

[215] A much more mundane explanation would seek to attribute the court's failure to rule on the ouster issue in *Omar* and *Ngqumba* to the existence of uncertainty as to whether the ouster clause actually applied to the regulations at issue in those cases, regulations which had been promulgated and in *Omar*'s case had already expired before the ouster clause became law on 26 June 1986 as part of the Public Safety Admendment Act 67 of 1986. I do not believe this explanation can hold, for three reasons. First, the statutory language in the ouster clause does not contain any exception for previously promulgated regulations. Second, the regulations at issue at *Ngqumba* were promulgated only 14 days before s. 5B took effect, and do not appear to have been altered in any relevant respect during the remaining 351 days of the 1986–7 emergency. It seems likely, too, that the *Ngqumba* case did not begin until after s. 5B took effect, for it was heard as a matter of urgency in the lower court beginning on 14 Aug. 1986. *Nqumba* [sic] *and Others* v. *State President and Others*, 1987 (1) SA 456 (E) at 456, 459. It is implausible to believe that the court would have read s. 5B as inapplicable under these circumstances. Third, there is no evidence that the court *did* adopt such a reading, for the Appellate Division never mentions this timing question.

[216] S. 5B, Public Safety Act 3 of 1953.

and that if they do not fall under it then the courts are free to review and set them aside despite the existence of the ouster clause.[217]

Therefore the issue is whether vague regulations are none the less regulations made under the Public Safety Act. Rabie's conclusion is clear.[218] He argues:

> The State President relied in the promulgation of all the regulations on the power conferred on him by s. 3(1)(*a*), and even if it were so (as found by the court *a quo*) that some of the regulations are so vague that they must be regarded as invalid, they are still regulations made by the State President by virtue of his power in terms of s. 3(1)(*a*). One could say that he, in the exercise of his power, failed to make some of the regulations as clear as the law demands of him, or that he made some regulations which are ineffective on account of their vagueness and which can therefore not be applied, but in my opinion he still did not act, in the making of such regulations, other than in terms of, or under, the power granted him by s. 3(1)(*a*). An imperfect or ineffective exercise of his competence by making regulations which are vague, does therefore to my mind not mean that the State President overstepped his authority and thus acted *ultra vires*.[219]

This passage bluntly states Rabie's conclusion. It sheds less light on the reasoning supporting the result.

One possibility is that Rabie is arguing that officials act 'under' a statute even if they violate its express or implied requirements, so long as they have endeavoured to act under it and do not fall into such manifest or egregious breaches of its requirements as, say, fraud.[220] Acting, let us say, in good faith, officials may misunderstand the scope of their statutory authority or commit

[217] Rabie ACJ does not expressly endorse this view, but his discussion of the ouster clause issue is framed, as this view would dictate, as a discussion of whether vague regulations constitute action under the Public Safety Act. See *United Democratic Front*, 1988 (4) SA 830 (A) at 853F (judgment of Rabie ACJ). Hefer JA more expressly adopts this framework. Ibid. 866G.

[218] Rabie ACJ's judgment on the ouster clause question appears to represent the views of four members of the court, for Hefer JA and Vivier JA expressly concur (ibid. 856I), while E. M. Grosskopf JA (with whom Hefer and Vivier also concur) states that he agrees generally with Rabie's judgment (ibid. 873D) and writes only on another issue.

[219] Ibid. 853C–F (judgment of Rabie ACJ).

[220] Such an argument might be suggested by language in *Union Government* v. *Fakir*, 1923 SA 466 (A) at 470, in which Innes CJ wrote that '[t]he fact that an order purports to be done under the Act will not exclude the interference of the courts, where there was no jurisdiction to deal with the matter at all or where it has been dealt with not *bona fide* but fraudulently'. In *During NO* v. *Boesak and Another*, 1990 (3) SA 661 (A) at 676G–I, Botha JA also suggests that there may be 'certain instances of the improper exercise of a discretion' that do constitute 'exercise[s] of the functionary's powers'. Lawrence Baxter observes, somewhat similarly, that the actual intention of most legislators enacting ouster clauses is probably 'to preclude review in circumstances where there are no "manifest defects" in the action concerned': Baxter, *Admin. Law* (cit. n. 80), 727. He goes on to argue, however, that since it is up to the courts to determine whether 'manifest defects' are present, this partial ouster can in practice be no ouster at all (ibid. 727, 729–31). Ultimately Baxter seems to approve of the outcome reflected in his observation that '[i]n practice ouster clauses have usually only encouraged a degree of restraint on the part of some judges' (ibid. 730).

a variety of other errors in breach of their statutory duties. In the normal course of things, such violations of the law would be subject to review and correction in court, for they *are* violations of law. But if a statute forbids inquiry into the validity of actions taken under it, then these violations cannot be reviewed by the courts; the conduct in question, despite its unlawful aspects, remains action 'under' the statute.[221] It seems to me that in principle one can understand such a distinction between errors so serious as to require judicial invervention and others that, although unfortunate, do not demand judicial action.[222]

There are indeed hints of such an argument in Acting Chief Justice Rabie's judgment for the court in *United Democratic Front*. The passage just quoted seems to place some emphasis on the State President's reliance on, and attempted exercise of, the powers granted him by the relevant statute. Just after this passage, moveover, Rabie writes that '[t]o qualify as a regulation issued in terms of s. 3(1)(*a*) of the Act and therefore protected by s. 5B of the Act against a declaration of invalidity, a regulation need not in my opinion meet all the requirements for validity'.[223] Rabie finds support for this proposition in two immigration cases, which can be read to indicate that the immigration officials in question were acting under their authorizing statute despite having violated implied (or perhaps even express) statutory requirements governing their actions.[224]

[221] Thus—though not in the context of an ouster clauser—the US Supreme Court has recently observed, in addressing the question of whether a failure to hold a pretrial detention hearing at the time required by law entitles the detainee to release, that '[i]t is conceivable that some combination of procedural irregularities could render a detention hearing so flawed that it would not constitute [in the words of the statute] "a hearing pursuant to the provisions of subsection (f)" for purposes of ... [the statute]. A failure to comply with the first appearance requirement, however, does not so subvert the procedural scheme ... as to invalidate the hearing.' *United States* v. *Montalvo-Murillo*, 58 USLW 4652, 4654 (US 29 May 1990).

[222] But see Haysom and Plasket, 'War against Law' (cit. n. 6), 328 n. 123 (characterizing Baxter's 'manifest defect' approach, described in n. 220 above, as not being 'conceptually clear').

[223] *United Democratic Front*, 1988 (4) SA at 853F (judgment of Rabie ACJ).

[224] *Narainsamy* v. *Principal Immigration Officer*, 1923 AD 673, 675; *Barday* v. *Passport Control Officer and Another*, 1967 (2) SA 346 (A) at 356–8. The crux of each of these cases, as the courts saw them, seems to have been a challenge to the treatment of a particular individual by the immigration authorities, rather than a challenge to any regulations issued by those authorities. Van Heerden JA contends in his dissenting judgment that these cases, whose validity he declines to address, deal with 'executive' or 'administrative' action. In *United Democratic Front*, on the other hand, the challenge to the vagueness of the regulations 'concerns something totally different, namely the "defects" which attach to delegated legislation'. *United Democratic Front*, 1988 (4) SA at 859D–F (dissenting judgment of Van Heerden JA). (The same distinction can be made with respect to a case Rabie ACJ does not cite, *Winter* v. *Administrator-in-Executive Committee*, 1973 (1) SA 873 (A), in which the Appellate Division declared that in the face of a valid and sufficiently broad ouster clause 'the ambit of the Court's jurisdiction is limited indeed': ibid. 887D.) This argument goes to the weight of these cases as precedent, but does not directly address the possibility that *some* conduct might violate *some* statutory prohibitions and yet remain conduct 'under' the statute in question. Van Heerden's judgment hints, however, that for him the validity of *Narainsamy* and *Barday* would turn not on this notion but rather on whether these cases correctly determined which limitations on administrative action were and were not implied in the relevant legislation. *United Democratic Front*, 1988 (4) SA at 859F. One

This theory, however, had a major flaw. This was that it was very hard to square with the *Hurley* case. In *Hurley*, Rabie had concluded that an officer responsible for an arrest under the statutory provision in question had to have reasonable grounds for the arrest, and that an arrest by an officer who lacked such reasonable grounds would not be an arrest under the statute, just as an arrest by an officer who lacked the rank required by the statute also would not be an arrest under the statute. It would have been easy to formulate an argument that the officer's mistake of judgement, in concluding that certain facts provided a reasonable basis for an arrest when, in the court's eyes, they did not, was by no means such an egregious departure from the statute's requirements as to make the arrest not 'under' the statute. Yet the court in *Hurley* does not so much as raise this possibility, nor does it cite any of the cases—*Fakir*, *Narainswamy*, and *Barday*—which Rabie invokes in *United Democratic Front*. Moreover, in *Hurley* Rabie expressly finds support for his position in the views of two of the justices in the earlier Appellate Division case of *Schermbrucker* v. *Klindt, NO.*[225] Neither of these justices, Trollip AJA and Rumpff JA, showed any sign of embracing the notion that the ouster clause in that case applied to actions, purportedly under the statute, that were actually 'unlawfully'[226] committed or violated 'the explicit and implicit provisions' of the statute.[227]

Rabie ACJ does not mention *Hurley*'s handling of the ouster clause issue in *United Democratic Front*, nor do any of the members of the *United Democratic Front* court. Yet Rabie seems to have been haunted by it none the less, for after developing the framework for an argument that action may be under a statute despite violating some of the statute's requirements, Rabie in the end does not rely on this argument. Instead, he describes the contention of the court below that the Public Safety Act impliedly requires the State President not to make vague regulations, and then writes:

> As will appear from what I have said above, this view of the matter is in my opinion not correct. It is to my mind artificial and impure, and I think that vagueness must be seen as an independent ground on which subordinate legislation such as that in the case in hand can be challenged, and not as an instance of *ultra vires*.[228]

reason that Van Heerden does not pursue at length the idea of action under, yet in violation of, statutory authority may be that Rabie himself ultimately does not appear to embrace it, as indicated in the text below.

[225] *Schermbrucker* v. *Klindt, NO*, 1965 (4) SA 606 (A), discussed in *Hurley*, 1986 (3) SA 568 (A) at 584I–586A.

[226] *Schermbrucker* v. *Klindt, NO*, 1965 (4) SA 606 (A) at 623F–G (judgment of Trollip AJA), quoted by *Hurley*, 1986 (3) SA 568 (A) at 585I. Trollip AJA may have been referring to non-statutory as well as statutory unlawfulness, but that would only underline the narrow reach he apparently was giving to the ouster clause in that case.

[227] *Schermbrucker* v. *Klindt, NO*, 1965 (4) SA 606 (A) at 613B–C (Rumpff JA, dissenting), quoted in *Hurley*, 1986 (3) SA 568 (A) at 585G.

[228] *United Democratic Front*, 1988 (4) SA at 855G.

This passage appears to endorse the view that the rule against vagueness is not a statutory requirement but rather an independent, presumably common-law, injunction. But in what he had 'said above', Rabie certainly had not developed any clear rationale for this conclusion, for he had not until this passage articulated the idea that the prohibition against vagueness, or any other legal requirement, existed independent of statute. Nor does he offer such a rationale here, for the passage I have just quoted simply does not contain an argument. The only explanation he musters is the pained statement that to encompass vagueness within *ultra vires* is 'to my mind artificial and impure'. This is a *cri de cœur* and no more.

A broad view of the ambit of *ultra vires* was certainly not unprecedented. A well-known lower court decision had averred forty years earlier, in a different but related context, that:

> [i]n considering whether the proceedings of any tribunal should be set aside on the ground of illegality or irregularity, the question appears always to resolve itself into whether the tribunal acted *ultra vires* or not. ... If then, a tribunal, whether as a consequence of misconstruing its powers or otherwise, does something which it is not empowered to do, or fails to do something which it is obliged to do, it simply acts *ultra vires*, i.e., in a manner not contemplated by the Legislature.[229]

In the 1980s, moreover, Lawrence Baxter, the author of one of South Africa's leading treatises on administrative law, had strongly endorsed this wide conception of *ultra vires*, and contended that it was 'supported by dozens of cases'.[230]

Rabie ACJ's position logically required him to offer some criterion by which courts would decide which of the many grounds for challenging the validity of subordinate legislation are statutory requirements, and part of *ultra vires*, and which, like vagueness, are not. Far from providing this criterion, however, Rabie ACJ appears to treat so many of these grounds as *ultra vires* matters, here and in *Omar*, that his exclusion of vagueness begins to seem simply *sui generis*. Thus in *United Democratic Front* Rabie considers at length, and rejects on the merits, the argument that the State President breached Parliament's intentions and thus acted *ultra vires* when he delegated to a subordinate official 'a discretion which must, in terms of the statute, be exercised by the State President himself, and which he is not permitted to abdicate'.[231] Rabie also

[229] *Estate Geekie* v. *Union Government and Another*, 1948 (2) SA 494 (N) at 502.

[230] Baxter, *Admin. Law* (cit. n. 80), 308; see ibid. 307–12. As noted in n. 220, however, Baxter did not appear to endorse the view that statutory ouster clauses should be interpreted into oblivion.

[231] *United Democratic Front*, 1988 (4) SA 830 (A) at 844B–F, quoting *United Democratic Front and Another* v. *State President and Others*, 1987 (3) SA 296 (N) at 328B–C. I will not examine here the court's handling of this issue, on which Van Heerden JA dissented. Haysom and Plasket do take up this matter and sharply criticize the court's reasoning, which they view as 'startling' and, in at least one respect, as 'fly[ing] in the face of ... well established principle': 'War against Law' (cit. n. 6), at 313, 314.

addresses, and again rejects on the merits, arguments that the regulations issued by the State President were *ultra vires* because they could not possibly serve any of the purposes for which he was permitted to make regulations.[232]

In *Omar*, Rabie ACJ seemed to recognize an even wider range of arguments as embraced within *ultra vires*. Most clearly, he did not quarrel with the characterization of subordinate legislation as *ultra vires* if it involved '"such oppressive or gratuitous interference" with the rights of the subject as can find "no justification in the minds of reasonable men."'[233] This formulation derives from *Kruse* v. *Johnson*, an English case much cited in South African decisions. Lord Russell CJ had explained in *Kruse* that:

> If, for instance, they [in that case, by-laws] were found to be partial and unequal in their operation as between different classes; if they were manifestly unjust, if they disclosed bad faith; if they involved such oppressive or gratuitous interference with the rights of those subject to them as could find no justification in the minds of reasonable men, the Court might well say, 'Parliament never intended to give authority to make such rules; they are unreasonable and *ultra vires*.'[234]

Rabie ACJ also discusses the requirement that the State President apply his mind as going to the question of whether the State President 'went beyond the powers given to him by the Act', although he does not expressly attach the label *ultra vires* to this ground for relief.[235] To be sure, the import of Rabie ACJ's discussion in *Omar* may be qualified because, as he tells us, he found it unnecessary to address the ouster clause issue.[236] None the less, *Omar* is at least consistent with a broad understanding of the scope of *ultra vires*.

If claims such as these are *ultra vires* arguments, it requires no great leap to conclude that vagueness claims—the claims at issue in *United Democratic Front*—also are *ultra vires* issues. Indeed, a judgment now more than half a century old stands for this conclusion. In the words of *R.* v. *Shapiro and Another*: '[S]tatutes do not empower the authorities to make regulations so uncertain that people will not know how to comply with them or whether they are subject to them or not. So if a regulation is found to be void for uncertainty, that is one way of arriving at the conclusion that it is *ultra vires*.'[237] To this another court had added that '[t]he requisite measure of clarity is therefore seen as a condition implicit in the enabling statute, subject to which the subordinate legislation is authorised'.[238] In what has been called 'the leading

232 See *United Democratic Front*, 1988 (4) SA at 840I–843G.

233 *Omar*, 1987 (3) SA at 893B, quoting *Kruse* v. *Johnson*, [1898] 2 QB 91.

234 *Kruse* v. *Johnson*, [1898] 2 QB 91 at 99–100.

235 *Omar*, 1987 (3) SA at 894E–F.

236 Ibid. 904C.

237 *R.* v. *Shapiro and Another*, 1935 NPD 155, 159. Van Heerden JA endorses this 'axiom' in his *United Democratic Front* dissent, 1988 (4) SA at 850.

238 *S.* v. *Meer and Another*, 1981 (1) SA 739 (N) at 740H. The decision in *Meer* was reversed by the Appellate Division, *S.* v. *Meer en 'n Ander*, 1981 (4) SA 604 (A), the Appellate Division

case on vagueness', *R.* v. *Pretoria Timber Co. (Pty), Ltd. & Another*,[239] Van den Heever JA appears to endorse the same view, and while he does so in a dissenting judgment, on this score no other judge expresses disagreement.[240] In *Metal and Allied Workers Union and Another* v. *State President and Others*,[241] Didcott J. invoked this reasoning in ruling that emergency regulations which were void for uncertainty were not made 'under' the Public Safety Act, and so were not protected from judicial review by the Act's ouster clause.[242] We simply do not know from Rabie ACJ's judgment why this decision was wrong.

Perhaps recognizing this gap, Hefer JA offers in his judgment, with which two other members of the court (but not Rabie ACJ) expressed agreement,[243] a much more serious effort to articulate a legal theory leading to the same result. Existing South African law did not foreclose this effort. As Hefer JA's judgment demonstrates, there *was* dispute about the reach of the concept of *ultra vires* in South African law.[244] Some commentators had urged a narrow understanding of *ultra vires*,[245] and Hefer JA is able to point to a modest amount of support for such a view in the case-law,[246] although he does not

did not mention this doctrinal formulation in its judgment. Cf. in *Metal and Allied Workers Union and Another* v. *State President and Others*, 1986 (4) SA 358 (D) at 366B–C (full bench).

[239] *R.* v. *Pretoria Timber Co. (Pty) Ltd. and Another*, 1950 (3) SA 163 (A). Haysom and Plasket say that this case 'is generally regarded as the leading case on vagueness'. 'War against Law' (cit. n. 6), 323.

[240] *R.* v. *Pretoria Timber Co. (Pty) Ltd. and Another*, 1950 (3) SA at 181E–182F (dissenting judgment of Van den Heever JA).

[241] *Metal and Allied Workers Union and Another* v. *State President and Others*, 1986 (4) SA 358 (D) (full bench).

[242] Ibid. 365–7.

[243] Vivier JA expressly concurred in Hefer JA's judgment, *United Democratic Front*, 1988 (4) SA 830 (A) at 873C. E. M. Grosskopf JA expressed general agreement with Hefer JA's reasoning. Ibid. 873D. (Hefer and Vivier JJA also concurred in Rabie ACJ's judgment, and Grosskopf JA expressed general agreement with it too.)

[244] *United Democratic Front*, 1988 (4) SA 830 (A) at 868D–872E (concurring judgment of Hefer JA).

[245] Among the commentators, Lawrence Baxter's broad view of *ultra vires* has already been mentioned. See text at n. 230 above. Other commentators, however, have urged narrower views. For example, Wiechers prefers a narrower understanding of *ultra vires*, but his central concern appears to be that use of the *ultra vires* rubric will generate a concentration on the statutory language (as the source of *vires*) and therefore risk an abridgement of legal protections that do not seem to fit within that language. Wiechers, *Admin. Law* (cit. n. 80), 176–8. See also e.g. L. Rose Innes, *Judicial Review of Administrative Tribunals in South Africa* (Cape Town: Juta, 1963), 93. Baxter suggests that those who have argued for a narrow understanding of *ultra vires* 'have done so in order to ensure that the grounds of review remain wide rather than narrow': *Admin. Law* (cit. n. 80), 311. If so, Hefer JA's adoption of this doctrinal position as a basis for abridging judicial review of an emergency regulation has given it a much different effect than its advocates intended.

[246] Perhaps the most direct case-law support that Hefer JA offers consists of four Appellate Division cases which he sees as 'distinguish[ing] between exceeding one's authority and other review grounds': *United Democratic Front*, 1988 (4) SA at 868J. They cannot be considered a powerful collection of authority. Two of them, *Union Government* v. *Fakir*, 1923 AD 466, and *Narainsamy* v. *Principal Immigration Officer*, 1923 AD 673, both cited by Rabie ACJ as well, deal with immigration decisions and do not, so far as the judgments reveal, turn on the extent of any delegated authority to make regulations. (Compare van Heerden JA's discussion of

identify any case which contended that the making of vague regulations was *intra vires*.[247]

Hefer JA develops an argument for a narrow understanding of *ultra vires*, and thus for giving effect to the ouster clause, an argument which paradoxically relies primarily on the independence of the courts to justify their ouster. Hefer JA emphasizes the creative role of the courts in the shaping of a range of grounds for review.[248] From this perspective, he argues that these grounds of review are really judge-made law rather than genuinely implicit statutory requirements. Judge-made law is law, but it is not statutory law, and so action in breach of such judge-made provisions is not *ultra vires*, and hence is shielded from review by an ouster clause.

It must be said at once that this is a dramatic, potentially 'radical', reformulation of the judicial role in South Africa.[249] It is also noteworthy that it apparently was 'the result of his [Hefer JA's] own research and was not fully argued in open court'.[250] The cases which Hefer JA invokes in support of this characterization by no means go as far as he does.[251] This is not to deny the force of Hefer JA's observation that South African judges do make law under the rubric, or guise, of statutory interpretation; indeed, this is a point I have sought to demonstrate as well.[252] It is one thing, however, to say that the

Narainswamy and *Barday*, described in n. 224 above.) The other two are dissenting judgments—which Hefer JA contends were not disputed on this score—which argued for maintaining 'the distinction between excess of power and unreasonableness': *Sinovich* v. *Hercules Municipal Council*, 1946 AD 783, 802 (dissenting judgment of Schreiner JA); *Arenstein* v. *Durban Corporation*, 1952 (1) SA 279 (A) at 287H (dissenting judgment of Centlivres CJ). In fact, however, it is by no means clear that the other judges in *Sinovich* accepted Schreiner JA's view. See *Sinovich*, 1946 AD 783, 791–2 (judgment of Watermeyer CJ); ibid. 797–9 (judgment of Greenberg JA); ibid. 817 (judgment of Feetham JA). In *Arenstein* Centlivres refers to this point only in a single sentence, and the other judges' failure to disagree with him hardly seems to demonstrate agreement. Whatever the validity of this distinction, it sheds no light on whether vagueness is or is not an instance of 'excess of power'.

247 Haysom and Plasket maintain that prior to the *United Democratic Front* decision 'it was clear that vagueness, in our law, is treated as a part of the *ultra vires* doctrine'. 'War against Law' (cit. n. 6), 316.

248 *United Democratic Front*, 1988 (4) SA at 869E–870E.

249 I adopt the term 'radical' from Haysom and Plasket, who call Hefer JA's approach 'radical to say the least': 'War against Law' (cit. n. 6), 321.

250 Ibid. 332.

251 See n. 246 above. Hefer JA also cites several cases dealing with the basis for courts' application of the *audi alteram partem* requirement. Of these, the one providing the most explicit support for Hefer's thinking is the judgment of Corbett JA in *Attorney-General, Eastern Cape* v. *Blom and Others*, 1986 (4) SA 645 (A). Corbett JA suggests that the *audi alteram partem* principle should be understood as applicable whenever the government prejudicially affects the property or liberty of an individual, unless it is expressly or impliedly excluded by statute. He contrasts this to an approach which first assumes that a statute permitting such governmental action impliedly incorporates the *audi* principle, and then asks whether the particular statute impliedly excludes it, an approach which he feels does not differ from the other in substance but is 'logically less satisfactory'. Ibid. 662G–J. This careful effort to clarify a particular doctrinal difficulty seems quite distant from Hefer JA's broad-gauged reinterpretation of South African law.

252 See Ch. 2 above.

courts enjoy substantial interpretive freedom which the legislature cannot readily or entirely check; it is quite another to imply that a substantial body of law is not interpretation at all but is instead invention—and to approve of it as such. And it is often a radical step to pierce popular fictions, however fictional they may be. The result of Hefer's formulation, should it become a new conventional wisdom, might well be to give the courts a sense of greater lawmaking freedom—perhaps to abridge the protections of doctrines hitherto seen as implicitly embodied in legislative commands, but perhaps, instead, to expand them in ways that Hefer JA would be unlikely to welcome.[253]

Etienne Mureinik argues that for courts to invalidate actions authorized by statute on the basis of extra-statutory, judge-made law (as Hefer JA claims they do) would be inconsistent with the bedrock principle of parliamentary sovereignty.[254] If so, then Hefer JA's position would be not only radical but actually untenable within South African law; but on this point I believe Mureinik is mistaken. It is possible to square the existence of judge-made grounds for review with parliamentary sovereignty by affirming that the judge-made grounds have legal force only so long as Parliament allows them to have it, or that Parliament has impliedly authorized the courts to fashion such rules. Thus Hefer JA's position does not necessarily violate this fundamental premiss of South African law. Indeed, as a formal matter all that Hefer JA has really done is to change the focus of statutory interpretation from asking whether Parliament has impliedly incorporated the various judge-made rules of review to asking whether Parliament has impliedly excluded them.[255]

This formal issue points, however, to a different respect in which the principle of parliamentary supremacy is relevant to this case. Hefer JA's position must be that Parliament has acquiesced in the existence and judicial enforcement of the various judge-made grounds for review (since he agrees that they are law), but that Parliament has chosen *not* to incorporate them, implicitly, into the statutes themselves. Indeed, Hefer JA says almost exactly this. He writes:

> I am prepared to accept that the legislator proceeded on the assumption that a delegated competence will be exercised within the limits of the rules; but I find the elevation of such an assumption to an actual condition (with already-mentioned consequences [that is, the potential for a finding of *ultra vires* based on a breach]) unacceptable.[256]

But this is an issue of statutory interpretation. The question is whether statutes that are wholly silent about the various judge-made rules of review should be interpreted to make these rules parts of the statutes themselves or

[253] See Haysom and Plasket, 'War against Law' (cit. n. 6), 321.

[254] Mureinik, 'Pursuing Principle' (cit. n. 103), 71. Haysom and Plasket develop a similar objection in 'War against Law' (cit. n. 6), 320–1.

[255] In this sense, Hefer JA's position *is* similar to the view which Corbett JA took of the legal status of the *audi alteram partem* protections. See n. 251 above.

[256] *United Democratic Front*, 1988 (4) SA at 872G (concurring judgment of Hefer JA).

rather parts of their environments. Even if Hefer JA were right that the 'environmental' interpretation would make more sense and—a much more dubious proposition—fit better with South African legal precedent, it is hard to maintain that these silent texts unambiguously express agreement with Hefer JA's position. If the statutes are admitted to be ambiguous, however, and if (as *United Democratic Front* demonstrates) an interpretation which reads these rules into the statutes preserves them from the effect of ouster clauses elsewhere in those statutes, then there is considerable basis for choosing this interpretation. Adopting this view, after all, is consistent both with the presumption against interference with the jurisdiction of the courts and with the rule that ambiguous statutes should be read *in favorem libertatis*. Perhaps Hefer JA would dispense with these somewhat fictional rules of interpretation as well—but then what would take their place? Hefer JA's statement that he finds such a reading 'unacceptable', like Rabie's assertion that a similar position is 'artificial and impure', does not amount to a guide to interpretation.

Perhaps the most serious problem with Hefer JA's approach, however, is that it too fails to give a satisfactory answer to the question of which of the various grounds of review are to be seen as part of the statute and which are not. Hefer JA focuses on the judge-made rules for review, but it seems clear that he does not believe that all of these rules fall outside the bounds of *ultra vires*. If he did believe that, he might have had difficulty joining Rabie's judgment, for Rabie appears to accord *ultra vires* status to prohibitions on unauthorized delegation of authority and on use of authority for unauthorized purposes, prohibitions certainly not spelt out in the Public Safety Act.[257]

In one important respect, moreover, Hefer goes further in embracing non-statutory claims within the ambit of *ultra vires* than Rabie explicitly does. Hefer's judgment indicates that he believes that the State President would be *ultra vires* if he acted '*mala fide* or for an ulterior purpose or without proper consideration'.[258] Rabie does not address this issue in *United Democratic Front*, although, as we saw, he may have adopted a similar stance in *Omar*.[259] Hefer maintains that his position does not rest on the theory that the Public Safety Act makes compliance with these requirements an implied condition of the State President's action. But such action would evidently still be *ultra vires* because the State President 'would simply not be exercising the power which the Act granted him. For this reason a regulation made in such circumstances

[257] The Act specifies the purposes for which the State President may make emergency regulations, but does not state that the State President is forbidden to make regulations for other purposes. Public Safety Act 3 of 1953, s. 3(1)(*a*). It also specifies that, '[w]ithout prejudice to the generality of the powers conferred by this section' such regulations may delegate the power to make orders, rules, and by-laws, but does not state that no other delegations are permitted. Ibid., s. 3(2)(*a*)(i).

[258] *United Democratic Front*, 1988 (4) SA 830 (A) at 873B–C (concurring judgment of Hefer JA).

[259] See text at n. 235 above.

is not a regulation issued under s[ection] 3 [the provision authorizing the making of emergency regulations].'[260]

This explanation adheres to Hefer's rejection of the implied condition doctrine, but it does not otherwise support a limited view of statutory incorporation. In effect, Hefer has conceded that the rules prohibiting conduct that is *mala fide* or not based on proper consideration (surely as judge-made as any of the grounds of review) *are* incorporated in the statute.[261] It seems of little importance whether the theoretical vehicle for their incorporation is as implied conditions on otherwise valid action or as elements in the definition of valid action; indeed, it is difficult to grasp even the theoretical distinction between these two methods of incorporation. In any event, the upshot is that Hefer JA has acknowledged a wide scope for the process of incorporation.[262]

Having done so, he now faces the question of why vagueness too should not be incorporated. In his dissenting judgment, van Heerden JA suggests an argument that seems to make the task of formulating an answer to this question particularly elusive. Van Heerden argues that since vague regulations cannot be carried into effect, the State President would not have issued vague regulations if he had properly applied his mind to the task at hand.[263] Accordingly, the decision that 'apply the mind' issues are *ultra vires* questions should embrace vagueness challenges as well. Hefer does not directly respond to this argument.[264]

Hefer does, however, address the question of whether vagueness should be seen as incorporated directly (rather than via the 'apply the mind' doctrine) into the statute. He writes near the end of his judgment that even if vagueness is not an implied condition, 'the question remains whether [a vague regulation] can be regarded as *ultra vires* simply on the ground that the legislation does not authorize vague regulations'.[265] Hefer's response to this question is not

260 *United Democratic Front*, 1988 (4) SA at 873B–C.

261 This is particularly interesting because in *Dempsey* Hefer JA was at pains to assert that the 'apply the mind' doctrine was *not* a statutory precondition to lawful arrests. See text at nn. 102–5 above. Apparently he now would say that this doctrine was a statutory requirement, but not a precondition.

262 Thus I would not read Hefer JA's judgment, as Haysom and Plasket do, to place essentially all of the judicially inferred limits on administrative power potentially 'outside the *ultra vires* doctrine', 'War against Law' (cit. n. 6), 330 and n. 134.

263 *United Democratic Front*, 1988 (4) SA at 859I–860A (dissenting judgment of van Heerden JA).

264 Whether this argument by itself would have much assisted the challenge to the regulations in this case is, however, open to question. In the lower court, the challengers apparently disclaimed any intention to assert that the State President had failed to apply his mind—perhaps because such a claim would have opened the way for the state to introduce affidavit evidence of circumstances to which the State President would maintain he had given his attention. When the state sought to offer such evidence, the challengers opposed its admission, while also contending that if admitted this evidence supported an 'apply the mind' attack on the regulations. Since the evidence was not admitted, it appears that this case does not present an 'apply the mind' issue as such. See *United Democratic Front and Another* v. *State President and Others*, 1987 (3) SA 296 (N) at 301, 305–6.

265 *United Democratic Front*, 1988 (4) SA at 872H (concurring judgment of Hefer JA).

very illuminating, for he says that it 'has already been answered by the acting Chief Justice [Rabie]'.[266] He appears to be invoking Rabie's argument, already quoted,[267] that when the State President formulates regulations for the statutorily authorized purposes, he (in Hefer's words) 'is busy with an authorized act. If his formulation falls short of the requisite degree of clarity, it is defective and ineffective, but I find it difficult to accept that the act is suddenly converted into an *unauthorized* one'.[268] As we saw at some length earlier, Rabie's judgment fails to develop a coherent rationale for this conclusion.[269] Hefer, like Rabie, finds it 'difficult to accept' that vagueness is an element of *ultra vires*—but that is no answer to the question he himself has posed.

This question is all the more difficult because of the apparent unenforceability of vague regulations. Unlawfully vague regulations are regulations to which courts are unable to assign a reasonably clear meaning through the normal process of interpretation.[270] Each of the members of the court who speaks to the issue appears to agree that such regulations are unenforceable,[271] as indeed they must be to the extent that they are unintelligible. To make them enforceable, courts would have to assign them a meaning by some method other than the rules of interpretation ordinarily available and appropriate.

Must courts do such super-interpretation of vague emergency regulations? Van Heerden writes in dissent that '[n]o one suggested that if an accused is charged with the contravention of a vague regulation, a court is obliged to impute a meaning to it in one way or another',[272] and indeed none of the majority justices urges such a course. Apparently, therefore, vague regulations cannot be enforced in court. It is surprising to learn that the apparent intention of the legislature, by virtue of the ouster clause, was to permit the State President to issue regulations which courts could neither enforce nor invalidate: an intention Van Heerden JA calls 'nonsensical'.[273]

Sadly, there is a sense in which this intention, although deeply disturbing, is not nonsensical. For the result of the court's decision is that the State President is free to write vague regulations. To be sure, anyone prosecuted for violating those regulations will *probably* have a good defence against the charges, provided that the courts in the end agree that the regulations are vague. But until that trial, no one can say whether the regulations do or do not have the force of law, and anyone considering whether to act in ways that

[266] Ibid. 872H–I (concurring judgment of Hefer JA).
[267] See text at nn. 219 and 223 above.
[268] *United Democratic Front*, 1988 (4) SA at 872J (concurring judgment of Hefer JA).
[269] See text at nn. 220–42 above.
[270] See n. 204 above.
[271] See *United Democratic Front*, 1988 (4) SA at 853A (judgment of Rabie ACJ); ibid. 872J (concurring judgment of Hefer JA); ibid. 859D (dissenting judgment of van Heerden JA).
[272] Ibid. 860B (dissenting judgment of van Heerden JA).
[273] Ibid. 859G (dissenting judgment of van Heerden JA). Part of this paradox would be resolved if the ouster clause *did* compel the courts to enforce vague regulations, a possibility which van Heerden raises. Ibid. 860C (dissenting judgment of van Heerden JA). But no member of the majority argues for this reading of the ouster clause.

might violate these regulations must recognize the risk that in the end they will be upheld and enforced. Moreover, trials for violations of the emergency regulations appear to have been relatively rare; the state's extra-judicial emergency powers, such as its authority to arrest and detain without trial, were 'simpler and swifter than prosecuting suspected "law-breakers"'.[274] Those who exercise these extra-judicial powers are free to look to vague regulations, however unenforceable in court they may ultimately be, for guidance in their actions. In short, vague regulations can serve a very real purpose: they can deter conduct that even the elaborate emergency regulations do not actually make unlawful. The court may not have welcomed this effect, but it mustered the fragile arguments we have considered to render a decision which made this effect possible.

Thus the work of the emergency team. As usual, the only dissenting voice, a clear one to be sure, comes from a judge who was not part of the emergency team, van Heerden JA. By this time the Rabie era was less than five months from its conclusion, and it is more difficult to attach significance to the subsequent role of van Heerden JA in emergency cases than it was in the cases of Nestadt JA, who concurred in *Dempsey* on grounds quite different from those of Hefer JA, or of Hoexter JA, the *Omar* dissenter. None the less it deserves mention that van Heerden JA did not sit on any of the four Rabie-era emergency cases argued after this decision.[275]

The patterns in these cases are clear enough. What are we to make of them? I will postpone a full exploration of these questions until Chapter 5, but we have enough data now to offer certain observations. First, and most obviously, these decisions reflect the dominance of a small group of like-minded judges who were positioned to speak for the Appellate Division as a whole, a state of affairs which made the court's jurisprudence the expression of an even smaller range of South African understanding than would otherwise have been the case. Second, the Rabie court responded to human rights issues in ways that fell painfully short of carefully reasoned adjudication: with ill-explained doctrinal interpretation or development, with abrupt or even deaf responses to opposing arguments, and on occasion with startling recasting of existing doctrine. Third, despite (and in part because of) these decisionmaking methods, the court was repeatedly unable to generate persuasive justifications for its decisions. Fourth, the cases attest that the dominant judges shared what must be called a political view, a conviction that the emergency system had to be

[274] Haysom and Kahanovitz, 'Courts and the State of Emergency' (cit. n. 112), 197.

[275] These were *Bishop of the RC Church*, No. 165/87 (Appellate Division 29 Sept. 1988) (argued 16 Sept. 1988); *Swart*, 1989 (1) SA 295 (A) (argued 19 Sept. 1988); *Parker*, 1989 (2) SA 633 (argued 1 Nov. 1988); and *Van der Westhuizen*, 1989 (2) SA 242 (A) (argued 14 Nov. 1988). Unlike all other dissenters from these cases, however, van Heerden JA dissented in two. This was not because he was chosen for any emergency panels after his first dissent. Both of these cases, *United Democratic Front* and *Release Mandela Campaign*, were argued on 21 Mar. 1988 and decided on 13 Sept. 1988.

sustained despite its invasions of human rights. Fifth, and finally, we have repeatedly found reason to see these decisions as blows to human rights, blows that may well have contributed to the sweeping, largely unregulated, invasions of human rights of this era.

As dismaying and troubling as these judgments are, however, we have not yet fully taken the measure of the Rabie court. As we will see in Chapter 4, there are other cases to be studied in which the court actually granted relief to the targets of emergency power. There are also aspects of the cases we have looked at which we will need to highlight, in order to see the ways in which the Rabie court stopped short of adopting positions that would have undercut the jurisprudential bases for human rights protection even further. We will turn to these matters in the first two sections of the next chapter. When we have assembled the data more completely, we will then trace the elements of the court's perspective on emergency law, a perspective which underlies not only the grim decisions in *Dempsey, Omar,* and *United Democratic Front* but the other aspects of the Rabie court's emergency law. We will then be in a better position to understand the ways in which the Rabie court remained confined, by custom and by choice, within the toils of the law.

4

The Rabie Court's Protection of Human Rights

> The rhetoric and the rules of a society are something a great deal more than sham.... They may disguise the true realities of power, but, at the same time, they may curb that power and check its intrusions.[1]

E. P. Thompson wrote those words at the end of a study of what he called, two pages later, 'a bad law, drawn by bad legislators, and enlarged by the interpretations of bad judges'.[2] In offering a chapter on the Rabie court's protection of human rights, similarly, I do not mean to suggest that the emergency decisions of this period are an evenly balanced set. They are not. The most important cases, those involving the most far-reaching challenges to the emergency system, were all, without exception, decided in favour of that system, and these judgments sanctioned profound violations of human rights in the name of the emergency.

Even so, what we have seen so far is not a complete picture of the Rabie court's work. In this chapter, I want to add two important elements to that picture. The first will emerge from a return to the emergency cases we have just studied, in which we now need to highlight certain respects in which these cases preserved legal protections that might have been discarded altogether. The second will emerge from an examination of the three decisions of the Rabie court that unmistakably and often inventively protected the rights of emergency detainees.

When we have assembled the data, we will need to ask how these benign decisions, or features of decisions, could be the product of the same emergency jurisprudence—and the same emergency-team judges—responsible for the grim results in *Dempsey, Omar, United Democratic Front,* and elsewhere. I will argue that the Rabie court, as sensitive as it was to the demands of the emergency, should not be seen as fecklessly surrendering common-law protections to the whims of the executive. The court was prepared to risk invasion of human rights in order to avoid hampering emergency-law enforcement, but its own perception of that risk must be seen against the background of its trust in the authorities' conduct and in their avoiding abusive exercise of the

[1] E. P. Thompson, *Whigs and Hunters: The Origin of the Black Act* (New York: Pantheon, (1975), 265.

[2] Ibid. 267.

powers which they wielded. Moreover, there were limits to the court's tolerance. In general, the Appellate Division jealously guarded the courts' institutional role and capacity to enforce the law. In the rare cases where the court encountered what it saw as genuine abuse of authority by the state, its distaste for the police behaviour is quite evident and its disposition of the matters strict and vigilant. After examining the work of the Corbett court in Chapter 5, we will turn in Chapter 6 to the challenge of explaining the genesis and force of these conflicting judicial sentiments.

A. The Rights Not Lost

Let us look again at the cases we studied in the last chapter, and catalogue not the rights discarded but the rights, and rules of law, preserved. We will find that the list is surprisingly long. Heading it, perhaps, is a rule in part chosen rather than merely preserved: the principle that the powers wielded by the State President under the Public Safety Act are not plenary and unreviewable but rather are subject to judicial scrutiny on the various conventional grounds by which matters vested in government officials' subjective discretion can be tested. It was clearly open to the Appellate Division to decide, instead, that the State President's powers were equal, or almost equal, to those of Parliament. Had the court made this equation, it would have been explicitly accepting unlimited and autocratic authority, but it would not have been out of tune with perhaps the most apposite judicial precedent.[3]

Having denied that the State President's powers were so absolute as to be unreviewable, the court in fact went on to review them on a number of grounds. Thus the State President is not permitted to use his emergency powers for unauthorized purposes;[4] must not act in bad faith;[5] may not engage in unauthorized delegations to subordinate officials;[6] must apply his mind to the issues involved in the exercise of his powers;[7] may not exercise his powers in ways so grossly unreasonable that Parliament could not have meant to authorize such conduct;[8] and may not issue vague regulations.[9]

In addition, the court raises no question about the continued applicability of the usual tools for judicial interpretation of legislation. In particular, the court appears to accept that a regulation will not be read to invade fundamental common-law rights, such as the *audi* principle, unless it does so expressly or by necessary implication.[10] The court itself repeatedly reads into broad

[3] See Ch. 3, text at nn. 155–61 above.
[4] *Omar*, 1987 (3) SA 859 (A) at 892G–H.
[5] Ibid.
[6] See *United Democratic Front*, 1988 (4) SA 830 (A) at 843G–846I (judgment of Rabie ACJ); *Tsenoli*, 1986 (4) SA 1150 (A) at 1182B–J.
[7] *Omar*, 1987 (3) SA at 892G–H.
[8] Ibid. 892J–893D.
[9] *United Democratic Front*, 1988 (4) SA 830 (A) at 851I–J (judgment of Rabie ACJ).
[10] See Ch. 3, text at nn. 146–8 above.

regulations an implied requirement that the powers granted in those regulations be used only for the purposes of the emergency—although, to be sure, it does so in order to head off claims that unlawfully broad powers have been conferred by these regulations.[11] The only instance in which the court appears to challenge interpretive conventions is Hefer JA's judgment in *United Democratic Front*, but that judgment's striking features should not obscure the fact that Hefer JA does not suggest that characterizing the grounds for review as judge-made rather than statutorily implied will actually change the content of any of these grounds.[12]

The court also does not apply the Public Safety Act's ouster clause to any of these claims, except, of course, for the vagueness challenge at issue in *United Democratic Front*.[13] The vagueness claim, in turn, may be *sui generis*. Certainly the court's judgments do not offer criteria that compel the extension of this ouster doctrine to any other ground for review. Moreover, vague regulations have a special feature, namely that if they are indeed entirely unintelligible, then they are also entirely unenforceable.[14] Regulations which are invalid under the other grounds for review may be perfectly clear, and so, if they cannot be declared invalid because of an ouster clause, they may be enforceable; with vague regulations, the judges can take a 'second bite at the apple', if and when the state tries to enforce them in court.

Similarly, in *Dempsey* the Appellate Division preserves much of the doctrinal structure governing arrest cases even as it increases the difficulty of challenging an arrest. The court never questions that the 'apply the mind' doctrine does apply to arrests, and does not expressly go beyond quite discrete modifications in the elements of that doctrine.[15] At the same time, the court never questions that the general *onus* of justifying an arrest lies on the party defending the arrest, though it opens up an exception to this principle that could easily swallow the rule.[16] Moreover, in an aspect of *Ngqumba* which we have not yet considered, the court accepted the existence of a requirement, certainly not spelled out in the emergency regulations, that the police inform the arrestee as soon as reasonably practicable of the reasons for his or her arrest.[17] According to the court, '[i]t is hardly conceivable that the intention could have been that a person could be arrested, and be deprived of his liberty, without being given an indication of why he had been arrested.'[18]

[11] See *Tsenoli*, 1986 (4) SA at 1183A–1184F (finding that the Minister's power to extend detention must, 'by necessary implication', be exercised only for emergency purposes); *Omar*, 1987 (3) SA at 896I (holding that the power to deny a detainee access to a lawyer can be exercised 'only on grounds which are related to the emergency').

[12] Hefer JA's point, rather, is that the judge-made rules can be enforced without the fiction that they are legislatively implied. *United Democratic Front*, 1988 (4) SA at 870I (concurring judgment of Hefer JA).

[13] See Ch. 3 at nn. 216–74 above.

[14] See Ch. 3 n. 204 and text at nn. 270–1 above.

[15] See Ch. 3, text at nn. 77–85 above.

[16] See Ch. 3, text at nn. 89–111 above.

[17] *Ngqumba*, 1988 (4) SA 224 (A) at 265H, 268J–269B.

[18] Ibid. 265I–J.

In short, the list of doctrines not rejected is quite substantial. What is much less clear, however, is what the meaning of this list is. One explanation for the retention of these doctrines is simply that the court did not need to jettison them in order to reach the results it did. The force of this explanation cannot be denied, in light of the fact that the court *did* give effect to an ouster clause, when it might otherwise have felt constrained to overturn an emergency regulation, and in light of the undemanding cast which the court gave to many of the benign principles which it had preserved. I will argue, however, that the retention of these doctrines also reflects that the judges of the emergency team, despite their support for emergency authority, held to attitudes which significantly modulated the court's executive-mindedness. To develop the grounds for these benign explanations will require an examination of other aspects of the Rabie court's work and ultimately of South African legal culture. In this chapter we will begin that effort by looking at those decisions in which the court did grant relief to people whose rights had been invaded under the mantle of the emergency.

B. The Rights Protected

For evidence that the courts' preservation of certain potentially benign doctrines is related in any degree to a continuing judicial concern for the common law rights of South Africans, we need to find evidence that that concern was ever sufficient to tip the result in a case in favour of a victim of emergency power. For this purpose, it will not be enough to find that there are cases—in fact there are three from the Rabie era[19]—which are resolved in favour of the subjects of emergency action, for it might be that legal argument so pressed for this result that the court's action tells us little of its own convictions. But the existence of such a concern would be suggested by cases in which the court chose to resolve disputable legal issues in favour of those on whom emergency power had fallen, and in which the court's judgment conveys a sense of judicial disapproval of the state's conduct. Such cases exist.

Indeed, all three of the cases decided in favour of human rights claims during Rabie's tenure have at least something of this flavour. This is even true, though perhaps least so, of a decision by Hefer JA, usually a vigorous and ingenious defender of emergency authority. In this case, *Swart*, the Rabie court held for the first and only time that an emergency detention was unlawful. The basis for this decision was that the detainee had not been informed of the reason for his arrest—he had not even been told he was being arrested under

[19] These are, in order of decision (but not of reporting), *Apleni*, 1989 (1) SA 195 (A) (decided 26 Nov. 1987); *Nkwentsha*, 1988(3) SA 99(A) (decided 30 Mar. 1988), and *Swart*, 1989 (1) SA 295 (A) (decided 29 Sept. 1988). None of these cases appears to have been particularly difficult for the court, since each was decided, unanimously, within less than six weeks after being argued.

emergency powers—until he had actually been transferred out of police custody and into the prison in which he was to be detained (a period, it appears, of well over five hours).[20] This failure to inform him was a violation of the rule announced in *Ngqumba*, that such information must be given to the detainee as soon as reasonably practicable after his arrest.

Hefer JA's judgment does not offer us rhetorical flourishes on behalf of human rights, yet it is clear that the decision could have gone the other way. The detainee's affidavit confirmed that when he got to the prison, he *was* told that he was being held under the relevant emergency regulation. This was not much information, but the question of whether it was enough was an open one. Moreover, while this information was quite clearly late in terms of *Ngqumba*, *Ngqumba* did not foreclose, and perhaps invited, a decision that although the detention was invalid until this information was provided, at that point (and thereafter) it became valid. In *Ngqumba* Rabie ACJ (with whom Hefer JA concurred) had in fact said that if two detainees there were not informed of the reasons for their arrests as early as they should have been, the validity of the arrests 'would, in my opinion, have been rectified when they, while still under arrest, were informed of the reason for their arrest and detention'.[21] Hefer JA, reasoning that Swart was not informed of the reason for his arrest until he was no longer in police custody but in the prison, responds that '[i]t need hardly be stated that a situation where the detainee is informed of the reasons for his arrest by an outsider while he is no longer in police custody is entirely different.'[22] Different it is; but it is only 'entirely different' because the court is of that conviction.

Hefer JA's judgment also suggests that one factor important to the court's decision is its disapproval of the police affidavits. In one of these affidavits, the arresting officer 'confirms' his failure to inform the detainee of the reasons for his arrest. The court comments: 'This curious lapse is not explained.'[23] Another affidavit, the court writes, 'is equally uninformative .... [I]n the result the court has been left completely in the dark' as to why the detainee was not given this information more promptly than he was.[24] It seems clear that members of the court must have put this point bluntly to the lawyers for the state—who evidently found it unanswerable.[25] Whether the judgment's discontent on this score expresses a concern for human rights is debatable. What is strongly suggested, however, is that Hefer JA was concerned that the rules laid down should be followed, and was suspicious and irritated about the gaps in the police officers' affidavits.

[20] *Swart*, 1989 (1) SA at 299H–300D.

[21] *Ngqumba*, 1988 (4) SA at 271A–B, quoted in *Swart*, 1989 (1) SA at 300I–301A. The lower court in *Ngqumba* had made a similar point, in a more extended discussion. See *Nqumba* [sic] *and Others* v. *State President and Others*, 1987 (1) SA 456 (E) at 470C–H, quoted in *Swart*, 1989 (1) SA at 301C–H.

[22] *Swart*, 1989 (1) SA at 301H.

[23] Ibid. 300D.

[24] Ibid. 300F.

[25] See ibid. at 300H.

The *Swart* court also repulses an argument on behalf of the Minister of Law and Order that, even if the initial arrest and detention were invalid because of the failure to tell Swart why he had been arrested, the Minister's subsequent decision to extend Swart's detention should be sustained so long as the extension was, in itself, a valid decision. Hefer JA's response to this argument is that, if it 'were to be correct, all the [Supreme Court] divisions in the country, including this Court, have been wasting their time during the last few years in their punctilious enquiries into the validity of the arrest in cases where' the Minister had issued an extension order.[26] To Hefer JA, it would appear, these 'punctilious enquiries', however infrequently they have resulted in freeing anyone, are important. Indeed, for Hefer JA this case is 'really quite a simple matter'.[27]

The other two decisions in favour of human rights claims, *Nkwentsha* and *Apleni*, embody even greater doctrinal innovation than *Swart* and reflect more unmistakably the genuine weight which the court is giving to human rights concerns. These two cases deal with a critical and recurrent issue, namely the extent to which emergency detainees are sealed off from the outside world. In the face of an emergency regulation and a 1960s precedent which both pointed towards the conclusion that detainees were indeed without rights to access to the outside world, the court in each case, in unanimous decisions written by Vivier JA, found ways to ensure that detainees at least had access to court. In so holding, the Appellate Division was vindicating the promise of the *Hurley* case that the courts would not be ousted, or unavailable, for internal security cases.

To understand how far the court travelled to reach these results, we need to assay the obstacles which it confronted. The emergency regulation at issue in each of these cases was regulation 3(10), which provided as follows:

> No person, other than the Minister or a person acting by virtue of his office in the service of the State—
> (*a*) shall have access to any person detained in terms of the provisions of this regulation, except with the consent of and subject to such conditions as may be determined by the Minister or a person authorized thereto by him; or
> (*b*) shall be entitled to any official information relating to such person, or to any other information of whatever nature obtained from or in respect of such person.[28]

This regulation on its face appears to lock detainees away and give the Minister the only key. Moreover, the Appellate Division had already held in *Omar* that

[26] *Swart*, 1989 (1) SA 299B–C.
[27] Ibid. 302A. The court says this in a brief, impatient paragraph limiting the costs for which the state, as the losing party, will be responsible.
[28] Reg. 3(10), Proc. R. 109, *Government Gazette* 10280 (12 June 1986).

the effect of 3(10)(*a*) was, as this characterization would suggest, to deny detainees a right of access to counsel.[29]

The bleak import of this regulation was buttressed by the forbidding case of *Schermbrucker* v. *Klindt, NO*, a case decided in the period of government fear and repression following the Sharpeville massacre in 1960.[30] In *Schermbrucker* the Appellate Division had held that a court could not exercise its normal power to order any person to appear as a witness so as to require the state to produce a person, detained for interrogation under a statute providing for detention without trial, to testify on allegations that he had been tortured.[31] The Act itself did not specifically address this point. It did, however, on its face establish a regime of nearly incommunicado detention and interrogation. D. H. Botha JA concluded that allowing the detainee to be brought to court would undermine the purpose of the detention, which was, according to an earlier decision, to induce the detainee to talk by subjecting him to the rigours of incommunicado detention.[32] These 1960s cases in no way approved of physical torture, but they clearly did accept a form of incarceration that, as even the court recognized in one respect, might 'approximate to the application of a form of ... "psychological compulsion"'[33] *Schermbrucker*'s failure to require detainees to be brought to court to testify concerning allegations of physical torture surely aggravated the risk of abuse.[34]

In *Nkwentsha* and *Apleni* the Appellate Division does not actually overturn *Schermbrucker*. Without directly challenging this precedent, however, the court demonstrates a readiness to construe governmental power narrowly and judicial authority broadly that seems far removed from the stern approach of

[29] See Ch. 3, text at nn. 182–99 above. *Omar* dealt with the 1985 version of this regulation, but the 1986 text was almost identical.

[30] *Schermbrucker* v. *Klindt, NO*, 1965 (4) SA 606 (A). Two of the five judges dissented.

[31] The statute in question was s. 17 of the General Law Amendment Act 37 of 1963, the opening wedge by which the government introduced detention without trial into the ordinary law of the land. See A. Mathews and R. Albino, 'The Permanence of the Temporary: An Examination of the 90- and 180-Day Detention Laws', 83 *SALJ* 16, 23 (1966).

[32] Ibid. 619H (judgment of Botha JA); see ibid. 626A–C (judgment of Trollip AJA). The earlier case was *Rossouw* v. *Sachs*, 1964 (2) SA 551 (A). Sachs, then an advocate practising in South Africa, later left the country. Early in 1988, he was the victim of a car-bomb evidently planted by South African agents. Sachs lost an arm, and suffered other injuries, but survived to become, today, one of the leaders of the effort to shape a constitution for a new South Africa. For Sachs's own comments on this case, see A. Sachs, *Justice in South Africa* (Berkeley: University of California Press, 1973), 251–2.

[33] So the court in *Rossouw* v. *Sachs* characterized the deprivation of reading matter or writing materials 'for detainees who may broadly be classified as intellectuals': 1964 (2) SA at 565A.

[34] Cf. C. Forsyth, *In Danger for Their Talents: A Study of the Appellate Division of the Supreme Court of South Africa 1950–1980* (Cape Town: Juta, 1985), 144. Trollip AJA, with whom Steyn CJ concurred, may well have been troubled by this danger. He left open the possibility that the courts might be able to order detainees produced under a writ of *habeas corpus ad testificandum*—instead of under the court rule which Schermbrucker had invoked. He also argued that there were other methods by which the court might deal effectively with allegations of ill-treatment. *Schermbrucker* v. *Klindt, NO*, 1965 (4) SA at 625–7 (Trollip AJA, with whom Steyn CJ concurred). Trollip AJA's discussion of these alternatives does not make entirely clear whether even he believed that they would be *as* effective as permitting detainees to testify in court. For his part, Botha JA (with whom Steyn CJ also concurred) did not offer such a rationale.

Botha JA in this earlier case. Indeed, as we will discover, these cases display creative, even vigilant, judicial protection of detainees' rights.

In *Nkwentsha*, Lindiwe Monica Nkwentsha challenged the lawfulness of her husband's arrest. She was able to bring the suit because South African law, never abandoned during the state of emergency, permits third parties to invoke the South African equivalent to habeas corpus, the interdict *de libero homine exhibendo*, on behalf of people in detention.[35] Her ability to bring the case also depended on the courts having jurisdiction over it, and the Appellate Division brushed aside the emergency regulations' ouster clause.[36] To prove her case, however, Ms Nkwentsha needed her husband's testimony in open court.[37] But if he were to be brought to court, then wouldn't the lawyer representing his wife 'have access' to him and become the recipient of 'information obtained from or in respect of' him when he testified—all in violation of regulation 3(10)? Wouldn't the same be true of the judge and the state's lawyer? Wasn't it also possible that the detainee would succeed in having access to other people as well during the time that he was outside the gaol walls?

In answering these questions the Appellate Divison did not exploit the full range of potentially liberal interpretive tools available to the South African courts. Rather than asserting, say, that any possible ambiguities in the regulation should be construed in favour of the individual, the court considered itself bound by the sterner canon of construction, purporting to preclude a tilt in favour of either the state or the individual, laid down by *Rossouw* v. *Sachs*.[38] Yet this canon of construction, the same that *Schermbrucker* v. *Klindt, NO* had followed,[39] produced a result quite different from that of the earlier case.

In *Nkwentsha* the court ruled that the detainee could be brought to court to testify. The court decided that

> it cannot be said that when a witness is produced in Court and is then under the control of the presiding Judge, the latter or any person leading his evidence or cross-examining him would be having access to him in the sense in which the word is used in reg. 3(10). This was readily conceded by counsel for [the state].[40]

The court also maintained that the 'information' referred to in regulation

[35] See *Wood and Others* v. *Ondangwa Tribal Authority and Another*, 1975 (2) SA 294, 311 (A); Cameron, 'Legal Standing and the Emergency', in N. Haysom and L. Mangan (eds.), *Emergency Law: Papers Presented at a Workshop—Johannesburg, April 1987* (Johannesburg: Centre for Applied Legal Studies, University of the Witwatersrand, 1987), 61, 65–6, 74–5. *Hurley* and *Dempsey* were also cases of third-party suits for the release of detainees.

[36] *Nkwentsha*, 1988 (3) SA 99 (A) at 112J–113B.

[37] The affidavits presented by the parties in their papers, which included affidavits by Mr Nkwentsha and by officers involved in his arrest, presented diametrically different accounts of the facts. Ibid. 111.

[38] Ibid. 112F–I. For a discussion of this rule, see Ch. 2, text at nn. 123–28 above.

[39] *Schermbrucker* v. *Klindt, NO*, 1965 (4) SA at 617E–618C (judgment of Botha JA); see ibid. 626B–C (judgment of Trollip AJA). Even in *Schermbrucker*, however, the results of this approach were not foreordained, for it was also accepted as governing by Williamson JA in his dissent, ibid. 620F–H (dissenting judgment of Williamson JA).

[40] *Nkwentsha*, 1988 (3) SA at 115G.

3(10)(*b*) 'does not ... include a reference to evidence given in Court by the detainee. The prohibition is, furthermore, directed only against a person seeking to obtain the "information" and is not directed against the possessor of the information.'[41]

Moreover, the court expressed its confidence that the security authorities could prevent any unlawful access to the detainee by others during his presence in court.[42] The court did take note of the concern that the detainee, once arrived in court, might succeed in enjoying access to someone other than the judge and counsel. Surely Mr Nkwentsha would at least have enjoyed the opportunity to *see* his wife in court, since she would presumably have been entitled to be present as the actual applicant for relief; if his hearing were not held in camera (and the court did not say that it must be) he might see others as well.[43] It seems, however, that the court did not consider the chance for Mr Nkwentsha to see and be seen by those who cared for him to be prohibited 'access', for it does not mention these forms of contact.

Nkwentsha does address the possibility of a more substantial interaction between the detainee and the outside world. In 1965, this 'danger' had impressed Botha JA (with whom Steyn CJ concurred) in *Schermbrucker*. Botha JA wrote there that '[t]he prohibition against access to the detainee can ... be effectively enforced only while he is being detained in isolation from contact with the outside world at the place deemed fit by a commissioned officer of police, for no other effective machinery is provided for its enforcement and no sanction is prescribed for a contravention thereof.'[44] Without mentioning this language, or specifying any new components of 'effective machinery', the *Nkwentsha* court found it inconceivable 'that the security authorities would be unable to prevent any unlawful access to the detainee or that they would not be able to ensure his continued isolation when he is brought to Court to testify'.[45] This passage not only reflects impatience with the furthest flights of security arguments, but also may suggest an unwillingness to deprive detainess of the sight of their family or friends in court under the rubric of denying unlawful access.

In *Schermbrucker*, the members of the majority also maintained that a detainee brought to court would *ipso facto* no longer be at a place designated by the police, as the law required.[46] Although another of the emergency regulations

[41] Ibid. 115J–116A.

[42] Ibid. 115I.

[43] In addition, the case could be reported in the media, so that many, many others might eventually read the information presented in court—though not, by virtue of another emergency regulation, until after final judgment. See J. Grogan, 'Evidence from Detainees', 4 *SAJHR* 369, 374 (1988).

[44] *Schermbrucker* v. *Klindt, NO*, 1965 (4) SA at 619F.

[45] *Nkwentsha*, 1988 (3) SA at 115I. Perhaps the emergency regulations embodied newly 'effective machinery', such as the very severe penalties specified in reg. 14, Proc. R. 109, *Government Gazette* 10280 (12 June 1986), for breaches of the other provisions of the regulations, including reg. 3(10). The Appellate Division, however, does not rely on—or make—this point.

[46] *Schermbrucker* v. *Klindt, NO*, 1965 (4) SA at 619D–E (judgment of Botha JA); ibid. 626B (judgment of Trollip AJA). Steyn CJ concurred in both of these judgments.

gave the Minister or his delegee a quite similar authority to select the prison in which a detainee would be held,[47] *Nkwentsha* made no mention of the idea that bringing the detainee to court would undercut this authority.

It is true that *Nkwentsha* and *Schermbrucker* can be distinguished, but these distinctions are not powerful enough to account for the court's judgment—even though the court itself invokes one.[48] Thus it could have been argued that Nkwentsha was being brought to court to testify concerning the lawfulness of his arrest, while Schermbrucker would have testified concerning the treatment he was receiving while in detention. The force of this distinction is questionable, but in any event the court never makes this point. As a result, *Nkwentsha* suggests that emergency detainees should be entitled to testify concerning either of these issues.[49]

The distinction which *Nkwentsha* does identify is that the purpose of detention in *Schermbrucker*'s case was to induce the detainee to speak, while emergency detentions had a quite different purpose, namely to 'combat subversive activities of various kinds which threaten the maintenance of public order or the safety of the public or the safety of the detainee himself'.[50] The regime of investigatory detention at issue in *Schermbrucker is* a very harsh one, and virtual isolation might be said to be more integral to it than to emergency detention. Yet it may be significant that *Nkwentsha*'s discussion of this distinction occupies less than a paragraph,[51] and that *Nkwentsha* never in so many words reaffirms *Schermbrucker*'s correctness even in the context to which that case directly applied.

In any event this distinction might not have persuaded a court that was more reluctant to grant relief to emergency detainees. After all, the purpose of inducing the detainee to speak was not specifically enunciated in the statute at issue in *Schermbrucker*; rather, this purpose had been inferred by the court.[52]

[47] Reg. 3(4), Proc. R. 109, *Government Gazette* 10280 (12 June 1986).

[48] In a thoughtful analysis of the interpretive paradigms employed in *Schermbrucker* and *Nkwentsha*, David Dyzenhaus concludes that only judges committed to a Dworkinian (or, in Dyzenhaus's terms, 'common law') system of interpretation in light of presumed 'fundamental purposes or ideals of their legal system' would want 'to distinguish between the legislation in *Schermbrucker* and *Nkwentsha*'. 'The Disappearance of Law?', 107 *SALJ* 227, 243, 249 (1990). He ends with the tantalizing hope that Vivier JA, author of the *Nkwentsha* judgment, and other members of the Appellate Division may indeed be Dworkinian judges. Ibid. 249–50.

[49] In that case, *Nkwentsha*'s logic would support the result urged by Rumpff JA in his dissent 25 years ago in *Schermbrucker* v. *Klindt, NO*, 1965 (4) SA at 610–16. Rumpff argued there that while the detention statute permitted coercion by prolonged isolation, it did not permit coercion by any form of torture and that, accordingly, a detention in which torture was carried out was not a detention authorized by the statute. Since Rumpff believed that a court could order a detainee brought to court to testify concerning whether his detention was lawful, it followed that the court could order this testimony concerning whether the detention was accompanied by torture as well.

[50] *Nkwentsha*, 1988 (3) SA at 115E.

[51] Ibid. 115C–F.

[52] The inference was drawn in *Rossouw* v. *Sachs*, 1964 (2) SA at 560H–561B. Neither party to that case had defined the purpose quite this way, and in *Schermbrucker* itself one of the dissenters rejected *Rossouw*'s characterization. *Schermbrucker* v. *Klindt, NO*, 1965 (4) SA at 620–1 (dissenting judgment of Williamson JA).

The absence of an explicit announcement of such a purpose in the emergency regulations by no means precluded the court from inferring that one reason for emergency detention was to afford the state an opportunity to gather information. On the contrary, the emergency regulations specifically permitted such interrogation when needed for the purposes of the emergency,[53] as counsel for the state pointed out.[54] Moreover, it might have been claimed by the state that isolation was required to prevent detainees from continuing in some way or other to foment struggle against the government. Perhaps such isolation was needed to avoid information flowing from one person to another; perhaps it was required to cause the detainees to lose heart and thus to become less dangerous to the regime.[55] Harsh as *Schermbrucker* detention was, after all, emergency detention is a system to be used when the ordinary law of the land (which includes the modern version of the *Schermbrucker* statute) is inadequate. It could easily have been held that the considerations underlying *Schermbrucker* compelled the same result here.[56]

Nkwentsha should be seen, therefore, as a case in which the Appellate Division demonstrated a commitment to the principle that detainees should be able to testify concerning the lawfulness of their arrest—however hard it might be for them, in light of *Dempsey*, to prevail in their cases. That the court was acting out of such a commitment is confirmed by its treatment of one final objection to its authority, the argument that, even if the emergency regulations did not bar a detainee's being called to court, the court could not order this done, simply because no rule of law conferred such a power on the judiciary. The *Nkwentsha* court perceived, in one of the opinions in *Schermbrucker*, doubt as to whether South African courts had the power to grant a writ of *habeas corpus ad testificandum*.[57] In 1988, however, the Appellate Division was prepared not only to discern the requisite power in a not perfectly apposite

[53] Reg. 3(5), Proc. R. 109, *Government Gazette* 10280 (12 June 1986).

[54] *Nkwentsha*, 1988 (3) SA at 106F (argument of counsel).

[55] In fact the state did argue that ordering the detainee's appearance in court 'may attract public attention, stir emotions and may prove to be a very real threat to the maintenance of public order, the safety of the public or the detainee himself or for the determination [ending] of the state of emergency'. Ibid. 106E–F.

[56] This is not to say that the *Nkwentsha* decision was unprecedented. In fact, only a year after *Schermbrucker*, the Appellate Division had found its full rigours inapplicable in a case presenting the question of whether a person who was being detained under a provision for detention of material witnesses to certain crimes could consult counsel when he refused to testify as a witness in court, a refusal which subjected him to a potential penalty of a year's imprisonment. *S.* v. *Heyman and Another*, 1966 (4) SA 598 (A). Steyn CJ reasoned in *Heyman* that the statute providing for detention of material witnesses was not so intensely concerned with 'public order and the safety of the State' as the *Schermbrucker* statute, and that therefore there was more room for 'a more generous interpretation [of the statute] in favour of the rights of the individual': ibid. 605G. *Heyman*'s case by no means dictated the result in *Nkwentsha*, however, for emergency regulations are supposed to be quintessentially concerned with the safety of the state.

[57] *Nkwentsha*, 1988 (3) SA at 116E, discussing *Schermbrucker* v. *Klindt, NO*, 1965 (4) SA at 624F–625G (judgment of Trollip AJA). While Trollip suggests that there is no general statutory power to issue such a writ, he by no means rules out the possibility that such a judicial power might be 'inherent, implied or at common law': ibid. 625D–E.

rule of procedure,[58] but also 'would hold that such power is in any event authorised under the Court's inherent jurisdiction to regulate its procedure in the interests of the proper administration of justice'.[59]

Nkwentsha is not unique. In fact the court had made its concern for the 'proper administration of justice' apparent as well four months earlier in *Apleni,* a decision which undermined the effect of regulation 3(10) in equally startling ways.[60] *Apleni* was a case of alleged police assault on two emergency detainees, Apleni and Lamani, assault so severe that it resulted in the detainees' prolonged hospitalization.[61] Because the police denied having assaulted the detainees, the court was unable to determine the facts based on affidavits alone. But because the detainees were confined subject to regulation 3(10), the lower court took *Schermbrucker* to indicate that it could not order them produced in court to testify to their version of events. As a result, it appeared to the lower court that testimony could not be heard until the detainees were released from detention. The detainees accordingly asked the court to grant an 'interim interdict', prohibiting further unlawful assaults by the police until their release made a determination of the facts possible. The court refused this relief, however, on the ground that to order interim relief running until the end of the detainees' detention would amount to the grant of final relief while the facts were still in dispute.[62] Catch-22!

The Appellate Division, however, took a far different view. Clearly disturbed by the available evidence in the case (as the lower court had also been) the Appellate Division set out in some detail the evidence that Apleni and Lamani had been injured at the hands of the police. The court also called attention to a number of yawning gaps in the state's evidence,[63] and described the affidavits which the police had given as 'unsatisfactory and evasive'.[64] As in *Swart,* the Appellate Division grimly complains that the state's evidence before the lower court left that court 'totally in the dark' on a critical point, namely why the detainees had been hospitalized for so long.[65] In light of these facts, the Appellate Division decided that the lower court should 'at least' have granted interim relief pending a hearing following the detainees' release from

[58] *Nkwentsha,* 1988 (3) SA at 117C–E. As quoted by the Appellate Division, the rule in question, rule 6(5)(*g*), specifically permitted the court to 'order any deponent to appear personally or grant leave for him or any other person to be subpoenaed', and broadly empowered it to 'make such order as to it seems meet with a view to ensuring a just and expeditious decision'. Clearly neither portion in precise terms authorizes an order to a gaoler compelling him to produce a detainee in court.

[59] *Nkwentsha,* 1988 (3) SA at 117E.

[60] Though decided earlier than *Nkwentsha, Apleni* was reported later. Not all South African decisions are reported, and *Apleni* may not initially have been seen as a case that should be reported.

[61] *Apleni,* 1989 (1) SA at 198C.

[62] Ibid. 199B.

[63] Ibid. 199F–200H.

[64] Ibid. 199G.

[65] Ibid. 200G. The Appellate Division, hearing the case on appeal, must have been equally 'in the dark'.

detention.[66] In addition, however, the appellate court overturned the decision not to proceed to hear evidence 'as soon as possible', despite the detainees' apparent unavailability under regulation 3(10).

But how could the truth of the allegations be assessed if the court's power to hear evidence was circumscribed by this emergency regulation? *Apleni* gave two answers to this question, each in its own way potentially significant. One source of evidence, the court said, would be medical evidence concerning the detainees. The court took for granted that such medical evidence constituted 'official information', which, by virtue of regulation 3(10)(*b*), the state could not be compelled to produce.[67] If the court and the detainees lacked the power to insist that the medical evidence be produced, however, the court went on to point out that regulation 3(10) left the state free to present this evidence if it so chose. The court suggested that the state's failure to so choose would support an inference against it—an inference that might be so strong as to support judgment against the state![68]

A second source of evidence would be the detainees themselves. To be sure, *Apleni* does not challenge (though it also does not expressly address) the assumption that the courts could not insist on the detainees' being brought to court to testify.[69] So long as that prohibition stands, it might seem to follow that the courts could not issue orders directing that such detainees be produced in court to give testimony. In *Schermbrucker*, Botha JA reasoned on these lines, arguing that:

> no Court has power to order anything to be done which would be in conflict with an Act of Parliament. It follows that no Court can issue any order or process the effect of which would be to require or authorise an interference in any manner whatsoever with the kind of detention prescribed by ... [the statute], or which would be likely to defeat the purposes of that section.[70]

This reasoning did not commend itself to, and is not mentioned by, the *Apleni* court. Instead, *Apleni* asserts that the responsible Minister might—

[66] Ibid. 201D.

[67] In so holding, the court seems to have rejected, *sub silentio*, an available, narrower interpretation of the phrase 'official information'. In *Mkhize* v. *Minister of Law and Order and Another*, 1985 (4) SA 133 (N), a full bench of the Natal Provincial Division had suggested that '"official information" is confined to matters, directly or indirectly, relating to the reasons for, or the purposes of, the detention .... Information relating to the detainee's health and his treatment whilst in detention is clearly of a different nature. In the absence of very special circumstances such information could not, in any way, adversely affect the reason for, or the purposes of, the detention.' Ibid. 151J–152B.

[68] *Apleni*, 1989 (1) SA at 199H–I.

[69] Nor did *Nkwentsha*, when it was decided some months later, establish that detainees could testify concerning their mistreatment in detention, although I have suggested that the case points towards this conclusion. See text at n. 49 above.

[70] *Schermbrucker* v. *Klindt, NO*, 1965 (4) SA at 619C (judgment of Botha JA). The majority judgments in *Schermbrucker* offer quite different rationales for the result in the case, however, and Trollip AJA might not have dissented from the decision in *Apleni*, described in the text below, to test the state's willingness to produce the detainee.

indeed, might well—have given his consent to the detainees' production in court if oral evidence had been ordered. 'The mere fact that counsel for the [state] resisted the application for referral to oral evidence, does not mean that the Minister had refused to grant his consent or that he would do so if the order was made.'[71] The Appellate Division proceeded to direct that such a hearing be ordered 'as a matter of urgency'. In addition, it specified that this order would state (with an exception not relevant here) that '[t]he evidence shall be that of any witness whom the parties or any of them may elect to call', language that seems clearly meant to include the detainees themselves.[72] This language may stop just short of ordering the detainees produced, but it does in effect call on the state to produce them.[73] Thus, *Apleni* tells us, the proper role for the court faced with the possible limit on its authority created by regulation 3(10) is not to abandon the field but to press the matter as far as it can. Moreover, it may be (though *Apleni* does not address this point) that a court confronted with an obdurate refusal by the state to produce a detainee could draw an inference against the government on that basis, just as it apparently could if the government failed to produce salient medical evidence.

Apleni and *Nkwentsha* are, unmistakably, cases in which the Appellate Division responded to human rights claims not with hostility but with vigilance and doctrinal innovation in favour of those claims. *Swart* is less dramatic, but not inconsistent with the tenor of these bolder decisions. These cases are victories for human rights, as *Hurley* was, and they appear to be evidence that the Appellate Division, in the depths of the emergency, had not forsaken all concern for human rights. But this perspective on the Appellate Division is quite different, to say the least, from the view we took in Chapter 3. The final focus of this chapter will be to offer a portrayal of the Appellate Division's attitudes towards the conflict between emergency needs and human rights claims that can account for both faces of its emergency decision-making.

[71] *Apleni*, 1989 (1) SA at 199D. In *Schermbrucker*, the state 'had refused to grant permission to the detainee to come to Court in person': *Schermbrucker* v. *Klindt, NO*, 1965 (4) SA at 616G (judgment of Botha JA). *Apleni* and *Schermbrucker* are distinguishable, therefore, on the ground that in *Apleni* the government had not made its opposition to production of the detainees quite so plain. *Apleni*, however, never offers this (or any other) distinction between itself and *Schermbrucker*, and it does not seem to me that this distinction accounts for the general difference in approach reflected in Botha JA's judgment in *Schermbrucker* and Vivier JA's in *Apleni*. As a matter of technical reasoning, moreover, the distinction is not necessarily definitive, for we cannot know whether the responsible officials in *Schermbrucker* would have given their consent if faced with a court order such as that endorsed in *Apleni*.

[72] *Apleni*, 1989 (1) SA at 201E–G.

[73] In this sense, therefore, I disagree with John Grogan, who reads *Apleni* as not actually deciding 'whether reg 3(10) prevented the courts from calling on a detainee to testify in person': 'Evidence' (cit. n. 43), 371.

C. The Demands of the Emergency against the Claims of Human Rights

The emergency decisions of the Rabie court are *all* the product of the members of the emergency team. The justices who were part of this team were not fungible, and it is reasonable to assume that there were various shadings of view among them. But they never disagreed on the result of a case, and it is safe to say that their positions on emergency issues were broadly in harmony. To explain the cross-cutting patterns of the emergency decisions, therefore, we may usefully seek a portrayal of their thinking in light of which these cases can be seen as expressions of a single judicial perspective.

In addition, I believe that such a portrayal must eschew the temptation to explain the benign decisions of the Appellate Division as mere window-dressing, mere 'Potemkin jurisprudence'. Such an explanation would be mistaken for three reasons. First, the decisions in favour of human rights claims are not so insignificant as this idea suggests. It is quite true that the court consistently rejected the most far-reaching challenges to the emergency system, cases such as *Dempsey, Omar,* and *United Democratic Front*. But the cases in which it stretches most to grant relief, *Nkwentsha* and *Apleni,* are not trivial. The state did not concede these cases, and regulation 3(10), especially read in light of *Schermbrucker,* hardly seemed to invite the court's decisions. It was entirely plausible, from the state's point of view, to say that the system would run more smoothly if detainees could not come to court at all without the state's permission, if the courts would not press the state to grant that permission, and if the state's exercise of its prerogative to withhold information about detainees carried no penalty—but *Nkwentsha* and *Apleni* deny the state all of these boons. These cases, and in its narrow sphere *Swart* as well, are a genuine check on abuse of emergency power, though they are not, and are not meant to be, a check on its lawful use.

Second, a 'Potemkin' theory should be rejected because it rests on an implausible view, or views, of judicial functioning. One such view would be suggested by Potemkin's own sham villages, by which he consciously intended to deceive his audience. There is no reason to imagine that South African judges in general are guilty of such a design. On the contrary, as we will see in Chapter 6, the judiciary prides itself on its integrity and independence, and it is hardly likely that these public professions are honoured only in the breach. This is not to say that South African judges are, unlike all other men and women, incapable of bending their principles, or of deciding that one principle trumps another. The dominant presence of the emergency team on every emergency case, in particular, cannot reasonably be explained as a product of neutral and apolitical selection of panels, yet such selection surely is important to sustaining the ideal of judges as objective, austerely sober decisionmakers.[74] But it is more likely that we can explain even this disturbing pattern, and much

[74] For South African expressions of this ideal, see Ch. 3, text at nn. 52–5 above.

more likely that we can explain the votes of the various judges of these cases, as the uneasy product of the judges' conflicting principles rather than as deliberate, cynical deception.

An alternative theory to account for the production of 'Potemkin' jurisprudence would be that although the judges who decided these cases were sincerely trying to perform their duties, their conduct was ineluctably driven by some social forces which determined that the only benign decisions these judges would produce would be mere glosses on an oppressive reality. I very much doubt the strength of such deterministic explanations in general, and the distinctly better performance of the Corbett court, which we will consider in Chapter 5, casts particular doubt on this way of accounting for the Rabie court's decisions. Even if this theory were true, however, it would be incomplete, for it would not explain how these social forces find their way into the actions of individual human beings. Presumably this missing mechanism would have something to do with the generation, in individual judges, of attitudes and actions that comport with the driving social forces—and so we would need, once again, an account of those attitudes.

Third, the idea that *Swart*, *Nkwentsha*, and *Apleni* could be explained as window-dressing is undercut by their substantial failure to have the 'prettying-up' or legitimizing effect that such a theory would look for. By itself, this failure to legitimize is not a conclusive argument, for the court might have high hopes for legitimation even from decisions that prove not to win approbation at all. (We will see in Chapter 6 that such miscalculations by whites with respect to the attitudes of black South Africans, in particular, are entirely likely.)[75] But still it is worth noting that as vehicles for legitimizing the emergency system, or the Appellate Division's emergency jurisprudence, these cases were far from a success. At the end of the Rabie era, emergency detainees turned to the use of hunger strikes as a way to gain their release, and declared in a statement smuggled out of prison, 'We have tried all available means. We have gone to the courts; we have petitioned Ministers of Government; we have met representatives to no avail.'[76] Some of their lawyers fasted in solidarity with them, and issued their own statement that '[t]he South African legal system has failed our detainee clients'.[77] Etienne Mureinik wrote of 'the despair with which lawyers around the country are responding to the supine performance of the Appellate Division in the exercise of its supervisory jurisdiction over emergency powers'.[78] Liberal academic criticism of the Rabie court's decisions was intense and sometimes outspoken.[79] Decisions such as

[75] See Ch. 6, text at nn. 98–9 below.

[76] 'Strikers Spark New Spirit in South Africa', 31 *Africa News* (No. 4) at 2 (20 Feb. 1989).

[77] Ibid.

[78] E. Mureinik, 'Pursuing Principle: The Appellate Division and Review under the State of Emergency', 5 *SAJHR* 60, 60–1 (1989).

[79] See e.g. D. Davis and H. Corder, 'A Long March: Administrative Law in the Appellate Division', 4 *SAJHR* 281 (1988); N. Haysom and C. Plasket, 'The War against Law: Judicial Activism and the Appellate Division', 4 *SAJHR* 303 (1988); Mureinik, 'Pursuing Principle' (cit.

Nkwentsha could be seen as modest grounds for hope, but certainly were not portrayed as compensating for the damage done in other decisions.[80]

Rather than viewing these decisions as a combination of nothing but power and pretence, therefore, we need to seek an account of the judges' thinking that identifies the cross-cutting, but genuine, commitments that could combine to produce the decisions we have examined. Such an account will of necessity be an inference about the judges' thinking, rather than a direct transcription of their thoughts. But we will find evidence to guide it in what the judges have actually said and decided, and the result will, I suggest, be a more complete and more sensitive description of the concerns of the Rabie court than a Potemkin explanation could provide.

None the less, we can hardly explain the court's handling of emergency cases without giving full recognition to the court's attentiveness to the needs of emergency law enforcement. No judgment offers us a concise and explicit account of the sources of this attentiveness, and so we can explore this matter only by teasing out the implications of what the court says and does. I suggest that the court's understanding of the needs of the emergency system had three distinguishable strands: an acceptance of the existence of a genuine emergency; a trust in the good faith of the state, and especially of its most senior officials; and a sympathetic perception of the burdens on law enforcement officers. These three themes help to make up the 'executive-mindedness' of the Appellate Division.

There is, first of all, striking evidence of the court's belief that it faced a real emergency. Dennis Davis has called attention to the quite explicit comments of Acting Chief Justice Rabie himself on this score. In a newspaper interview in 1987, Rabie commented on the inadequacy of the common law and observed that 'the situation in the country is pretty near that of a civil war. It is naive to think you can quell it by bringing people to court.'[81] In saying this, Rabie ACJ did no more than to concur in the view, long and vigorously proclaimed by the government, that South Africa faced a 'total onslaught' against which it had to defend itself.[82] Davis observes that invoking the 'total onslaught' had 'become almost standard practice' in defending emergency regulations in court.[83] A 'siege mentality ... dominate[d] white politics',[84] and it is no cause for surprise that many of the white judges on the Appellate Division shared this widespread sense of threat.

The judges' acceptance of the reality of the emergency goes far to explain their deference to the government's emergency measures. If an emergency exists, a situation in which the ordinary law of the land really is insufficient,

n. 78); C. Forsyth, 'The Sleep of Reason: Security Cases before the Appellate Division', 105 *SALJ* 679 (1988); and the articles collected in 'Focus on Omar', 3 *SAJHR* 295–337 (1987).

[80] See Davis and Corder, 'Long March' (cit. n. 79), 302; Grogan, 'Evidence' (cit. n. 43), 375.

[81] D. Davis, 'The Chief Justice and the Total Onslaught', 3 *SAJHR* 229, 231 (1987).

[82] The government also *believed* in this view, as Dennis Davis has emphasized to me. See A. Sparks, *The Mind of South Africa* (New York: Knopf, 1990), 309–15, 354–60.

[83] Davis, 'Chief Justice' (cit. n. 81), 229.

[84] E. Cameron, 'Judicial Endorsement of Apartheid Propaganda: An Enquiry into an Acute Case', 3 *SAJHR* 223, 228 (1987).

then it is entirely reasonable for judges to accept the abridgement of the rights which that ordinary law would secure in better times. It is also reasonable, indeed inevitable, that courts would defer to the countless judgment calls which those directly responsible for dealing with the emergency and best informalabout its contours—in short, the government—must make. None of this is to say that the court should have taken this deference as far as it did; indeed, even in a just society the preservation of restrictions on emergency powers is important to the protection of liberty.[85]

Here I mean only to trace the roots of the court's choices, and the court's judgments do point to this source. In *Omar*, for example, Rabie ACJ responded to the argument that security risks resulting from detainees' access to their lawyers could be avoided by measures short of denying the very right to access, in these words: 'This may, or may not have been, feasible. I do not know. It may even be that the State President and the Minister of Justice considered measures of the kind suggested but decided against them on the ground that they would be impracticable.'[86] Similarly, in *United Democratic Front*, Rabie ACJ is at pains to demonstrate that restrictions on publicity for lawful meetings were not, as the lower court asserted, utterly unrelated to the purposes of the emergency. To Rabie's mind, it is 'not difficult to understand why the State President would have deemed ... [such restrictions] necessary or expedient'.[87]

The emergency decisions suggest, secondly, that the Appellate Division trusted the good faith of the officials responsible for dealing with this threat. It would have been painful for the judges not to have such trust, for these officials were, inevitably, the people who would have to handle the emergency. But the court's faith does not seem to be only the product of necessity. Thus *Apleni* in particular can be read as an expression by the Appellate Division of its faith that abuse of detainees is the exception rather than the rule, and that responsible officials of the government will co-operate with judicial efforts to root out such conduct. In this vein, the court avers 'that the Minister may well have given his consent for the [detainees] to give *viva voce* evidence in Court in view of the serious nature of the allegations against the Police and the strongly expressed disapproval of the respondents' [affidavit] replies' by the lower court.[88]

Omar's treatment of the denial of detainees' right of access to their counsel suggests a similar attitude. The detainees had challenged the access regulation in part on the ground that the regulation left it up to the government whether they would get to see their lawyers or not. Rabie ACJ answered that 'it is ... not to be supposed that the Minister or the Commissioner of Police may, or

[85] See Ch. 6, text at nn. 415–16 below.

[86] *Omar*, 1987 (3) SA at 897E–F. Rabie ACJ asserts that this answer is called for by legal doctrine, but it is at least as clearly supported by the logic of a belief that a genuine emergency existed.

[87] *United Democratic Front*, 1988 (4) SA at 842H (judgment of Rabie ACJ).

[88] *Apleni*, 1989 (1) SA at 199D–E.

will, refuse leave for the necessary access on just any ground whatsoever'.[89] To be sure, Rabie ACJ finds in the relevant rule an implied requirement 'that leave can be refused only on grounds which are related to the emergency',[90] but his apparent confidence that the Minister will obey this restriction suggests his belief that the government does obey the law's commands. In fact, Rabie's vote of confidence comes immediately after he has quoted at length from the affidavit of the Minister of Justice, who expresses his recognition that 'the right of access to a legal representative is a basic right' and his consequent desire 'to ensure that such access be restricted only if good reason exists for it'.[91] For this reason, the Minister says, he has placed the responsibility for approving or disapproving such visits at 'the highest level only ... Thereby I have ensured that the most responsible persons would consider the applications'.[92]

Another striking example of such deference to senior officials appears in an aspect of *Ngqumba* which we have not previously examined. Besides challenging their arrests, the detainees in *Ngqumba* challenged the Minister's decision to extend their detentions. They argued that because the Minister had failed to submit an affidavit justifying his decisions, it was impossible to conclude that he had properly decided on the necessity of their continued detention. The court, however, did not even suggest that it would have been *better* if the Minister had submitted an affidavit. Instead, the court finds sufficient evidence of what the Minister considered in a subordinate's affidavit detailing, with the authorization or on behalf of the Minister, what information the subordinate had provided to the Minister.[93] In support of this decision, Rabie ACJ invokes a Second World War case in which a judge had inferred an official's holding the requisite opinion from the sheer fact that he had taken action which would have been unlawful if he had not held that opinion![94]

It is less clear that the court had the same sort of faith in the police officers who exercised the powers of the emergency at the 'front lines'. The sharp comments of the *Swart* and *Apleni* judgments about the inadequacy of the police affidavits reflect, at the least, that the court was capable of suspecting lower-level officers of misconduct. Acknowledging this possibility would have provided the court with a way to square the repeated, sometimes very highly publicized allegations of security force misconduct—up to and including murder—with its confidence in more senior officials' good faith.[95] This selective trust, in turn, would tend to produce the pattern that in fact exists in the case-

[89] *Omar*, 1987 (3) SA at 896I.

[90] Ibid. 896I–J.

[91] Ibid. 896F (Afrikaans affidavit trans. by Nadine Havenga).

[92] Ibid. 896F–G.

[93] *Ngqumba*, 1988 (4) SA at 254I–255D.

[94] *Seedat* v. *R.*, 1942 NPD 189, 195 (judgment of Hathorn JP), cited in *Ngqumba*, 1988 (4) SA at 225D–J. See also *Seedat* v. *R.*, 1942 NPD 189, 192–3 (judgment of Carlisle J.)

[95] For example, according to the Human Rights Commission, a human rights monitoring group in South Africa, as of late 1988 '[d]uring the 25 years of detention without trial, there have been 67 deaths in detention, an average of almost three each year': M. Zondi, 'There've Been 15 More Bikos Since June '86', *Weekly Mail*, 8 (2–8 Dec. 1988), quoting the Commission.

law, of occasional sharp responses to allegations of misconduct by low-level police, combined with consistent rejection of charges of unlawful action by senior officials.

It would not be inconsistent with this pattern of selective trust for the court to believe that *by and large* even the actions of lower-level officers were appropriate and in good faith. This position would be an easy one for judges to hold, entailing as it would an implied comparison of the likelihood that the servants of the state, or their revolutionary opponents who challenged their conduct, were telling the truth. If the court did hold this belief, it would help explain the decision in *Dempsey* to impose much of the *onus* in arrest cases on the party challenging the arrest. The decision could then be understood as expressing the court's view that such challenges are, ordinarily, not well-founded, and therefore should not be upheld where the available evidence does not press in their favour.

This supportive judicial attitude towards emergency arrests would mesh well with the third feature of the court's executive-mindedness: its sympathetic perception of the burdens which in an emergency law-enforcement officers face. This sympathy is the natural corollary of a belief that the country does face a genuine emergency against which it must defend itself, a feeling which we have identified as a source of the deference the court shows to the decisions of senior officials in *Omar* and *United Democratic Front*. The court's sympathy also extends, however, to the much less senior people on the front lines.

This sympathy seems to be at work in *Ngqumba*. There the court justified its rejection of a general requirement that arresting officers tell the court what alternative law enforcement steps under the ordinary law of the land they had considered. The court said that an arresting officer will 'probably ... as well as he is able to in the circumstances', address this matter, and emphasized that these officers 'are not lawyers' and may not always know of available alternatives under the ordinary law of the land.[96] One inevitable result of such ignorance is that arresting officers may use emergency powers when they actually do not have to, but for the court this is a matter for understanding rather than condemnation. The validity of the arrest does not turn on the objective accuracy of their judgment, after all, but only on their actually and honestly making the subjective assessment of the need for arrest.[97] If the court believes that the arresting officers are doing their imperfect best, considering the difficulties under which they labour and their own limitations of expertise, then it will not be of a mind to step in.

Fear of an assault on the state, trust in its senior officials, and sympathy for its lowest officers make up a heady brew. Those who drink of it might conclude that no restrictions whatsoever should be placed upon the state, that even the occasional excesses of which it might be guilty should be accepted as part of the price of withstanding a total onslaught. But this is not the conclusion

[96] *Ngqumba*, 1988 (4) SA at 252E, 254A.
[97] See Ch. 3, text at nn. 66–72 above.

which the Appellate Division reaches. Instead, the examination we carried out earlier in this chapter points to a set of more benign attitudes which the court held, attitudes which qualified its executive-mindedness. Again there are three strands to the court's stance: a determination to preserve a legal order in South Africa, a jealous guarding of the institutional role of the judiciary, and a genuine disapproval of abuse.

To say that the court was determined to preserve a legal order in South Africa may seem implausible, in light of the extent to which the emergency system was meant precisely to remove legal accountability[98] and of the extent to which the court's decisions protected that system. I am not saying, however, that the court meant to subject emergency powers to close judicial scrutiny, or to preserve the human rights protections embodied in many formulations of the rule of law. I am saying only that the court was determined to maintain that South African governmental power was conferred by law and was confined within boundaries, however wide, that were set by law.

There are three features of the cases we have examined which support this conclusion. The first is the court's decision that when the State President makes emergency regulations he is still subject to judicial review, because he is exercising the authority of a subordinate legislator. As we have seen, existing precedent offered the court the option of embracing a more autocratic characterization of the State President's powers, but the court firmly turned aside from this option. The second is the court's retention of so many of the doctrines of interpretation of legislation and of review of official action. The court was capable of revising these principles, and Hefer JA did so with considerable vigour, but Rabie ACJ's approach, which remained dominant, usually eschewed overt doctrinal innovation. These doctrines might be applied loosely, but they were not simply erased.

The third sign of the court's determination to preserve a legal order in South Africa is the court's insistence, perhaps most evident in *Swart* and *Apleni*, that the rules of the game be adhered to. *Swart* is a particularly significant case as a clue to the court's thinking, because it is written by Hefer JA, who surely did not easily find against the state in emergency decisions. Swart, as we have seen, was not told the reasons for his arrest until he had been transferred from police custody to prison. Then, however, he *was* told that he was being arrested under the emergency regulations, and thereafter the Minister decided to extend his detention. It would have been quite possible to hold that Swart's detention became valid once it was 'explained' at the prison, and possible (though much more doctrinally wrenching) to hold that it became valid when the Minister assessed and extended it. But Hefer JA will have none of this. There is a rule that people arrested are to be told the reasons for their arrest promptly, and the reasons for the officers' 'curious lapse' in not doing so are 'not explained', with the result that the court is 'left completely in the dark'. (*Apleni*'s detailed explication of the 'unsatisfactory and evasive' police evidence

[98] See Ch. 1, text at n. 83 above.

in that case has much the same flavour.) And for the court to ignore the breach of the rules in *Swart* because of the Minister's subsequent approval of detention would mean that the judiciary's 'punctilious' examination of one emergency arrest after another had all been a waste of time. The rule which the court enforces here is a very modest constraint indeed on the immense arrest power conferred on emergency officers, but it is a rule, and the court does want it obeyed.

Closely linked to its determination that a legal order be preserved is the Appellate Division's jealous protection of the institutional role of the courts. The court was willing to have its role circumscribed by the broad language of the Public Safety Act and of its implementing regulations, as the judicial deference to emergency decisionmaking reflects. But the court was not prepared to accept easily the idea that it had no role whatsoever. On the contrary, its insistence that it did have a role to play is repeatedly reflected in the cases. The assertion of the reviewability of the State President's power is, after all, an assertion of its *judicial* reviewability. The retention of so many doctrines by which the courts interpret and control government action is also a reaffirmation of the judicial role. The refusal to accept the ouster of the court's jurisdiction, except in the perhaps special context of vague regulations, extends a long-standing South African judicial resistance to such legislative diminution of the courts.[99]

The Appellate Division's attention to the preservation of the role of the courts is particularly apparent in *Nkwentsha* and *Apleni*. *Nkwentsha* ensures that detainees can come to court to testify concerning the lawfulness of their being detained, does so in the face of ample legal ground for a contrary result, and ultimately invokes the inherent powers of the court as a source of the requisite judicial power. *Apleni* stops short of *ensuring* that detainees can come to court to testify concerning their treatment while in detention, but it devises one doctrinal move after another to provide a vigorous judicial response to allegations of brutality against detainees. The court's willingness to grant an interim interdict without the detainees' testimony, to pressure the state to present medical evidence which the relevant emergency regulation was taken to shield from compulsory disclosure, and to call on the state to produce the detainees themselves, all attest to the court's vigilance. In these cases, as John Grogan says of *Apleni*, 'the Appellate Division was not prepared lightly to deprive the courts of their responsibility to take what steps were necessary to get at the truth in matters before them'.[100] Moreover, the court was prepared to grant relief once it had ascertained the facts—or even, as in *Apleni*, to grant

[99] The disturbing possibility that the court did not reach the issue of the meaning of the Public Safety Act's ouster clause until the strength of a challenge to an emergency regulation made resort to the ouster clause 'necessary', see Ch. 3, text at nn. 170–7 above, ironically confirms the court's reluctance to declare the existence of any such ouster.

[100] Grogan, 'Evidence' (cit. n. 43), 371. Davis and Corder suggest similarly that *Nkwentsha* reflects the fact that 'the Appellate Division has traditionally guarded its own jurisdiction jealously against executive interference': 'Long March' (cit. n. 79), 302.

an interim interdict when the emergency regulations themselves might make the facts unascertainable.

Third, and finally, the Appellate Division dislikes abusive conduct by the state. As with each of my arguments about the benign side of the court's attitudes, this one needs to be put carefully. The court did not readily conclude that government conduct was abusive, as its willingness to accept an abrogation of *audi alteram partem* in *Omar* and its limitation of the 'apply the mind' requirements in *Dempsey* and *Ngqumba* reflect. The court also did not make the avoidance of the risk of abuse a decisive feature of its emergency jurisprudence. The shift of *onus* in *Dempsey* inevitably risked that some valid challenges to arrests would be defeated for reasons of burden of proof rather than of truth. The decision in *Omar* that there was no right of access to counsel, but that detainees could only be denied access for reasons connected to the emergency, risked the *sub rosa* denial of counsel for other reasons, reasons which would inevitably be difficult or impossible to prove in court. The refusal to invalidate vague regulations in *United Democratic Front* risked that unlawful regulations would continue to exercise an *in terrorem* effect on those against whom they might be wielded.

None the less, where the court encountered what it recognized as abuse it did not like it. The court showed no sympathy for illegal, or possibly illegal, arrests in *Nkwentsha* and *Swart*. Its attitude towards abuse, however, is most apparent in *Apleni*, which dealt with conduct whose abusiveness was unambiguous: police assaults on detainees. Vivier JA's judgment offers not the faintest hint of a rationalization of this sort of conduct. Instead, Vivier JA refers to 'the serious nature of the allegations against the police',[101] and unmistakably treats them as serious matters indeed. One cannot read the court's detailed recounting of the evidence of the detainees' mistreatment, nor consider its grant of an interim interdict, without feeling that the court wanted this conduct to *stop*. And while this judgment and *Nkwentsha* were written by Vivier JA, who perhaps was particularly concerned about these matters, Rabie ACJ and Hefer JA concurred without qualification in both of these decisions.

With this portrayal of the thinking of the Appellate Division, or rather of those members of the court who dominated the emergency cases, we can indeed understand the pattern of decisions that it reached in a way that is more nuanced than the suggestion that some of these decisions must be dismissed as mere efforts to disguise the grim reality of the rest. All of these cases are real. Most of them are decided against human rights claims, and they reflect the court's intense fear of revolutionary onslaught, and its trust and sympathy for those dealing with it. These sentiments take the court very far indeed, and may well have contributed to the sweeping violations of human rights during the state of emergency, but they do not lead the court to complete indifference to human rights concerns. Instead, both the cases that

[101] *Apleni*, 1989 (1) SA at 199D–E.

affirm human rights claims and those that do not mark out boundaries beyond which the court will not permit the government to go: beyond a legal order altogether, beyond judicial supervision altogether, or into the realm of deliberate, unambiguous abuse. South Africa has had its share of state-supported hit squads, but the Appellate Division even in its darkest period set its face against such truly naked power. In doing so the court may have helped to slow—though it certainly did not stop—South Africa's descent from authoritarian law to state or vigilante terrorism. In Chapter 6 we will look to an understanding of the role of law in South African culture to help us understand this modicum of judicial restraint. Before we develop this explanation, however, we must first further enlarge the data that we are considering, by examining the emergency decisions of the Appellate Division after Rabie's retirement. As we will see in Chapter 5, these decisions are strikingly different in tone and result from most of those we have been examining until now.

5

The Corbett Court and the Emergency

> The trumpet of a prophecy! O Wind,
> If winter comes, can spring be far behind?[1]

On 31 January 1989 Rabie ACJ retired. He was replaced as chief justice by Justice Michael Corbett. As his name suggests, Corbett CJ is a member of the English-speaking white South African community—though he speaks Afrikaans, and in some of his speeches he turns to Afrikaans with the apparent goal of communicating more fraternally with Afrikaners in his audience.[2] At the age of 18 he enlisted in the South African armed forces, and served in Egypt and Italy during the Second World War. Educated at the University of Cape Town, one of the leading English-speaking universities of South Africa, he earned a second law degree at Trinity Hall, Cambridge, and then joined the Cape Bar in 1948. He became a senior counsel in 1961 and in 1963 was appointed to the bench of the Cape Provincial Division. In 1974 he joined the Appellate Division and so, in 1989, he was a very senior member of the court.[3]

Corbett CJ's concern for human rights had been apparent for many years before his appointment as chief justice. In 1979 he gave the opening address at the First International Conference on Human Rights in South Africa, held at the University of Cape Town, and told his audience that two years earlier he had made his first visit to the United States and become acquainted with the Bill of Rights and the American system of judicial review. In his words, 'I returned home a convert to that system.'[4] A longtime member of the anti-apartheid South African Institute of Race Relations,[5] a man concerned about the injustice of South Africa's society.[6] In a speech to this Institute, he described his understanding, in 1976, 'that sooner or later—and the sooner the better—

[1] P. Shelley, 'Ode to the West Wind' (1819), 11.69–70.

[2] See M. Corbett, 'Human Rights: The Road Ahead', 96 *SALJ* 192, 201 (1979); M. Corbett, 'Speech to Johannesburg Bar', *Consultus* 73, 73 and 74–5 (Oct. 1989). In my experience, educated Afrikaners are normally fluent in English; the Afrikaans of English-speaking whites seems less comfortable. My impression is that Corbett's use of Afrikaans is a somewhat distinctive gesture on his part.

[3] Much of the information in this paragraph is drawn from 'Mr Justice MM Corbett', *De Jure* (No. 1) 1 (1979).

[4] Corbett, 'Human Rights' (cit. n. 2) at 196.

[5] Corbett mentioned this himself in an address to the Institute, *Guaranteeing Fundamental Freedoms in a New South Africa* (Johannesburg: South African Institute of Race Relations, 1990), 12.

[6] See Corbett, 'Human Rights' (cit. n. 2), at 195.

a new political dispensation would have to be negotiated in South Africa by *all* interested parties'.[7] And as a judge he believes that 'in the grey areas of uncertainty [of statutory meaning] ... our common law and our legal tradition require that the importance of human rights should be kept well to the fore'.[8]

But Chief Justice Corbett is not a radical. In his speech to the Institute of Race Relations, he went on to say that it was evident in 1976

> that this new dispensation, while giving full rights of citizenship to all, would have to take account of the plurality of South African society and the fear of minority groups of being dominated. It then struck me with all the force, suddenness and clarity of a spiritual revelation that, especially as regards the latter, the answer was possibly to be found in the American example [of a Bill of Rights enforceable by the courts].[9]

While there are many minority groups that might fear domination in South Africa, one of the most visible such groups today consists, bluntly, of whites. Corbett's words hint at considerable sensitivity to white anxieties, together with his recognition of whites' injustice to blacks. As a judge, he has declared his recognition that current law permits legislation restricting human liberty, and maintains that where such legislation's 'language is plain or the validity clear, then the proper administration of justice demands that it be given effect'.[10] Unlike some critical observers of judicial behaviour, moreover, he believes in the possibility of a 'professional objectivity which transcends [judges'] personal predilections'.[11]

Why did the government appoint this liberal jurist as chief justice? Had the government wished to do so, it could have appointed him two years earlier, rather than asking Rabie to stay on past his retirement age as acting chief justice. Now, in 1989, the government might have prevailed upon Rabie to stay on in that capacity even longer, or it might have chosen a more junior member of the court, such as Hefer JA, to serve as chief justice. In the event, however, the government appointed Corbett. It is possible to speculate on a number of factors that may have played a role in this decision. Perhaps relatively moderate forces within the government enjoyed more influence when this decision was made than they had two years earlier. Perhaps other forces in the government felt that the greatest exigencies of the emergency were behind them, and that the precedents established in the jurisprudence of the Rabie court would be hard to dislodge. But there are also tantalizing rumours that pressure from the Appellate Division itself contributed to this

[7] Corbett, *Guaranteeing* (cit. n. 5), at 14.

[8] Corbett, 'Speech' (cit. n. 2), at 75.

[9] Corbett, *Guaranteeing* (cit. n. 5), at 14. Elsewhere in the same speech Corbett refers to 'the fervent desire of minority groups [in South Africa] not be [sic] be dominated or overwhelmed'. Ibid. 12.

[10] Corbett, 'Speech' (cit. n. 2), at 75.

[11] Corbett, 'Human Rights' (cit. n. 2), at 199.

decision.[12] If these rumours are correct, then Corbett's appointment may reflect a disquiet within the court itself about the manipulations of the past years.

Whatever the genesis of Corbett's appointment, the transformation in the Appellate Division since he became chief justice has, if anything, exceeded the hopes of those who welcomed his selection. In a series of different legal contexts the court has worked, not a velvet revolution, but surely a velvet reform in South African law, especially in internal security cases.[13] One of those areas has been emergency law, and the upshot of the Corbett court's work has been that the Appellate Division's stance towards emergency cases has significantly changed, and that the chances of human rights claims prevailing against the government's use of emergency powers have strikingly improved—although by no means all such claims have prevailed even before the Corbett court.

This chapter will first explore the dimensions of this change, and trace the strands of the court's enhanced concern for human rights claims as well as of its continued acceptance of the broad and discretionary character of emergency lawmaking. We will then need to understand how the Appellate Division could change so significantly in so short a span of time, and I will suggest that two factors, the change in the composition of the court's panels and the change in the political climate of the country, help explain this transition. Chapter 6 will go on to look more deeply at the roots of the Appellate Division's response to the emergency under both of its chief justices.

[12] Thus I have heard the suggestion that another senior judge was approached to take the appointment instead of Corbett, but refused, as well as the possibility that members of the court conveyed to the government their belief that Corbett must be appointed.

[13] Many of these decisions have dealt with internal security prosecutions. See *Minister of Law and Order* v. *Pavlicevic*, 1989 (3) SA 679 (A) (holding that crime of subversion requires an intention to achieve a proscribed goal rather than just knowledge that one's conduct may cause such a result); *S.* v. *Tshoba*, 1989 (3) SA 393 (A) (restrictive interpretation of statutory definition of terrorism and of common law fraud); *S.* v. *Nel*, 1989 (4) SA 838 (A) (following *Pavlicevic* with respect to crime of sabotage); *S.* v. *Malindi*, 1990 (1) SA 962 (A) (overturning terrorism and treason convictions of leaders of the United Democratic Front and others). Others have dealt with closely related issues. See *Masuku* v. *Minister of Justice and Others*, 1990 (1) SA 832 (A) (establishing the jurisdiction of the courts to grant stays of death sentences pending appeals to the State President on the basis of new evidence, and setting out generous guidelines for the grant of such stays); *Ellispark Stadion Bpk.* v. *Minister van Justisie*, 1990 (1) SA 1038 (A) (holding the banning of a concert under the Internal Security Act invalid); *S.* v. *Toms*; *S.* v. *Bruce*, 1990 (2) SA 802 (A) (holding that the 6-year penalty for draft resistance was a maximum sentence rather than a mandatory one). Still others have affected other aspects of the changing South African society. See e.g. *Administrator, Transvaal, and Others* v. *Traub and Others*, 1989 (4) SA 731 (A) (expanding the applicability of *audi alteram partem* protections); *SA Breweries Ltd.* v. *Food and Allied Workers Union and Others*, 1990 (1) SA 92 (A) (holding that certain concerted refusals to work overtime are not a strike, and therefore are not subject to the Labour Relations Act's requirements for a lawful strike).

A. The Change in the Court's Decisions

We can measure the difference between the Rabie and Corbett courts, roughly but usefully, simply by asking how many cases of the Corbett court have been decided in favour of those challenging the use of emergency power. As of the end of 1990 there have been six reported emergency decisions by the Appellate Division since Corbett became chief justice,[14] and of those four have granted at least some relief against the state's use of its emergency authority,[15] whereas under Rabie only three of the twelve emergency cases did. In these four cases, the Corbett court overturned portions of a restriction order imposed on a former detainee after his release;[16] overturned a press censorship order on the ground that it was not authorized by the emergency regulations;[17] invalidated an emergency arrest on the ground that the arresting officers lacked the power to make it;[18] and invalidated an emergency detention because the state did not produce any order which directed that the detainee be held in the particular prison in which he was held.[19] In a fifth case, in which the court did not grant relief, it *did* decide to overrule *Dempsey*'s position that in a challenge to an emergency arrest the detainee bears the *onus* to prove that the arresting officer failed to apply his mind properly.[20]

As striking as these results are, the full extent of the differences between the Corbett and Rabie emergency cases emerges only from a closer look at the Corbett-era cases. As we will see, the Corbett cases reflect a revitalized insistence on the importance of fundamental human rights, a newly declared willingness to endorse quite fundamental doctrinal innovation for the sake of such rights, and an increased stringency in the court's supervision of the state's compliance with the law's requirements. These changes, to be sure, are by no means unqualified, and we will need to consider the limits on the Corbett court's reformation of this field of law. But these limits should not obscure the

[14] The Corbett court's cases, based on the *South African Law Reports* through Dec. 1990, are *Visagie* v. *State President and Others*, 1989 (3) SA 859 (A) (hereafter cited as *Visagie*); *Minister of Law and Order, KwaNdebele, and Others* v. *Mathebe and Another*, 1990 (1) SA 114 (A) (hereafter cited as *Mathebe*); *Minister van Wet en Orde* v. *Matshoba*, 1990 (1) SA 280 (A) (*Minister of Law and Order* v. *Matshoba*, hereafter cited as *Matshoba*); *Catholic Bishops Publishing Co.* v. *State President and Another*, 1990 (1) SA 849 (A) (hereafter cited as *Catholic Bishops*); *Minister of Law and Order and Another* v. *Argus Printing and Publishing Co. Ltd. and Another*, 1990 (1) SA 1058 (A) (hereafter cited as *Argus*); and *During NO* v. *Boesak and Another*, 1990 (3) SA 661 (A) (hereafter cited as *Boesak*). I do not include an unreported decision, issued without opinion by the chief justice alone (and without any formal panel sitting on the case), in which the chief justice in 1990 declined to grant condonation for the untimeliness of the filing of a petition for leave to appeal from a judgment upholding the seizure of copies of the *Weekly Mail* newspaper.

[15] The cases in which no relief was granted were *Catholic Bishops*, 1990 (1) SA 849 (A), and *Boesak*, 1990 (3) SA 661 (A). *Boesak*, however, altered pre-existing doctrine in a way that clearly improved the chances of successful challenges to emergency arrests.

[16] *Visagie*, 1989 (3) SA at 869B–871G.

[17] *Argus*, 1990 (1) SA 1058 (A).

[18] *Mathebe*, 1990 (1) SA 114 (A).

[19] *Matshoba*, 1990 (1) SA 280 (A).

[20] *Boesak*, 1990 (3) SA at 663G (judgment of Nestadt JA).

gap between the work of the Corbett court and that of its predecessor.

First, the Corbett decisions express, for the first time, intense and explicit concern about the impact of emergency power on fundamental *rights*. *Visagie* is one example. There the Appellate Division considered the validity of a restriction order which sharply constrained the life of a former detainee, forbidding him to leave a particular area, to participate in several organizations, to be involved in producing or distributing any publications, or to 'attend any gathering at which any form of government or any principle or policy of, or conduct or intended conduct by the Government of the Republic of South Africa is attacked, or criticized'.[21] Let us look at the court's handling of two issues presented by this grim order: the question of whether those subject to such orders had any *audi alteram partem* rights in connection with them, and the question of whether the final, quoted portion of the order was so grossly unreasonable as to be invalid.

The *audi* issue prompts the Appellate Division to express itself in a language of rights heretofore almost wholly absent from its emergency decisions. The lower court had suggested that the *audi alteram partem* maxim did not apply to such orders, because the *audi* principle operated only where the state deprived someone of a valuable right, and a detainee who was released from prison with a restriction order was freer, rather than less free, than he had been before.[22] The Appellate Division disagreed. Hoexter JA wrote for the court: 'The subject's liberty is his supreme right; and true liberty is liberty unimpaired. In the instant case the conditions of release involved very serious invasions of the appellant's liberty. They drastically curtailed his right of freedom of movement; his rights of free association; and his right of free self-expression.'[23] So they did, but one would look in vain for similar language in any of the judgments for the Rabie court in emergency cases, though those cases dealt with regulations working equally great, or even greater, intrusions on South Africans' common-law rights. The language of rights is never more than faint in these earlier judgments,[24] even in cases such as *Nkwentsha* and *Apleni* which actually protect such rights. Emotive use of this language was altogether unheard.[25]

The court's rationale for finding the last portion of the restriction order invalid reflected the same vigorous concern for the protection of citizens'

[21] *Visagie*, 1989 (3) SA at 862G–863A.

[22] Ibid. 863G–H (quoting the lower court judgment).

[23] Ibid. 864D–E.

[24] For an instance of such faint reference to the 'freedom of assembly' in a Rabie-era judgment upholding emergency authority to ban meetings, see *Van der Westhuizen NO* v. *United Democratic Front*, 1989 (2) SA 242 (A) at 251B–C. There Hefer JA, 'without derogating in any way from the importance of the freedom of assembly', concludes that 'there is every reason to believe' that the emergency regulation in question made the Commissioner of Police the 'sole arbiter of the necessity or expediency of exercising his powers to ban meetings'.

[25] Visagie did not win any relief on the basis of this aspect of the court's judgment, however, because the court also concluded that in this context the *audi* principle required only a hearing after a restriction notice was delivered, rather than before, and Visagie had not 'avail[ed] himself' of this right. *Visagie*, 1989 (3) SA at 865I–866A.

rights. The emergency regulation providing for restriction orders contained no express limits on the kinds of order that could be issued, nor on the considerations which might lead the responsible Minister to issue such an order.[26] The Appellate Division declared, moreover, in terms reminiscent of and in fact more sweeping than *Dempsey*, that this regulation left it up to the Minister to decide which facts were relevant and which were not.[27] But the court also ruled that the Minister could only exercise this power for the purposes of the emergency, and that the prohibition on attending gatherings was 'so manifestly extravagant' that it was 'legally impeachable in its entirety'.[28]

The court acidly specified the details of this extravagance. The restriction order barred attendance of 'any gathering at which any form of government ... is attacked, or criticized'. This appeared to mean that Visagie could not have attended 'a purely academic constitutional law lecture devoted to a critical analysis of such a topic as, for example, the forms of government in ancient Greece, or in medieval Italy, or in modern Switzerland', even if South Africa's government was never mentioned.[29] The order also prohibited Visagie from attending any gathering at which 'any principle or policy of, or conduct or intended conduct by the Government of the Republic of South Africa, is attacked, or criticized'. The court commented that 'few if any topics of commonplace and daily discussion do not directly or indirectly touch upon either the principles or the policies or the actions of the government'. Applied to Visagie, a clergyman, this prohibition would have 'consign[ed] him to an existence of intolerable and near-monastic seclusion'. This 'drastic ... inhibition of the appellant's rights of freedom of association and freedom of expression' could not, the court concluded, 'be fairly and reasonabl[y] related' to the purposes of the emergency, and was therefore void.[30] The Appellate Division had decided that the Minister had improperly exercised his discretion[31]—the first and only time the Appellate Division has invalidated emergency action because it was a misuse of discretion rather than because it violated some specific, and non-discretionary, rule.[32]

[26] Reg. 3(6), Proc. R. 109, *Government Gazette* 10280 (12 June 1986), provided: 'The Minister may at any time by a notice in writing signed by him order that a person detained in terms of this regulation, be released on such condition or conditions, if any, as may in his discretion be determined by the Minister in such notice.'

[27] *Visagie*, 1989 (3) SA at 867I–868F. For a critical assessment of this aspect of the case, see J. Grogan, 'Restricting the Power to Restrict', 5 *SAJHR* 431, 435–6 (1989).

[28] *Visagie*, 1989 (3) SA at 870G.

[29] Ibid. 870I–871A.

[30] Ibid. 871B–G.

[31] See ibid. 870D–E, 871F–G.

[32] The distinction between misuse of discretion and violation of rules is not an absolute one, since the Minister's misuse of discretion did violate a legal rule that emergency powers must be used for the purposes of the emergency. But this rule focuses quite closely on the judgment of the official in question. By contrast, rules like the one at issue in *Swart*—that an arrestee must be told the basis for his arrest as soon as reasonably practicable—call for little discretionary judgment by those who wield emergency power. The dissenting judgment in *Boesak*, 1990 (3) SA 661 (A), provides another instance of critical assessment of discretionary judgment, albeit only by two justices. They offer a notably stringent analysis of what they find to be a failure

The court returned to its explicit emphasis on the protection of rights in *Matshoba*, and also demonstrated in this case the second of the notable features of the Corbett era, the express willingness to make new and innovative law in order to provide this protection. The particular details of fact which led to Matshoba's release are probably the least important aspect of the case; the principles which led the court to give these facts significance are much more far-reaching. The facts were that Matshoba had been arrested under the state of emergency and, in due course, the Minister of Law and Order had issued a written notice to the head of Worcester Prison, directing that Matshoba continue to be held in that prison. A few days later, however, he was transferred to another prison. When Matshoba brought litigation to compel his release, the state offered no justification for the fact that Matshoba was not in the prison in which the Minister had ordered him to be kept. The Appellate Division held on this basis that Matshoba was entitled to his freedom—a welcome result for him, but not one likely to win freedom for many other detainees, since normally the state will no doubt be able to explain why a detainee is in one prison rather than another.[33]

The procedural posture of this case is the key to its importance. Matshoba had never asserted that he was being held in the wrong prison or that he was entitled to release on that basis. Rather, the gist of his plea for relief was that there was no valid basis for his arrest or for the Minister's decision to extend his detention.[34] To be sure, he had never conceded that he was being held in the right prison, or expressly disclaimed any intention to seek relief because he was in the wrong prison—but neither had he identified this as an issue. Even after the state, in its reply to Matshoba's opening affidavit, submitted the Minister's order for his placement in the first prison to the court, Matshoba did not raise this point in his reply papers.[35] Eksteen JA, who dissented from the court's decision, argued that it was unfair to require the state to meet a claim that had never been asserted. 'Fairness and justice would, in my humble opinion, have required that the Minister should have been given the opportunity to deal with an objection in an affidavit before it became an important basis of a Court's judgment.'[36]

The members of the majority took a very different view of what should be required of the pleadings of a person seeking his or her liberty, and they did

to apply the mind on the part of a Divisional Commissioner of Police who banned a concert in celebration of Nelson Mandela's birthday. Ibid. 680C–681I (dissenting judgment of E. M. Grosskopf JA). Grosskopf JA also endorsed a demanding formulation of the requisites of applying one's mind, ibid. 671J–672D, and passed over without a mention the less stringent formulation Hefer JA had offered in *Dempsey*. See Ch. 3, text at nn. 78–83 above.

[33] The regulations permitted detainees to be transferred 'if the Minister or a person authorized by him in writing so directs': Reg. 3(4), *Government Gazette* 10280 (12 June 1986).

[34] See *Matshoba*, 1990 (1) SA at 300H–301E (dissenting judgment of Eksteen JA). Eksteen JA argued, moreover, that Matshoba's only basis for challenging the Minister's decision on extension was that the initial arrest and detention had been invalid. Ibid. 301H–302B.

[35] See ibid. 307I–J (dissenting judgment of Eksteen JA).

[36] Ibid. 308J–309A (dissenting judgment of Eksteen JA).

so precisely, and expressly, because liberty was at stake. E. M. Grosskopf JA, with whom the remaining three justices concurred,[37] agreed that judgment should not be given on a point 'not pertinently raised' by the detainee *if* that would be unfair. Whether it would be unfair, however, depended on what the detainee was required to plead in order to place on the state the burden of justifying his arrest.[38] (It also depended on what was required of the state to meet that burden, an issue to which we will turn in a moment.)[39] Grosskopf JA invokes the analogy of the *rei vindicatio*, a procedure for recovery of property in which the property owner need only allege that he is the owner of the item in question and that the defendant is holding it, to place the *onus* on the defendant to indicate his basis for claiming the right to possess the owner's property.[40] Then Grosskopf JA writes:

> The right to personal liberty is more fundamental than the right to own property, and in my opinion there can be no doubt that a person who objects to his detention, need in the first place not have to allege more than that he is being detained by the defendant or respondent (probably he need not even allege that the detention is unlawful or against his will ...). The onus then rests on the defendant or respondent to justify the detainee's detention.[41]

The right to liberty also bears on how the court will interpret what the detainee alleges if the detainee chooses to allege more than this minimum. The issue now is not whether Matshoba raised the issue of his imprisonment in the second prison, as Eksteen JA understood the matter, but rather whether he somehow excised this issue from what would otherwise be the state's *onus*. Grosskopf JA argues that Matshoba nowhere in his papers made any 'express admissions of fact' which would reduce the state's burden of proof, and that his papers' 'emphasis' on the invalidity of his arrest did not impliedly abjure any other grounds for attack on his detention.[42] Again Grosskopf JA points to the right at stake (though he develops other arguments as well): 'Particularly when a party's liberty is in issue, a Court will not readily accept that such a party has by implication admitted important elements of the other party's case.'[43]

[37] Botha JA did not expressly concur but stated at the beginning of his separate judgment that he agreed with Grosskopf JA's conclusion and reasoning. Ibid. 291B–C (concurring judgment of Botha JA). Corbett CJ and Milne JA expressly concurred in the judgments of both Grosskopf JA and Botha JA. Grosskopf JA did not expressly concur in, or comment on, Botha JA's judgment. Thus Grosskopf JA's judgment represents the views of four members of the court, while Botha JA's expresses the views of three.

[38] Ibid. 285E–G (judgment of E. M. Grosskopf JA).

[39] For discussion of this issue, see text at nn. 46–52 below.

[40] I am here paraphrasing E. M. Grosskopf's language, *Matshoba*, 1990 (1) SA at 286A–B.

[41] Ibid. 286B–D (judgment of E. M. Grosskopf JA) (citation omitted).

[42] The quoted phrases are to be found at ibid. 287B, 287E. Grosskopf JA develops his argument at 287F–288H. For the similar reasoning of Botha JA, see ibid. 298F–299H (concurring judgment of Botha JA).

[43] Ibid. 287I (judgment of E. M. Grosskopf JA).

What I have said so far does not fully illuminate the innovation entailed in the pleading rule which Grosskopf JA articulates. This is the focus of Botha JA's concurring judgment, in which, on behalf of a majority of the panel, he recognizes the extent of this innovation and wholly accepts it, once again on the express ground that the right at stake requires it. What made this pleading rule particularly novel was that it was to apply to proceedings by 'motion' (expedited proceedings in which the pleadings are not normally permitted to multiply as they can in a regular 'action'). In motion proceedings, Eksteen JA maintains, the applicant must 'allege in his founding affidavit not only the legal grounds on which he relies but also all the facts on which the application rests'.[44] The *rei vindicatio* precedents, Botha JA indicates, did not make clear what pleading rules should apply in motion proceedings, and Botha JA assumes for the sake of argument that in motion proceedings involving property the minimal pleading endorsed by Grosskopf JA would not be permitted.[45]

None the less, Botha JA argues, precisely this sort of opening pleading should be permitted in motion proceedings challenging arrests, because liberty is at issue. This is so even though, in Botha JA's view, the result of permitting the case to begin with so opaque an initial pleading is that the number of affidavits and counter-affidavits which will be needed to bring the case to the point at which it can be adjudicated will have to expand well beyond what is normally permitted in motion proceedings. Botha writes:

> It would clearly constitute a radical deviation from the normal rules of practice applicable in motion proceedings. The question is whether this should be allowed. In my view the answer is: yes. In my opinion, an exceptional approach in these kind[s] of cases [is] justified because of the fundamental nature of the right to personal liberty. The protection of that right of the individual by our Courts against unauthorized or improper violation by authorities should not be hampered by the normal rules of practice.[46]

The court's concern to protect the right to liberty also plays a part in resolving the question of whether, given (now) that the detainee's pleading was sufficient to place on the state the *onus* of justifying the arrest and detention, the state had to justify the detainee's being in one prison rather than another in order to carry that *onus*. The court resolves this issue in favour of the detainee despite the distinctly contrary tenor of the Rabie-era decision in *Dempsey*. There, the Appellate Division had held that the state had to show that the arresting officer actually held the opinion that the arrest was necessary for the purposes of the emergency, as the regulation in question required, but that the state did not have to show that the officer had properly applied his mind in coming to this opinion. One ground for the court's position was that

[44] Ibid. 303C–D (dissenting judgment of Eksteen JA). Botha JA essentially agrees with this characterization, ibid. 294C–D (concurring judgment of Botha JA).
[45] Ibid. 292B–293A (concurring judgment of Botha JA).
[46] Ibid. 293E–G (concurring judgment of Botha JA).

it would be unfair to require the state to address all possible grounds for the invalidity of an arrest in response to a bare allegation that the arrest was unlawful.[47]

Matshoba does not overrule *Dempsey*, but its unsympathetic response to this charge of unfairness clearly pointed the way towards the eventual rejection of *Dempsey*'s *onus* rule in *Boesak*.[48] According to *Matshoba*, the state must show 'at least' that it 'had complied with all the formal requirements of the enabling legislative provision on which it relies', requirements which include providing a legal basis for the detainee's being held at the place where he is in fact being held.[49] Botha JA writes that he is 'well aware that this standpoint has not been pertinently formulated in our case law before, but to my mind it is a logical and natural outcome of our existing law'.[50] He continues, in by now familiar vein:

> I am further of the opinion that it is in accordance with healthy legal policy, because of my view of the importance of the role which our Courts must play in the protection of the individual's right to personal freedom, and against deprivation of it by the authorities, with the exception of action by the authority which clearly falls within the framework of empowering statutory measures.[51]

As a result, Botha JA contends, the question of fairness simply falls away. 'There is no room for an enquiry into the question whether it was fair or unfair to expect the Minister to produce the absent notice [explaining why Matshoba was in the second prison]; he was obliged in law to do it so as to discharge his onus of proof.'[52] Since the rule creating this obligation had only just been announced, it is clear that the court is taking its newly articulated concern for human rights quite seriously indeed.[53] In sharp contrast, while we have seen that the Rabie-era court was also, on occasion, prepared to shape the law so as to favour human rights, no emergency decision from that period was prepared to *say* that it was fashioning doctrinal innovations for that purpose.

The Corbett court's willingness to reshape doctrine is nowhere more evident,

[47] See Ch. 3, text at n. 98 above.

[48] Botha JA hints that *Dempsey* may face imminent judicial revision (ibid. 294F) and characterizes broad and seemingly contrary language in *Dempsey* as 'not authoritative' on the issue in *Matshoba* (ibid. 297J). For another Corbett-era decision vigorously distinguishing *Dempsey*, in this instance on the extent of an arresting officer's *onus* in defending arrests under s. 29 of the Internal Security Act 74 of 1982, see *Minister of Law and Order and Others* v. *Pavlicevic*, 1989 (3) SA 679 (A) at 692G–693C (judgment of Corbett CJ). *Pavlicevic*, too, can be seen as part of the gradual solidification of the court's conviction that *Dempsey* was clearly mistaken.

[49] *Matshoba*, 1990 (1) SA at 289B–C (judgment of E. M. Grosskopf JA); ibid. 298A–B (concurring judgment of Botha JA).

[50] Ibid. 298B–C (concurring judgment of Botha JA).

[51] Ibid. 298C–D (concurring judgment of Botha JA).

[52] Ibid. 299F (concurring judgment of Botha JA).

[53] The court also gives short shrift to the state's argument that if Matshoba's presence in the second prison is unjustified, all that he is entitled to is an order placing him in the right prison—despite the fact that the court has not found any other legal flaw in his detention. Ibid. 289H–290J (judgment of E. M. Grosskopf JA).

however, than in *Boesak*. In that case, the judicial rumblings in *Matshoba* and elsewhere[54] come to the surface. E. M. Grosskopf JA, with whom Milne JA concurs, sets out an extensive and firm critique of *Dempsey*.[55] Nestadt JA, writing for the three-judge majority, begins his judgment by expressing his agreement with Grosskopf JA 'that the decision ... in *Dempsey*'s case was clearly wrong and should not be followed'.[56] Thus all five members of the panel agree that *Dempsey*'s allocation to the detainee of the *onus* to prove that the arresting officer failed to apply his mind properly was clearly mistaken—a judicial forthrightness all the more striking because, for the majority of the panel, the expression of this conclusion is clearly unnecessary to the decision of the case and so is *obiter dictum*.[57] As a result, it now appears to be the law that the state must carry the *onus* on this issue as well as on the question of whether the officer actually held the opinion that the arrest was necessary (on which *Dempsey* agreed the state had the *onus*) and on the issues addressed in *Matshoba*. Among the judges concurring, silently, in the overturning of *Dempsey* on this score is Joubert JA, who had concurred in the very *Dempsey* judgment that is now, in this respect, overruled. Nestadt JA, the author of the majority judgment in which Joubert JA concurred, was the sole member of the *Dempsey* panel who had declined to join the majority on this issue.[58]

The majority in *Boesak* choose not to elaborate on their reasons for rejecting *Dempsey*, but the judgment of Grosskopf JA exemplifies the Corbett court's use of the language of human rights. Grosskopf JA makes clear that a central basis for his rejection of *Dempsey* is that 'it is proper and fair—as a matter of policy—that a person who encroaches upon the freedom of the individual, ought to bear the onus of proving that his conduct is lawful'....[59]

The third feature of the Corbett emergency cases may already be evident: the court approaches emergency issues with a new insistence on confining the powers of the state and a correspondingly diminished attention to the exigencies, as seen from the state's perspective, of emergency law enforcement. I have argued that the Rabie court was also concerned to hold the state to compliance with the rules of the game. What is different in the Corbett era is that the court is clearly more prepared to identify rules and limits, rather than to leave emergency power, as the Rabie court so often did, almost without

[54] See text at nn. 48–53 and n. 48 above.

[55] *Boesak*, 1990 (3) SA at 673E–679G (judgment of E. M. Grosskopf JA).

[56] Ibid. 663G (judgment of Nestadt JA, with whom Joubert and Botha JJA concurred).

[57] See ibid. 663G–H (judgment of Nestadt JA). The question of *onus* in *Dempsey* dealt with a challenge to an emergency arrest. In *Boesak* the issue was the validity of an emergency banning of a public concert. The majority simply assumes for purposes of argument that the *onus* to justify this banning fell entirely on the state, as it would—given the rejection of *Dempsey*—in an arrest case.

[58] In *Dempsey*, Nestadt JA expressed doubt about Hefer JA's splitting of the *onus*, but did not decide the matter. *Dempsey*, 1988 (3) SA 19 (A) at 42G (judgment of Nestadt JA). Instead, he assumed for purposes of decision that the state did have the *onus* even on the 'apply the mind' question (ibid. 42G–H) and on that basis went ahead to find that the state had satisfied its burden of proof.

[59] *Boesak*, 1990 (3) SA at 673G (judgment of Grosskopf JA).

any limits at all. Thus in *Visagie* the court for the first time finds that the purposes of the emergency, broad as they are, are not broad enough to sustain a profound breach of individual rights. As John Grogan points out, the court had repeatedly declared in earlier cases that emergency powers could only be used for emergency purposes, but this limit had never been used to overturn anything the government had done.[60]

Similarly, in *Matshoba*, the court shows no sympathy for the litigation burdens which its new pleading rules will impose on the state. I do not mean to say that the court has become indifferent to law enforcement concerns. Indeed, Botha JA assures his readers that '[n]aturally that function [of maintaining law and order] must not be slighted, and it would not do to approve of a form of procedure which would place an unnecessary or improper hindrance on the execution of that function'.[61] But it is clear from *Matshoba* that the court is not being 'astute' to discern such damage,[62] and is, instead, rather urgently concerned to eliminate what it views as unnecessary or improper hindrance to detainees' challenges to the lawfulness of what has been done to them. And if *Dempsey*'s allocation of burden of proof rested in part on a desire to protect the state from unmeritorious claims, as I have inferred,[63] *Boesak* insists instead on an allocation of the burden of proof which requires the state to demonstrate its basis for the intrusion on liberty entailed in an emergency arrest.

Mathebe offers another example of the court's new-found stringency towards the state. Mathebe and two other men had been arrested in Johannesburg on the basis of the emergency regulations. What made their arrest legally problematic was that they had not been arrested by South African police as such, but rather by police from the 'self-governing territory' of KwaNdebele.[64] Complicating matters even further, the so-called KwaNdebele police were actually South African police who had been 'seconded' to service on the KwaNdebele police force. The Appellate Division decided, however, that for the purposes of this case the arresting officers should be considered only as KwaNdebele police,[65] and then held that the emergency regulations did not authorize the police of a self-governing territory to make arrests in South Africa proper. The court reached this conclusion despite the fact that the

[60] Grogan, 'Restricting' (cit. n. 27), 439.

[61] *Matshoba*, 1990 (1) SA at 294E–F (concurring judgment of Botha JA).

[62] Thus it is heeding the often-quoted injunction of Van den Heever JA that '[w]here Parliament has conferred vast powers of legislation upon the Executive, the Courts should not in my opinion be astute to divest themselves of their judicial powers and duties, namely to serve as buttresses between the Executive and the subjects': *R.* v. *Pretoria Timber Co. (Pty), Ltd, and Another*, 1950 (3) SA 163 (A) at 182A (dissenting judgment of Van den Heever JA).

[63] See Ch. 4, text following n. 95 above.

[64] A self-governing territory—in theory, a 'homeland' for blacks of a particular ethnic group, in this case the Ndebele—is a part of South Africa rather than an independent state. Although products of apartheid and thoroughly enmeshed in the social system of apartheid, such territories do have some attributes of independence. *Mathebe* describes KwaNdebele as a 'separate and largely independent political entity': *Mathebe*, 1990 (1) SA at 119D.

[65] Ibid. 117E–118G (judgment of Smalberger JA).

relevant emergency regulations authorized members of a 'security force' to make emergency arrests (and stated no geographic limitation on this power),[66] and also expressly included the police of self-governing territories within the term 'security force'.[67] Plainly these regulations could have been read to permit any member of such a force to make arrests anywhere in South Africa. On this reading, the effect of the regulations would have been to leave it up to the security forces to determine who would make which arrests, and where.

The court, however, invokes the tools of South African statutory interpretation in favour of a quite different reading. The court reaches its conclusion by deciding, first, that under normal South African law the police of such a territory are not empowered to make arrests outside the territory's boundaries. This view seems entirely plausible, but it apparently had never been established before, for the court cites no case as doing so.[68] Once this norm is discerned, however, the interpretive question is transformed. Now the issue is whether the emergency regulations alter the normal state of affairs. 'To extend their powers beyond such territorial limits', Smalberger JA writes for the court, 'would constitute a radical departure from the norm. Any such departure would have to be authorized in clear terms. In the case of doubt the norm must prevail.' He concludes:

> At best for the appellants [the state] there is considerable doubt whether the State President intended reg 3(1) to confer extraterritorial powers of arrest on members of the police force of a self-governing territory. As there is a presumption against interference with an existing state of affairs, in the absence of clear language to the contrary, reg 3(1) must be interpreted in a manner consonant with the normal position ...[69]

A court concerned to preserve the executive's freedom of manœuvre in the face of emergency circumstances could have found less doubt, or clearer language.[70] And—although this can be said of much statutory interpretation—one may well doubt whether the authors of the emergency regulations had fully understood that the court would demand such certainty on the basis of a 'normal' rule which had not yet been announced!

[66] Reg. 3(1), Proc. R. 96, *Government Gazette* 10771 (11 June 1987).

[67] Reg. 1, Proc. R. 96, *Government Gazette* 10771 (11 June 1987) (definition of 'security force', subsection (*c*)).

[68] See *Mathebe*, 1990 (1) SA at 118H–119I.

[69] Ibid. 121A–B.

[70] Such a court might also not have been so ready to conclude that the illegality of the arrest invalidated Matshoba's subsequent detention, which did take place in KwaNdebele. There was precedent, which the court acknowledges, for the view that an accused who has been illegally seized in a foreign nation may none the less be tried in the courts of the country which brought about the seizure. See *Nduli and Another* v. *Minister of Justice and Others*, 1978 (1) SA 893 (A); *Abrahams* v. *Minister of Justice and Others*, 1963 (4) SA 542 (C). While there was also precedent, in particular in the *Swart* case, for the view that an emergency detention cannot be valid if the underlying arrest was invalid, it was not a foregone conclusion that this latter principle would be held to apply where the flaw in the underlying arrest was its extraterritoriality—perhaps especially where, as here, it was not self-evident that the extraterritorial arrest had been illegal in the first place.

The court's effort to understand emergency powers as limited rather than unlimited is reflected in *Argus* as well. *Argus* is the first case in which the Appellate Division has suggested that one of the emergency regulations themselves might well be *ultra vires*.[71] The court did not rule on this issue, but it did strike down a press censorship order issued by the Commissioner of Police on the ground that the emergency regulations did not authorize it, and this was the first time that the Appellate Division had struck down an order of general applicability issued on the strength of emergency regulations.[72] The court did so, moreover, despite its acceptance of the view that the 'wide and uninhibited language' of the regulations on which the Commissioner sought to rely was, if 'literally interpreted', 'certainly wide enough' to cover the order the Commissioner had issued.[73]

To the *Argus* court, giving these regulations their literal meaning would 'have led to glaring absurdity and a result manifestly contrary to the intention of the Legislature, as shown by the context'.[74] This glaring absurdity was that this reading would have rendered other regulations, which contained 'certain specific and, on the whole, circumscribed provisions impinging on what the Press might publish', redundant. 'Moreover, whatever limitations or safeguards might have been contained' in these other regulations 'would have been overridden', and 'powere specifically vested in the Minister of Law and Order would have been exercisable by the Commissioner' of Police, a less senior official.[75] This perhaps is not the stuff of high drama. It does, however, suggest a preference for limited rather than unlimited power, and it invalidates an exercise of authority that might have been symptomatic of the state's ready assertion of an almost unlimited emergency authority.

[71] *Argus*, 1990 (1) SA at 1065C–D. The court does not rule on this point, however, and so its observation is *obiter dictum*.

[72] The cases granting relief against emergency detentions had in effect held detention orders invalid, and *Visagie* had held a restriction order invalid in part, but all of these orders had applied only to single individuals. John Grogan, however, writes that *Visagie* can also be seen as 'something of a watershed', as the first case in which the Appellate Division 'struck down executive action of a legislative character': 'Restricting' (cit. n. 27), 431.

[73] *Argus*, 1990 (1) SA at 1066F–I. The broader of the two regulations permitted the Commissioner to issue orders 'relating to any other matter the regulating, control or prohibition of which in his opinion is necessary or expedient with a view to the safety of any member or members of the public or the maintenance of the public order, or in order to terminate the state of emergency, the generality of the powers conferred by this paragraph not being restricted by the provisions of the preceding paragraphs'. Reg. 7(1)(*d*), Proc. R. 109, *Government Gazette* 10280 (12 June 1986). The Commissioner's order forbade the editors of newspapers and periodicals to permit the publication of any matter calculated either to improve the image of an unlawful organization or (*semble*) to defend any of such an organization's policies of resistance or subversion. This order is quoted in *Argus*, 1990 (1) SA at 1063D–F.

[74] Ibid. 1066J–1067A.

[75] Ibid. 1066F–J. The court also pointed out that when the Commissioner actually issued his order, new media regulations had been proclaimed with the apparent intention of 'collect[ing] ... all the prohibitions and controls affecting what may be published'. Ibid. 1067D. Since the regulations on which the Commissioner's order purported to rest were not among those collected in the media regulations, the court felt that it was now even less likely that the regulations on which the state was relying applied to press censorship. Ibid. 1067D–E.

B. The Common Doctrinal Ground of the Corbett and Rabie Courts

As this review of its decisions reflects, the Corbett court has become significantly more responsive to human rights claims against emergency action than the Rabie court was. Exciting as this change is, it has not *transformed* South African law; this is spring, but not yet summer. Just as the Rabie court retained some concern for human rights, sensitive as it was to the needs of the state, so the Corbett court has by no means challenged every aspect of emergency power. That the court's activism does know limits becomes clear in *Catholic Bishops*, the one Corbett emergency case which granted no relief, and worked no significant doctrinal improvements, against the exercise of emergency power. It is also evident in the majority judgment in *Boesak*, despite the fact that that case, in a sense parenthetically, overrules *Dempsey*.

In *Catholic Bishops* the Appellate Division, in a judgment written by Corbett CJ, upheld the state's use of emergency powers to close an important anti-government newspaper, the *New Nation*, for three months. This result was dismaying in itself. But the case is notable on two other scores as well. The first is the generally cool tone of the judgment, and its lack of the rhetoric of rights so evident in certain of the Corbett-era cases. This may be no more than Corbett's distinctive style, evident in *Argus* as well; the more vivid judgments were written by other judges. Moreover, the judgment in a sense has the virtue of its defects, for it avoids the pro-executive passion and, generally, the conclusory reasoning that infuse much of Rabie's emergency decisionmaking. None the less it serves as a reminder that the more rights-focused judgments represent only one mode of the new court's reasoning.

The second noteworthy feature of the *Catholic Bishops* judgment is its reiteration of some of the doctrinal foundations of the Rabie era's emergency jurisprudence. For example, the court embraces the Rabie era's recognition of the broad scope of the State President's emergency powers.[76] It invokes these broad powers to turn back a challenge to the State President's delegation of authority in the regulations providing for newspaper closures, and finds confirmation of its view in a Rabie argument from *United Democratic Front*.[77] Perhaps most important, however, the *Catholic Bishops* court had before it a challenge to the decision in *United Democratic Front* that the Public Safety Act's ouster clause deprived the court of jurisdiction over claims that emergency regulations were invalid by reason of vagueness. The *Catholic Bishops* court rejected this challenge, and did so in a strikingly abrupt fashion, quite out of keeping with most of the judgment. After citing the South African rule that a prior decision, part of the *ratio decidendi* of a case and a considered judgment, 'should be followed unless, at the very least, we are satisfied that it is clearly

[76] *Catholic Bishops*, 1990 (1) SA at 861E–I.

[77] Ibid. 862H, 863B.

wrong',[78] Corbett CJ said only the following about his reasons for adhering to *United Democratic Front*:

> Mr *Browde* [counsel for the *New Nation*] advanced various arguments aimed at showing that the majority decision in the *United Democratic Front* case (AD) *supra* was an incorrect one. I do not propose to deal with these arguments in detail. I have carefully considered them, but I remain unpersuaded the majority decision in the *United Democratic Front* case (AD) on this particular point is clearly wrong.[79]

Corbett's judgment does not give the sense, as Rabie's did, that he is anxious to avoid addressing the merits of the vagueness arguments, but the result of this refusal to overrule *United Democratic Front* is, of course, that those arguments do go unconsidered.

Boesak, too, demonstrates that the court is by no means prepared to overturn all the work of the Rabie court. For although *Boesak* unanimously overturns *Dempsey*'s allocation of the *onus* in challenges to emergency arrests, the actual decision in the case is that a Divisional Commissioner of Police's order prohibiting a Nelson Mandela birthday concert in 1988 (when Mandela was still a prisoner) was a lawful order. In the course of resolving this question, the majority of the panel declines to decide whether the state should bear the same *onus* to defend its emergency banning of a public gathering that it now must bear to defend an emergency arrest.[80] The principle that the *onus* should be on the party interfering with fundamental rights, if accepted, would be a very far-reaching one, for it would impose the *onus* on the state in every challenge to its emergency measures—but the court has not yet embraced so sweeping a rule.[81]

In addition, the majority declines to overturn another emergency decision, *Van der Westhuizen NO* v. *United Democratic Front*.[82] This Rabie-era case, on which we have not focused until now, dealt with the power to ban gatherings. The relevant regulation authorized Divisional Commissioners of Police

> for the purpose of the safety of the public, the maintenance of public order or the termination of the state of emergency, and without prior notice to any person and without hearing any person, [to] issue orders not inconsistent with these regulations ... whereby any particular gath-

[78] *Catholic Bishops*, 1990 (1) SA at 866H.

[79] Ibid. 866H–I.

[80] Nestadt JA assumes *arguendo*, however, that the *onus* in such a case is on the state. Boesak, 1990 (3) SA at 663H (judgment of Nestadt JA).

[81] So, too, in *Catholic Bishops*, the Appellate Division seemed to take it for granted that the *New Nation* bore the *onus* on its claim that the Minister had relied on 'extraneous factors' in deciding to close the newspaper. The fact that the Minister *had* used some information which he had not identified to the court was clear from his own affidavit. But because there had been no effort to develop further evidence on this matter (e.g. to show *what* information had been used), the court held that the *New Nation* had not discharged its *onus*. *Catholic Bishops*, 1990 (1) SA at 871F–872D. Had the *onus* been on the Minister, the decision might well have gone the other way.

[82] *Van der Westhuizen NO* v. *United Democratic Front*, 1989 (2) SA 242 (A).

> ering, or any gathering of a particular nature, class or kind, is prohibited at any place or in any area specified in the order.[83]

In *Van der Westhuizen* the Appellate Division held, in a judgment by Hefer JA, that in making such orders the Divisional Commissioner exercised a discretion which was not objectively justiciable. That is to say, the Appellate Division decided that the courts had no authority to decide whether the Divisional Commissioner had correctly judged that such a ban would serve the purposes of the emergency; they could only assess whether the Divisional Commissioner *thought* it would, in good faith and after properly applying his mind.

Van der Westhuizen's conclusion overrode serious objections raised on behalf of the United Democratic Front.[84] First, there was good reason to think that the regulation at issue here had been promulgated in response to a lower court case which had invalidated another regulation because its explicit grant of a subjective discretion constituted an excessive delegation of power by the State President; it was plausible to infer that the new regulation was meant to remove the subjective-discretion issue.[85] Second, if the regulation had said that the Commissioners could make such orders when *in their opinion* the orders would serve these purposes, cases such as *Hurley* would have left little doubt that the orders were not objectively justiciable—but that language was rather conspicuously absent. Third, the court's reading clearly made this regulation an even greater intrusion on the freedom of assembly than it would otherwise have been, and this consideration might have been expected to weigh against acceptance of this reading. Hefer JA responded, in part, that:

> without derogating in any way from the importance of the freedom of assembly, but taking into account matters such as the nature and purpose of the powers, the status of those on whom they were conferred, and the fact that they were conferred and are to be exercised in a declared state of emergency, there is every reason to believe that the intention was to constitute the Commissioner the sole arbiter of the necessity or expediency of exercising his powers.[86]

As this passage suggests, *Van der Westhuizen* was a particularly clear instance of the Rabie court's embrace of the grant of broad, subjective discretion to emergency authorities, and of its concern to protect those authorities' power to respond to the challenge of the emergency.

In *Boesak*, however, the Corbett court does not accept the invitation to declare *Van der Westhuizen* clearly wrong.[87] Moreover, the majority's reasons for declining this invitation are set out extremely tersely, albeit not quite as

[83] Reg 7(1)(*b*A), Proc. R. 225, *Government Gazette* 10542 (28 Nov. 1986).

[84] See *Van der Westhuizen*, 1989 (2) SA at 249H–250J.

[85] The lower court decision was *Natal Newspapers (Pty) Ltd. and Others* v. *State President and Others*, 1986 (4) SA 1109 (N) at 1126J–1128B.

[86] *Van der Westhuizen*, 1989 (2) SA at 251B–C.

[87] The dissent does not propose to overrule *Van der Westhuizen* either, but a judgment on this matter would not have been necessary to the dissenters' approach to the case.

opaquely as in *Catholic Bishops*. Nestadt JA declares that he 'do[es] not propose to detail the argument advanced',[88] and then says that he 'remains unpersuaded' by the legislative history argument and is not 'prepared to say' that Hefer JA's reliance on the emergency context as a guide to the regulation's interpretation (in the passage quoted above) was error.[89] Why he remains unpersuaded or not prepared to say, Nestadt JA does not explain.

Boesak and *Catholic Bishops* remind us that the Corbett court is not a radical institution. They point to three more specific lessons besides. First, they help identify the limits on the court's challenge to emergency governance. While the Corbett court does not seem preoccupied with the fear of onslaught that appeared to haunt the Rabie court, it shows no inclination to challenge the executive assertion of an emergency or the generous overall standard articulated in the Rabie days for the judicial evaluation of the State President's exercise of his discretion to frame emergency regulations. Similarly, the court does not appear committed to interpreting these regulations, where possible, to confer limited rather than broad powers on subordinate emergency authorities. Though cases such as *Matshoba* and *Argus* do suggest a preference for such constrained readings, *Boesak* indicates that the court has not foresworn the option of interpreting those regulations to convey broad, subjective discretion. The court may also still share some of the Rabie era's apparent faith in the conduct of high (or relatively high) officials, such as the Minister in *Catholic Bishops* and the Divisional Commissioner of Police in *Boesak*.[90] Similarly, the court has not altered the verbal formulas for the review of such discretionary authority when it has been granted, although it has given signs, in *Visagie* and (more faintly) in *Boesak*, that these formulas will be applied more vigorously than they once were.[91]

Second, these cases offer some hints, albeit only hints, about the sorts of emergency invasions of rights that most concern the judges. Two of the three cases in which the Corbett court has granted relief have been detention cases, and the third involved detention's closest cousin: a restriction order imposed on a detainee as a condition for his release. By contrast, the three judges in the majority in *Boesak* do not suggest that they see the banning of the Mandela

[88] *Van der Westhuizen*, 1989 (2) SA at 863I (judgment of Nestadt JA).

[89] Ibid. 863I–864A (judgment of Nestadt JA).

[90] In *Catholic Bishops* the emergency decision, namely to close the *New Nation*, appears to have received considerable personal attention from the relevant Minister, the Minister of Home Affairs and of Communications, though the court does not explicitly place any emphasis on this feature of the case. The passage from *Van der Westhuizen* which Nestadt JA in *Boesak* is not 'prepared to say' is erroneous expressly takes into account 'the status of those on whom they [the banning powers] were conferred' as one ground for interpreting those powers not to be objectively justiciable. *Van der Westhuizen*, 1989 (2) SA at 251B–C.

[91] Nestadt JA upholds the banning at issue in *Boesak*. He does say, however, that if the banning had rested only on one vague piece of information (a report that black youths were going to stone state vehicles or buses on Mandela's birthday, which was also the occasion and focus of the gathering), 'it may be that he [the Divisional Commissioner of Police] did not show that he properly exercised his discretion'. *Boesak*, 1990 (3) SA at 864H (judgment of Nestadt JA).

birthday celebration as a specially troubling invasion of human rights; indeed, the language of rights is absent from this majority judgment as it was from *Catholic Bishops.* The court's attitude towards press censorship may also be somewhat less vigilant than its view of detentions, although here the record is mixed, since *Argus* overrides a censorship order while *Catholic Bishops* upholds the temporary closure of a newspaper. Perhaps one explanation for *Catholic Bishops* is that the court felt that the fairly elaborate procedural preliminaries to a closure order, procedures of which the newspaper in question took full advantage, imposed some constraint on the threat to liberty which this power to close newspapers would otherwise have represented.[92] By contrast, procedural protections clearly were not a *sine qua non* in *Boesak,* where the banning decision was apparently made, as the regulation's language on its face permitted,[93] without any process whatsoever—a further sign, perhaps, of the majority's attitude to such decisions.

Third, the cases suggest the court's reluctance to alter too visibly or too quickly the work of the Rabie court. In part this reluctance may reflect agreement with the earlier decisions; Nestadt JA's comments in *Boesak* faintly hint at this. *Catholic Bishops'* rejection of the challenge to the Rabie court's ruling on the ouster clause question, however, is so completely silent about the arguments at issue that even faint hints of approval are hard to discern. This complete silence has the effect of withholding the court's endorsement, even partial endorsement, of any particular rationale for the *United Democratic Front* ouster decision.

Catholic Bishops' opacity on this score may illuminate the Corbett court's sense of the constraint of precedent. One interpretation of its silence is that the court wanted to avoid foreclosing future challenges to the Rabie view on this issue. That could suggest that it meant to await the kind of accretion of authority that preceded *Boesak*'s overruling of an aspect of *Dempsey,* and wanted to avoid the appearance or reality of abrupt abrogation of the decisions of the Rabie court. A second interpretation, quite consistent with the first, is that the court wanted to avoid undercutting any of the arguments raised against *United Democratic Front,* not because it was convinced that they proved *United Democratic Front* clearly wrong but because it believed that these arguments had enough force to guide results in other, comparable contexts in which *United Democratic Front* was not directly binding. In this light, the startling abruptness of this aspect of *Catholic Bishops* would not betoken an indifference to human rights arguments—an indifference that would be quite out of kilter with the other work of the Corbett court—but rather a desire to

[92] Although the *New Nation* challenged the adequacy and fairness of these procedural steps on a number of grounds, the court rejected these attacks. *Catholic Bishops,* 1990 (1) SA at 868B–872E. Whatever the validity of these challenges, it is clear that the newspaper received notice of the impending action against it and at least some account of the Minister's reasons for considering such action, and that it responded to these notices with documentary submissions to the Minister totalling hundreds of pages. Ibid. 857H–859A.

[93] See text at n. 83 above.

explore and employ those arguments without undermining the rules of precedent, and the atmosphere of legal stability, of South African law. Fidelity to precedent in the Rabie court operated to help preserve the basis for human rights claims; in the Corbett court a similar concern constrains and even retards the flowering of the same sorts of claim.

C. The Immediate Causes of the Change in the Court's Approach

In this section I do not mean to explore the deep roots of the sentiments of South African judges for and against the emergency. That will be the focus of Chapter 6. The difference between the emergency decisions of the Rabie and Corbett courts, however, poses a question that needs to be answered before we undertake that broader inquiry. How could the same court render decisions so different? The answer is not that the Corbett court is a completely different body from the Rabie court; in fact, the great majority of the judges serving on the Corbett court during the emergency were members of the court under Rabie as well. The Corbett court is a different court, however, in the sense that the judges who have sat on its emergency cases are a very different group from those who dominated the Rabie era's emergency jurisprudence. Yet we should be wary of attributing all of the change of judicial mood to this shift in the selection of the court's panels, important as it is. South Africa has become a society in transition during the tenure of Chief Justice Corbett, and it is entirely likely that the court has been affected by the new orientation of the government.

Let us look first at the sharp change in the composition of the court's panels. With the retirement of Rabie ACJ and of Viljoen JA,[94] the emergency team's dominance was placed at risk, as only Hefer, Joubert, and Vivier JJA remained on the court. Moreover, during the Rabie years the composition of the Appellate Division had evolved, to the point that the court in early 1990 included a few liberals and quite a number of relative moderates, with the more conservative judges perhaps a minority.[95] (It is important to a full

[94] According to the lists of judges in the *South African Law Reports*, Viljoen JA retired as a full member of the court in early 1988, though he is listed as an Acting Judge of Appeal through to the end of that year.

[95] The most recent of the Corbett cases covered in this book is *Boesak*, 1990 (3) SA 661 (A), which was argued on 20 Mar. 1990. At that time, according to the Mar. 1990 issue of the *South African Law Reports*, there were 19 permanent or acting judges on the Appellate Division. Although these classifications are inevitably imprecise, the liberals of this group might have included Milne JA and two of the acting judges, Friedman AJA and Goldstone AJA (both of whom have since become full permanent members of the court). Among the relative moderates might have been Corbett CJ and Botha, E. M. Grosskopf, Hoexter, Kumleben, Smalberger, and Van Heerden JJA, as well as a third acting judge, Nicholas AJA. More conservative, but not unqualifiedly so, might have been Eksteen, F. H. Grosskopf, Nestadt, and Vivier JJA. The most solidly conservative justices would have included Hefer, Steyn, and Joubert JJA. (The remaining emergency team members on the court were Vivier, Hefer, and Joubert JJA, all at the

understanding of Rabie's role—of his attachment to law as well as his support for emergency power—to remember that, as Chief Justice, he may well have influenced the government's decisions to appoint many of these judges.)[96] Even so, the change in the court's panels goes well beyond what was dictated by the shifts in the court's membership.

There have been six emergency decisions by the Appellate Division since Corbett became chief justice. Members of the emergency team played only a small role in these cases. They did, it is true, make up a majority of the court in the first of these cases, *Visagie*, on which Hefer, Joubert, and Vivier JJA all sat. Since then, however, Hefer JA has not sat on an emergency case, while Vivier JA and Joubert JA have each sat on only one more (and not the same one).[97]

At the same time, judges who took little or no part in the emergency jurisprudence of the Rabie years have assumed a much more prominent role.[98] Corbett CJ himself, after sitting on only one emergency case during Rabie's tenure, has now served on four more. Botha, who never sat on a Rabie-era panel, has now served on three emergency cases. Kumleben, Milne, and Smalberger JJA, who also never appeared on any of the Rabie cases, despite being on the court for some or even most of the Rabie period, have now served on two cases each.[99] Two judges who disagreed in whole or in part with emergency team decisions during the Rabie era, and were not heard from thereafter, have also now served on two Corbett cases: Hoexter JA and Nestadt JA. The prominence of previously excluded judges can be measured on another index as well: not one of the judgments in any of these cases has been written by a member of the emergency team.

But the change in the Corbett court has not been from one emergency team to another. While the old emergency team has been deprived of its prominence, the Corbett court has not installed a clearly defined new team in its place.

conservative side of this spectrum.) These characterizations are based on comments of South African lawyers and my own impressions; I have been told that the Appellate Division has become the most liberal, or one of the most liberal, parts of the South African Supreme Court as a whole.

96 See Ch. 3 n. 43 above.

97 It is conceivable that the panel in *Visagie* was selected before Rabie ACJ's retirement, since panels are presumably selected at least somewhat in advance of the actual arguments. *Visagie* was not argued until 8 May 1989, however, more than three months after Rabie ACJ's retirement, and it is not clear that the usual 'lead time' is as long as this. Moreover, the panel in *Matshoba*, argued only 10 days later, contained no members of the emergency team.

98 The complete figures for judges and the number of cases on which they have served are as follows: Corbett (4), F. H. Grosskopf (3), Botha (3), E. M. Grosskopf (2), Hoexter (2), Joubert (2), Kumleben (2), Milne (2), Nestadt (2), Smalberger (2), Vivier (2), Eksteen (1), Hefer (1), Steyn (1), Van Heerden (1).

99 According to the *South African Law Reports*, Smalberger JA became a member of the court in the first quarter of 1986; Milne JA in the first quarter of 1988; and Kumleben JA in the second quarter of 1988, although he had been an acting judge earlier in this period. F. H. Grosskopf JA, who has now served on three Corbett emergency cases, also did not sit on Rabie-era cases, but he did not join the court even as an acting judge until the first quarter of 1989, during which Rabie ACJ retired.

Instead, the panels in the emergency cases heard by the Corbett court have been *both* less conservative and distinctly more representative of the court as a whole than were those of the Rabie era.[100] Every permanent member of the Appellate Division has served on at least one of these six emergency cases, all argued during Corbett's first fifteen months as chief justice. All but four members of the court have served on at least two of these cases.[101] Rabie presided over the Appellate Division from the time an emergency was first declared in 1985 until the end of January 1989, and during all that time there were six permanent members of the court who never found their way on to an emergency panel.[102] Moreover, although some judges have served more than others during Corbett's era, their relative role in these six cases is much less dominant than the role of the emergency team members in the first cases of the Rabie period.[103] It may well be, as a result, that the Corbett decisions

[100] The composition of internal security case panels in general (as categorized in the *South African Law Reports*) appears to resemble that of the emergency cases in particular (not surprisingly, since emergency cases make up much of this category). Kidd's data (covering the period up to May 1990), supplemented with the data for *Boesak*, demonstrate that only two members of the court had not sat on at least two out of the ten cases in this category, and these two (Eksteen JA and Friedman AJA) do not fall into a single political grouping. See M. Kidd, 'Internal Security and Specialist Judges: A Study of the Composition of the Appellate Division Bench in Internal Security Cases from 1986 to the Present', 6 *SAJHR* 417, 421, 423 (Table B). While certain important cases not falling in this classification, but involving closely related concerns, have been decided by notably liberal panels, see *S.* v. *Toms*; *S.* v. *Bruce*, 1990 (2) SA 802 (A) (Corbett CJ, Botha, Kumleben, and Smalberger JJA, and Nicholas AJA); *S.* v. *Malindi and Others*, 1990 (1) SA 962 (A) (same panel as in *Toms*); *S.* v. *Malinde* [sic] *and Others*, 1990 (1) SA 57 (A) (panel of Corbett CJ, Botha JA, and Nicholas AJA) (a procedural decision in the *Malindi* appeal just cited), there appears to be no core group which plays the consistent, numerically dominant role that the emergency team did in the Rabie-era emergency cases.

[101] Three of the four judges who have sat only once are among the more conservative members of the court (Hefer, Steyn, and Eksteen JJA). Other relatively conservative judges have served twice or even three times, however, while the fourth of the one-case judges, Van Heerden JA, is not on the conservative side of the court's spectrum. Moreover, a single additional case could alter the current picture substantially.

[102] See Ch. 3, text at n. 35 above, for data on the judges' service on emergency cases during the Rabie era. Those who did not sit on a single case, but were permanent members of the court during all or part of the period from 1986 onward, when all of the Rabie-era emergency decisions were rendered, were Botha JA (on the court throughout this period); Jacobs JA (on the court from 1986–8); Kumleben JA (a full member of the court beginning in the second quarter of 1988); Milne JA (on the court from the first quarter of 1988); Smalberger JA (on the court throughout this period); and Trengrove JA (on the court throughout 1986). Two acting judges, Nicholas and Galgut, also did not sit during Rabie's tenure; no acting judge has sat on an emergency case during Corbett's tenure either.

[103] In the first 6 Corbett emergency cases, 11 judges have sat at least twice, and of these only 3 have sat more than twice (F. H. Grosskopf and Botha JJA three times each, and Corbett CJ four times). In the first 7 Rabie cases (I use 7, rather than 6, because the last two of these cases, *Release Mandela Campaign* and *United Democratic Front*, were heard and decided by the same panel in the same period), Rabie himself sat in every case, Hefer JA in 5, and Joubert, Viljoen, and Vivier JJA in 4 each. Two other judges, Van Heerden and E. M. Grosskopf JJA, sat in 3 each, and no one else sat in more than one. In two pairs of the Corbett cases, three judges from one of the pair have also been on the panel of the other. These were *Mathebe* and *Argus*, in both of which Corbett CJ, F. H. Grosskopf JA, and Smalberger JA sat, and *Matshoba* and *Boesak*, in both of which Botha, E. M. Grosskopf, and Milne JJA sat. Obviously, the judges in common from the first pair are entirely different from the judges in common on the second.

do not represent so unitary a vision as the Rabie court's judgments did. What we see in the Corbett cases, therefore, is the pull of different judges' philosophies as well as of the different elements in the thinking of a single group of men.

We may be seeing, in addition, the influence of the dramatic recent changes in South African politics. The first intimations of these changes were being felt even as Corbett took office, for in early 1989 emergency detainees began a bold campaign of hunger strikes against their detention. Hunger strikes were not a new tactic, but in 1989 they suddenly became a powerful source of pressure on the state. For a number of reasons—among them the absence of then-State President P. W. Botha, who had been incapacitated by a stroke—the government adopted a conciliatory position towards the hunger strikes and within a matter of months had released hundreds of long-term detainees. Though the detainees' freedom was bittersweet, limited as it often was by harsh restriction orders, none the less their victory was palpable.

Meanwhile the National Party began throwing off the influence of P. W. Botha. Botha, while still remaining State President, chose to step down as head of the party, and F. W. de Klerk won this post over Botha's candidate. Quickly the presence of different men as State President and head of the National Party became untenable, and later in 1989 P. W. Botha was eased (none too easily) out of office and F. W. de Klerk took his place. Black organizations meanwhile took advantage of the stirrings of reform sentiment to begin mobilizing again, despite the continuing presence of the state of emergency.

Under its new leadership the National Party won re-election from the white electorate. Though the very conservative Conservative Party increased its strength, the government chose to see the election as a victory for the forces of reform (among whom it classed its erstwhile liberal opposition, the Democratic Party). Then, faster than most people might have dreamt, came more substantial changes, as the government loosened the state of emergency, legalized the African National Congress and other organizations, and finally freed Nelson Mandela. By doing so the government set in motion the process of 'talks about talks' and now, it appears, of negotiations themselves. In June 1990 the government lifted the state of emergency except in the province of Natal, and in October 1990 the state of emergency in Natal came to an end too.[104] In August 1990, in an agreement with the African National Congress known as the Pretoria Minute, the government committed itself to amnesty and indemnity for a wide range of political offences, and promised to 'give immediate consideration' to repealing certain provisions of the Internal Security Act. For its part the African National Congress formally suspended its armed struggle.[105] The stage seems at last to be set for negotiations about a post-apartheid South Africa—though even now, in mid-1991, obstacles remain,

[104] See Ch. 1, text at nn. 63–7 above.

[105] See Lawyers' Committee for Civil Rights Under Law, *Update on the Transition Process—Paper III: The Pretoria Minute and Working Group Report of August 6, 1990* (14 Aug. 1990).

including sad and widespread violence that has involved both competing black political and ethnic groups and the government's police and armed forces.

In one sense, none of this exciting political movement bears directly on the decisions of the Appellate Division in state-of-emergency cases, for all of these cases have arisen under the emergency regulations of years gone by. But the members of the Appellate Division have surely seen in these events the government's adoption of a strategy of negotiation and liberalization in place of the much more authoritarian mode of previous years. It seems entirely likely that this sense of opening in the society at large has touched a responsive chord among the judges as well. We need now to understand the genesis of that responsive chord, and more generally to understand the sources of the judicial attitudes which the members of the Appellate Division have expressed, in varying voices and intensities, under both Chief Justice Rabie and Chief Justice Corbett.

6

Explaining the Court's Performance: Visions of Law in South Africa

The past isn't dead. It isn't even past.[1]

We must explain the actions of two courts—very similar in membership, but very different in performance. We have already seen the immediate sources of the difference between the two. The Rabie court, so far as the emergency was concerned, was decisively dominated by the five members of the emergency team. It is these judges' jurisprudence, developed in a period of stern government repression directed against what was seen as total onslaught, that we must explain. The emergency jurisprudence of the Corbett court, on the other hand, is much more the work of the Appellate Division as a whole, and it is work carried on in a time of both continued government repression and hesitant, but gathering, hope of broad racial reconciliation in South Africa.

The Rabie court's protection of emergency power is patent, and yet, as we have seen, not altogether without limits. Perhaps what is at first blush most surprising about this performance is, that there were any limits at all, and I believe we must therefore ask why the Rabie court was not worse. As we will see, courts, and the countries of which they are a part, can be worse than the Appellate Division and South Africa were, even in the darkest days of the emergency. I will argue that South Africa was *not* worse in good part because a widely shared sentiment of white South African culture, evident in the Appellate Division but echoed and buttressed in the society at large, accepted adherence to law as an important value. The reasons for this adherence to law are complex and not always edifying, but the adherence is real and its impact on the court and the country real as well. The decisions of the Rabie court attest to this adherence, though they suggest as well the limits of legality's grip on South African thinking.

When we turn to the Corbett court, we must explain why, in the midst of South African oppression, the country's highest court charted a course of moderate, albeit hardly radical, improvements in South African emergency law. It might have turned out that the rest of the Appellate Division saw emergency issues just as the Rabie court's emergency team had. This proved

[1] W. Faulkner, *Requiem for a Nun* (New York: Random House, 1951), 92.

not to be the case, and I will argue that a crucial reason for the better performance of the Corbett court is that South African legal institutions provided support for a strain of legal thinking that was decidedly concerned not only with adherence to law but also with protection of rights. Moreover, unlike antislavery jurisprudence in the pre-Civil War United States, this mode of legal reasoning remained well established in legal culture and compatible with accepted jurisprudential premisses, and this foundation lessened whatever tension judges might otherwise have seen between their more liberal aspirations and their duties as judges. Concern for human rights has by no means dominated South African law, and no doubt that reality goes far to explain the moderation of the Corbett court's legal reforms, but, again, such concern is real and its effects have been felt.

Thus the explanation of the Appellate Division's performance that I propose is a story of the force of visions of the rule of law, whether as a mandate for government by law or as a call, in addition, for government that respects its subjects' rights. This account links the particular decisions of this group of men to the larger features of their culture. This is not a venture in which we can hope for absolute certainty. To confirm this theory more conclusively would ultimately require the nuanced detail of biographical studies of the individual judges. Even then, the task of understanding would rest on the sureness of empathy and inference rather than on ineluctable logic. Moreover, these empathetic perceptions would be guided, explicitly or implicitly, by the biographers' sense of what to look for, and so I am offering an explanation which I hope will play its part in future inquiry. In the mean time, the strength of this cultural explanation on its own lies in its capacity to illuminate what we know of both the particular cases and the broader society. The residual concern for the preservation of a legal order which the Rabie court judgments display fits with the legalism of South African white society; the Corbett court's greater attention to human rights likewise fits with the relatively liberal thinking long nurtured within the South African legal profession. Thus cultural explanation, in short, reveals a coherence between two quite different sets of data, and that coherence suggests the value of the cultural account.

I do not want to make this story a happier one that it really is. South Africa has been and still is a profoundly unjust society, which in both its ordinary laws and its emergency regulations deprives its people of countless protections which have been associated with the emotive concept of the rule of law. But that is precisely why understanding the force of the rule of law in South Africa is important. In seeking this understanding we are asking what the rule of law can mean, not in a society where its protections are so firm that they are taken for granted, but in one where they are still very much in dispute and in jeopardy. We are asking, too, what cultural and institutional factors might contribute to the sustenance of concern for law and even human rights in the midst of great injustice. I will close the chapter by suggesting the lessons which this examination of South African experience carries for the protection of human rights not only in South Africa but also in other countries now, or yet to be, under profound stress.

A. The Rabie Court: Adherence to Law in South African Culture

The Rabie court affirmed the legal underpinnings of the sweeping emergency powers claimed by the government beginning in 1985. It did so out of a perception that the nation faced a genuine emergency, a genuine onslaught on its fundamental social order, and out of trust in the good faith of the government officials who were trying to meet this crisis, and out of sympathy for the difficulties of the front-line officers who were deployed against it. Given these perceptions, it was not surprising that the court would broadly support executive authority; its doing so was consistent with the Appellate Division's own history and with the behaviour of judiciaries elsewhere in comparable circumstances. Indeed, the court might have done worse; some courts have. That the Rabie court did no worse than it did requires explanation.

1. The Court's Performance in Comparative Perspective

Whether or not the Rabie court manifested a genuine adherence to law, it certainly manifested a genuine support for the powers the government exercised under the state of emergency. In doing so, as we have seen, the Rabie court was frequently on thin, or cracking, doctrinal ice, but it must be said that the court was not out of line with an important aspect of South African legal tradition. Writing of the Appellate Division from 1910 to 1950, Hugh Corder has traced the court's reaction to cases of 'resistance and rebellion'. He finds in the court's decisions in this sphere 'a strong tendency to uphold state authority'.[2] Christopher Forsyth, considering the Appellate Division's attitudes towards security legislation in the years 1950 to 1980, concludes that 'the court has, throughout the period under review, shown, in general, a considerable preference for the executive interest over that of the individual'.[3] We need not measure the precise force of this tradition to suspect that similar sentiments help explain the decisions of lower courts during the 1960 state of emergency that offered support for a broad view of executive emergency powers.[4] Actually, the Rabie court adopted a characterization of these powers that was decidedly *narrower* than one of these earlier cases had endorsed.[5]

[2] H. Corder, *Judges at Work: The Role and Attitudes of the South African Appellate Judiciary, 1910–50* (Cape Town: Juta, 1984), 224; see ibid. 91–2.

[3] C. Forsyth, *In Danger for their Talents: A Study of the Appellate Division of the Supreme Court of South Africa from 1950–80* (Cape Town: Juta, 1985), 178.

[4] See *R.* v. *Maphumolo and Others*, 1960 (3) SA 793 (N); *Stanton* v. *Minister of Justice and Others*, 1960 (3) SA 353 (T); *Ex parte Hathorn: In re O.C., Durban Prison Command and Another*, 1960 (2) SA 767 (D). A case that did circumscribe the state's authority during this emergency was *Brink and Others* v. *Commissioner of Police*, 1960 (3) SA 65 (T).

[5] See Ch. 3, text at nn. 155–61, above.

Similarly, it must be said that the Rabie court's deference to executive emergency authority resembled the positions taken in prominent decisions of other courts, in countries such as the United States and Britain. In the United States, for example, local governments coping with urban riots in the 1960s 'not infrequent[ly]' imposed curfews or other emergency measures in response.[6] The mayor of Milwaukee, Wisconsin, confined all city residents except 'doctors, nurses and others performing essential services' to their homes for twenty-six hours, with two brief pauses to permit food shopping.[7] Riot curfews were 'generally upheld' by the courts.[8] The mayor of Philadelphia proclaimed a state of emergency pursuant to a local ordinance after the assassination of Martin Luther King, Jr., and banned almost all types of outdoor gatherings of twelve or more persons. Although the United States Constitution contains no explicit, general authorization of emergency invasions of constitutional rights,[9] the Supreme Court found that an appeal challenging arrests under this state of emergency did not present a substantial federal question.[10]

Two cases exemplify the furthest extensions of such deference by the Supreme Court. In one, *Ex parte McCardle*,[11] the Supreme Court gave broad effect to what it saw as an 'ouster clause' authorization, contained in the constitution itself, which granted Congress the power to make exceptions from the Supreme Court's appellate jurisdication.[12] The court held that this clause authorized Congress to divest it of jurisdiction over a habeas corpus appeal which would have called into question the constitutionality of the post-Civil-War military governments in the Southern states. The court accepted its loss of jurisdiction in this case despite the fact that the ouster statute in question became law only after the court had heard oral argument! *McCardle*'s meaning remains ambiguous, in part because Congress had not eliminated an alternative procedural path to the Supreme Court.[13] Moreover, the lower federal courts were not divested of their habeas jurisdiction.[14] None the less it is clear that ouster is not wholly alien to United States law.

[6] Comment, 'The Riot Curfew', 57 *Calif. L. Rev.* 450, 461 (1969).

[7] Ibid. 464.

[8] Note, 'Assessing the Scope of Minors' Fundamental Rights: Juvenile Curfews and the Constitution', 97 *Harv. L. Rev.* 1163, 1164 n. 7 (1984).

[9] See S. Ellmann, 'A Constitution for All Seasons: Providing Against Emergencies in a Post-Apartheid Constitution', 21 *Colum. HRLR* 163, 172–3 (1989).

[10] *Stotland* v. *Pennsylvania*, 398 US 916 (1970) (dismissing appeal for want of a substantial federal question). Such a dismissal, issued without full briefing and argument, carries less precedential weight than a decision rendered after plenary consideration, and might even reflect a tacit, discretionary desire not to hear the case rather than solely an assessment of its merits. None the less such a dismissal is a judgment on the merits. See P. Bator, P. Mishkin, D. Shapiro, and H. Wechsler, *Hart and Wechsler's The Federal Courts and the Federal System* (Mineola, NY: Foundation Press, 2nd edn., 1973), 648–9.

[11] *Ex parte McCardle*, 74 US (7 Wall.) 506 (1869).

[12] US Const., art. III, s. 2, cl. 2.

[13] *Ex parte McCardle*, 74 US (7 Wall.) 506, 515 (1869).

[14] For an analysis of the relevant statutes, see Van Alstyne, 'A Critical Guide to *Ex Parte McCardle*', 15 *Ariz. L. Rev.* 229, 233–42 (1973).

In the second of the cases, *Korematsu* v. *United States*,[15] the court did have jurisdiction; what has made this case notorious is the court's decision on the merits. The case grew out of the decision by Second World War military authorities to exclude from the Pacific Coast area all people of Japanese descent, including American citizens, and to confine many of them in internment camps. The Supreme Court upheld the constitutionality of Korematsu's conviction for disobeying an exclusion order.[16] I do not mean to suggest that every American emergency decision has been so accepting of executive power, for in fact there have been important decisions that did constrain emergency authority,[17] but it is plain that broad deference to the executive is not incompatible with American legal practices.

In Britain, the Second World War decision of *Liversidge* v. *Anderson*[18] reflected such intense judicial concern for the exigencies of the war that it well deserved to become, as it did, a basis for executive-minded decisionmaking in South Africa. In that case, the House of Lords decided that a regulation permitting the Secretary of State to detain anyone whom he had 'reasonable cause to believe' satisfied certain criteria actually meant that the Secretary could detain anyone of whom the Secretary in good faith *thought* there was reasonable cause.[19] *En route* to this conclusion, Viscount Maugham declared that the rule that ambiguous legislation should be construed *in favorem libertatis* 'has "no relevance in dealing with an executive measure by way of preventing a public danger"' when the safety of the state is involved.[20] The sole dissenter, Lord Atkin, did not take issue with this proposition,[21] though he did sharply

[15] *Korematsu* v. *United States*, 323 US 214 (1944).

[16] The majority declined to address in *Korematsu* most aspects of the constitutionality of detentions which followed on the exclusions, *Korematsu* v. *United States*, 323 US 214, 221–3 (1944), although two dissenters argued that the detentions were part and parcel of the programme to which Korematsu had been subjected. Ibid. 226–30 (Roberts J. dissenting); ibid. 243 (Jackson J. dissenting). Clearly more uncomfortable about the detentions than about the exclusions by themselves, the court ordered the freeing of a detainee in another case decided the same day, *Ex parte Endo*, 323 US 283 (1944). Four decades later the United States apologized for its wartime treatment of people of Japanese ancestry, and authorized payments in restitution to the victims. See 50 USCA ss. 1989*a*(*a*), 1989*b* to 1989*b*-8 (Supp. 1989).

[17] See e.g. *Youngstown Sheet & Tube Co.* v. *Sawyer*, 343 US 579 (1952) (invalidating President Truman's seizure of most of the nation's steel plants, despite the President's contention that the seizure was necessary to forestall a strike that would directly jeopardize the war effort in Korea). For a discussion of other Supreme Court decisions limiting emergency authority, see Ellmann, 'Constitution' (cit. n. 9), 176–7.

[18] *Liversidge* v. *Anderson*, [1942] AC 206 (HL).

[19] Ibid. 219–20 (judgment of Viscount Maugham).

[20] Ibid. 218–19 (judgment of Viscount Maugham), quoting *R.* v. *Halliday*, [1917] AC 260, 270 (HL). Lord MacMillan, who concurred in Maugham's interpretation of the regulation, offered a somewhat different interpretive guide-line. He appeared to say both that courts should be more vigilant than usual in wartime to be sure that 'the law is duly observed, especially in a matter so fundamental as the liberty of the subject', and that since laws should be interpreted so as to realize their objects, 'it is right so to interpret emergency legislation as to promote rather than to defeat its efficacy for the defence of the realm'. Ibid. 251–2 (judgment of Lord MacMillan). See also ibid. 260–1 (judgment of Lord Wright).

[21] Ibid. 238–9, 244 (dissenting judgment of Lord Atkin).

attack 'the attitude of judges who on a mere question of interpretation when face to face with claims involving the liberty of the subject show themselves more executive minded than the executive'.[22] While it is Lord Atkin's strong dissent that has stood the test of time,[23] again it is clear that British legal practices could encompass very broad deference to the executive.[24]

There are, indeed, strong pressures on judges to reach such decisions as these. An emergency exists—or is said to, and said by the senior officials of the state. It places the nation in danger. It must be dealt with by the political authorities of the country, for certainly the courts are in no position to undertake the task. The judges are part of this state, presumably drawn from the ranks of its more powerful and privileged citizens, and no doubt owing their appointment directly or indirectly to the trust and confidence of the governing authorities, the very authorities who now see themselves facing emergency. It is not to be expected that judges would lightly cast aside the account of the necessities of the emergency which their government puts before them. Presumably this pressure is one of the factors which make emergency rule so attractive to so many governments; in 1978 at least a fifth of all the world's countries were in states of emergency.[25]

None of this means that the Rabie court's decisions were inevitable. The court might have done better, as the Corbett court has. But it might also have done worse, as the German judiciary did. The behaviour of the German judiciary, which as late as 1933 could be said to have 'some serious claims to be regarded as the best in Europe',[26] deserves our attention as a measure of what might have been in South Africa. Later in this chapter we will look more closely at some of the underlying causes of the differences between South African and German judicial conduct;[27] here, it will suffice simply to sketch what German courts and judges did. 1933 was an extraordinary year for German law, a year in which law was put to the service of injustice in staggering ways. The day after the Reichstag fire, 28 February 1933, the Nazis promulgated the 'Decree for the Protection of the People and the State', which invoked the emergency provision of the constitution to annul 'almost all of

[22] *Liversidge* v. *Anderson* [1942] AC at 244 (dissenting judgment of Lord Atkin).

[23] On the subsequent rejection of the majority position, see Ch. 2, n. 123 above.

[24] For an effort to identify the conservative and libertarian attitudes 'towards order and order-maintenance' that underlie British and American free speech law, see R. Gordon, 'Law and Disorder', 64 *Ind. LJ* 803 (1989).

[25] International Commission of Jurists, *States of Emergency: Their Impact on Human Rights* (Geneva: International Commission of Jurists, 1983), 413; see Ellmann, 'Constitution' (cit. n. 9), 167–9.

[26] R. Ensor, *Courts and Judges in France, Germany, and England* (London: Oxford University Press, 1933), 52. Ensor concluded his book with the observation that '[a]t the time of going to press, German politics appear to have crossed the frontier between legality and revolution; and it would be unfair to estimate the normal working of a judicature by what may conceivably happen under revolutionary conditions.' Ibid. 141.

[27] See text at nn. 176–98, 297, 328–34 below.

the basic rights' which the constitution safeguarded.[28] Yet '[o]nly a few weeks after Hitler had abrogated the most important basic rights enshrined in the Constitution, and only a few days after the Nazis had terrorized their political opponents, the Confederation of German Judges declared "its full trust in the Government".'[29] On 7 April 1933, the Nazis adopted the 'Law for Restoration of the Professional Civil Service', a law which 'decree[d] the permanent removal from the civil service of all judges and other officials who were Jews, Social Democrats or otherwise "politically unreliable"'.[30] The judiciary's response to this fateful purge was, in the words of one German scholar, 'servile'.[31]

Even this kowtowing was not, it seems, enough to win Hitler's trust,[32] and the Nazis carried out the worst of their oppression outside the domain of the traditional courts and even of law, through 'the special non-judicial courts, the Gestapo, S.S., and S.A., and concentration camps'.[33] The German judges at least to some extent acquiesced in the shaping of this new machinery of oppression. John Dugard cites an instance in which a German court 'ruled that the orders and actions of the Gestapo were not subject to judicial review'.[34] Müller comments more sweepingly that '[t]he police on the one hand and scholars and administrators of the law on the other agreed that political matters should not come under review by the courts.'[35]

In many of the cases which did come before them, moreover, German judges lent their considerable ingenuity to the task of interpreting German law in the service of Nazi obsessions. So, for example, the German scholar Udo Reifner describes a case in which a court avoided an argument that a law forbidding sexual relations between Jews and 'Aryans' applied only to conduct in Germany by reasoning that 'Germany' exists wherever two Germans

[28] I. Müller, *Hitler's Justice: The Courts of the Third Reich*, trans. D. Schneider (Cambridge, Mass.: Harvard University Press, 1991), 29.

[29] L. Fernandez, 'The Law, Lawyers and the Courts in Nazi Germany', 1 *SAJHR* 124, 129 (1985).

[30] Müller, *Hitler's Justice* (cit. n. 28), 37.

[31] Ibid. Müller reports that a leader of the German judiciary named Linz met Hitler on the day this law was promulgated, and announced after his meeting: 'We have placed everything in his hands with complete confidence. The chancellor [Hitler] was clearly in agreement with out [sic] remarks and assured us that he would continue to maintain the independence of judges, even though certain measures would be necessary. We may therefore rest assured that the regulations contained in the law on the civil service will be dropped again as soon as possible.' Ibid. 'These servile words', Müller writes, 'were the extent of the protest ventured by the Federation of Judges on the removal from office of its numerous Jewish members—643 in Prussia alone.' Ibid. Apparently, however, the same group did later respond to a Nazi 'Boycott Day' of attacks on Jews by asking Hitler 'to allow their Jewish colleagues to resume their work'. U. Reifner, 'The Bar in the Third Reich: Anti-Semitism and the Decline of Liberal Advocacy', 32 *McGill L. Rev.* 96, 122 (1986).

[32] See ibid. 129–30; M. Osiel, 'Sources of Judicial Resistance to Oppressive Law: A Sociological Reappraisal of the Hart/Fuller Debate' (unpubl., Nov. 1988), 41–3.

[33] Ibid. 37; D. Richards, 'Terror and the Law', 5 *HRQ* 171, 180 (1983).

[34] J. Dugard, 'The Judiciary in a State of National Crisis: With Special Reference to the South African Experience', 44 *Wash. and Lee L. Rev.* 477, 484 n. 43 (1987). See also Müller, *Hitler's Justice* (cit. n. 28), 47.

[35] Ibid. 49.

commit this crime—including, apparently, Prague. This ludicrous reasoning carried with it the death penalty.[36] In another case under the same law, the Hamburg County Court considered two young people's relationship 'so grave and vile that no mitigating circumstances can be found. It is a prime example of Jewish effrontery, Jewish contempt for German laws, Jewish lasciviousness, and Jewish unscrupulousness'.[37] Dugard characterizes the judges' conduct as closer to 'collaboration' than 'abstention'.[38] Contemporary German scholars, who are opening up this obscured chapter of German legal history, might be even more harsh in their judgments.[39]

Examples of judicial subservience to oppressive governments are by no means confined to Nazi Germany. In Pinochet's Chile, a team of human rights observers 'found no reason to question' the view 'that, at least in those cases that matter to the military government, most Chilean judges—and certainly the Supreme Court—can be counted on to do the government's bidding'.[40] Of over 10,000 petitions for the release of prisoners filed during a thirteen-year period, only three achieved even 'a small measure of success'.[41] In Argentina, the military dismissed approximately 80 per cent of the judges, and required those who remained to take loyalty oaths.[42] Surprisingly, the Argentine courts on a number of scores adopted a critical, though sympathetic, stance towards the regime.[43] In certain respects, however, their performance has been sternly criticized. Thus, while Argentina was notorious for the many people who 'disappeared' when the country was under military rule, Alejandro Garro wrote in 1983 that '[n]ot even one out of the many thousands of petitions for habeas corpus has succeeded in recovering a missing person alive.'[44]

[36] Reifner, 'Bar in the Third Reich' (cit. n. 31), 101.

[37] The court's judgment is quoted in Müller, *Hitler's Justice* (cit. n. 28), 104.

[38] Dugard, 'Judiciary in Crisis' (cit. n. 34), 484. For similar judgments, see Fernandez, 'Law, Lawyers' (cit. n. 29), 130 (observing that '[o]n the whole, judges were wont to interpret racially discriminatory laws even more extensively than the regime expected them to'), and Richards, 'Terror' (cit. n. 33), 180 (characterizing the judiciary as 'completely subserved to party aims').

[39] For examples of this scholarship in English, see Müller, *Hitler's Justice* (cit. n. 28); Reifner, 'Bar in the Third Reich' (cit. n. 31); A. Kaufmann, 'National Socialism and German Jurisprudence from 1933 to 1945', 9 *Cardozo L. Rev.* 1629 (1988); M. Reimann, 'National Socialist Jurisprudence and Academic Continuity: A Comment on Professor Kaufmann's Article', 9 *Cardozo L. Rev.* 1651 (1988). See also D. Vagts, 'International Law in the Third Reich', 84 *Am. J. Int. L.* 661 (1990).

[40] W. Zabel, D. Orentlicher, and D. Nachman, 'Human Rights and the Administration of Justice in Chile: Report of a Delegation of the Association of the Bar of the City of New York and of the International Bar Association', 42 *Assoc. of the Bar Record* 431, 439 (1987).

[41] Ibid. 465.

[42] S. Klitzman, 'Judicial Process: Defending Lawyers, Judges, and the Rule of Law', 31 *Federal Bar News and Journal* 219, 221 (1984).

[43] See Osiel, 'Sources' (cit. n. 32), 47–70.

[44] A. Garro, 'The Role of the Argentine Judiciary in Controlling Governmental Action under a State of Siege', 4 *HRLJ* 311, 335 (1983). Another Argentinian lawyer calls the judges' failure to exercise their investigatory powers in habeas corpus cases 'the major contributing factor in the establishment of the methodology of 6,000–20,000 "disappearances" as a means to control political opposition'. J. Mendéz, 'Some Patterns of Violation of the Independence of Judges and Lawyers', 76 *Am. Soc. Int. L. Proc.* 316, 319 (1982).

Various Communist countries have also thoroughly undermined the independence of the judiciary. Richard Neumann has eloquently written of the compromised character of the judiciary in East Central Europe. Throughout this area, when a judge was said to have received 'a telephone call', everyone knew from whom the call had come and what its purpose was.[45] In China, Hiroshi Oda reports, the Cultural Revolution 'attacked the law and the legal system as a whole.... Instructions were given by Mao to smash the *Gongjianfa*, which consisted of the police, the courts, and the Procuracy.'[46] Decades after the Cultural Revolution, courts in China are obliged in certain cases 'to request the instruction of superior Party committees'—a reform of an earlier, long-standing 'practice of preliminary review of court judgments by the local party committees'.[47] An unwritten rule called 'five major rejections' bars courts from accepting various types of cases, including (with some exceptions) 'suits against the state for infringement of a citizen's rights of [sic] interests'.[48] Meanwhile, in North Korea, 'little information on the legal system is available because it currently is classified'![49] In short, a range of regimes, using a variety of mechanisms, have profoundly undercut the potential value of the courts as protectors of their people.

2. The Sources of South African Whites' Adherence to Law

To explain fully why South Africa has not travelled very far down such routes as these would call for a study going vastly beyond the focus on the legal system which is this book's concern. One part of the explanation, however, is our concern. As we saw when we looked at the cases decided by the Rabie court, its decisions exhibited not just a disapproval of abuse, a stance which might be rooted much more in moral than legal principle, but also a determination to preserve a legal order in South Africa and a concomitant desire to preserve the institutional role of the courts. I suggest that these characteristics of the Rabie court reflect the broad acceptance of the importance of adherence to the law among the white citizens who rule South Africa. Because

[45] R. Neumann, 'From an Insurrection' *Yale J. L. and Human.* 157, 171 (1991). For an explication of the 'clearly subservient position' of the judges in Poland, see S. Frankowski, 'The Procuracy and the Regular Courts as the Palladium of Individual Rights and Liberties: The Case of Poland', 61 *Tul. L. Rev.* 1307, 1323–35, 1338 (1987). For a detailed, and trenchant, analysis of the East German legal system, see Otto Kirchheimer's chapter on '"Democratic Centralism" and Political Integration of the Judiciary' in his *Political Justice: The Use of Legal Procedure for Political Ends* (Westport, Conn.: Greenwood Press, 1980), 259–303. The telephone is useful elsewhere as well; the Inter-American Commission on Human Rights of the Organization of American States found 'justice by phone' and other forms of executive control of the judges in Paraguay: *Annual Report of the Inter-American Commission on Human Rights 1979–1980* (Washington, DC: Organization of American States, 1980), 117.

[46] H. Oda, 'The Procuracy and the Regular Courts as Enforcers of the Constitutional Rule of Law: The Experience of East Asian States', 61 *Tul. L. Rev.* 1339, 1346 (1987).

[47] Ibid. 1361. Apparently Vietnam and North Korea also provide for Party oversight of the courts. Ibid.

[48] Ibid. 1348.

[49] Ibid. 1352.

those who have governed South Africa for the past forty years have predominantly been Afrikaners, and because the members of the emergency team (Rabie ACJ and Viljoen, Joubert, Vivier, and Hefer JJA) were all Afrikaners, it is worth making clear that adherence to the law is valued on both sides of the deep ethnic divide within the white community of South Africa, that is, among South African whites of both Afrikaner and English-speaking backgrounds.[50] (Approximately 1.7 million of South Africa's 4.9 million whites are part of the English-speaking community.)[51] Adherence to law has deep roots among South African blacks too,[52] and blacks outnumber whites in South Africa by more than five to one,[53] but because the apparatus of emergency law has been constructed and maintained by whites, it is whites' legal culture on which we need to focus here.

That South African whites do consider adherence to the law important is suggested both by what their leaders say and by how they govern. What their leaders say is exemplified by the comments of H. J. Coetsee, the Minister of Justice, while dedicating a new police station and magistrates' court in January 1986. The *Los Angeles Daily Journal* reported: '"Our legal system cannot be outclassed," Coetsee said. He added, "The truth is there are no courts anywhere in the world whose judges' and magistrates' integrity is higher than ours."'[54] Later that year Louis le Grange, then the Minister of Law and Order, discussed the government's reaction to judicial decisions against its positions: 'Where a court, for example, points out a deficiency in a regulation, the executive authority sees it as a guideline and new regulations are not intended as a clash with the court's standpoint or judgment, but rather as a

[50] I do not mean to suggest, or imply, that all Afrikaners are conservatives or devotees of white supremacy, or that all conservatives or whites supremacists are Afrikaners. Neither generalization is true. As Allister Sparks tellingly points out, it was English-speaking whites of southern Africa who led Rhodesia into a bitter war in their desperation to stave off black rule. A. Sparks, *The Mind of South Africa* (New York: Knopf, 1990), 49–50.

[51] Ibid. 47.

[52] Allister Sparks comments that early white travellers in what would become South Africa 'were impressed ... with the application of the rule of law through a sophisticated court system presided over by the chiefs but in which the chiefs themselves were beneath the law and could be tried and fined by their own councillors'. Ibid. 15. According to Albie Sachs, '[t]he ease with which Africans in the Cape adapted themselves to British-type courts came as a surprise to many persons unacquainted with African traditional legal procedures.' A 19th-century observer considered 'the ordinary native ... far superior, as a rule, to the ordinary European in the witness box', and attributed this ability to what Albie Sachs calls the 'popular participation in the traditional African lawsuits': *Justice in South Africa* (Berkeley, Calif.: University of California Press, 1973), 96–7. For discussion of the extent to which Africans' long-standing appreciation of the value of law now carries over to acceptance of the legal order which whites have constructed in South Africa, see text at nn. 83–96 below.

[53] The South African Institute of Race Relations estimates the total 1988 population of South Africa (including the so-called 'independent homelands' of Transkei, Bophuthatswana, Venda, and Ciskei) as 35,978,284 people, including approximately 26,974,284 Africans (74.9% of the total), 928,000 Asians (2.6%), 3,127,000 'Coloureds' (8.7%), and 4,949,000 whites (13.8%). C. Cooper *et al.*, *Race Relations Survey 1988/89* (Johannesburg: South African Institute of Race Relations, 1989), 149.

[54] K. Jost, 'S. African Judges Test Their Power Against State Fiat', *Los Angeles Daily Journal*, 1 (7 Feb. 1986).

supplement to fill the gap in line with the finding.'[55] We need not take the sincerity of these statements for granted to recognize that the politicians who give voice to them *at least* believe that what they are saying will be well received by some portion of their audience.

Perhaps a clearer measure of South Africa's adherence to law is its intense use of it. Compared to other tyrants, Joseph Lelyveld writes, 'South Africa's white rulers have been unusually conscientious about securing statutory authority for their abuses'[56]—although this tendency is less unusual than Lelyveld suggests, for it has been noted repeatedly in other places as well.[57] In the words of the historian Martin Chanock, '[t]he oppressions of apartheid have, until the beginnings of its disintegration, characteristically been imposed not by the random terror of the death squad, but by the routine and systematic processes of courts and bureaucrats.'[58] Not all South African governance has been by legal processes, to be sure. Detainees have been tortured and killed, and at least since the 1980s death squads have indeed been set up and done their vicious work. Even these descents into illegality, however, do not completely escape the realm of law. The death squads became the subject of an investigatory commission consisting of a judge of the Supreme Court (though its results were inconclusive).[59] Similarly, despite the recurrent, brutal treatment of detainees, Allister Sparks observes that:

> after all this concealment and remoteness from the protection of the law, if anyone should die in this brutal and secret process, as many have, an inquest is held in open court where often the most horrifying details become public. In the end the police are always exonerated by the state-employed magistrates who preside over these inquests, but the disclosures are hugely embarrassing nonetheless. Thus a brutal authoritarianism presents periodic glimpses into its own gulag.[60]

[55] South African Press Association, 'Courts are independent' (18 Oct. 1986), (copy on file with author).

[56] J. Lelyveld, *Move Your Shadow: South Africa, Black and White* (New York: Times Books, 1985), 81.

[57] Thomas Friedman finds a similar phenomenon in Israel, in *From Beirut to Jurusalem* (New York: Farrar Straus Giroux, 1989), 352–60. Observers have pointed to the 'punctiliousness' of Pinochet Chile's adherence to 'the forms of legality'. Zabel, Orentlicher, and Nachman, 'Human Rights in Chile' (cit. n. 40), 436. Joan Hartman has commented that '[o]ne of the most disturbing and yet fascinating aspects of thoroughly oppressive states of emergency is the regime's typical effort to cloak repressive policies with the trappings of legality and officiality through the issuance of minutely detailed and prolix "decree-laws."' 'Book Review' (of International Commission of Jurists, *States of Emergency: Their Impact on Human Rights* (Geneva: International Commission of Jurists, 1983)), 6 *HRQ* 125, 131 (1984).

[58] M. Chanock, 'Writing South African Legal History: A Prospectus', 30 *J. Afr. Hist.* 265, 265 (1989).

[59] See Ch. 1, n. 92 above.

[60] Sparks, *Mind* (cit. n. 50), at 37. Not all suspicious deaths receive this exposure, however, for there is also an 'informal' inquest procedure which 'allows the magistrate simply to make a decision on the basis of affidavits before him, without hearing oral evidence, or witnesses being cross-examined'. L. Levin, P. Benjamin, and D. Smuts, 'Human Rights Index: 1 November 1987–31 January 1988', 4 *SAJHR* 110, 117 (1988).

It might be thought that adherence to the law would have lost its attraction in a society engaged in the working of such profound injustices as South Africa has undertaken. Certainly South African laws have violated many of the principles which Westerners often associate with the rule of law, and have enacted in their stead systems of discrimination and repression which in some ways have few parallels even in a world as full of injustice as our own. I do not at all mean to argue that all white South Africans, or all those in positions of power, believe in the importance of adherence to law.

The persistent legalism of unjust states, however, should signal to us that injustice does not necessarily imply lawlessness. Similarly, we should not be content to assume that because unjust states manifestly find legal forms *useful*, the legalism of such countries is solely the product of calculations of *realpolitik* by the oppressors. The truth is that injustice and adherence to law can coexist. Self-interested calculations, moreover, can coalesce with other sources of support for law to maintain a culture that values law even as it practises or acquiesces in oppression. It is important to understand the multiple ways that law can take root, even in an unjust society, if we are to gauge the potential that law has to serve as a limit on rather than merely an instrument of injustice.

South African whites' adherence to law has such diverse roots, and these roots go deep. First, law is useful as a method of control. Second, adherence to law has power as a potential source of legitimation for South African whites' society, in the eyes (so South African whites may hope) of foreign observers and of South African blacks, and also in the eyes of whites themselves. But adherence to law is not merely effective or legitimizing. Its third source is a sincere belief in the value of law, a belief rooted in quite early South African history and reflected, perhaps strengthened, in more recent struggles between Afrikaner and English-speaking South African whites. Each of these sources contributes to a climate in which courts are likely to impose, and the government likely to endure, some legal limits on emergency powers.

(a) The Law's Utility.

The first source for the government's desire to work its will largely through legal rather than extra-legal coercion, as I have suggested, is the recognition that legal regulation can be effective.[61] This is a cynical explanation, but no less important for that. Law is the characteristic mode of regulation in a complex, industrial, modern nation. South Africa has a sophisticated legal system in use for the direction and resolution of a wide array of non-political matters, and the use of similar mechanisms to deal with the enormous tasks of establishing and defending apartheid must have seemed, and may well have been, natural and efficient. From this perspective, what is unusual about South Africa is not that it achieves its governmental objectives through the elaborate

[61] For Martin Chanock, 'in the South African state law is a way of creating, extending and exercising power rather than limiting and controlling it'. 'Writing' (cit. n. 58), 267.

use of law—many nations do that—but rather that its objectives are so repellent.

The South African law of race and internal security may be particularly efficient, from the state's point of view, because it tends to confer such broad discretion on state officials. For example, the elaborate array of laws which until recently governed blacks' right to live and work in urban areas was 'designed to create a system of government by administration rather than by rules of law'.[62] The law that governed blacks conferred broad discretion on the officials who did the governing;[63] all the more reason to find resort to the law convenient. The essence of the emergency security machinery has also been said to be 'an attempt to confer upon the police the capacity to operate in the grey areas between an (extended) legality and wanton illegality, to impose order without law'.[64] Taken to this extreme, South Africa's use of law verges on the legalization of illegality. South Africa is not the only oppressive regime to write itself such a blank cheque; in colonial Virginia a statute dealing with runaway slaves took this tendency even further. This law decreed that after suitable proclamations had been placed on church doors, it was 'lawful for any person or persons whatsoever, to kill and destroy such slaves by such ways and means as he, she, or they shall think fit, without accusation or impeachment of any crime for the same'.[65]

It deserves to be said, however, that even if South Africa's use of law were based solely on its efficiency, the decision to rely on law would have a price for the state. As we have seen in our study of the emergency cases, the government's desire to immunize its conduct from review did not in fact mean that it would altogether escape judicial scrutiny. Lawyers were prepared to test the government's claim that its conduct fell within the law, and doctrinal resources for performing such tests were available, however unwelcome these cases were to the government. The very ubiquitousness of legal regulation in South Africa has meant the development of legal principles by which courts can review not only the treatment of blacks and demonstrators but also the commercial, governmental, and personal relations of the white population. Doctrines shaped in decisions about the ordinary lives of whites inevitably are capable of application in other contexts as well. Not to apply these rules

[62] W. Dean, 'The Legal Regime Governing Urban Africans in South Africa: An Administrative-Law Perspective', 1984 *Acta Juridica* 105, 129 (1985). The hateful 'pass laws' and other aspects—though by no means all—of the legal apparatus regulating blacks' right to live and work in urban areas were repealed in 1986. For an early appraisal of the new legal regime, see H. Schoombee and D. Davis, 'Abolishing Influx Control: Fundamental or Cosmetic Change?', 2 *SAJHR* 208 (1986).

[63] See generally Dean, 'Legal Regime' (cit. n. 62).

[64] N. Haysom, 'Legal Intervention and the State of Emergency', in N. Haysom and C. Plasket (eds.), *Developments in Emergency Law* (Johannesburg: Centre for Applied Legal Studies, University of the Witwatersrand, 1989), 1, 2.

[65] Aviam Soifer calls this the 'legalization of lawlessness'. 'Slavery and the Law: A Study in Contradiction', 56 *Tex. L. Rev.* 1319, 1321 (1978) (reviewing A. Higginbotham, *In the Matter of Color: Race and the American Legal Process—The Colonial Period* (New York: Oxford University Press, 1978), in which this statute is quoted at p. 56).

more generally may be hard to justify logically, and if such doctrines are generally applied, then courts cannot rework them too sharply in any one context without risking injury to other aspects of the social order that powerful interests protect.

One way for South African whites to enjoy the efficiencies of legalistic control over blacks while denying them the benefit of legal doctrines that protect whites would have been to carve off a separate body of law applicable only to the subjects of apartheid. There have indeed been such bodies of law, of which the pass laws were perhaps the most notorious example.[66] Complete categorization, however, may be very hard for a legal system to achieve.[67] Moreover, this denial of the interconnectedness of the law has become less tenable, and in my judgment less frequent, as the broader South African racial and political scene has shifted and as human rights advocacy has pressed for the making of connections.

The resultant doctrinal drag, as it might be termed, provides one explanation for the stability of so many doctrinal formulas in the Rabie emergency decisions. The court's treatment of the *audi alteram partem* maxim is a case in point. *Audi* protections are important throughout administrative law, much of which is very much the concern of the white, government-supporting population. In *Omar* the Rabie court was prepared to find *audi* rights excluded by regulation in emergency law, but it was not prepared to do so on the basis of a reformulation of the rules governing the determination of whether the *audi* maxim applied. This judicial reluctance did the detainees in *Omar* itself little good, but the continued viability of pre-emergency doctrines meant at least that they remained available for a fight another day.

(*b*) *The Law's Legitimacy.*

Law's efficacy, however, is not the only reason for its embrace by the government. South Africa's reliance on the law offers it a basis for claiming legitimacy, by enabling it to assert its fidelity to the principle of the rule of law, an ideal that seeks to guarantee that the power of government is restrained

[66] See generally M. Chanock, 'An Ecology of Coercion: Criminology, Criminal Law and the New State. South Africa 1902–1930' (unpubl., 1990), 25–9 (on statutory reversals of the usual *onus* of proof in certain classes of cases 'affect[ing] a large number of black rather than white accused'); Sachs, *Justice* (cit. n. 52), 168–74 (on prosecutions under 'race-statutes', laws in practice or by definition focused on blacks); N. Steytler, 'Criminal Justice and the Apartheid State', in A. Rycroft, L. Boulle, M. Robertson, and P. Spiller (eds.), *Race and the Law in South Africa* (Cape Town: Juta, 1987), 68, 75–7 (on the unfairness of process in the commissioners' courts, exclusively dealing with the cases of blacks, and in the magistrates' courts, in which many blacks are tried); R. Suttner, 'The Judiciary: Its Ideological Role in South Africa', 14 *Int J. Soc. L.* 47, 55 (1986) (on aspects of South African law which categorized by race or, as part of the government's effort to divide blacks, by 'tribe').

[67] Mark Tushnet argues that 'Southern slave law was characterized by a failed attempt to develop rigid categories'. He attributes the failure in part to features of Southern political economy, and in part to 'the inevitable openness of reasoning by analogy'. *The American Law of Slavery 1810–1860: Considerations of Humanity and Interest* (Princeton, NJ: Princeton University Press, 1981), 40.

by the staying hand of legal rights. South Africa does in fact make this claim, as the Ministers' comments already quoted reflect. In 1968, its Department of Foreign Affairs produced a sixty-eight page pamphlet with the title *South Africa and the Rule of Law,* meant to refute 'the impression that the rule of law has been discarded. Nothing', said the Department, 'is further from the truth.'[68] As one South African judge has commented, 'I know that it is popular, particularly for South African politicians and diplomats, to proclaim with considerable pride (vicarious pride, I should say) that whatever else can be said about South Africa, its legal system and its system of courts and justice is [sic] above criticism.'[69]

Such claims can be of value for three different audiences. First, the claim of adherence to the rule of law speaks to international concerns. South African policy-makers must consider the reactions and the potential sanctions of foreign observers, and this audience may be impressed by government according to law. Moreover, the risk of international reaction has a significance for South Africans that goes beyond political or economic considerations. Many South Africans of all political stripes are very conscious of the world beyond their borders. Many South African whites, especially, want to consider themselves part of the Western world, faithful to its traditions and sharing in its aspirations and achievements,[70] yet '[a]partheid label[s] them as racist backwoodsmen'.[71] The international boycott of South African sport has been so painful to some in part because it denied white South Africans membership in the club. The cultural boycott of South Africa has been painful even (perhaps particularly) for opponents of apartheid, and has now been modified in order to permit progressive, anti-apartheid South African artists to share in the world's cultural developments.[72]

Lawyers too are subject to this desire for a place in the sun of the Western world: we can hear its reverberations in the 1970 boast of a South African judge that he was 'told on good authority that the English judges, who are

[68] The Dept.'s words are quoted by the respected South African advocate Arthur Suzman, who dissected the Dept.'s claims in 'South Africa and the Rule of Law', 85 *SALJ* 261, 261 (1968). Suzman's article is itself evidence that the question of whether the government respected the rule of law was important to critics as well as supporters of the government's policies.

[69] J. Kriegler, 'Extracts of an Address Delivered by Mr Justice J. C. Kriegler at the Annual General Meeting Of Lawyers For Human Rights, Pretoria, 16 November 1985', 2 *SAJHR* 204, 205 (1986).

[70] Joseph Lelyveld describes an issue of *Fair Lady,* a popular South African magazine read mainly by whites, which featured a series of photographs of a black South African model, photographs taken in Spain. '"The Fair Lady team" had been flown to Madrid from Johannesburg, a caption said, by Iberia Airways. ... To do it justice, *Fair Lady* has a social conscience that periodically permits it to slip in an article about hunger in the black rural areas. But when it hands an Iberia ticket to a black model, it is imitating *Vogue,* showing its readers that *they* have risen above apartheid and joined a wider world.' Lelyveld, *Move Your Shadow* (cit. n. 56), 38–9.

[71] Sparks, *Mind* (cit. n. 50), 317. Sparks is speaking specifically of Afrikaners, but the point seems applicable to all South African whites.

[72] For a discussion of the 'selective boycott', see I. Powell, 'The "Desk" has Put the Bad Old Days Behind Now', *Weekly Mail* 25, 25–6 (21–7 July 1989).

undoubtedly the most eminent judges in the world, consider only the South African judges as their equals'.[73] Sydney Kentridge, one of South Africa's most eminent anti-apartheid lawyers, captured a similar sentiment in his account of a speech he gave 'at a law dinner at which some Supreme Court judges were present. ... I said that I believed that we still had the best judiciary in Africa. It was clear that those most immediately concerned thought this compliment wholly inadequate.'[74] Each interference with the ideal of the rule of law takes a certain toll on this international cultural affiliation, and it is reasonable to infer that South Africa oppresses by law in part to stake a claim to sharing in the Western tradition of the rule of law.[75]

Second, law's claim to moral standing may help to make it an efficient method of controlling people, for if they accept the rightness of the controls then they will obey by choice rather than only by coercion. In particular, on this theory, the state's adherence to a system of law should tend to win black South Africans' approval and obedience. Whether people's obedience to law is based partially on its perceived legitimacy, even in more just societies than South Africa, is a matter of some debate, but that debate need not occupy us here.[76] For our purposes, it is enough to recognize that South African whites are concerned about blacks' attitudes towards their power—the white fear of the total onslaught attests to this concern—and that they are quite likely to believe that rule by law can lay claim to legitimacy in the eyes of blacks. This sentiment is captured in the words of South Africa's first chief justice, J. H. de Villiers, who declared that '[i]t must tend to enlist the natives on the side of the law if they know that the Courts of Law are as ready and willing to protect their legal rights as they are to punish them for offences against the law.' On celebrated occasions, de Villiers practised what he preached.[77]

A 1977 speech by then Chief Justice Rumpff gives us a sense of the hopes South African whites may entertain on this score.[78] Rumpff, speaking at the

[73] C. Claassen, 'Retain the Bar and Side-Bar', 87 *SALJ* 25, 25 (1970).

[74] S. Kentridge, 'Telling the Truth about Law', 99 *SALJ* 648, 651 (1982).

[75] A similar effect may contribute to the often positive impact which international trial observers evidently have in various countries on the trials they observe, see D. Weissbrodt, 'International Trial Observers', 18 *Stan. J. Int. L.* 27, 113–14 (1982). One explanation for this impact may be the finding of experimental psychology, cited by Weissbrodt, that an 'observed person will tend to behave more in conformance with societal norms in the presence of an observer who shares those norms'. Ibid. 111.

[76] Alan Hyde has cogently set out reasons to doubt 'the supposedly significant contribution of law and legal institutions to popular belief in legitimacy and hence to political action or nonaction of various types': 'The Concept of Legitimation in the Sociology of Law', 1983 *Wisc. L. Rev.* 379, 383–5. For a critique of Hyde's argument, and a critical legal studies perspective on the legitimating effects of the law, see M. Kelman, *A Guide to Critical Legal Studies* (Cambridge, Mass.: Harvard University Press, 1987), 262–95.

[77] *Sigcau* v. *The Queen*, 12 SC 256, 271 (1895). *Sigcau* itself is an instance of Lord de Villiers' applying this admonition, and freeing a black chief, Sigcau, whom the colonial governor had ordered held, indefinitely, without trial. See text at nn. 243–4 below.

[78] 'Centenary of the Transvaal Supreme Court', *De Rebus Procuratoriis* 393, 394–8 (1977) (hereafter cited as 'Rumpff Speech').

centenary celebration of the Transvaal Supreme Court, observed that the people of the Transvaal

> called this building, where we are, the Palace of Justice and gave it one entrance for Blacks and Whites and they allowed Blacks and Whites to sit in the same open court at a time when, judged by Western standards, the Blacks were very primitive and had only just come into contact with the Western culture and way of life.[79]

The Chief Justice did not mention that when the construction of this Palace of Justice began, the Transvaal—then the South African Republic—had a provision in its constitution declaring that 'the People desire to permit no equality between colored people and the white inhabitants, either in Church or State'.[80]

Instead, Rumpff emphasized the boon which he believed white law had been to blacks, and blacks' supposed receptiveness to this new system. 'As time went on', he declared, 'the Blacks were not deprived of any justice under our common law.' He continued:

> Because of its inherent fairness our common law was acceptable to them, and this was particularly so in respect of our criminal law.... Under the accusatorial system people who are guilty are perhaps more often acquitted. To the mind of the Black man that has always been a source of wonder and to the accused an agreeable surprise.[81]

Now, moreover, '[t]he Blacks in the white cities and towns are willingly and often keenly taking over the White way of life', and '[i]t is ... clearly our duty to produce, in co-operation with the Black universities and all other universities, non-White lawyers and jurists into whose willing hands our legal heritage can be placed, to be enjoyed not only in the Republic [of South Africa] but also in the independent [black] homelands.'[82] Rumpff said all this one year after the Soweto uprising.

Rumpff's appraisal of black attitudes to the system of justice is painfully condescending and naïve. Today there are frequent suggestions that blacks have lost respect for South African law because of its injustice.[83] A recent news report quoted a former black magistrate as saying that 'You can expect very little protection from the law because the law favours the white man, not the black man.... So you have a very good example of the law of the jungle.'[84] In the course of the massive black mobilization of the 1980s, one of the new

[79] Ibid. 396.

[80] J. Dugard, *Human Rights and the South African Legal Order* (Princeton, NJ: Princeton University Press, 1978), 20.

[81] 'Rumpff Speech' (cit. n. 78), 396.

[82] Ibid. 397.

[83] See e.g. Kriegler, 'Extracts' (cit. n. 69), 205; Chanock, 'Writing' (cit. n. 58), 267–8. Judge Higginbotham takes a similar view, in A. Higginbotham, 'Racism in American and South African Courts: Similarities and Differences', 65 *NYU L. Rev.* 479, 568–70 (1990).

[84] K. Jost, 'Violence among an Excluded People', *Los Angeles Daily Journal* 2 (27 Jan. 1986).

tactics was to establish 'alternative structures', among them 'people's courts', as one part of freeing black townships from state control.[85] But these views are not only a phenomenon of the past decades political mobilization. In 1962, fifteen years before Rumpff spoke, Nelson Mandela, himself an attorney, challenged the right of the court to try him for criminal charges, and told the presiding magistrate that he felt that he was 'a black man in a white man's court'.[86]

If there were no basis for the idea that blacks accord some legitimacy to the law, then we might well doubt whether any value that whites place on the law can be attributed to their believing that it is having a legitimizing effect among blacks. There is evidence, however, that even under the weight of oppression black South Africans do accord some respect to the laws that oppress them. Thus Lucie White has noted that the black villagers of Driefontein, facing removal from their land by the government, in the course of conversations with a sympathetic, white community organizer 'initially expressed deference to the authority of South African law'.[87] Perhaps cruel laws ironically function, as they may have in eighteenth-century England, to reinforce deference to those, such as judges, who hold the power to ease this cruelty.[88]

[85] Sparks, *Mind* (cit. n. 50), at 338. For a careful study of people's courts in the Cape Town area, see S. Burman and W. Schärf, 'Creating People's Justice: Street Committees and People's Courts in a South African City', 24 *Law and Soc. Rev.* 693 (1990). Burman and Schärf point out that alternative African courts, existing in relationships of competition and collaboration with the state, are a long-standing phenomenon in South Africa. Ibid. 696. '[F]or a large sector of Cape Town's African population,' they write, 'the formal rather than the informal courts of South Africa are peripheral.' Ibid. 706.

[86] N. Mandela, '"Black Man in a White Court": First Court Statement, 1962', in N. Mandela, *The Struggle is My Life* (London: International Defence and Aid Fund for Southern Africa, 1978), 125, 129.

[87] L. White, 'To Learn and Teach: Lessons from Driefontein on Lawyering and Power', 1988 *Wisc. L. Rev.* 699, 728 and n. 118. White thoughtfully considers whether the Driefontein villagers' expressions of deference to the authority of South African law were sincere or not, ibid. If they were sincere, White does not suggest that they reflected a belief on the part of blacks that apartheid laws were *just*. Rather, she sees attitudes towards these laws as being, perhaps, a form of 'ideological static', blunting people's perception of the possibility and rightfulness of political challenge. Personal communication from Lucie White, 8 Mar. 1990.

Sandra Burman quotes the words of a magistrate from more than a century ago, extolling the quality of white justice—in the eyes of blacks—in terms faintly reminiscent of Rumpff's. S. Burman, 'Symbolic Dimensions of the Enforcement of Law', 3 (2) *Brit. JL and Soc.* 204, 213 (1976). Burman appears to say that as African society was disrupted and altered by whites, the white magistrates' claim that they offered better, more impartial justice than the chiefs did have some validity. Ibid. Burman also comments that the growing number of Christian Africans opposed the magistrates' use of African law to decide Africans' cases. Ibid. 210. For the example of a famous black South African Christian, Sol Plaatje, who had an abiding faith in the courts, see B. Willan, *Sol Plaatje: South African Nationalist 1876–1932* (Berkeley, Calif.: University of California Press, 1984), 48–9, 117–18, 144–5, 206, 215–16.

[88] Douglas Hay, in his analysis of 18th-century English criminal law, argues that England then 'was a society with a bloody penal code, an astute ruling class who manipulated it to their advantage, and a people schooled [by this system] in the lessons of Justice, Terror and Mercy. The benevolence of rich men to poor, and all the ramifications of patronage, were upheld by the sanction of the gallows and the rhetoric of the death sentence.' 'Property, Authority and the Criminal Law', in D. Hay, P. Linebaugh, J. Rule, E. Thompson, and C. Winslow, *Albion's*

But even people who, like Nelson Mandela, are hardly deceived about the realities of South African power, may well hold a measure of respect for South African law. When Mandela, an attorney, challenged the bias of the 'white man's court' which tried him in 1962, he still abided carefully by its forms and disclaimed any personal challenge to the magistrate's fairness; instead, he assured the magistrate that 'I hold Your Worship in high esteem and I do not for one single moment doubt your sense of fairness and justice.'[89] Mandela obtained a postgraduate degree in law while serving his sentence of life imprisonment, and, Anthony Sampson reports, 'encouraged other political prisoners to take up the law. I begin to realize how much of Mandela's optimism depends on his respect for the law, and his trust in the integrity of another lawyer, President de Klerk.'[90]

The decisions of black South African litigants, or potential litigants, give us another hint of black assessment of South African law. If black South Africans considered the legal system wholly bankrupt, they might also conclude that there was nothing to be gained from participating in it—or at any rate nothing that outweighed the moral and educational value of publicized non-participation. Viewing the legal system this way, they would not only refrain from bringing litigation that sought to use the state's law against the state, but also decline to offer any defence when they were brought to trial by the state. It would be hard to measure the numbers of cases not brought for this reason (though my impression is that they are few),[91] but it is quite clear that the number of cases in which people accused by the state refuse to defend themselves is very small indeed. The rare exceptions to this rule are newsworthy precisely because they are exceptions—and even some of the prominent refusals have been distinctly qualified.[92]

Fatal Tree: Crime and Society in Eighteenth-Century England (London: Allen Lane, 1975), 17, 62–3. Cf. E. Genovese, *Roll, Jordan, Roll: The World the Slaves Made* (New York: Vintage Books, 1976), 40 (broad discretion of slaveholders to ignore severe Southern slave laws 'confirmed the power of the master'). For sharp criticism of Hay's article, and a defence of the contrary view that '[t]he criminal law and its procedures existed to serve and protect the interests of the people who suffered as victims of crime, people who were overwhelmingly non-élite', see J. Langbein, 'Albion's Fatal Flaws', *Past and Present* 96, 97 (Feb. 1983).

[89] Mandela, 'Black Man' (cit. n. 85), 125.

[90] A. Sampson, '18 Days: A South African Journal', *NY Times Magazine* (18 Mar. 1990), 38, 44.

[91] Every one of the emergency cases decided by the Appellate Division is an example of litigation brought against the state, since each of them was a challenge to emergency power rather than a state-initiated proceeding to enforce emergency authority. While many of these cases resembled criminal prosecutions in that they involved efforts by detainees to obtain their freedom, others were brought (and brought by activist groups) to challenge quite different aspects of emergency authority. Among the latter were the Rabie-era cases of *United Democratic Front, Release Mandela Campaign,* and *Van der Westhuizen NO* v. *United Democratic Front,* as well as the Corbett-era decision in *Boesak.*

[92] One such exception was the 1989 trial of *S.* v. *Masina and Others,* in which members of Umkhonto we Sizwe (the ANC's military arm) took the position that '"civilian courts"' had no authority to try them and 'refused to plead and participate in the court proceedings'. Though they declined to have advocates appear for them, they were represented by a Johannesburg firm of attorneys. V. Gunene, 'No Remorse as Delmas Trio Convicted', *Weekly Mail* 4 (3–9

Evidence of this sort, however, falls far short of establishing the kind of legitimation which echoes in Chief Justice Rumpff's words. I will argue in Chapter 7 that it is most unlikely that state of emergency litigation, in particular, leads blacks to confer any broad legitimacy on the South African social order.[93] More generally, the vigorous black opposition to apartheid suggests that most South African blacks, like American black slaves before the Civil War, welcome whatever protections they can secure in the midst of injustice, but are not confused by these benefits into forgetting that there are other rights they have been denied.[94]

Blacks' use of the courts then would attest to their belief that there is some potential advantage to be gained there, but would not imply a belief that the system is entitled to anything approaching unalloyed respect. Thus Abdullah Omar, the advocate whose detention was the subject of the *Omar* decision by the Appellate Division, recently told an American interviewer that in legal work on behalf of the victims of apartheid '[i]t is not a question of using South African laws. It is a question of defending people against the laws.... But you must go to court to fight injustice even though the laws are weighted against you.'[95] Albie Sachs's observations on blacks' use of lawyers suggest a similar view. He discusses evidence that, by the beginning of the twentieth century, 'Africans throughout South Africa had become accustomed to the use of lawyers, who, if they could not secure rights for them, could at least soften their disabilities.... It might even be argued that the more unfavourably Africans felt towards the laws, the more well-disposed they were towards the lawyers.'[96]

None the less these ambiguous hints of support provide a 'hook' on which

Mar. 1989). Ultimately evidence in mitigation of sentence in this case was led, unsuccessfully, by counsel 'instructed by the families of the accused men'. V. Gunene, 'Judge Outvoted—So Three Will Hang', *Weekly Mail* 1 (28 Apr.–4 May 1989). (The death sentences were later overturned on appeal.) David Halberstam describes another instance of rejection of counsel in 'The Fire to Come in South Africa', *Atlantic Monthly* (May 1980), 81, 86–7. In this case the accused directed their advocates to withdraw after the trial judge decided to hold parts of the trial *in camera*. *S.* v. *Mange*, 1980 (4) SA 613 (A) at 616E–617B. Though they made this decision with the expectation that they would be executed, see Halberstam, 'Fire', 86, only one of the accused was sentenced to death. On his appeal, he was once again represented by counsel—and the appeal against the death sentence was successful. *S.* v. *Mange*.

[93] See Ch. 7, text at nn. 36–7 below.

[94] Genovese, *Roll, Jordan* (cit. n. 88), 31, 48–9. For the very caustic assessments of South Africa's legal system by black lawyers whom a visiting American interviewed in 1988, see R. Wilkins, 'The South African Legal System: Black Lawyers' Views', 7 *Transafrica Forum* (No. 3) 9 (Fall 1990). Moreover, Judge Higginbotham may well be right that blacks' recognition of the limited potential of the South African courts has led them to adopt other, more radical strategies for change, 'Racism' (cit. n. 83), 569, though these strategies characteristically appear to encompass use of the courts as and when necessary.

[95] 'What Does Mandela Want?', *Human Rights* 31, 46 (Fall/Winter 1990) ('Interview with Abdullah Omar by Vicki Quade'). This assessment is consistent with Otto Kirchheimer's observation that 'those who have suffered from the hands of the wielders of official or unofficial power will generally not want to miss whatever chance the resort to court proceedings may open up for them, regardless of whether such resort remains their only weapon or serves only as one among several interconnected means of defence or counterattack': *Political Justice* (cit. n. 45), 178.

[96] Sachs, *Justice* (cit. n. 52), 202.

whites can hang their hopes.[97] It is all too easy for South African whites to project their hopes about blacks on to reality because the whites know so little of the reality. As Allister Sparks points out, '[t]hough only a few miles separate their living areas, though they spend much of their days working together, the black South African world is as distanct [sic] from the white world as Outer Mongolia; its mind a closed book to all but a handful of whites who keep in touch with it'.[98] Those whites who form their judgments about blacks solely from interactions with them as servants, supplicants, or subjects of governmental power are not likely to encounter a blunt acknowledgement of the extent of blacks' disaffection. Neither the condescension nor the *naïveté* of Rumpff's views is likely to be unique to him.[99]

Whether or not blacks can still be impressed by South African legal forms, therefore, it is very possible that many South African whites believe that they can be—and so the hope of inducing black obedience may well be one motive for the use of law. Indeed, even if the government is less hopeful on this score than Rumpff, it may well consider the matter important. Such considerations may underlie the 1988 decision by the South African Commissioner of Police to ban a protest meeting related to a decision in a major treason trial then under way. The Commissioner observed 'that the manner in which the judgment was being attacked had the effect of heightening emotions and making the administration of justice "suspect"'.[100] In similar vein, the state attempted to punish the establishment of alternative 'people's courts', in at least one important case by making their creation a basis for a treason

[97] Stanley Greenberg recounts a bizarre incident exemplifying whites' desire to win some form of approval from blacks even in the midst of military operations in black townships. In Operation Palmiet, Greenberg writes, 'The army supervised South African Police counter-insurgency units that conducted house-to-house searches [in Sebokeng, a black township near Johannesburg] looking for weapons and protest leaders. Yet even as it visibly represented the state's reliance on direct coercion, the army sought to cultivate other images. The armed troops kicked around soccer balls, played with the children—presumably after they had laid down their stones—and passed out pamphlets to the detained residents announcing, incongruously, "I am your friend."': *Legitimating the Illegitimate: State, Markets, and Resistance in South Africa* (Berkeley, Calif.: University of California Press, 1987), 3.

[98] Sparks, *Mind* (cit. n. 50), p. xvii.

[99] For an even more disparaging appraisal of blacks by a white judge, see K. Jost, 'A Conservative of Afrikaner Stock', *Los Angeles Daily Journal* 19 (7 Feb. 1986). Jost reports that George Munnik, the Judge President of the Cape Provincial Division of the Supreme Court, left his previous judicial position in the putatively independent black 'homeland' of Transkei 'with the belief that the form of government that best suits black Africans is "a benevolent dictatorship". ... He sees greater social progress by the Cape's mixed-race population, who he says are "quicker mentally" than blacks. "They rise because they are able to rise," he says. "After all, they are our offspring."' Rumpff's condescension has not always been as benign as in the Centenary speech. In a judgment two years after that speech, he commented that '[a]pparently the counsel for the defence and the trial Court have not yet gained the experience that Coloured and Black men indeed stab people sometimes without any reason, except for an apparent desire to stab'. *S.* v. *Augustine*, 1980 (1) SA 503 (A) at 506A (trans. from Afrikaans). Judge Higginbotham sternly criticizes this remarkable observation in 'Racism' (cit. n. 83), 520.

[100] E. Cameron, G. Marcus, and D. van Zyl Smit, 'The Administration of Justice, Law Reform and Jurisprudence', in *Annual Survey of South African Law, 1988* (Cape Town: Juta, 1989), 500, 521–2 (quoting *The Citizen* (7 Dec. 1988)).

prosecution.[101] In short, even if whites have grown less sanguine about the legitimizing effect of their law on blacks, they may well wish to retain whatever remaining legitimacy they can, and that in itself would be a reason for continued use of the law.

The third audience for whom South Africa's reliance on law as a means of governance may have legitimating value is South Africa's white population itself. To the extent that whites see adherence to law as a part of a good social order (and we will see shortly that whites' belief in the law is a long-standing feature of South African culture),[102] it will naturally matter to them whether South Africa satisfies this standard. If South Africa appears to act lawlessly, some whites might be more likely to challenge the government's acts; others might simply lose heart and so give less firm support to the government's policies. Both groups may be quicker to accept the propriety of oppression carried out through the forms of the legal process than they would be to approve of wholly extra-legal government action. For example, the revelation in the 1970s that senior South African officials were covertly using government money to generate pro-South African progaganda created a major scandal, and led to the resignations of Prime Minister Vorster and Minister of Information Mulder. Although no one was 'held accountable before the law', these events, in a 'party that prided itself on its probity', were 'a shock to many rank-and-file Nationalists'.[103] So, too, the brutal death of Steve Biko at the hands of the police undercut, even for Afrikaners, 'the hitherto claimed innocence of Afrikaner rule'.[104]

Legalism may also have other, more indirect, legitimizing value for whites. In an insightful article, Martin Chanock has argued that '[t]he image of legalism, its justice, discernment, and restraint is a counterpoint of and component of the opposing image of savagery, impulse and transgression.'[105] Writing of the first three decades of this century, Chanock urges that '[t]he judgments of courts were a crucial part of the discourses which divided self and other; ruler and ruled; white and black.'[106] We can sense this flavour even in the 1970s, in Chief Justice Rumpff's proud declaration that: 'Long before 1877 our ancestors, both English and Afrikaans, had introduced in South Africa this way of life, a culture based on the concept of individual freedom, law and religion, a culture which was poles apart from the way of life of the primitive Blacks.'[107]

Rumpff revisited this theme, in more somber mood, in a 1980 Appellate

[101] See *S.* v. *Mayekiso and Others*, 1988 (4) SA 738 (W) at 738H–739E. Mayekiso and the other accused were acquitted in 1989.

[102] See text at nn. 116–52 below.

[103] D. Harrison, *The White Tribe of Africa: South Africa in Perspective* (London: Ariel Books, 1985), 223, 228.

[104] H. Adam, 'Perspectives in the Literature: A Critical Evaluation', in H. Adam and H. Giliomee, *Ethnic Power Mobilized: Can South Africa Change?* (New Haven, Conn.: Yale University Press, 1979), 16, 28–9).

[105] Chanock, 'Ecology' (cit. n. 66), 31.

[106] Ibid. 32.

[107] 'Rumpff Speech' (cit. n. 78), 396.

Division decision reviewing a trial in which the accused discharged their counsel and then disrupted the proceedings with 'loud singing and an "ear-splitting war cry"'.[108] There Rumpff wrote that:

> One can only admire the extreme patience which the trial Judge [Hefer, later a leading member of the emergency team] displayed during the hearing of the case. For many weeks he conducted himself with dignity and courtesy in an atmosphere of *savage* hostility which, fortunately, is completely strange in our Courts, where justice is dispensed in a *civilized* manner.[109]

Chanock's account suggests two distinct functions of this differentiation between rulers and ruled. The first, and the more apparent in Chief Justice Rumpff's speech, is to provide a justification for whites' sweeping and obviously undemocratic domination over blacks. That justification lies in whites' perception of themselves as the carriers of a superior culture, one element of which is its embodiment of the rule of law, and in their perception of others as, in Kipling's words, 'lesser breeds without the Law'.[110] The second is not so much to justify white power as to deflect attention from its grimmest features. Thus the Supreme Courts of South Africa can proclaim the beneficent values of the rule of law, while the magistrates' courts and similar tribunals perform the bulk of the law's nitty-gritty task of controlling blacks. In this world, as a magistrate whom Chanock quotes says, the magistrate's job is to 'punish, punish, punish'.[111]

Like utility, the legitimating function of the law is a constraint on the decisions that courts can hand down and on the response that the government can make to them. Chanock's emphasis on legitimation as a veil hiding bleak reality is an apt reminder that a state's quest for legitimation may not greatly constrain its use of its power, but we should not altogether discount legitimation as a source of pressure for justice. This is especially so in the case of emergency litigation, for all of this litigation has taken place in the Supreme Courts rather than in lower courts, and so has implicated as directly as possible the values of legality. Illusions, moreover, are harder and harder to maintain, the more informed and critical the audience to be fooled becomes. South Africa has faced increasingly demanding audiences, abroad and at home, over recent

[108] *S.* v. *Mange*, 1980 (4) SA 613 (A) at 617B.

[109] Ibid. 617E–F (emphasis added). The writer David Halberstam, after describing the accused's conduct during the trial, says that the trial judge 'was enraged': 'Fire' (cit. n. 92), 87. Halberstam continues, 'He sentenced the leader, James Daniel Mange, to death by hanging ("How far is a traitor to be allowed to go before the death penalty is imposed?" he asked).' Ibid.

[110] R. Kipling, *Recessional*, l. 22. I am grateful to John Leubsdorf for pointing Kipling's poem out to me.

[111] H. Corder, *The Truth and Nothing But* (Cape Town: Juta, 1946), 96–7, quoted in Chanock, 'Ecology' (cit. n. 66), 24. Until the abolition of the pass laws in 1986, the pass-law courts provided a particularly egregious example of such assembly-line justice, to which only blacks were subject. For appalling accounts of the operation of these courts, see J. Carlson, *No Neutral Ground* (London: Quartet Books, 1977), 5–12, 25–63; Kevin Boyle *et al.*, *South Africa: Imprisonment Under the Pass Laws* (New York: Amnesty International USA, 1986).

years. Under these circumstances, E. P. Thompson's admonition is particularly telling:

> If the law is evidently partial and unjust, then it will mask nothing, legitimize nothing, contribute nothing to any class's hegemony. The essential precondition for the effectiveness of law, in its function as ideology, is that it shall display an independence from gross manipulation and shall seem to be just. It cannot seem to be so without upholding its own logic and criteria of equity; indeed, on occasion, by actually *being* just.[112]

Whites' desire for legitimacy, then, presses the courts and the state to acknowledge some legal limits. Politicians may respond to this desire merely by factoring it into their calculations of *realpolitik*, but for judges the impact of the concern for legitimacy is more indirect and less insincere. As I suggested in Chapter 4, the Appellate Division did not hand down decisions such as *Swart*, *Nkwentsha*, and *Apleni* because the members of the emergency team cynically decided to go just this far in favour of the subjects of emergency power in order to create a veneer of legitimacy.[113] Rather, honest people need to justify themselves on grounds which they themselves accept, and South Africa, as Eugene Genovese wrote of the slaveholding American South, is 'a world inhabited, like most worlds, by men who strove to be considered decent'.[114] Hence adherence to law is a much more viable basis for South African whites' claim to legitimacy to the extent that whites themselves accept that adherence to law is part of a good society. As a result, the desire for legitimacy itself becomes a motive, conscious or unconscious, for whites' adoption of a belief in the law. But judges, for whom the law is so much of their life, will need little encouragement to believe in what they are doing. They are surely particularly likely to accept this value, at least so long as it is not denied by the society around them.

Thus we can say that the concern for legitimacy played a part in the Rabie court's emergency decisions because it contributed to the judges' own sense of the meaningfulness of their commitment to the law. The Rabie court's insistence that the rules of the game—loose as they are—be adhered to and its effort to keep the courts open and able to act effectively against cases of governmental abuse appear to reflect just such judicial conviction. Perhaps they reflect it all the more clearly precisely because these cases, considered coldly, had such modest impacts on the emergency system and, as we have seen, so little success as ways of securing the legitimacy of that system.[115]

[112] E. Thompson, *Whigs and Hunters: The Origin of the Black Act* (New York: Pantheon, 1975), 263. See also, to very similar effect, Genovese, *Roll, Jordan* (cit. n. 88), 27.

[113] See Ch. 4, text at nn. 73–80 above.

[114] Genovese, *Roll, Jordan* (cit. n. 88), 48.

[115] See Ch. 4, text at nn. 75–80 above.

(*c*) *Whites' Belief in the Law.*

Whites may come to believe in the law because it is so useful to them, or because they cannot easily claim that it confers legitimacy on their rule unless they themselves accept its value. Beliefs may have such roots and yet be held without conscious insincerity. But I suggest that South Africans whites' belief in the law cannot be reduced to the overt or unconscious product of such calculations of self-interest. On the contrary, belief in law is directly rooted in South African whites' broader traditions and values as well, and these historical and cultural factors reinforce the impact of considerations of utility and legitimation on South African thinking.[116] And this is true not only of English-speaking white South Africans but also of Afrikaners, though the legal principles which these two groups have embraced have sometimes been far from the same.[117] This cultural tradition surely has not been honoured in equal measure by all members of either the English-speaking or Afrikaner white communities, and future research may fruitfully trace the gradations in the strength of adherence to law among South African whites *and* blacks.[117a] But it is a genuine element of South African culture none the less.

The history of both white groups confirms their acceptance of the value of law. The British brought their law with them when they took over the Dutch colony at the Cape of Good Hope at the beginning of the nineteenth century. 'British justice', as Albie Sachs has emphasized, both served as 'an instrument for extending Imperial control', and 'was proclaimed as the guardian of the property and liberty of all British subjects, whether white, brown or black, English-speaking or Afrikaans'.[118] In the words of an early British governor of the colony,

> We are to bear in view that in the dispensation of justice no distinction is to be admitted, whether the complaint arose with the man of wealth, or the poor man, the master or the slave, the European or the Hottentot, the same patient and equal attention is to be paid to the representation and the most careful inquiry is to ensure, that unbiased justice follow, I will not entertain the doubt.[119]

Moreover, legalism fitted well with the 'conservative, antirevolutionary, middle class' culture of the British colonists who began arriving in 1820.[120] In such a culture, legalism has a clear, though hardly liberatory, niche. Allister Sparks

[116] Richard Abel pointed out to me the significance of tradition as a reason for whites' use of law.

[117] Not all South African whites are of either English-speaking or Afrikaner descent, but these two groups represent the major components of the white population.

[117a] On what is *lawless* in South African society, see generally R. Malan, *My Traitor's Heart: A South African Exile Returns to Face His Country, His Tribe, and His Conscience* (New York: Atlantic Monthly Press, 1990).

[118] Sachs, *Justice* (cit. n. 66), 33.

[119] These words of Governor John Cradock, written in 1812, are quoted in G. Frederickson, *White Supremacy: A Comparative Study in American and South African History* (Oxford: Oxford University Press, 1981), 147.

[120] Sparks, *Mind* (cit. n. 50), 56–7.

maintains, however, that from the start a minority of the British immigrants 'established a liberal tradition that has endured through six generations'.[121] Within fourteen years, the British had outlawed slavery throughout their empire and in South Africa had given 'Hottentots and other free persons of colour ... all the rights to which any other of His Majesty's subjects ... are entitled'.[122] British missionaries could and did assist the Khoikhoi, early victims of white domination in southern Africa, to litigate their grievances against their masters.[123]

The case of the Afrikaners is more complex. The British imposed their norm of formal legal equality on the Afrikaners, 'some of whom—the Voortrekkers—'found it so alien and intolerable that they emigrated into the wilderness rather than accept it'.[124] Moreover, the Voortrekkers did not leave British control in order to establish a comparably rule-bound life for themselves. These were the descendants, after all, of what Allister Sparks has called 'one of the most remarkable settlements in the history of colonialism. A small and scattered community of white men drifted beyond the effective reach of any law or administrative arm and lost themselves like so many Robinson Crusoes in the vastness of Africa for a century and a half.'[125] They tended to be 'natural anarchists', even amongst themselves, and they claimed the right to wield a patriarchal power over their black servants that seems to have been even harsher than that of American slaveholders.[126] And they were coming to believe that they were God's chosen people.[127] George Frederickson writes that '[f]or the Voortrekkers ... religion was the only available source of intellectual authority'.[128]

But we should not infer, even from this picture of patriarchal anarchists fired with religious zeal, that Afrikaners were indifferent to law. For one thing, by no means all Afrikaners left the Cape in response to British rule; a great many stayed, prospered (some of them as lawyers), and became the first 'intellectual élite' of the Afrikaner people.[129]

Those who did leave were not lawless either. As Albie Sachs writes, '[t]his was not the departure of outlaws, but the migration of a community determined

[121] Sparks, *Mind* (cit. n. 50), 50. Tom Karis has emphasized the extent to which Cape liberalism was a tradition imposed from outside, and one which did not particularly flourish in South African soil. T. Karis, 'South Africa', in G. Carter (ed.), *Five African States: Responses to Diversity* (Ithaca, NY: Cornell University Press, 1963), 471, 479–80. As he puts it, '[t]he nineteenth-century Cape liberal tradition, that is, the tradition of racial tolerance and color blindness, had for over a century [as of the period following the 2nd World War] inspired only a small number of whites, although a larger number of whites in the Cape had become accustomed to it.' Ibid. 479.

[122] Sachs, *Justice* (cit. n. 52), 39, quoting Ordinance 50 of 1828.

[123] Sparks, *Mind* (cit. n. 50), 66; Frederickson, *White Supremacy* (cit. n. 119), 164–5.

[124] Frederickson, *White Supremacy* (cit. n. 119), 138; see Sparks, *Mind* (cit. n. 50), 30.

[125] Sparks, *Mind* (cit. n. 50), 39.

[126] Frederickson, *White Supremacy* (cit. n. 119), 168–9.

[127] Ibid. 171–5; Sparks, *Mind* (cit. n. 50), 26–33.

[128] Frederickson, *White Supremacy* (cit. n. 119), 173

[129] Sparks, *Mind* (cit. n. 50), 116.

to maintain what it considered to be proper relations between masters and servants.'[130] To be sure, those relations gave Afrikaners tremendous, highly personal power over their black servants, whose status was not dramatically distinguishable from that of slaves, and this sort of unchecked personal dominion is in a sense beyond the realm of law. But Southern planters in the United States exercised comparable dominion over their slaves, and although Northerners indicted them for not living according to law, by the Southerners' own lights they were entirely law-abiding.[131] '[P]lanters', a historian has suggested, 'thought their actions were no more lawless than the operations of a court of equity'.[132] This legalization of dominion could be (though it rarely was) taken to a particularly stark and explicit extreme, as Judge Ruffin of North Carolina once did. He praised what he saw as 'a mildness of treatment, and attention to the comforts of the unfortunate class of slaves',[133] but nevertheless declared that in the absence of contrary statute:

> The power of the master must be absolute, to render the submission of the slave perfect. I most freely confess my sense of the harshness of this proposition, I feel it as deeply as any man can. And as a principle of moral right, every person in his retirement must repudiate it. But in the actual condition of things, it must be so. There is no remedy. The discipline belongs to the state of slavery.[134]

Law can and often does mark out areas of life largely free of legal regulations; the Afrikaners' claim that their treatment of blacks was one of those areas should not be understood as a claim that they were bound by no law, but rather as a statement that the law which bound them gave them this sweeping

[130] Sachs, *Justice* (cit. n. 66), 68.

[131] See C. Sydnor, 'The Southerner and the Laws', 6 *J. So. Hist.* 3, 13, 20 (1940).

[132] Ibid. 13. Mark Tushnet suggests that a dominion regulated only by the demands of 'sentiment' rather than by law is in 'fundamental contradiction' with 'the idea of a law of slavery': *Law of Slavery* (cit. n. 67), 230. He contends that Southern law sought to resolve this contradiction, but did not succeed. So long as the law 'tolerated' its contradictions, as Tushnet suggests it did, ibid. 230, Southern planters no doubt were able to maintain their view of themselves as law-abiding.

[133] *State* v. *Mann*, 13 NC (2 Dev.) 263, 268 (1824).

[134] Ibid. 266. Few judges were so relentless, perhaps because, as Genovese comments, 'no civilized community could live with such a view': *Roll, Jordan* (cit. n. 94), 36–7. North Carolina subsequently distinguished *Mann* in *S.* v. *Will*, 18 NC (1 Dev. and Bat.) 121, 171 (1834) and found that a slave who had killed his overseer after the overseer shot the slave was guilty only of manslaughter rather than murder. To have found malice in these circumstances, the court felt, would have been to accept 'an arbitrary and inflexible rule so sanguinary in its character, and so repugnant to the spirit of those holy statutes which "rejoice the heart, enlighten the eyes, and are true and righteous altogether."' Ibid. As Genovese notes, *Roll, Jordan*, 36, Judge Ruffin did not dissent. (For further discussion of *Mann*, see Tushnet, *Law of Slavery* (cit. n. 67), 54–65. Though Tushnet here criticizes Genovese's treatment of this case—and Genovese has suggested Tushnet's critique is well founded, E. Genovese, 'Slavery in the Legal History of the South and the Nation' (Book Review), 59 *Tex. L. Rev.* 969, 988 n. 112 (1981)—Tushnet himself emphasizes that '[n]o legal system can sustain itself unless participants in the legal process believe that its operations are somehow connected to doing justice—in a slave society, to protecting harmonious, and largely paternalistic, relations between masters and slaves': *Law of Slavery*, 67.)

discretion. Both Southerners and Afrikaners maintained, moreover, that their conduct was justified by another source of law, the law of God.[135]

In fact the Voortrekkers seem to have been very concerned to set out laws by which they could live, despite the fact that their legal institutions were initially 'rudimentary' and their legal knowledge slight.[136] Chief Justice Rumpff declares that 'the Voortrekkers and their descendants in effect brought with them a legacy consisting of a triad of freedom, law and religion.... Their interest in the application of the law was remarkable.'[137] Barend van Niekerk, himself an outspoken and courageous Afrikaner advocate of human rights, observes that a particular Dutch law treatise, Van der Linden's *Koopmans Handboek*,

> was the most popular of the old authorities amongst the old South African pioneers. Together with the Holy Scriptures and the *Trap der Jeugd* grammar book, it found its place in many an ox-wagon kist during the Great Trek. In a very direct fashion therefore Van der Linden contributed monumentally to the preservation of Roman-Dutch law in southern Africa.[138]

In the mid-nineteenth century, the Afrikaner South African Republic went so far as to declare particular Roman-Dutch treatises legally binding, a measure both of the citizens', or burghers', desire to be rid of English law and of their intention to live by another law instead.[139]

In their struggle to free themselves of British imperial control, the Afrikaners became republicans, and as republicans they showed another form of attentiveness to law: they became constitutionalists. The constitution of the Orange Free State was heavily influenced by the United States constitution, some portions of which were 'accepted almost verbatim and translated into Dutch'. Although only whites were permitted to be citizens, the Orange Free State even guaranteed equality before the law, and judicial review of the constitutionality of legislation was viewed 'as an inherent feature of the Constitution'.[140] The Free State selected a Cape Town law professor as its president, and '[s]o great was the prestige of the judges that when one of them ventured

[135] American Southerners contended that they were more faithful both to the constitution and to the Bible than their Northern critics. Sydnor, 'Southerner' (cit. n. 131), 4–6. On Afrikaners' claim of religious sanction for their domination over blacks, see Frederickson, *White Supremacy* (cit. n. 119), 172–3, and T. Dunbar Moodie's synthesis of the Afrikaner 'civil religion', in *The Rise of Afrikanerdom: Power, Apartheid, and the Afrikaner Civil Religion* (Berkeley, Calif.: University of California Press, 1975), 2–11.

[136] See Sachs, *Justice* (cit. n. 52), 69–70.

[137] 'Rumpff Speech' (cit. n. 78), 395.

[138] B. van Niekerk, 'Translator's Preface to Van der Linden's Address on Advocacy', 88 *SALJ* 84, 84 (1981). Rumpff quotes this passage, 'Rumpff Speech' (cit. n. 78), at 396.

[139] The *Koopmans Handboek* was 'declared to be the main source of the law in the South African Republic in 1859'. Van Niekerk, 'Translator's Preface' (cit. n. 138), 84 n. 2. The Republic also made 'the law-book of Simon van Leeuwen and the *Introduction* of Hugo de Groot' binding. 'Rumpff Speech' (cit. n. 78), 396.

[140] Dugard, *Human Rights* (cit. n. 80), 19. The guarantee of equality of the law proved to have little value for blacks. See ibid.

outside of Bloemfontein [the capital] on the court's first circuit, he was received with immense enthusiasm, and returned home suffering from nervous strain and exhaustion.'[141]

It is true that in the South African Republic, the other long-standing Afrikaner republic, '[c]onstitutionalism was less successful'.[142] The South African Republic's *Grondwet* or constitution was haphazardly drafted, and its High Court's effort to exercise a power of constitutional review was decisively defeated. It was at the end of this fight that the President of the Republic, Paul Kruger, declared that '[t]he testing right is a principle of the Devil'. But Kruger's position was hardly lawless. As John Dugard has pointed out, what Kruger endorsed was no more than the British principle of parliamentary supremacy, under which—to use Kruger's words—'[t]he Court is free as it were as a fish is free to swim in a net.'[143] Among those who supported his position was the Cambridge-educated Afrikaner advocate, Jan Smuts,[144] who would in later years fight against the British in the Anglo-Boer War and then play a dominant role in post-independence South African politics as an advocate of a South Africa in which whites, whether Afrikaners or English-speakers, would become one people.

The twin desires of Afrikaners to be ruled by law, and by their own law rather than that of the British, have been evident in this century as well, before and after the National Party, the party of Afrikaner nationalism, came to power in 1948. Legal education at Afrikaans-language universities was expanding well before the Nationalists came to power, and so increasing numbers of Afrikaner lawyers, and law teachers were being trained.[145] The Nationalist government for a time adopted a conscious policy of adding Afrikaners to the Supreme Court bench (one of many forms of pro-Afrikaner affirmative action which South Africa has seen)—though this step may well have reflected greater concern with power than with law.[146]

In addition, Afrikaner legal academics and judges pursued a vigorous effort, sometimes called the purism movement, to rid South African legal doctrine of what they saw as alien, English usurpations of the Roman–Dutch law.[147] Such

[141] Sachs, *Justice* (cit. n. 52), 72.

[142] Dugard, *Human Rights* (cit. n. 80), 20.

[143] Dugard quotes both of Kruger's remarks. Ibid. 24. Kruger misses the holes in the net, which in a sense are the subject of the present book.

[144] Ibid. 22–3.

[145] Forsyth, *In Danger* (cit. n. 3), 223.

[146] J. Mervis, 'How the Nats have Eroded the Pillars of Justice for 30 Years', *Rand Daily Mail* (18 Oct. 1980).

[147] See E. Cameron, 'Legal Chauvinism, Executive-Mindedness and Justice: L. C. Steyn's Impact on South African Law', 99 *SALJ* 38, 43 (1982). Forsyth distinguishes the purists, who he says proposed not only to use but also to modernize Roman–Dutch Law, from the antiquarians, who he believes simply wished to return to the Roman–Dutch law formulated in the 17th cent. in Holland. Forsyth, *In Danger* (cit. n. 3), 183–5. Adrienne van Blerk, much more sympathetic to the general enterprise than Cameron, agrees that this movement meant to excise English principles which had been adopted 'in conflict with the cardinal principles of our own law': 'The Irony of Labels', 99 *SALJ* 365, 368 (1982). She argues, however, that '[e]ssentially the goal of the "purists", then, was for a more modern, effective and equitable legal system ...

ethnic struggles over legal traditions are not unique to South Africa.[148] In the end, the purism movement by no means led to the excision of all English doctrine,[149] although it has had significant effects on South African law.[150] Perhaps, from a broader perspective, its most important effect has been that it may have reassured Afrikaners that the system of law under which they lived was responsive to them, that it was 'our own law',[151] and so assuaged the nationalist sentiments that surely played a role in the genesis of the movement.[152] In the end, therefore, the purism movement may have cemented Afrikaners' adherence not only to law in the abstract, but to the law of South Africa.

Adherence to the law, in short, is a widely shared value among white South Africans, with deep historical and cultural roots as well as, to be sure, important practical and symbolic uses. The strong cultural foundation of this value suggests that it will be honoured even in circumstances where a fresh calculation of its effects might cause a wholly uncommitted person to dispense with it. Law is a real force in white South Africa, and its violation correspondingly a real affront to values that whites accept.

We can now understand well why the South African courts would have engaged in what Hefer JA called their 'punctilious' review of emergency claims, and why they would have been as reluctant as they were to allow emergency power to become a wholly extra-legal, or overtly abusive, affair. Just as Southern appellate judges in the United States, in Mark Tushnet's words, 'attempted to place slavery in the moral framework of Western law', and in part for that reason 'rather consistently enforced the same procedural technicalities in trials of slaves and whites',[153] so South African judges, too,

[B]y introducing the comparative method—including comparison with English law—they were in reality following what has [sic] become the best traditions of Western European jurisprudential methodology.' Ibid. 376.

[148] See R. Luckham, 'The Political Economy of Legal Professions: Toward a Framework for Comparison', in C. Dias, R. Luckham, D. Lynch, and J. Paul (eds.), *Lawyers in the Third World: Comparative and Developmental Perspectives* (Uppsala: Scandinavian Institute of African Studies (Uppsala) and International Center for Law in Development (New York), 1981), 287, 297.

[149] See Cameron, 'Legal Chauvinism' (cit. n. 147), 51–2.

[150] Forsyth, *In Danger* (cit. n. 3), 220–4.

[151] So Cameron, 'Legal Chauvinism' (cit. n. 147), 47, translates a phrase from the judgment of Steyn CJ, the first judge appointed by the Nationalists to rise to the post of chief justice, in *Trust Bank van Afrika Bpk.* v. *Eksteen*, 1964 (3) SA 402 (A). For further information on Steyn's judicial career, see n. 328 below.

[152] Edwin Cameron has argued that 'the doctrine of legal purism exhibits a significant similarity of impulse with its racial counterpart'—that is, with the ideology of apartheid. Cameron, 'Legal Chauvinism' (cit. n. 147), 51. Van Blerk writes that 'it must be conceded that there was more than just a tinge of anti-English, Afrikaans nationalistic sentiment in the early writings of some of the "purists"', a sentiment to which she feels English-speaking South Africans responded in kind. Van Blerk, 'Irony' (cit. n. 147), 375.

[153] Tushnet, *Law of Slavery* (cit. n. 67), 23–4. A. E. Keir Nash has written extensively on the character, often relatively benign, of the work of the Southern appellate courts. See e.g. A. Nash, 'Fairness and Formalism in the Trials of Blacks in the State Supreme Courts of the Old South', 56 *Va. L. Rev.* 64 (1970); 'Reason of Slavery: Understanding the Judicial Role in the Peculiar Institution', 32 *Vand. L. Rev.* 7 (1979).

have been constrained by law even in the midst of injustice. Surely judges, as compared to other white South Africans, must be particularly sensitive to this constraint. Later in this chapter we will consider certain distinctive features of South African lawyers and judges which might heighten this sensitivity, by contributing to judicial independence and even to a human rights tradition within the South African legal profession.[154] It requires no special discussion of South Africa's legal profession, however, to suggest that throughout their legal careers judges are likely to be schooled in valuing the law. As judges, moreover, they are called upon to hear opposing arguments and then to offer reasoned judgments that must speak in legal terms. These burdens of their role, in South Africa as in the American slave states,[155] no doubt reinforce what judges promise in typical oaths of office—that they will enforce the law.[156]

(d) Afrikaner Nationalism and the Limits on Adherence to Law.

It would be a mistake to think that a group's attitudes to the law have all been compassed when we say that that group does, or does not, value adherence to the law. While adherence to the law may well have modestly constrained the Rabie court and the Nationalist government during the state of emergency, two other characteristics of Afrikaners' historic attitudes towards the law may also have had an effect, and not in favour of legalistic constraint. The first of these is Afrikaners' sensitivity to the claims of a higher, or deeper, law than what is on the books. The second is Afrikaners' lack of sympathy, until very recently, with the rhetoric of human rights.

Afrikaners' willingness to disregard South African law in favour of a deeper law has been a vivid feature of South African history. Eleven of the eighteen cases of 'resistance and rebellion' which Hugh Corder examines in his study of the Appellate Division from 1920 to 1950 grew out of Afrikaner rebellion or attempted rebellion during both of the World Wars.[157] Among the Afrikaners interned by South Africa for security reasons during the Second World War were a future judge, Kowie Marais, and a future prime minister, John Vorster;

[154] See text at nn. 260–354 below.

[155] Mark Tushnet suggests that evidence that local justice in one Southern state was harsher than appellate justice reflects 'that appellate judges had to explain what they were doing, whereas local magistrates and slave patrols had only to do it': *Law of Slavery* (cit. n. 67), 24. A. E. Keir Nash contrasts the Southern judges' focus on 'the individual Negro, or his counsel, standing before him seeking justice' with the more 'general' (perhaps one should say institutional, or even *realpolitik*) view that a legislator might take of slavery issues: 'A More Equitable Past? Southern Supreme Courts and the Protection of the Antebellum Negro', 48 *N. Ca. L. Rev.* 197, 239–40 (1970).

[156] The Supreme Court Act No. 59 of 1959, s. 10(2)(*a*), specifies the oath to be taken by each judge of the South African Supreme Court: 'I will in my capacity as a judge of the Supreme Court of South Africa administer justice to all persons alike without fear, favour or prejudice, and, as the circumstances of any particular case may require, in accordance with the law and customs of the Republic of South Africa or of the territory of South-West Africa.' (The reference to South-West Africa reflects that that territory, now the independent nation of Namibia, was under South African rule until 1990.)

[157] See Corder, *Judges at Work* (cit. n. 2), 71–92.

Marais 'gave lectures on law to his fellow internees at what was called the *Boere Universiteit* that they themselves had organized'.[158]

The source of these rebellions was not simply a sense of continued oppression at the hands of English-speaking South Africans. Instead, Afrikaners had come to see their history as describing a sacred course, in which the Afrikaner chosen people placed its faith in God in the midst of terrible trials. As J. C. van Rooy, a leader of the Broederbond (a powerful and secret Afrikaner organization), said in 1944:

> In every People in the world is embodied a Divine Idea and the task of each People is to build upon that Idea and to perfect it. So God created the Afrikaner People with a unique language, a unique philosophy of life, and their own history and tradition in order that they might fulfil a particular calling and destiny here in the southern corner of Africa. We must stand guard on all that is peculiar to us and build upon it. We must believe that God has called us to be servants of his righteousness in this place.[159]

To fulfil this calling nothing less was required than that the Afrikaner must achieve a 'free, sovereign, and independent ethnic existence'.[160] Put more bluntly, as van Rooy and a colleague did in a 1934 circular to the members of the Broederbond, 'the main object is ... that Afrikanerdom shall reach its ultimate destiny of domination in South Africa'.[161]

Afrikaners, in other words, saw themselves as bound by a greater law than man's to seek their own freedom from others' domination, or even their domination of others. The vindication of rebellion for the cause of national freedom is expressed in the words of an important Afrikaner poet, N. P. van Wyk Louw, in a verse play, *The Deeper Law*, which he wrote in 1938, the year of an extremely emotional centenary of the Great Trek.[162] In this play, the Afrikaners of the Trek (the Voortrekkers), and their Advocate, described as 'one of the highest officials of Justice',[163] appear in the Hall of the Eternal Justice and must justify their having rebelled in pursuit of their liberty. In the play's most famous lines, which today are quoted on both the right and the left of the South African political spectrum, the Afrikaners' advocate declares, 'When you oppress a proud people, rebellion against the law becomes its right'.[164] The Voice of Justice ultimately speaks, and says:

[158] Harrison, *White Tribe* (cit. n. 103), 124.

[159] This speech is trans. and quoted in Moodie, *Rise of Afrikanerdom* (cit. n. 135), 110–11.

[160] These are the words of E. C. Pienaar, quoted by Moodie in ibid. 185. Moodie calls Pienaar 'the foremost Cape Broederbonder of his day'. Ibid. at 186.

[161] This statement too is quoted by Moodie. Ibid. 113.

[162] N. van Wyk Louw, *Die Dieper Reg: 'n Spel van die Oordeel oor 'n Volk* (Cape Town: Nasionale Pers Beperk, 1947). No trans. of this play has been published; I rely primarily on a trans. prepared by Ms Nadine Havenga.

[163] Ibid. 9.

[164] In the original Afrikaans: 'As jy 'n trotse volk verkneg, | word opstand teen die reg *sy* reg.' Ibid. 16. The trans. in the text is guided by Professor Johann van der Westhuizen, who also told me about the prominence of these lines, and the diverse causes in whose favour they are now invoked. Personal communication, 31 Aug. 1990.

Go forth and know that your law
and deed can stand before God....

They will not die, their life
is so soaked into that land
and has been absorbed in it
that they will remain for
as long as it cliffs jut out above
the long foam-rings of the sea,
separate and proud and free![165]

While rebellion against unjust authority is obedience to a deeper law, Afrikaner thinking has, until recently, shown little fondness for the notion of individual rights against *just* authority. This is not to say that Afrikaners approved of lawless government, or did not recognize that a government bound by law was indeed a constrained government. What Afrikaners did not welcome was the ideology of 'human rights'. In 1983 H. J. Coetsee, the Minister of Justice, identified two sources of this feeling. One reason was, simply, resentment. The Minister observed that 'one is faced with the fact that South Africa has over a long period of time been the target of institutions which have employed human rights concepts against us'.[166]

The other reason stemmed from the contrast between 'the humanistic overemphasis of individual rights vis-à-vis government authority with on the other hand the Afrikaner with his Calvinistic background who tends rather to emphasize State order and the maintenance thereof'.[167] This sentiment is far from the natural anarchism of the early Afrikaner; the change in Afrikaner thinking seems to owe a great deal to the shared experience of struggle in the Anglo-Boer War and thereafter.[168] The unity of the Afrikaner people was a recurrent theme during the slow rise of Afrikaner power leading up to 1948. Not only did the chosen people need to be united, but also, according to one strand of civil religion thought, linked to German nationalist thinking, the individual could only find himself in the nation. Nicolaas Diederichs, much later the Minister of Finance, argued in 1935 that: 'Without the uplifting, ennobling and enriching influence of this highest inclusive unity which we call a nation, mankind cannot reach the fullest heights of his human existence. Only through his consecration to, his love for and his service to the nation can man come to the versatile and harmonious development of his human

[165] Van Wyk Louw, *Die Dieper Reg* (cit. n. 162), 27–8. 'Separate' in the final line could also be trans. as 'detached'.

[166] H. Coetsee, 'Hoekom nie 'n verklaring van menseregte nie?', 1984 *TRW* 5, 6 ('Why Not a Bill of Rights?', trans. by Nadine Havenga). Coetsee urged, however, that such 'past prejudices must be forgotten'. Ibid.

[167] Ibid. 6. I should add that Coetsee's point was not to disparage the legal protection of liberty, but to argue against a bill of rights and a concomitant power of judicial review under such a statement of rights.

[168] On the unity forged in war and the pressures for conformity in the political struggles thereafter, see Sparks, *Mind* (cit. n. 50), 127–8.

existence'.[169] Hence '[f]reedom is not simply a task which must be fulfilled, but seen from the angle of the nation, freedom is also a *duty*.'[170]

For similar reasons, perhaps, Afrikaners have not been enamoured of the notion of the 'rule of law'.[171] Again, Afrikaners might have wholeheartedly accepted certain elements in formulations of the rule of law—say, the idea that governmental action should take place in accordance with previously adopted legal rules.[172] But the concept of the rule of law can mean much more than that, from due process to a very broad compendium of rights.[173] In the 1970s an Afrikaner scholar argued that advocates of the rule of law 'all presuppose the notion of "fundamental rights" accruing to the individual as against (state, government) authority'. This in turn must depend on a humanistic assumption that 'man is ... the measure', and so, 'if humanism cannot be considered to be the prevailing political philosophy in a country, then the Rule of Law has no place in that land'. Because the South African constitution acknowledged the sovereignty of God, its fundamental intention was Christian, and hence in 'radical opposition to the humanistic point of departure, which makes *man* the sovereign consideration'. This scholar called, therefore, not for the rule of law but for 'Christian government, necessarily including juridical ordering and administration of justice with a distinct Christian accent'.[174] And more recently Paul van Warmelo, the Dean Emeritus of the University of Pretoria School of Law (an Afrikaner university), has written that '[t]he Rule of Law is, in my opinion, nothing but an ideology belonging to a small minority which has had the good fortune to impose it on the majority.'[175]

If these sentiments—the ardent willingness to breach the law for the sake of Afrikaner survival, and the potentially authoritarian indifference to the claims of human rights—had been in full flower in the 1980s, the course of the emergency and of emergency law might have been much worse than it was. The fact that a country values the law is not, as Nazi Germany among others teaches us, a guarantee of its good conduct.

The mystic, chauvinistic nationalism of Nazi Germany—sadly not unrelated to the civil religion of Afrikaner nationalism[176]—generated its own 'juris-

[169] N. Diederichs, *Nationalisme as Lewensbeskouing en sy verhouding tot Internasionalisme* (Bloemfontein: Nationale Pers, 1935) (*Nationalism as a* Weltanschauung *and its Relation to Internationalism*), quoted and trans. in Moodie, *Rise of Afrikanerdom* (cit. n. 135), 156–7.

[170] Diederichs, *Nationalisme* (cit. n. 169), quoted in Moodie, *Rise of Afrikanerdom* (cit. n. 135), 158.

[171] Personal communciation from Johann van der Westhuizen, 31 Aug. 1990.

[172] For an illustration of this understanding of the rule of law on the part of a National Party minister, see A. Mathews, *Freedom, State Security and the Rule of Law: Dilemmas of the Apartheid Society* (Cape Town: Juta, 1986), 1.

[173] See Ibid., pp. xxviii–xxx, 1–30.

[174] F. Venter, 'The Withering of the "Rule of Law"', 8 *Speculum Juris* 69, 86–7 (1973).

[175] P. van Warmelo, 'Law, Ideology and Justice' in J. Hung (ed.), *Law and Justice in South Africa* (Johannesburg: Institute for Public Interest Law and Research, and Cape Town: Centre for Intergroup Studies, 1988), 161, 163.

[176] So e.g. Diederichs declared in 1937 that 'In South Africa we believe that the Afrikaner worker is still the best and most reliable Afrikaner. He must be drawn into his nation in order to be a genuine man. There must be no division or schism between class and class. May the

prudence' (if that is not too generous a term). It is chilling to learn that, as the German scholar Arthur Kaufmann points out, 'the great majority of legal philosophers settled into the Third Reich with little difficulty'.[177] In place of the sober 'legal scientific positivism' of the nineteenth century,[178] one scholar now affirmed 'the knowledge that the essence of justice is the direct expression of the blood community of the "volk"'. Another replaced the virtue of parliamentary debate as a path to truth with 'trust in the Führer to find what is right at a given moment'. Still another, more extreme than most, 'mystically spoke of a great Führer ... the personification of the German soul'.[179] In Müller's bitter words,

> There was virtually no outrage perpetrated by the Nazis which was not praised [by the law professors] during the regime as 'supremely just' ....
>
> It is almost impossible to overestimate this contribution [of jurists to Nazi terror] ... for it was in the writings of these scholars that the judges of the Third Reich found guidelines for their verdicts and lethal interpretations.[180]

This jurisprudence of the Volk was not the sole factor impelling the German courts towards their collaboration with Nazism. Other factors, including the old tradition of positivism and the judges' susceptibility to pressures of various sorts from the state, probably played a role as well, and we will consider these

day break here as is the case in Italy and Germany, where the worker may comfort himself with the thought: "What I do here I do as a worker, but I do it in service of my nation."' Moodie, *Rise of Afrikanerdom* (cit. n. 135), 168–9. Moodie comments that '[t]he Nazi influence in this attitude to class conflict is obvious.' Ibid. 169 n. 21. David Harrison writes that the Ossewabrandwag (trans. by Moodie as the 'Oxwagon Sentinel', ibid. 189), a nationalist organization with 'a distinctly military flavour', gained popularity in 1939, 'with many Afrikaners drawing inspiration from the way National Socialism had united Germany and brought Hitler to power. The parades, the Hitler Youth, the stress on ethnic purity, all found their echoes in South Africa.' Harrison, *White Tribe* (cit. n. 103), 115. While the National Party ultimately split with the Ossewabrandwag, the split was due more to inter-organizational competition than to 'ideological differences, which tended to cut across organizational lines'. Moodie, *Rise of Afrikanerdom*, 221. Before the split Dr D. F. Malan, later a Prime Minister of South Africa, 'sought to steal the civil religion thunder' of the Ossewabrandwag, and his party 'went as far as to declare Malan *volksleier* ("leader of the People") as well as the party leader'. Ibid. 218.

[177] Kaufmann, 'National Socialism' (cit. n. 39), 1633. In general, the Nazis found it 'relatively easy to get control of universities and their law schools', Vagts, 'International Law' (cit. n. 39), 671. In the process, however, many academics left Germany; few legal philosophers were among those who chose to leave. Kaufmann, 'National Socialism', 1633.

[178] The phrase is David Richards's. Richards, 'Terror' (cit. n. 33), 178. The decline of positivism had already begun even before the Nazi take-over. Richards has suggested that the German judiciary's 'strict allegiance to the rule of law when the law was that of the authoritarian bureaucracy of Imperial Germany' was modified during the republican years, when the judiciary began to affirm 'its own capacity to articulate moral values'. Ibid. 179. Moreover, most members of the judiciary—for decades a very conservative institution—had 'kept their distance from the [Weimar] republic'. Müller, *Hitler's Justice* (cit. n. 28), 10; see ibid. 6–9. In many trials during the Weimar years, 'the courts continued to take the Nazi side of the ongoing political struggle, sometimes openly, sometimes behind the façade of legal manœuvres'. Ibid. 17. Positivism, Müller urges, fell victim to judicial conservatism even before 1933. Ibid. 219.

[179] Kaufman, 'National Socialism' (cit. n. 39), 1638–40.

[180] Müller, *Hitler's Justice* (cit. n. 28), 68.

later in this chapter.[181] For many judges the guiding force in their decisions was probably neither jurisprudential theory nor personal ambition or anxiety, but rather active sympathy with much of the Nazis' programme.[182] One way for such sympathy to find legal expression, however, would have been through jurisprudence. The force and impact of nationalist feelings in the law emerge starkly in the stunning and fateful case of the Bavarian beer-hall *putsch* in 1923. Adolf Hitler was tried for treason for his role in this *putsch*, and convicted. The relevant statute required the deportation of foreigners convicted of this offence, but the court refused to deport Hitler (who was an Austrian citizen). The court explained that '[i]n the case of a man whose thoughts and feelings are as German as Hitler's, the court is of the opinion that the intent and purpose of the law have no application.'[183]

I do not mean to argue that if the Afrikaner civil religion had remained stronger, South Africa would have descended to the depths of the Nazis. South Africa's ruling white minority (Afrikaner and English-speaker alike) did *not* seek the extermination of an entire ethnic group, and did not need the methods that such an objective calls forth. On the contrary, South African whites have never been able to do without the services of the black majority, however much whites have sought to impose their will on their black fellow citizens.

In particular, it is unlikely that South Africa's courts would have yielded entirely to the fires of white nationalism had those fires been burning freely during the years of the state of emergency. Even in the 1960s, when nationalist sentiment was more intense and unquestioning than it has since become, and when the courts rendered some very harsh decisions, they were not incapable of 'a more generous interpretation in favour of the rights of the individual'.[184] Just as judges' vocation and experience make them particularly likely to value the law, so they may be particularly unlikely to cast this value aside in response to the call of other passions. The prestige and traditional independence of South African judges and the persistence of a modest human rights tradition within the South African legal profession—to which we will turn shortly[185]—would augment the judges' insulation. None the less it is chilling to imagine what might have been, had the emergency decisions been rendered under the brunt not only of fear but also of unbridled ethnic passion. Ouster clauses might easily have been read sympathetically rather than with almost unremitting

[181] See text at nn. 333–4, 361–2 below.

[182] See Reimann, 'National Socialist Jurisprudence' (cit. n. 39), 1658 n. 35. Müller sees such sympathy as central. *Hitler's Justice* (cit. n. 28), 294–6.

[183] This decision is quoted in ibid., 16.

[184] Thus in the grim era when the Appellate Division decided such cases as *Rossouw* v. *Sachs*, 1964 (2) SA 551 (A) (see Ch. 2, text at nn. 123–7 above) and *Schermbrucker* v. *Klindt, NO*, 1965 (4) SA 606 (A) (see Ch. 4, text at nn. 30–59 above), it also decided *S.* v. *Heyman and Another*, 1966 (4) SA 598 (A), in which Chief Justice Steyn found room for precisely such an interpretation in favour of individual rights even though the case had internal security implications. Ibid. 605B-G.

[185] See text at nn. 237–354 below.

narrowness; the State President's exercise of his emergency powers could have been held altogether beyond judicial review; common law protections might have been bluntly abrogated, with the admonition *salus reipublicae est suprema lex*, or even *inter arma silent leges*.[186] These rulings were never made.

In fact, however, these passionate sentiments had faded substantially by the time the state of emergency began in 1985. Afrikaners came to power, by lawful means, in the 1948 elections, and the National Party has governed ever since. In the decades of power, much of the fire of this civil religion has burnt out. In part, it faded just because such 'chiliastic' fires can never be renewed indefinitely.[187] In part, it lost its grip because it had been so successful as a programme of Afrikaner ethnic advancement; Afrikaners tasted the good life, and then drank deeply of it, and like so many others elsewhere began to experience the temptations of ease and the discomfort of privilege.[188]

These discomforts must have become more acute as it became clear that the programme of apartheid which Afrikaner nationalism had embraced was in other respects more costly, and less workable, than many whites had once dreamt. Apartheid subjected Afrikaners to world-wide contempt and certain tangible sanctions as well; the subjective cost may actually have been the greater one.[189] Perhaps, too, the modest liberal white opposition over the years within South Africa exacted some moral cost, although as an electoral force white liberalism has not been very significant for decades.[190] The growth of anti-apartheid law practice, reflected in the formation of such organizations as the Legal Resources Centre, the Centre for Applied Legal Studies, Lawyers for Human Rights, and the Black Lawyers Association, contributed to this moral cost by calling attention to injustice, and won modest victories that interfered with aspects of apartheid's programme.[191]

A central part of the grand design of apartheid—the dream of an all-white South Africa, whose black menial employees would find their political destiny in independent black homelands—turned out to be unachievable. Economic pressures inevitably drew blacks out of their homelands and into the cities, all the more so when the government decided that economic growth was essential to its security.[192] At the same time, black political mobilization and militancy turned out to be resilient and impossible to ignore. Black opposition can be

[186] That is, that 'the safety of the nation is the highest law' or that 'amidst the clash of weapons the laws are silent'.

[187] Sparks, *Mind* (cit. n. 50), 315–16.

[188] Sparks emphasizes the temptations of ease. Ibid. 316–17.

[189] On the subjective costs, see ibid. 317 and text at nn. 70–5 above.

[190] Ibid. 46–8, 70–1.

[191] So e.g. litigation contributed to the demise of the influx control system by which the state sought to keep South African blacks from establishing permanent residence in South Africa's cities. (These cases are discussed in Ch. 2 at n. 137 above.) For an instance of advocacy on behalf of a community facing forced removal, see White, *To Learn and Teach* (cit. n. 87). And for one of a host of cases in which lawyers have made effective use of a reformist labour statute to secure rights for black workers, see *Marievale Consolidated Mines* v. *President, Industrial Court*, 1986 (2) SA 485 (T).

[192] Sparks, *Mind* (cit. n. 50), 199–202, 314–15.

and has been punished again and again,[193] but since the development of the black consciousness movement led by Steve Biko, beginning in the late 1960s, new movements have arisen repeatedly from the ashes of the old.[194] In every walk of South African life, from education to music, drama, medicine, law, and of course in politics, opposition to the government is vibrantly expressed.[195] Among all the forces weakening the confidence and moral certainty of Afrikaner nationalism, African nationalism has been central.

For all these reasons, the civil religion weakened. Allister Sparks at one point in his recent book, *The Mind of South Africa*, goes so far as to say that '[t]he Afrikaner revolution is over, and all that is left of it is the politics of survivalism. The fortress of the *volk* is to be defended, but there is no faith within its walls.'[196] This may be too strong,[197] but it is clear that many Afrikaners have come to hope for a future of co-operation with South Africa's other people, from English-speaking whites to 'Coloureds', Indians, and Africans.[198] Undoubtedly this change of heart, as well as pragmatic calculations, have contributed to the gradual opening of South African politics.

Just as the passions of the civil religion have cooled, so have Afrikaner attitudes to human rights warmed. In 1986 State President Botha claimed that '[w]e believe in the sovereignty of the law as the basis for the protection of the fundamental rights of individuals as well as groups. We believe in the sanctity and indivisibility of law and the just application thereof.'[199] In the same year the Minister of Justice, whose explanation of opposition to a bill of rights I have already mentioned, asked the South African Law Commission to study the desirability of adopting a bill of rights in South Africa.[200] Perhaps to the government's surprise, the Commission proceeded to put together an extensive working paper which urged the adoption of a generally liberal bill

[193] Leaders of the African National Congress, the Pan Africanist Congress, the South African Students Organization, and the United Democratic Front, as well as many other less prominent people, have suffered severe penalties for their acts in the struggle against apartheid.

[194] The most striking recent example is the emergence of the 'Mass Democratic Movement', an amorphous but prominent grouping which filled part of the gap created by the government's use of its emergency powers virtually to ban the United Democratic Front in Feb. 1988.

[195] For examples of the diverse fields of anti-apartheid struggle, see P. Molefe, 'NECC Meets to Discuss "Education for All"', *Weekly Mail* 4, col. 2 (15–20 Dec. 1989) (education); T. Mkhwanazi, 'Sweet Potato Freedom', *Weekly Mail* 27, col. 4 (15–20 Dec. 1989) (anti-apartheid nursery rhymes); Z. Dobson, 'The Musical's Revitalized—But Not the District', *Weekly Mail* 23, col. 1 (8–14 Dec. 1989) (musical); 'Snubbed SACOS Links Up with PAC', *Weekly Mail* 35, col. 1 (1–7 Dec. 1989) (sport). For an overview of 'the revolt of the eighties', see Sparks, *Mind* (cit. n. 50), 329–61.

[196] Ibid. 328.

[197] Compare ibid. 32 (saying that the civil religion 'has lost some of its animating force in recent years').

[198] For an illustrative, although already dated, expression of such sentiments by Willem (Wimpie) de Klerk, a prominent Afrikaner journalist (and brother of the current State President, F. W. de Klerk), see W. de Klerk, *The Second Revolution* (Johannesburg: Jonathan Bull, 1984).

[199] These words were part of Botha's opening address to Parliament on 31 Jan. 1986, and are quoted in South African Law Commission, *Working Paper 25—Project 58: Group and Human Rights* (n.d., ?1989) 265.

[200] Ibid. 266.

of rights.[201] Moreover, the Commission marshalled evidence from a range of sources to demonstrate that its proposal in fact was consistent with what had become the dominant, or at least significant, religious and political sentiments of the nation and of its white population.[202] Martin Chanock characterizes the Commission's report as seeking to effect 'a fundamental change in political direction' by offering 'a mass of objective legalism' to support it—an ironic appraisal that points, however, to the appeal that legalism may have, at least for the Commission's likely audience of powerful white South Africans.[203]

South African, and Afrikaner, thinking *is* changing, as these political and cultural developments reflect, and I suggest that these changes helped insulate the Appellate Division from the potential temptation to cast off the bounds of law. But the change is hardly complete. Survival has been at stake, in the eyes of the government, and even a sterile politics of survivalism can be a source of profound pressures. Just as the concern for survival has persisted despite the waning of the civil religion, so we should not be too quick to assume that the idea of law as a guarantee of rights—everyone's rights—against the state enjoys universal white approbation. Encouraging as the Commission's evidence is, it also includes polling data indicating that only 19.6 per cent of South African whites unequivocally believe that all groups in South Africa should have equal rights; 48.1 per cent 'conditional[ly]' agree with this proposition, and 32 per cent simply disagree with it.[204] This data is only suggestive, to be sure, but it offers us further reason to doubt that in a crisis of survival white sentiment would provide strong support for the notion of law as a protector of the rights of those who constituted the threat to whites' survival.

Events of the emergency suggest that both the willingness to breach ordinary law for the sake of Afrikaner (or white) survival and the distaste for the idea of rights against a just authority may have played a role in some whites' actions. Certainly it would be a mistake to characterize the conduct of the security forces during this period as having hewed to the boundaries, wide as they were, fixed by the law. Murders and bombings, and widespread mistreatment of detainees, all had their part in the handling of the total onslaught which whites thought they faced. People faced with threats to their own survival often end up compromising their principles, however benign those principles may be, for extreme conditions breed extreme conduct. The particular threads of Afrikaners' views of the law, however, may have helped bring South Africa to this point.

Did what remained of such sentiments play a role in the disturbing features

201 Ibid. 321–3. For the Commission's proposed draft of a bill of rights, see ibid. 471–80.

202 See ibid. 183–214, 260–81, 293.

203 M. Chanock, 'A Post-Calvinist Catechism? Reading the South African Bill of Rights Debate' (unpubl. 1991), 14.

204 South African Law Commission, *Group and Human Rights* (cit. n. 199), 279, quoting (in trans.) a Human Sciences Research Council memorandum to the Commission, 'Geesteswetenskaplike Oorwegings ten opsigte van 'n Akte van Menseregte' (Nov. 1987).

of the Rabie court's emergency judgments? Let me be clear that I do not contend that any member of the court consciously violated any rule of law for these (or any other) reasons. None the less several matters require explanation. First among them is the existence of the emergency team itself, a phenomenon for which the only apparent explanation is that it was felt—by Rabie himself if he picked these panels, as seems likely, or by whoever else did the picking if he did not—that other panels, more representative of the court as a whole, might be less reliable. That Rabie remained on the court during this period as acting chief justice is disturbing as well. It is also important to recall the extent to which the judgments of the members of the emergency team fell short of being carefully reasoned adjudication, instead resorting to often unpersuasive arguments and to abrupt, even deaf, responses to opposing views and displaying an apparent willingness to take whatever doctrinal steps were necessary to fend off broad challenges to the emergency system.

The evasion of the constraints of neutral judicial process—both in selection of judges and in marshalling of logic—are telling. Indeed, the Rabie Appellate Division's emergency jurisprudence has something of the flavour of the Taney United States Supreme Court's judgment in the *Dred Scott* case in 1857.[205] That case held that no black person descended from slaves could be a citizen of the United States, or of any state within it, under the federal constitution,[206] and decided as well that Congress could not constitutionally bar slavery from territories of the United States that had not yet become states.[207] The case's handling was marked by a number of irregularities of judicial process—including the communication to the President-elect of much, at least, of the expected decision's outcome more than a week before the judgments were actually handed down.[208] Moreover, '[t]he so-called opinion of the Court included a considerable amount of material that few if any of the other justices

[205] *Scott* v. *Sandford*, 60 US (19 How.) 393 (1857) (*Dred Scott*).

[206] Ibid. 403–27.

[207] Ibid. 431–52.

[208] Chief Justice Taney is said to have had a 'rigorous sense of propriety', D. Fehrenbacher, *The Dred Scott Case: Its Significance in American Law and Politics* (New York: Oxford University Press, 1978), 306. None the less Fehrenbacher quotes a 23 Feb. 1857 letter from Justice Grier to President-elect Buchanan, in which Grier writes that he has agreed to concur with Taney, predicts the number of votes on a central issue in the case, and declared that 'we [apparently Grier, Taney, and Justice Wayne] have thought due to you to state to you in candor and confidence the real state of the matter'. Ibid. 312. At his inauguration on 4 Mar. 1857, Buchanan then disingenuously declared that when the Supreme Court handed down its decision he, 'in common with all good citizens ... [would] cheerfully submit, whatever this may be'. Ibid. 313. Before Buchanan's speech, Taney had administered the oath of office to him, and observers had noted that the two men spoke briefly. The *Dred Scott* decision was announced two days later, on 6 Mar., and this conversation became the basis for charges that Taney had told Buchanan at his inauguration what the court's decision would be. Fehrenbacher maintains 'that no such revelation was necessary because the President already knew, and the Chief Justice knew that he knew, what the Court would decide'. Ibid. Taney's biographer offers a similar, though less blunt, conclusion. See C. Swisher, *Roger B. Taney* (New York: Macmillan, 1935), 498–9, 520–2.

heard or read before its publication.'[209] That opinion, by Chief Justice Taney, contained what Don Fehrenbacher has called an 'extraordinary cumulation of error, inconsistency, and misrepresentation, dispensed with ... pontifical self-assurance'.[210] Fehrenbacher concludes that Taney's 'true purpose' was 'to launch a sweeping counterattack on the antislavery movement and to reinforce the bastions of slavery at every rampart and parapet'.[211] Fehrenbacher's judgment that in *Dred Scott* 'law and history were distorted to serve a passionate purpose'[212] suggests that the similar features of the Rabie court's decisions may have reflected a comparable infection.[213]

But there are some signs that this infection, severe as it may have been, was not so virulent as the disease that assailed the United States Supreme Court when it decided the *Dred Scott* case. The Rabie court's judgments, as we have seen, did not defend 'every rampart and parapet' of state power but instead left standing a number of doctrinal principles of potential value as limits on governmental authority. The rhetoric of the Rabie court, in addition, does not reach the emotional pitch of Chief Justice Taney's opinion, which invokes, *inter alia*, as insistent emphasis on whites' contempt for blacks and a barbed celebration of the memory of the founding fathers in support of its

[209] Fehrenbacher, *Dred Scott Case* (cit. n. 208), 320–1. This bizarre situation was the result of Taney's decision to make major revisions in his opinion after the decision had been announced. Taney had already read his opinion in open court on 6 Mar. 1857, but he did not release it for publication at that time. The two dissenters, McLean and Curtis, had released their opinions to the press without delay, however, and Taney resented the 'definite advantage in the war of words' which opponents of the decision enjoyed as a result. Ibid. 315. He seems to have expanded his opinion before its publication by approximately 50% in order to meet the dissenters' arguments. Ibid. 317–21. Meanwhile, the court's term had ended with the announcement of the decision, Swisher, *Roger B. Taney* (cit. n. 208), 512, and most members of the court had left Washington. Only Taney and two other members of the *Dred Scott* majority remained, and the three of them directed the clerk of the court not to release any opinions until they were published in the court's official reports. On this basis, Taney blocked Justice Curtis, one of the dissenters, from even seeing the revised majority opinion until it was published! Fehrenbacher, *Dred Scott Case*, 316–18; see Swisher, *Roger B. Taney*, 512–15. Whether Taney's opinion deserved to be called, as it was, the 'opinion of the court' is debatable on another ground as well. There has been controversy since the case was decided over whether Taney's opinion actually expressed the views of a majority of the justices. See Fehrenbacher, *Dred Scott Case*, 324–5. Fehrenbacher's conclusion is that Taney did speak for a majority, ibid. 333–4, but the debate is not over. See D. Currie, 'The Constitution in the Supreme Court: Article IV and Feberal Powers, 1836–64', 1983 *Duke LJ* 695, 730–2 (characterizing 'Taney's "opinion of the court" label' as 'misleading').

[210] Fehrenbacher, *Dred Scott Case* (cit. n. 208), 559. David Currie is also blunt in his evaluation. 'From a lawyer's viewpoint [*Dred*] *Scott* was a disreputable performance. The variety of feeble, poorly developed, and unnecessary constitutional arguments suggests, if nothing else, a determination to reach a predetermined conclusion at any price.' Currie, 'Constitution' (cit. n. 209), 737.

[211] Fehrenbacher, *Dred Scott Case* (cit. n. 208), 341.

[212] Ibid. 559.

[213] One reason for Taney's untempered writing may have been the pain and guilt he must have felt from the death of his wife and one of his daughters just a few months before *Dred Scott* was argued. See R. Barnett, 'Professionalism and the Chains of Slavery' (Book Review), 77 *Mich. L. Rev.* 655, 661–3 (1979). If Taney's work is the product of both personal and political emotion, however, it would remain a measuring rod for the presence of distorting passion in a judge's work.

conclusions.[214] One of Taney's colleagues is not just intense but overheated: he is 'revolted' by one argument, and compelled to 'antipathy and disgust' by another.[215]

Though we must be careful in explaining the contrasting work of courts of separate eras and nations, one source of the differences between the Taney and Rabie courts may have been that the judges of the emergency team approached their task with cooler heads than did Chief Justice Taney and many of his colleagues in *Dred Scott*.[216] Passion there may have been among the South African judges, but it found expression in decisions that are more determined, even relentless, than fiery. If the members of the emergency team had tempered their passion, then we may also infer that their adherence to the law, which we have seen had strong roots in South African culture and in the judicial vocation, remained real as well. For judges who sought to harmonize their determination to protect the emergency order with their fidelity to law, the sense that these two goals were in tension would have been disquieting indeed. Perhaps it is just such disquiet that helps explain the alacrity of the Rabie court's response in such cases as *Nkwentsha* or *Apleni*, where it could, without undercutting the fundamental features of the emergency system, once again vindicate the integrity of law.

214 The most notorious passage of this discussion argues that the constitution embodies the view held by whites, at the time of the constitution's adoption, that blacks were 'beings of an inferior order, and altogether unfit to associate with the white race, either in social or political relations; and so far inferior, that they had no rights which the white man was bound to respect ...'. *Dred Scott*, 60 US (19 How.) at 407. Taney expands on this point, which he is obviously determined to drive home conclusively; for a more extended excerpt, see Ch. 2 n. 68 above. Two pages later he reiterates the 'absolute and despotic power' which whites intended to claim over blacks, and the 'stigma, of the deepest degradation', which whites had placed on blacks. Ibid. 409. Shortly afterwards Taney turns to the words of the Declaration of Independence, and asserts that an interpretation of the Declaration that extended its noble sentiments to blacks would require the conclusion that the founding fathers' actions were 'utterly and flagrantly inconsistent with the principles they asserted [in the Declaration]; and instead of the sympathy of mankind, to which they so confidently appealed, they would have deserved and received universal rebuke and reprobation'. Ibid. 410. Fehrenbacher speaks of the 'flat judicial prose' of Taney's opinion, Fehrenbacher, *Dred Scott Case* (cit. n. 208), 388, but in these passages Taney's prose, if not purple, is certainly vivid and emotive.

215 *Dred Scott*, 60 US (19 How.) at 480, 488 (Daniel J. concurring).

216 The cooler tone of the Rabie court should not be attributed only to the differences in ardour of the Supreme Court majority in 1857 and the Appellate Division's emergency team in the late 1980s. Tone is also a function of conventions of rhetorical style. Moreover, the Rabie court did not *need* to say as much as the Taney court did, for its task was only to uphold the emergency structure shaped by the executive, rather than, as the Supreme Court tried in *Dred Scott*, to reshape the law of a country so as to resolve a crisis which the political branches of government had been unable to handle. (Fehrenbacher writes that *Dred Scott* 'remains the most striking instance of the Supreme Court's attempting to play the role of *deus ex machina* in a setting of national crisis'. Fehrenbacher, *Dred Scott Case* (cit. n. 208), 5.) Perhaps the Rabie court would have revealed greater passion if it had been called upon to do so. But the relatively narrower purview of the South African courts, compared to their United States counterparts, could also insulate the South African courts somewhat from the full force of the storms of political opinion, and so encourage the judges to be somewhat more dispassionate, even in the midst of ideological fires, than judges with more explicit political roles. Difference in function, therefore, offers additional support for the inference in text of a difference in frame of mind as well.

B. The Corbett Court: The Bar and the Judiciary as Carriers of a Human Rights Tradition

It is clear from the cases that the Corbett court (which is to say, the Appellate Division as a whole) approaches questions of emergency law in a decidedly different fashion from the members of the emergency team who dominated the Rabie court's decisions. As we saw in Chapter 5, the decisions of the Corbett court reflect real and explicit concern about the preservation of rights under the emergency, together with a diminished attention to the exigencies of the emergency as seen from the state's perspective, and a willingness to innovate in the law to give expression to these perspectives. As with the Rabie court, a full explanation of the Corbett court's judgments and motivations would require a vast field of study (and even then we could hardly expect certainty). But one part of this explanation is, again, squarely within our focus.

I will maintain that the Corbett court's performance reflects the role that South African lawyers and judges have played as carriers of a human rights tradition even in the long years when dominant white opinion gave that tradition short shrift. Looking again at South African legal history, we will trace the emergence of this attention to human rights in the midst of a system of racial oppression to which white lawyers and judges alike gave their assent. Then we will examine three features of the legal community which have helped sustain and reinvigorate this tradition during the years of the Nationalists' rule: the great prestige of many of the individual lawyers (and judges) who have shared in this tradition, the institution of the independent bar, and the tradition of judicial independence. (These traits have a broader significance as well, for they surely helped give life to the value of adherence to the law, particularly for lawyers and judges, during this same period.) Finally I will argue that the human rights tradition in South Africa fitted quite comfortably with the positivist jurisprudence which has long held sway, and with the principle of parliamentary supremacy which is its central dictate, and that the profession's assimilation of this jurisprudence to the cause of human rights has in turn contributed to the tangible, though very incomplete, success that the cause of human rights has enjoyed. None of this is to say that the Corbett court could not be better, but it will help us to understand why this court *is* better than its predecessor.

This analysis seeks to inform our understanding of the legal profession's capacity to act as a protector of human rights. Thus it continues the effort, initiated in the first part of this chapter, to identify those factors that can make law a limit on governmental power even in a profoundly unjust society. The role of the legal profession in this task is an important matter for South Africa, which may soon need to consider which aspects of the present legal system to retain and which to jettison. It is also important to an understanding of the role of lawyers in unjust societies in general. Lawyers in settings as diverse as Argentina,[217] Brazil,[218] Chile,[219] Spain,[220] France,[221] Russia,[222] Ghana,[223] Kenya,[224] the West Bank,[225] Syria,[226] India,[227] Malaysia,[228] Bangladesh,[229] and the United States[230] and in other lands as well[231] have at

[217] Terence Halliday reports that Argentina's 'national bar association sharply criticized the military dictatorship': 'Legal Professions and the State: Neocorporatist Variations on the Pluralist Theme of Liberal Democracies', in R. Abel and P. Lewis (eds.), *Lawyers in Society: Comparative Theories* (Berkeley, Calif.: University of California Press, 1989), iii. 375, 404. Juan Ernesto Mendéz, writing in 1982, comments that since the military take-over in Argentina in 1976 'at least 90 lawyers have disappeared, more than 100 have been or still are in administrative detention without charges, and hundreds have been forced into exile as a result of threats and harassment'. Mendéz himself, an Argentinian, was 'legally expelled' from the country. Mendéz, 'Some Patterns' (cit. n. 44), 320–1.

[218] According to Joaquim Falcão, the authoritarian government which took power in 1964 in Brazil shut down many of the 'institutions of civil society: unions, political parties, student associations, and professional bodies.... One of the few institutions that managed to maintain its autonomy and identity was the OAB [the Brazilian Bar Association]. Therefore it (as well as the Catholic Church) were transformed into the institutional leaders of civil society in the redemocratization of the country.' J. Falcão, 'Lawyers in Brazil', in R. Abel and P. Lewis (eds.), *Lawyers in Society: The Civil Law World* (Berkeley, Calif.: University of California Press, 1988), ii. 400, 425. Falcão believes that the commitment of law graduates (including many who do not practise law) 'to liberal political ideals has been extremely important at such crucial moments as the bloodless abolition of slavery, the proclamation of the Republic, [and] the overthrow of the Vargas dictatorship in 1945' as well. Ibid. 412. He also comments, however, that lawyers' day-to-day practice reflects an uncritical formalism, ibid. 402, 434, and so lawyers 'have helped to implement most of the authoritarian legislation that still shapes the daily lives of Brazilians'. Ibid. 434.

[219] In Pinochet's Chile, 'the presentation of judicial petitions seeking judicial remedies for people whose human rights were violated ... was the first organized response to the installation of the authoritarian regime'. H. Frühling, 'Repressive Policies and Legal Dissent in Authoritarian Regimes: Chile 1973–1981', 12 *Int. J. Soc. L.* 351, 352 (1984). Other observers have been impressed with the human rights efforts of 'a small but committed number of Chilean lawyers', who have done their work despite facing 'a level of intimidation which lawyers in most civilized societies would find difficult to imagine'. Zabel, Orentlicher, and Nachman, 'Human Rights' (cit. n. 40), 439.

[220] 'From the late 1960s', according to Carlos Viladás Jene, the bar associations in Madrid and Barcelona 'were platforms for opposition to the [Franco] regime, publicly and continuously criticizing police methods and the trials of political activists': 'The Legal Profession in Spain: An Understudied but Booming Occupation', in Abel and Lewis (eds.), *Lawyers in Society: The Civil Law World* (cit. n. 218), ii. 369, 374. José Juan Toharia reports that lawyers in Spain were sharply opposed to the State Security Tribunal (Tribunal de Orden Público), which was seen as having an 'undisguised political character': 'The Spanish Judiciary: A Sociological Study—Justice in a Civil Law Country Undergoing Social Change under an Authoritarian Regime' (unpubl. doctoral dissertation, 1974), ii. 405. The Spanish Bar Association in 1970 unanimously endorsed a statement calling for its dissolution, and 'during 1970 and 1971, most lawyers tended to boycott the functioning of [this court] simply by refusing to defend their cases before it', although this was considered a punishable contempt of court. Ibid. 406.

[221] In the 1830s, the orders of advocates 'continued to provide a refuge for opponents of the new regime [of Louis Philippe]. Their members were among the few who could speak openly against it and the only ones to defend its victims'. M. Burrage, 'Revolution as a Starting Point for the Comparative Analysis of the French, American, and English Legal Professions', in Abel and Lewis (eds.), *Lawyers in Society: Comparative Theories* (cit. n. 217), iii. 322, 331. Burrage writes that 'the bar became the center of opposition to every postrevolutionary regime' until the fall of France's Second Empire. Ibid. 334.

[222] In Tsarist Russia 'the bar, or *advokatura,* was not introduced until 1864. Despite its late beginning, however, the prerevolutionary Russian bar flourished brilliantly in the later nineteenth and early twentieth centuries. It became famous at home and abroad for its integrity and skill, and especially for its courage in the defense of persons charged with political and

ideological crimes.' D. Barry and H. Berman, 'The Soviet Legal Profession', 82 *Harv. L. Rev.* 1, 12 (1968). Barry and Berman report that even in Communist Russia 'we do know of some important political cases in which Soviet lawyers have unsuccessfully used all possible means to prevent the conviction of their clients, as well as some political cases of less importance in which they have succeeded'. Ibid. 15–16 (footnote omitted).

[223] Robin Luckham describes the prominent role Ghanaian lawyers played, not only in the early nationalist movement, but also in opposition of Nkrumah and to the governments that followed. See R. Luckham, 'Imperialism, Law and Structural Dependence: The Ghana Legal Profession', in Dias *et al.* (eds.), *Lawyers* (cit. n. 148), 90, 94–9. Although Ghana's ruling groups 'consciously manipulated' law and lawyers to secure their power, lawyers proved an awkward group to manipulate. Ibid. 96. During the period of military rule beginning in 1972, '[t]hey were (after the suppression of the last remnants of a free press) virtually the only body of organized public opinion that was able to voice such criticisms [of military justice] in public.' Ibid. 98. Reacting to reported abuses, 'members of the Bar collectively refused to continue representing clients before military tribunals', and in 1977 lawyers 'played a prominent role' in organizing a strike by professionals in an unsuccessful attempt 'to force the soldiers back to the barracks'. Ibid. Robert Cover has also commented to 'the incredibly courageous resistance of several Ghanaian judges to the perpetrators of a military coup' in 1979. R. Cover, 'The Supreme Court, 1982 Term—Foreword: *Nomos* and Narrative', 97 *Harv. L. Rev.* 4, 59 and n. 164 (1983).

[224] In Kenya, the *Nairobi Law Monthly* was attacked in Parliament in 1990 by an Assistant Minister for being 'subversive'. The same official charged the editor of the *Monthly*, a lawyer named Gitobu Imanyara, with 'permanently abusing the government'. Lawyers Committee for Human Rights, *In Defense of Rights: Attacks on Lawyers and Judges in 1989* (New York: Lawyers Committee for Human Rights, 1990), 71. Subsequently, Imanyara was detained and then, after being released, faced a charge of sedition. Another lawyer, Gibson Kamau Kuria, was also detained and went into exile. In personal conversation, Kuria has told me that lawyers' increasing advocacy of human rights during the 1980s and since has led the bar into direct conflict with the government.

[225] In 1989 lawyers who practised in the Israeli military courts of the West Bank boycotted these courts in protest against the injustice of this system of law. See V. Sherry, *Background Memorandum: Boycott of the Military Courts by West Bank and Israeli Lawyers* (Lawyers' Committee for Human Rights: July 1989), 13–16. See also 'Palestinian Lawyers Boycott Courts', *The Guardian* 7 (3 Jan. 1989).

[226] Stephen Klitzman reports that 'the government, in March 1980, dissolved the Syrian Bar Association (founded in 1912) after its leadership participated in a one-day protest of the prolonged Syrian "state of emergency"'. Klitzman, 'Judicial Process' (cit. n. 42), 221.

[227] The most famous human rights activist from the bar in India was of course Mahatma Gandhi, who before his leadership of the struggle for independence in India had been '[t]he first dark-skinned professional lawyer in South Africa', Sachs, *Justice* (cit. n. 66), 205, and had there begun his practice of non-violent civil disobedience. Ibid. 206. Other lawyers as well were 'deeply involve[d] ... in the independence movement' in colonial India. J. S. Gandhi, 'Past and Present: A Sociological Portrait of the Indian Legal Profession', in R. Abel and P. Lewis (eds.), *Lawyers in Society: The Common Law World* (Berkeley, Calif.: University of California Press, 1988), i. 369, 377. J. S. Gandhi sharply taxes Indian lawyers now for participating in politics to seek 'personal gains by aligning themselves with a particular party', ibid. 379, but Luckham refers to 'the resistance put up by the courts and organized legal profession in India during the Emergency under Mrs [Indira] Gandhi'. Luckham, 'Political Economy' (cit. n. 148), 333.

[228] Param Cumaraswamy, a former President of the Malaysian Bar, has described that Bar's vigorous campaign against the government's suspension of six Supreme Court judges, and subsequent dismissal of three of them. For example, '[a]rmbands, badges and car stickers were used by lawyers to show the public the Bar's solidarity with judicial independence. Now the Bar Council ends all its correspondence with the words "return the independence of our judiciary". The Council has called upon all lawyers to do likewise in their correspondence with clients and others.' P. Cumaraswamy, 'The Independence of the Legal Profession', 63 *Law Institute Journal* 128, 132 (1989).

[229] According to Cumaraswamy's 1989 article, 'about two years ago the lawyers in Bangladesh displayed admirable unity and courage when they successfully protested over the appointment of the Chief Justice, who was alleged to be aligned to the Executive. It is learned

times played signficant roles in opposing governmental oppression. Aryeh Neier, the executive director of Human Rights Watch, has commented that '[l]awyers are often in the forefront of the struggle for human rights.'[232] These lawyers are members of legal professions that have varying structures, histories, and traditions, and a study of a single country's lawyers cannot supply any simple formula to explain this widespread activism. Nor is it likely that such a formula exists. But this study *can* contribute to the task of identifying the range of factors which can lead lawyers to take on the task of resisting oppression.

In the process, this examination will also contribute to the broader enterprise of understanding the characteristics of the legal profession. Some recent scholarship has sought to cast a clear, even harsh, light on the selfish objectives of market power and status which the legal profession may seek behind a veil of high ideals.[233] Richard Abel, a leader of this effort, has examined the rules of ethics of the American legal profession and commented that their purpose 'is not to describe reality or even to prescribe right behavior, but rather to

that as a result the Chief Justice does not sit on the Bench but is confined more to administrative work.' Cumaraswamy, 'Independence' (cit. n. 228), 132.

[230] Lawyers have worked in defence of human rights in the United States through such organizations as the Lawyers Committee for Human Rights, the NAACP Legal Defense Fund, Inc., the Southern Poverty Law Center, the Legal Services Corporation, and others. This is not to say, of course, that all lawyers have supported these efforts. During the timorous days of McCarthyism, for example, Jerold Auerbach contends that the few lawyers who resisted 'professional complicity in Cold War repression' were generally 'an alienated and disaffected professional group whose members shared similar career patterns, friendship bonds, political values, and Lawyers Guild membership'. J. Auerbach, *Unequal Justice: Lawyers and Social Change in Modern America* (New York: Oxford University Press, 1976), 256. For a more generous assessment of the work of one bar association during this period, see T. Halliday, 'The Idiom of Legalism in Bar Politics: Lawyers, McCarthyism, and the Civil Rights Era', 1982 *ABF Res. J.* 911. It is not my purpose in this book, however, to offer an assessment of the overall performance of the American bar.

[231] The Lawyers Committee for Human Rights has recently reported on the 'harassment and persecution of 277 members of the legal community in 1989. These lawyers, judges, law professors, and law students have been targeted, at least in part, because of their representation of unpopular clients or causes, or their advocacy of human rights.' M. Posner, 'Preface', in Lawyers Committee for Human Rights, *In Defense of Rights* (cit. n. 224), p. v. The lawyers in question come from 48 different countries.

[232] Neier's words are quoted in K. Jost, 'A Killing Field: Lawyers Risk Death, Persecution for Human Rights Work', *Los Angeles Daily Journal* 7, col. 3 (9 Dec. 1988). But see Neumann, 'Insurrection' (cit. n. 45), 168–79.

[233] '[T]he theory of the "professional project"', as Richard Abel has described it, R. Abel, 'Lawyers in the Civil Law World', in Abel and Lewis (eds.), *Lawyers in Society: The Civil Law World* (cit. n. 218), ii. 1, 9, 'argues that an occupational category of private practitioners who wish to professionalize must seek control over the market within which they sell their services and simultaneously assert and enhance their status'. Ibid. 8. Abel himself has used this theory to help analyse the legal professions of a wide range of countries. R. Abel, 'Taking Professionalism Seriously', 1989 *Annual Survey of American Law* 41, 42. For critical appraisals of this theoretical focus, see M. Osiel, 'Lawyers as Monopolists, Aristocrats, and Entrepreneurs', 103 *Harv. L. Rev.* 2009 (1989) (reviewing R. Abel and P. Lewis (eds.), *Lawyers in Society*, 3 vols. (Berkeley, Calif.: University of California Press, 1988–9); S. Sterrett, 'Comparing Legal Professions', 15 *Law and Social Inquiry* 363 (1990) (reviewing Abel and Lewis, *Lawyers in Society*, i. and R. Abel, *The Legal Profession in England and Wales* (Oxford: Basil Blackwell, 1988)).

create a myth about what lawyers might be in order to disguise what they are'.[234] Like large companies describing their oligopoly as a free market, '[l]awyers propagate a mythic view of reality that exalts a similar value: independence.'[235] This study will suggest that lawyers' stated values are not entirely mythic—a point Abel might well accept[236]—and will help us to recognize the circumstances in which such ideals as independence can indeed become elements in lives of real commitment, sacrifice, and courage.

1. The Human Rights Tradition of South African Law

Chief Justice Corbett recently recalled in a speech to the Johannesburg Bar that '[g]oing back plus-minus 50 years to the pre-war days of my youth, I would venture to say that one never heard the term "human rights".'[237] He comments that 'World War II and its aftermath changed all that,'[238] but I will argue that South Africa's human rights tradition dates back not only to before the Second World War but into the nineteenth century. Like many traditions, however, it did not always bear the same label. Martin Chanock emphasizes that liberal legal discourse from the 1950s to the 1970s was built around the idea of the rule of law rather than of human rights.[239] But where the rule of law is elaborated as a 'protection of basic rights', in which '[t]he basic freedoms of person, conscience, speech, information, movement, meeting and association shall be equally guaranteed by the law to all citizens of the society', as the South African scholar Anthony Mathews has urged,[240] then it has become a component of a human rights tradition. As we explore the relevant history, I believe readers will recognize the precursors of 'rights talk' in the language of judges who wrote many decades ago. Never the dominant focus of the legal community, this concern was also never extinguished, and has grown in strength in recent years.

We have already touched on the beginnings of this human rights tradition, in the early decisions by the British to free the slaves and to offer people of every race access to the courts to litigate their grievances.[241] This tradition grew under the influence of the judges of the Cape Colony, the most developed area of what would later be South Africa. Of these judges the pre-eminent one was J. H. de Villiers, who swore himself in as chief justice of the Cape

[234] R. Abel, 'Why Does the ABA Promulgate Ethical Rules?', 59 *Tex. L. Rev.* 639, 668 (1981).

[235] Ibid. 669. Claiming independence from the state may also enhance lawyers' status, one of the central tasks of the 'professional project'. See Abel, 'Lawyers in the Civil Law World' (cit. n. 233), 9.

[236] See R. Abel and P. Lewis, 'Putting Law Back into the Sociology of Lawyers', in Abel and Lewis, *Lawyers in Society: Comparative Theories*, iii. (cit. n. 217), 478, 482–3 (discussing the possibility that professional training and identity may encourage 'challeng[ing] the state in the name of law').

[237] M. Corbett, 'Speech to Johannesburg Bar', *Consultus* 73, 74 (Oct. 1989).

[238] Ibid.

[239] Chanock, 'Post-Calvinist' (cit. n. 203), 6–9.

[240] Mathews, *Freedom, State Security* (cit. n. 172), 15, 20.

[241] See text at nn. 118–23 above.

Colony at the age of 30 in 1874[242] and later became the first chief justice of South Africa as well. An imposing figure, he was also the author of decisions ordering the release of alleged black rebels. In the first of these, decided in 1879, de Villiers commented that:

> it is said the country is in such an unsettled state, and the applicants are reputed to be of such a dangerous character, that the Court ought not to exercise a power [to release an unlawfully detained prisoner] which under ordinary circumstances might be usefully and properly exercised. The disturbed state of the country ought not in my opinion to influence the Court, for its first and most sacred duty is to administer justice to those who seek it, and not to preserve the peace of the country.[243]

He repeated these words in 1895, in a case in which he admonished a black chief 'that if ever he should be found guilty of transgressing any of the laws of his country, this Court will be as ready to punish him with the heavy hand of the law as it now is to protect him against illegal interference with his rights of personal liberty'.[244] De Villiers was no subverter of governmental power—nor do I suggest the South African courts have ever been that—but he was a defender of the rights of the subject.

De Villiers's influence was widespread. Sachs writes that de Villiers and William Porter, an older advocate who transmitted to de Villiers 'a deep respect for justice through law', were 'the individuals who did the most to establish the traditions and ethics which South African barristers like to feel characterize their profession'.[245] Men from the Cape became leading judicial figures in the Orange Free State and the South African Republic.[246] In the Orange Free State, Sachs writes, the judges were 'not afraid to assert themselves against the Executive or the Legislature',[247] and in the Transvaal Chief Justice Kotzé, later a member of the Appellate Division, asserted in another case of the detention of a black chief that the court was 'bound to do equal justice to every individual within its jurisdiction, without regard to colour or degree, except where in the particular instance the law expressly provides to the contrary'.[248] Neither of these Republics' High Courts even remotely sought to restructure the racial order of their states, but, again, they stood for the ideal of judicial protection of those subject to governmental power.

[242] Sachs, *Justice* (cit. n. 52), 44. He swore himself in because 'it was expected that the passed-over judges would refuse to administer the oath to him'. Ibid.

[243] *In re Willem Kok and Nathaniel Balie*, 9 Buch. 45, 66 (1879).

[244] *Sigcau* v. *The Queen*, 12 SC 256, 270 (1895).

[245] Sachs, *Justice* (cit. n. 52), 48. Elsewhere Sachs speaks of 'a liberal tradition in the legal profession'. Ibid. 136.

[246] Ibid. 70, 72, 76. A Cape advocate also served on the Natal bench and attempted, perhaps not very radically, to show a Cape evenhandedness there. The political authorities in Natal, however, forced him out of office, and the Natal bench for many decades achieved neither high legal quality nor, it would seem, the critical distance from state policies displayed by such judges as de Villiers. Ibid. 85–8.

[247] Ibid. 73.

[248] Ibid. 78. As Sachs notes, however, Kotzé CJ did not in the end order the chief's release. Ibid.

Sachs considers Sir James Rose-Innes and Oliver Schreiner the 'most influential successors' to the tradition established by de Villiers and Porter.[249] It was Innes who declared in 1920, as chief justice of the Appellate Division, that '[i]t is a wholesome rule of our law which requires a strict construction to be placed upon statutory provisions which interfere with elementary rights.'[250] Schreiner played a lonelier role a generation later, becoming in 1956 the only member of the Appellate Division to dissent from the court's eventual acceptance of the Nationalists' removal of Coloured voters from the common roll of voters in the Cape Colony (the only part of South Africa in which they had the franchize).[251] Though he was alone in the last round of this struggle, however, it bears remarking that the Appellate Division as a whole twice turned back the government's efforts to achieve this result—the only occasions on which the Appellate Division has ever overturned parliamentary action as contrary to the South African constitution.[252] He was twice passed over for appointment as chief justice, but enjoyed instead tremendous respect from many members of the legal community.[253] After retirement from the Appellate Division bench, both Innes and Schreiner spoke out for the rights of blacks.[254]

The existence of this human rights tradition by no means led the Appellate Division to any broad challenge to the contours of South African government. Hugh Corder has argued, in fact, that the cases in which the Appellate Division did protect individuals' rights in the years before 1950 were characteristically those in which the righting of an individual injustice did not threaten the larger system.[255] He finds that the court was in greatest harmony with state policy in rebellion and resistance cases, and in cases dealing with racial issues—the very areas where challenges to that policy might have been most disruptive.[256] Despite the 'generally liberal backgrounds of the judges ... [and] the common-law emphasis on the equal treatment of all legal subjects',[257] he concludes that '[t]he main feature of the AD's record ... is manifest in the form of a strong commitment to legislative policy and the ideology of the ruling group'.[258] Christopher Forsyth is similarly bleak in his assessment of the Appellate Division's performance between 1950 and 1980. This period began, he writes,

[249] Ibid. 48. One advocate who practised in South Africa had less influence on the South African legal profession, but much more on the world: Gandhi. See ibid. 205–9.

[250] *Dadoo, Ltd. and Others* v. *Krugersdorp Municipal Council*, 1920 AD 530, 552 (A).

[251] *Collins* v. *Minister of the Interior and Another*, 1957 (1) SA 552 (A).

[252] For accounts of this constitutional crisis, see Dugard, *Human Rights* (cit. n. 80), 28–34; E. Kahn, 'Oliver Deneys Schreiner: A South African', in E. Kahn (ed.), *Fiat Justitia: Essays in Memory of Oliver Deneys Schreiner* (Cape Town: Juta, 1983), 1, 35–48; Ch. 1, text at nn. 9–13 above.

[253] See Kahn, 'Oliver Deneys Schreiner' (cit. n. 252), 54–5.

[254] See Corder, *Judges at Work* (cit. n. 2), 25, 32; Kahn, 'Oliver Deneys Schreiner' (cit. n. 252), 85–6. So indeed did Centlivres CJ and (by no means radically) Fagan CJ, both of whom served with Schreiner JA on the Appellate Division. See Corder, *Judges at Work*, 31; Kahn, 'Oliver Deneys Schreiner', 86.

[255] Corder, *Judges at Work* (cit. n. 2), 231, 238.

[256] Ibid. 222–3, 229.

[257] Ibid. 216.

[258] Ibid. 229.

with some notable judicial resistance to government actions (such as the constitutional cases mentioned earlier), and he comments that even after that, in cases raising 'no questions of high policy', the courts generally maintained their role 'of keeping the executive within the bounds of law'. In cases involving controversial government policy, however, Forsyth finds a pattern of 'subservience to executive policy' brightened by only a few exceptions.[259] But while the courts have rarely played a radical part in South African life, I suggest that during these years a strand of at least some lawyers' and judges' world-view has been a concern for the protection of human rights, and that the force of this concern made itself felt in the emergency jurisprudence of the Corbett court. Let us now consider the institutional forces that have helped to sustain this liberal tradition.

2. The Sources of the Human Rights Tradition

(*a*) *The Prestige of Lawyers Committed to this Tradition.*

First, this tradition has been nurtured, even in the midst of South Africa's sweeping discrimination and repression, by the extraordinary prestige of many of the individual lawyers who have chosen to use the law to challenge these policies of the state. Among these lawyers we should of course include judges such as Innes CJ and Schreiner JA, but there are others enjoying comparable respect who have not been appointed to the bench.[260] The prestige of individual lawyers who have opposed apartheid is of institutional importance because their presence and status lend protection (indeed, even the weight of tradition) to less prominent men and women who hope to undertake similar work. In some societies, perhaps, lawyers who adopt an anti-government stance tend to become pariahs within their own profession, generally tolerated, occasionally able to obstruct, but rarely enjoying open respect from their peers. In South Africa, however, some of the most successful and prestigious lawyers have also been firmly opposed to significant aspects of government policies.

While the fact that such highly regarded lawyers are involved in challenges to apartheid surely helps others to join in the struggle, we must also ask why opposition to the government has not destroyed the prestige of these prominent lawyers. The answer to this question lies partly in the historic independence of the bar and of the judiciary, to which we will turn in a moment. So, too, the adversary responsibilities of courtroom lawyers give them a justification for taking stands against the government in court—stands which, difficult as they are for the lawyers to undertake, might be even more awkward or risky for others. Thus enabled to express opposition to the

[259] Forsyth, *In Danger* (cit. n. 3), 225–6.

[260] For an unusual public listing of highly respected lawyers who have not been appointed to the bench, seemingly at least in part for political reasons, see the statement by John Didcott, himself a member of the Natal bench, in 'The Didcott Memorandum and Other Submissions to the Hoexter Commission', 97 *SALJ* 651, 662 (1980).

government, lawyers may then win admiration and prestige precisely for doing so, perhaps even from observers who disagree with the positions being advocated.[261]

The echoes of other conflicts in South African society, however, may also play a part. In particular, many of these eminent lawyers have been English- rather than Afrikaans-speaking, and it may be that the historic, multi-faceted division within the white community between the English and the Afrikaners (a division with class, cultural, and political ramifications) has helped to fuel lawyers' opposition to the state. Moreover, many of these lawyers were not only English-speaking but Jewish.[262] Jews in South Africa after the Second World War may well have found the policies of the Nationalist government particularly unattractive because of the presence in the National Party of people who had sided with the Nazis during the war or had sharp anti-Semitic views.[263] For English-speaking and Jewish lawyers, part of the reason that anti-apartheid work has not robbed them of their prestige may be that they have looked to communities alienated from the Afrikaner government for the measure of their reputation.

Perhaps the most celebrated of all these lawyers, however, was an Afrikaner, Abram Fischer.[264] Fischer's life illustrates not only the extent to which some lawyers have taken their commitment against apartheid but also the almost tangible quality of the prestige which certain lawyers have enjoyed in South Africa. Fischer was a prominent advocate, so highly regarded by his fellow lawyers that after his indictment in 1964 for membership and support of the Communist Party he was granted bail and allowed to leave South Africa to argue a case in England, despite the obvious possibility that he would escape

[261] Michael Burrage suggests that the advocates' courtroom opposition to the government 'considerably enhanced the prestige of the [advocates'] profession' in France during the 19th-cent. Second Empire. Burrage, 'Revolution' (cit. n. 221), 334. In Brazil, lawyers' image as liberators gives the Bar Association 'great moral authority'—and 'compels the [Bar Association] to engage in political activities'. Falcão, 'Lawyers in Brazil' (cit. n. 218), 425.

[262] As of 1979 the Johannesburg bar, perhaps the most liberal in South Africa, had 108 Jewish members and 143 non-Jews. The source of this statistic is itself an indication of the continued force of the ethnic prejudice referred to in the text. These figures apparently were offered by a former member of the Supreme Court (Judge Hiemstra) in the course of arguing against 'the old-type of ultra-conservatism (bekrompenheid) which had people continually talking of the Johannesburg "liberal" or "Jewish" Bar'. E. Hugo, 'Can Justice REALLY be Done?', *Rand Daily Mail* 7, (22 Aug. 1981). Hiemestra reported that it was still being argued '"that the character of the judicature in Johannesburg would assume a totally perverse direction"' if a separate Johannesburg division of the Supreme Court, drawn from this bar, were to be established. Ibid. (quoting Judge Hiemstra). This, the judge maintained, was highly unjustified, apparently because in fact there were 81 Afrikaans-speaking advocates among the 143 non-Jews, 'making it [Johannesburg] close to one of the biggest Afrikaans-speaking Bars in the country'. Ibid.

[263] On this aspect of Afrikaner politics, see Harrison, *White Tribe* (cit. n. 103), 114–32. Afrikaner nationalist thinking also showed the influence of Nazism, as discussed in n. 176 above. (I am grateful to Gail Gerhart for calling the role of Jewishness to my attention.)

[264] Fischer is a model for Dr Burger in Nadine Gordimer's novel, *Burger's Daughter* (1979). Cf. A. Sampson, 'Heroism in South Africa', *NY Times*, s. 7 (Book Review), 1 (19 Aug. 1979) (reviewing *Burger's Daughter*). For a poignant memory of Fischer's life, see M. Benson, 'A True Afrikaner', 19 *Granta* 197 (Summer 1986).

trial by failing to return. His lawyer told the court 'that Mr Fischer's colleagues at the Bar are confident of the fact that Mr Fischer, no matter what he is charged with here, is the sort of man that will stand his trial and they equally would put up any sum of money at all, no matter how large it is, to guarantee his return'.[265]

(b) The Structure of the South African Legal Profession.

Such prestige is a justified tribute to lawyers' ability and integrity, but it is also, I believe, a product of a second institutional feature: the structure of the South African legal profession. That structure, as we will see, has highly traditional and élitist features, which may well have quite unedifying effects, such as the protection of lawyers' income or the securing of their status. I will suggest, however, that these very features may encourage, and surely provide insulation for, lawyers who take up the cause of challenging apartheid.

We must first understand the basic contours of the South African legal profession. In the United States, the bar is formally an egalitarian institution: any duly admitted lawyer can generally handle any case in or out of court. By contrast, South Africa, like England, has a divided legal profession—divided, that is, between some 1,115 advocates, who alone are empowered to argue cases in South Africa's highest courts (the Supreme Courts),[266] and 8,300 attorneys, who can and do appear in lower courts but otherwise are limited to out-of-court work and to 'briefing' advocates for Supreme Court cases.[267]

[265] *Society of Advocates* v. *Fischer*, 1966 (1) SA 133 (T) at 134E. The members of the bar held this view despite the fact that Fischer had been an active Communist before the party had been outlawed, already had a criminal conviction as a result of the 1946 African Mineworkers' strike, and had also been 'banned' by the state. See S. Clingman, *Bram Fischer* (Rhodes Scholars Against Apartheid, Dec. 1988), 5–6. Fischer did return to South Africa, but ultimately chose to go underground. As a result he was struck from the roll of advocates (that is, he was disbarred), to his 'great anguish'. Ibid. 8. After his capture he was sentenced to life imprisonment. Before his sentencing he told the court that: 'It was to keep faith with all those dispossessed by apartheid that I broke my undertaking to the court, separated myself from my family, pretended I was someone else, and accepted the life of a fugitive. I owed it to the political prisoners, to the banished, to the silenced and those under house arrest, not to remain a spectator, but to act'. Benson, 'True Afrikaner' (cit. n. 264), 221 (quoting Fischer's words to the court). As M. Chanock points out, the fact that the Johannesburg bar took the initiative to seek Fischer's disbarment is evidence that the liberal tradition had its limits, even in this relatively enlightened part of the South African bar. Personal communication from Martin Chanock, 14 Apr. 1990.

[266] There is an exception to the advocates' exclusive right of appearance in the Supreme Courts: 'the court may permit an attorney to discharge the functions of an advocate in any proceedings pending before it if there is no advocate available or willing to act'. K. van Dijkhorst, 'Advocates' in W. Joubert (ed.), *The Law of South Africa* (Durban: Butterworths, 1981), xiv. 213, 214. (Years after this book was published, Van Dijkhorst, a judge of the Supreme Court, selected Joubert, the editor of this series of volumes, to serve as an assessor in the Delmas treason trial. It was Van Dijkhorst J.'s abrupt dismissal of Joubert during the trial that ultimately became the basis for the Appellate Division's decision to overturn all of the convictions in the case. See *S.* v. *Malindi*, 1990 (1) SA 962 (A).)

[267] These figures are based on information kindly provided by the General Council of the Bar (for South Africa and the 'independent' homelands) and the four provincial law societies in Aug. 1991. Perhaps with limited exceptions, both figures exclude non-practising lawyers and the figure for advocates includes only advocates in private practice (see text at nn. 268–73 below).

Because the advocates' profession (often called 'the bar') seems to have provided the more fertile soil for anti-apartheid lawyering, let us focus on it first.

In a broad sense the bar includes everyone who has been admitted by the Supreme Courts to the roll of advocates; admission to the roll suffices to entitle an advocate to appear in these courts.[268] It seems fair to say, however, that the core of the profession consists of the societies of advocates, or the 'bars', of particular cities and of the nation as a whole.[269] The societies of advocates are almost entirely associations of private practitioners. It is virtually impossible to engage in full-time private practice as an advocate in South Africa without having become a member of the society;[270] at the same time, advocates who are not engaged in full-time private practice—for example, those who are employed by the government as civil servants,[271] those who are engaged in any other trade or business,[272] and even those who are full-time law teachers[273]—are not *permitted* to join. As we will see, the rules and traditions of these societies play a central part in the institutional support for anti-apartheid lawyering.

Four features of the advocates' profession provide particularly significant sources of encouragement or protection for anti-apartheid lawyers. First, the

[268] See Van Dijkhorst, 'Advocates' (cit. n. 266), 216 n. 2.

[269] As of 1981, there were seven local bars in South Africa, located 'at the seat of every provincial and local division of the supreme court of South Africa although there is one bar for Pietermaritzburg and Durban and one bar for Grahamstown and Port Elizabeth'. Ibid. 215. The local bars 'are federated in the general council of the bar of South Africa'. Ibid. As of that time, Van Dijkhorst indicates, there was also a bar in what was then South-West Africa, and this bar was also part of the South African General Council of the Bar. In addition, there were bars in the 'independent homelands' of Transkei and Bophuthatswana. Ibid.

[270] What makes this so nearly impossible is that in most cases advocates do not appear on behalf of a client unless they have been 'briefed' to do so by an attorney. Briefing by an attorney is required in the great majority of civil cases, and is customary in criminal cases even though in some it is not required. Ibid. 214. Attorneys, for their part, generally will not be likely to brief people in private practice who are not members of the local society of advocates; to brief a non-member would mean forgoing the presumed ability and integrity of bar members. I am grateful to Arthur Chaskalson for helping me understand this and other aspects of the bar.

[271] Van Dijkhorst states that '[a]dvocates who are civil servants ... are not members of the societies'. Ibid. 215. Rule 4.15.1 of the *Uniform Rules of Professional Ethics of the General Council of the Bar, as Adopted by the Johannesburg Bar,* provides that '[a] practising member of the Bar is not entitled to accept salaried employment which may affect his professional independence.' Rule 4.15, ('No Right to Participate in Other Callings While in Practice at the Bar') in *Rules of Professional Ethics of the Johannesburg Bar* (1986). It is my understanding that prosecutors today are normally employees of the state rather than private practitioners retained on the state's behalf, see Dugard, *Human Rights* (cit. n. 80), 11–12, and that they are not generally eligible for membership in the societies of advocates, presumably on the basis of this rule. This exclusion, however, is apparently not absolute; the senior prosecutorial officials, beneath the Minister of Justice, are the attorneys general, and Van Dijkhorst notes that '[t]he attorney-general and his deputy are allowed to become members of certain bars': 'Advocates' (cit. n. 266), 216 n. 2.

[272] Rule 4.15.1 of the *Uniform Rules* (cit. n. 271), states that '[a] member of the Bar is not entitled to practise as an advocate while actively engaged in the carrying on of any other professional or commercial or industrial undertaking.'

[273] See Van Dijkhorst, 'Advocates' (cit. n. 266), 215. Part-time teaching is permissible, however, and there is a provision for 'Associate Members' to receive an exemption allowing them to teach full-time. *Uniform Rules* (cit. n. 271), Rule 4.15.2.

private bar in particular appears to enjoy considerable institutional prestige, and this status may well make it easier for anti-apartheid lawyers to persevere in their views, and in litigation expressing these convictions, despite widespread white disagreement with the causes they are aiding. No doubt this status, in South Africa as in England, is a product of a complex combination of factors, including the courtroom visibility of advocates, the distinguished conduct of particular individuals, and the fact that almost all judges, who themselves enjoy tremendous prestige in South Africa, come from the senior members of the private bar.[274] South African lawyers, like practitioners of the common law elsewhere, may also draw distinction from their mastery of the 'practical judgment' required for manipulation of common law legal materials.[275] The very independence, or reputation for independence, of lawyers may itself reinforce their prestige;[276] it is important not to underestimate the degree to which the quest for prestige may shape legal professions and so, in South Africa, may press lawyers to seek and earn a reputation for independence.[277] Whatever the sources of this stature, in any case, what is important for our purposes is simply that anti-apartheid lawyers are, by virtue of their profession, in a position to share in it.

Second, the bar itself is internally stratified, and this stratification enhances the prestige of those who rise within the hierarchy, among whom have been a number of anti-apartheid lawyers. The critical mark of eminence within the bar is designation as senior counsel, a credential which enables those private practitioners who have it to command higher fees for the ability and prestige they bring to the most difficult cases.[278] Advocates who seek this title must be reviewed by the Supreme Court and must ultimately receive the approval of the government. Those who rise to become senior counsel have so far almost all been white, and they are likely to share habits of mind acquired through the socialization processes of their profession. If they are far from representative of South African society as a whole, however, they do hold a wide range of political views. Whether or not the process of appointment of senior counsel generally escapes political distortion, it is beyond question that the Nationalist white government has approved the 'senior counsel' title for a number of determined opponents of apartheid. The result is that in a

[274] Richard Abel attributes the social status of British barristers to 'a composite of history, ascribed characteristics, functions, conventions of deference, the visibility of a few stars, and an exclusive relationship with the bench': 'England and Wales: A Comparison of the Professional Projects of Barristers and Solicitors', in Abel and Lewis (eds.), *Lawyers in Society: The Common Law World* (cit. n. 227), 23, 48.

[275] Mark Osiel develops the argument that common lawyers' practical judgment is integral to their prominent social role in Osiel, 'Lawyers' (cit. n. 233), 2054–64. For a philosophical exploration of the nature of judgment, and an argument that 'attain[ing] ... good judgment' is part of truly living the life of the law, see A. Kronman, 'Living in the Law', 54 *U. Chi. L. Rev.* 835, 873 (1987).

[276] See text at n. 261, and n. 261 above.

[277] Mark Osiel has forcefully argued this point in, 'Lawyers'(cit. n. 233), 2031–47.

[278] The senior counsel title is not confined to members of the private bar; in particular, the attorneys general, senior advocates in government employment, would also be senior counsel.

profession in which hierarchy is rather firmly entrenched, some of those who reap the prestige of the top rung of the ladder are leading anti-apartheid lawyers.

Third, advocates are heirs to a tradition of independence from outside control, a tradition guarded in a variety of ways in the rules and conventions of the societies of advocates. In particular, this tradition means, or at any rate asserts, that advocates are not subservient to clients, whereas solicitors may be. This independence arises, it is argued, from the structure of advocates' work.[279] In the United States, lawyers join corporate firms, or work for unions, or do plaintiffs' personal injury cases, or represent criminal defendants. Switching sides is relatively rare. In South Africa, each member of the society of advocates is, in effect, a sole practitioner, with no collective organizational imperatives to be satisfied.[280] In theory, moreover, every such advocate is normally bound to take cases in the order of their arrival in his or her chambers (the so-called 'cab rank' rule);[281] this limitation on advocates' discretion may operate to confirm the advocate's lack of obligation to, or identification with, any single client or cause. The fact that advocates do not normally receive their work directly from clients but rather from attorneys who 'brief' them may also make the advocates 'less subject to the centrifugal pressures of client loyalty'.[282] A number of rules and practices which bind counsel to the court may also tend to free the advocate from the domination of the client.[283]

[279] For an argument that similar features of the British bar contribute to its independence, see R. Alexander, 'The History of the Law as an Independent Profession and the Present English System', in American Bar Association, Tort and Insurance Practice Section, *The Lawyer's Professional Independence: Present Threats/Future Challenges* (American Bar Association, 1984), 1, 12–18.

[280] Rule 4.16 of the *Uniform Rules* (cit. n. 271), declares that '[n]o relation in the least degree resembling partnership in practice is permissible'. Advocates in private practice do, however, share expenses for support services in their 'chambers' or offices. Moreover, one advocate may do work for another, more senior, member of the bar as a 'devil', but this relationship is not supposed to become the equivalent of employment. 'Thus, although it is not improper for the member requesting such services to show his appreciation therefore in tangible form, any form of payment which obliges the devil to do work is undesirable.' *Uniform Rules*, Rule 4.26.1. I have been told that 'deviling' is nowadays not very widespread.

[281] See *Uniform Rules* (cit. n. 271), Rule 2.1.

[282] Abel, 'England and Wales' (cit. n. 274), 56.

[283] South African lawyers are expected to fight for their clients' interests, and to that end they are entitled to 'the free and unfettered statement of every fact and the use of every argument and observation that can legitimately, according to the principles and practice of law', assist the client, as Van Dijkhorst puts it, 'Advocates' (cit. n. 266), 238–9. But they have responsibilities to the court as well as to the client. For example, an advocate whose client in a criminal case confesses his guilt to the advocate must then explain to the client that he or she will not be permitted to 'assert that which he knows to be untrue nor may he connive at or attempt to substantiate a fraud or an untruth' in the client's defence. *Uniform Rules* (cit. n. 271), Rule 4.11. Similarly, counsel cannot confront an adverse witness with a theory of the case that he or she knows to be false and without basis, Van Dijkhorst, 'Advocates' (cit. n. 266), 239, even though a failure to 'put' one's theory to the opposing witnesses is likely to weaken the force of one's cross-examination. In addition, an advocate may not challenge a witness's credibility with cross-examination that attacks his character but is not otherwise relevant to the case, unless the advocate 'has reasonable grounds for thinking that the imputation conveyed by the question is well-founded or true'. *Uniform Rules*, Rule 3.3.1.

The extent of the independence from clients which these rules necessarily engender is somewhat unclear, and should not be exaggerated.[284] As in England, advocates are dependent on the attorneys who bring them work, and in this respect cannot be considered wholly independent.[285] Moreover, and again as in England, the cab rank rule's insulation of lawyers from identification with any given client is surely attenuated in actual practice.[286] Cases are likely to come to those advocates who have evinced an interest in doing them, and thus strongly pro- or anti-government lawyers, for example, will not be likely to find themselves switching sides. In addition, advocates can hardly escape the need for clients, and these clients no doubt tend, in South Africa as elsewhere, to be the powerful and privileged institutions and individuals of society. (Some members of the private bar may devote much of their time to litigating on behalf of the state itself.) The potential influence which powerful clients can wield is increased by the ethical rules' authorization for advocates to accept a retainer lasting up to one year from a client.[287] Powerful clients may discourage advocates from taking controversial cases—although it is conceivable that in South Africa the estrangement between the Afrikaner government and the largely English-speaking business community leads many private clients to find advocates' challenges to the system of apartheid more tolerable than they otherwise would.[288]

But even if these rules themselves do not secure advocates' independence, they buttress the belief that advocates are, and should be, firmly independent of mind. This belief in itself is a further encouragement of this independence, all the more so when it is reinforced in the daily interactions of the members of the bar, in what Robert Gordon calls the 'collectively maintained conventional

[284] For a cautious assessment of the relation between various aspects of lawyers' work and their degree of independence, see R. Gordon, 'The Independence of Lawyers', 68 *BU L. Rev.* 1, 30–48 (1988).

[285] See Abel, 'England and Wales' (cit. n. 274), 48.

[286] On the widespread circumvention and evasion of the 'cab rank' rule in England, see Gordon, 'Independence' (cit. n. 284), 21–2 n. 61; Abel, 'Taking Professionalism Seriously' (cit. n. 233), 54 n. 57.

[287] See *Uniform Rules* (cit. n. 271), Rule 5.2 (At least as of 1981, moreover, the one-year limit may have been applicable only to the Johannesburg bar. See Van Dijkhorst, 'Advocates' (cit. n. 266), 246 and n. 2.) Exceptions are also usually made to allow members of the societies of advocates to be employed by public-interest law organizations, and in such employment advocates may also have considerable discretion to act without the 'instructions' of an attorney that would normally be required. See *Local Rules and Practice of the Johannesburg Bar which should be read in Conjunction with the Uniform Rules of Professional Ethics*, Rule 3 ('Local Rules in Respect of the Legal Resources Centre') (*Annexure to Uniform Rules*, above).

[288] Allister Sparks writes that 'the English-speaking South Africans dominate their country's economy but are outsiders when it comes to the politically dominant Afrikaner Nationalist movement forged in opposition to them': *Mind* (cit. n. 50), 70. Robin Luckham has suggested that legal systems will offer greater 'scope ... for the expression of conflict ... where lawyers have a source of livelihood that is relatively independent of the dominant class(es) or political interests they oppose': 'Political Economy' (cit. n. 148), 334 and to some extent this condition may hold in South Africa. But Sparks also emphasizes the English-speaking community's 'reluctan[ce] to confront authority': *Mind*, 71, and this characteristic might operate to constrain the English-speakers' lawyers.

expectations of professional roles'.[289] Thus a South African advocate has argued that

> one of the most important elements in the training of an advocate is his presence in chambers, where his conduct is submitted to the scrutiny of his peers, where his integrity is shaped and controlled by other advocates and by attorneys who see him in the presence of his colleagues ... It is also an indefinable thing, but it is that element which rounds off his training, which helps to give him a detachment which is also important for the client. You know how often an attorney's zeal may run away with a client's true interest until he is confronted by a detached counsel without an axe to grind, without the necessity for retaining this very important client ...[290]

The attorneys who took issue with him suggested that their profession too was capable of such objectivity, but did not question that advocates possessed it.[291] Similarly, a liberal South African judge, A. J. Milne, declares that 'although every advocate is prejudiced to some degree, long practice at the Bar teaches one to recognize and discard one's prejudices so far as it is humanly possible, and to keep a cool head in the heat and clamour of litigation, however hot one's rhetoric'.[292]

These organizational and moral supports for the tradition of independence may indeed encourage advocates' psychological independence, their capacity to deliver even to powerful clients a detached and cool assessment of their legal situation. Independence is not an easily cabined virtue, however, and so men and women schooled to independence from the pressures of clients may also be prepared for independence from the broader pressures of white society and its government.[293] Thus Albie Sachs, noting that Natal did not have a divided bar until after the First World War, writes that it 'therefore never developed until after the First World War an élitist group of barristers on the English or Cape pattern, who regarded law as something standing apart from society in the same way as they stood aloof from the public'.[294] Even if these various features of the advocates' profession do not actually encourage such

[289] See Gordon, 'Independence' (cit. n. 284), 41.

[290] H. J. Preiss SC, in 'The Divided Bar: A Panel Discussion', *De Rebus Procuratoriis* 579, 587–8 (Sept. 1977).

[291] Ibid. 588, 590 (comments of C. L. Valkin and A. Gildenhuys, both attorneys).

[292] A. Milne, 'Speech by the Honourable Mr Justice A. J. Milne to the Natal Law Society', 97 *SALJ* 453, 455 (1980).

[293] One sign of the advocates' disposition to retain their independence from the government is that the advocates' profession is much less governed by statute than the attorneys' profession is. See K. van Dijkhorst and H. Mellet, 'Legal Practitioners', in W. Joubert (ed.), *The Law of South Africa* (Durban: Butterworths, 1981), xiv. 211, 213. (Van Dijkhorst's article on 'Advocates' has already been cited; this and Mellet's article on attorneys, cited in n. 297 below, make up the entry on 'Legal Practitioners' in this vol., but the introduction on p. 213 appears to be jointly authored.) As Arthur Chaskalson has pointed out to me, the societies of advocates administer the bar examination without statutory authority.

[294] Sachs, *Justice* (cit. n. 52), 86.

independence, moreover, they can still be important. For the tradition of independence can offer a shield against criticism of those advocates who do in fact take and press cases challenging the government, as Roman citizenship is said to have protected Saint Paul from whipping at the hands of his gaolers.[295] In the recent Delmas treason trial, for example, the trial judge accused the lawyers for the accused of unethical conduct. When the case was printed in the *South African Law Reports*, it included an editorial footnote reporting that the bar councils had found no impropriety in the lawyers' conduct.[296]

Fourth, the tradition of solidarity within the private bar may help to foster the conduct for which the standard of independence calls. (The absence of such cohesion among lawyers may have been one of the reasons that the Nazis so easily gained control over the German legal profession.)[297] Free (in theory) of indebtedness to any single client or interest, these advocates battle each other but also are bound to each other. As an attorney puts it, 'the strength of the bar is its insularity and the fact that it is a small disciplined body', a 'tight band of brothers'.[298] It is said of Schreiner JA that in his days as an advocate he 'participated fully in the spirit of camaraderie and helpfulness at the Bar', which Ellison Kahn, in his memoir of Schreiner, says with evident admiration might be 'the best club in Johannesburg'.[299]

It is important to remember how small and tight the South African bar is. Abel has commented that '[c]ertainly no contemporary national [legal] profession constitutes a meaningful community',[300] and this may be true, but within the South African legal profession the bar is well positioned to be such a community. In a country of almost 36,000,000 people there are roughly 1150 advocates in private practice. This is comparable to the English bar at the beginning of the nineteenth century![301] In this and certain other respects, conditions like those which Abel says 'facilitated informal social control' in England almost two centuries ago still have considerable reality in South Africa.[302] Almost all members of the societies of advocates have their 'chambers'

[295] See Acts 22: 25–9. As Roman citizenship shielded even an apostle of a reviled religion, so bar membership may have helped protect the advocates of the anti-apartheid cause.

[296] *S.* v. *Baleka and Others*, 1988 (4) SA 688 (T) at 707 and n. *. The attorneys in the case were similarly exonerated by their governing authorities. For the subsequent history of this case, see n. 266 above.

[297] Shortly after the 2nd World War, Norman Marsh argued that '[c]ontrol of the practising lawyer ... was facilitated by the fact that there was in Germany, even before 1933, no single body with comparable powers and prestige to that enjoyed by the General Council of the Bar and the Inns of Court or by the Law Society', all institutions of the English legal profession: 'Some Aspects of the German Legal System under National Socialism', 62 *Law Q. Rev.* 366, 371 (1946). The organization of South Africa's legal profession resembles England's, as to advocates, see n. 269 above, and as to attorneys, whose national professional body in South Africa is the Association of Law Societies. See H. Mellet, 'Attorneys', in W. Joubert (ed.), *The Law of South Africa* (Durban: Butterworths, 1981), xiv. 256, 265.

[298] C. L. Valkin, in 'Divided Bar' (cit. n. 290), 588, 590.

[299] Kahn, 'Oliver Deneys Schreiner' (cit. n. 252), 19.

[300] Abel, 'Taking Professionalism Seriously' (cit. n. 233), 59.

[301] See Abel, 'England and Wales' (cit. n. 274), 56, 73.

[302] Ibid.

or offices in just one or two buildings in South Africa's principal cities—a level of concentration again reminiscent of early nineteenth-century England, whose barristers were to be found 'within a few square blocks of London'.[303] This concentration of chambers in itself may well contribute to the bonding of the bar.[304] The role of attorneys in insulating advocates from client pressures has already been mentioned. In and out of court, finally, advocates are subject to the scrutiny of their fellow advocates, of the judges, and of attorneys; this continuous assessment affects advocates' income and their hopes for designation as senior counsel and elevation to the bench. The result is that the bonds and pressures of community can play a significant part in reinforcing advocates' professional norms. Indeed, the strength of this community undoubtedly constitutes a major pressure for conformity among advocates, but conformity within this community calls for some measure of independence towards those outside it.

At one time, advocates would virtually all have been white men, probably most of English-speaking background, and this homogeneity would have further cemented the ties of community. Yet I think the binding tradition has not spent its force, though the ranks of advocates have come to include more Afrikaners, as well as some women and blacks.[305] I spent time one day in 1988 with a black advocate in South Africa. During the course of the day we took a drive—in his BMW—through the parts of town where his parents had lived, but lived no longer because they had been forced out when these areas were restricted to whites. Later, in his chambers, he entertained the white advocate down the hall, whose father had signed the order years earlier that had 'banned' my friend from normal life. (It was no accident that another advocate was down the hall, given the centralized location of chambers.) And on our way out of the parking garage, my host exchanged pleasantries with a white advocate who had vigorously sought to keep blacks out of the ranks of advocates.[306]

[303] Ibid.

[304] See Claassen, 'Retain' (cit. n. 73), for an emphatic, indeed romantic, account of the value of the concentration of chambers, which the author calls '[t]he outstanding aspect of our system'.

[305] In fact, certain elements of this fellowship are enjoined upon advocates by rule. According to a 'Note' to Rule 1.3 of the *Uniform Rules* (cit. n. 271): 'A new member should introduce himself or herself to every other member of the Bar. This should be done by visiting each member in his or her chambers.... One member must not address or refer to another male member as "Mr". Surnames should be used except in those cases where members are on first names relationship. In the case of female members the usual rules of courtesy apply and they should be addressed and referred to as "Miss" or ["]Mrs" as the case may be.'

[306] I do not mean to suggest that black lawyers have been welcomed wholeheartedly into the legal profession. Duma Nokwe, one of the first black advocates, on being formally introduced to a white advocate, offered his hand and the white advocate responded, 'No money today ... out!' Sachs, *Justice* (cit. n. 66), 211. For many years it was illegal under the Group Areas Act for blacks to have offices in the business areas of cities, where all legal work was concentrated, and so black lawyers often had to be law-breakers in order to practise; this may have been true in some areas as late as the mid-1980s. See K. Jost, 'Black Lawyers in South Africa: Few, Beleaguered', *Los Angeles Daily Journal* 1, 20 (5 Feb. 1986). Today, although the difficulties facing blacks contemplating a legal career remain substantial (see ibid.), a significant number of

The ideal of a small élite group of lawyers beholden to no one but themselves (and the judges) is not an entirely attractive one. Nor do I mean to say that the bar's structure, to the extent it realizes this ideal, by any means ensures that an advocate will take an anti-apartheid role. Indeed, Alexis de Tocqueville argued long ago that lawyers were latent aristocrats, who 'derive from occupation certain habits of order, a taste for formalities, and a kind of instinctive regard for the regular connection of ideas, which naturally render them very hostile to the revolutionary spirit and the unreflecting passions of the multitude'.[307] The independence that lawyers enjoy may, on this account, as readily dispose them against dramatic reform as bolster their opposition to the government. In South Africa specifically, Hugh Corder has characterized the judges of the Appellate Division between 1910 and 1950 as coming from 'a narrow élite ... channelled along respectable and conservative lines by the collective socialisation of life at the Bar'.[308] And South African observers have noted '[t]he part played, in parliament and out, by practising or formerly practising advocates in the enervation of the principles of justice and the rule of law in this country over the past decades'[309]—an observation echoed in other countries as well.[310]

Thus the human rights tradition may never have been wholeheartedly embraced by more than a small fraction of the members of the bar. A reporter estimated in 1982 that only about forty white advocates (in other words, roughly six percent of some 686 advocates at the bar at that time) were prepared to take cases on behalf of those who faced legal trouble under apartheid laws.[311] No doubt many other factors besides the bar's tradition of independence contributed to the stance of these sixty individuals. I do suggest, however, that the tradition of élite independence of the bar played its part in encouraging lawyers to take up this role. Moreover, those South African advocates who have undertaken this work, whether as a result of experience at the bar or for other reasons, benefit from this tradition of independence, just as they make use of the technicalities of the law. In this way, too, the

blacks have entered the legal profession. According to a 1987 article, 695 out of 7,000, or slightly less than a tenth, of South Africa's lawyers were black (including 'Coloureds' and Indians). D. Mokgatle, 'The Exclusion of Blacks from the South African Judicial System', 3 *SAJHR* 44, 46 (1987). This is a sizeable increase from 1982, when it was reported that about 280 of South Africa's then 5,000 lawyers were black. J. Foisie, 'South Africa's Oppressive Laws Opposed by Some Lawyers, Black and White', *Los Angeles Times* (14 Nov. 1982). A recent sign of further progress has been the designation of the first African senior counsel, T. Lewis Skweyiya.

[307] A. de Tocqueville, *Democracy in America*, ed. P. Bradley, i (New York: Vintage, 1945), 283.

[308] Corder, *Judges at Work* (cit. n. 2), 48.

[309] E. Cameron, H. Rudolph and D. van Zyl Smit, 'Judicial Appointments—Public Confidence and the Court Structure: Proposals for a New Approach', *De Rebus* 430, 430 (Sept. 1980).

[310] See e.g. Cumaraswamy, 'Independence' (cit. n. 228), 129 (Singapore); Falcão, 'Lawyers in Brazil' (cit. n. 218), 425 (Brazil).

[311] Foisie, 'Oppressive Laws' (cit. n. 306) (*semble*; perhaps *60* such lawyers); the figure of 686 advocates was kindly provided by D. F. Joubert, Secy., General Council of the Bar. Modest as this number is, the willingness of South African advocates to take such cases has been compared

prestige and the protection against outside criticism which this hierarchical and exclusive structure can confer can contribute to fostering the 'indomitability in the pursuit of justice' that some members of the bar display.[312]

Moreover, there has, it would seem, been some broadening of the bar's endorsement of the human rights tradition in recent years. Arthur Chaskalson, the national director of the Legal Resources Centre, South Africa's oldest and largest public interest-focused law organization, recently noted 'within South Africa a vigorous human rights Bar, and a growing concern with public interest law', and he commented that '[l]eaders of the profession have helped to create space for and given their support to these forms of practice and have thereby helped to make them possible.'[313] In 1988 the General Council of the Bar, the bar's national governing body, unanimously adopted a 'motion expressing deepest concern at the reimposition of the state of emergency'. This motion stopped short of outright condemnation of the state of emergency; it was none the less significant, as John Dugard explained, 'because it was unanimous. Because of the structure of the council, previous motions on similar lines could be blocked by constituent members.'[314]

This activism, although certainly still very measured,[315] may draw strength from the very aristocratic habits of order that in some contexts are conservative. Tocqueville suggests, in rather Machiavellian vein, that 'the prince who, in presence of an encroaching democracy, should endeavor to impair the judicial authority in his dominions, and to diminish the political influence of lawyers, would commit a great mistake: he would let slip the substance of authority to grasp the shadow'.[316] The Nationalist government may well have made this mistake, through its decades of assault on the traditional protections of South African common law and, in particular, through its effort to abridge, or even excise, the role of the courts in the emergency.

favourably to that of the American legal profession during the 1950s and early 1960s. See J. Greenberg, 'South Africa and the American Experience', 54 *NYU L. Rev.* 3, 14 (1979).

312 The quoted phrase is from Cameron, Rudolph, and van Zyl Smit, 'Judicial Appointments' (cit. n. 309), 430. While strongly (and of course correctly) denying that only advocates possess this virtue, these writers do acknowledge 'much truth' in the argument that senior counsel are more likely to have such traits than lawyers in general. Ibid. 430–1.

313 A. Chaskalson, 'The Past Ten Years: A Balance Sheet and Some Indicators for the Future', 5 *SAJHR* 293, 300 (1989). For adjustments in the rules of ethics to facilitate public-interest practice, see n. 287 above.

314 T. Cohen and E. van der Merwe, 'Bar Council's "Deep Concern" at Emergency', *The Star* 1 (25 July 1988) (paraphrasing Dugard).

315 The 1988 resolution, after all, was not the most ringing denunciation of the state of emergency. The new chairman of the Bar called the decision very important—'but he would not expand on his statement because the wording of the motion had been drafted on the basis of unanimous agreement' (ibid.). Nor was the emergency new in 1988, yet apparently similar resolutions in the past had been blocked, no doubt because of political divisions within the bar. A new group of anti-apartheid lawyers, the National Association of Democratic Lawyers, urged in 1988 that the governing bodies of the advocates' and attorneys' professions should be barred from membership in international organization because they had 'either by ommission [sic] or action sided with the regime'. G. Davis, 'Lawyers Group Calls for "isolation" of Bar Councils', *Weekly Mail* 6 (27 May–2 June 1988).

316 De Tocqueville, *Democracy* (cit. n. 307), 285.

Even without adopting Tocqueville's grand view, we should not be surprised that lawyers are attached to the ideology of legalism (by which I mean simply the broad view that state power should be wielded through duly enacted law and fair process) and can stir themselves to action in its name, in South Africa as in the United States.[317] When Sachs describes the aristocracy of the bar as 'regarding law as something standing apart from society', he is pointing to the South African bar's embrace of this broad form of legalism. In other countries, such as the United States, lawyers have been legalists despite having professional structures very different from South Africa's, but the features of South Africa's legal profession have surely lent themselves to the cementing of this viewpoint. Perhaps in South Africa, where many of the values linked to the rule of law have been under such assault, the aristocratic community of the bar has been of special value as a buttress for commitments that might otherwise have been even more vulnerable.

What of the attorneys, who do not have the special institutional arrangements and status of advocates, but *do* handle a great deal of important legal work in South Africa? Historically, it appears that attorneys have been a more conservative group than advocates.[318] One reason for this may be that attorneys have had neither such strong structural self-protection[319] nor so

[317] See Gordon, 'Independence' (cit. n. 284), 44–5; Halliday, 'Idiom of Legalism' (cit. n. 230), 978–88. In somewhat similar vein, Bryant Garth has written that lawyers, '[a]s custodians of the language and tradition of legal rights ... can argue as experts about the contours of those rights': 'Independent Professional Power and the Search for a Legal Ideology with a Progressive Bite', 62 *Ind. LJ* 183, 202 (1987). Garth suggests with regret that 'lawyers' language of rights' no longer has much progressive force, but he feels that appeal can still be made to 'the core of international human rights', including such principles as the prohibitions on 'torture, disappearances, genocide, and pervasive racial discrimination'. Ibid. 206–7. As his listing of core principles suggests, however, the language of rights still has much to say in South Africa!

[318] One commentator has argued that as a result of government pressure on the courts the 'Incorporated Law Society' (that is, the Association of Law Societies), the official organization of attorneys, has been 'crush[ed] ... into a caricature of the custodian of a profession it is supposed to represent and uphold'. Mervis, 'How the Nats' (cit. n. 146). Some attorneys deeply involved in emergency practice sharply criticized the law societies, national and provincial, 'for failure to defend their interests, and the interests of some of their clients, during the State of Emergency'. P. Sidley, 'Lawyer Societies Deny Neglecting Detained Attorneys', *Weekly Mail* 9 (5–11 Sept. 1986). But the Association has, for example, opposed security legislation (ibid.), and 'prod[ded]' the Judge President of the Cape Supreme Court, Munnik JP, into beginning to 'visit political detainees in jail'. Jost, 'A Conservative' (cit. n. 99).

[319] Attorneys have their own professional associations, the law societies, and these societies may well secure for attorneys substantial professional independence. In certain respects, however, there is some reason to question whether the law societies have the same degree of insulation from state control as the societies of advocates do. Thus the relatively greater statutory regulation of attorneys (see n. 293 above) might suggest that attorneys' independence is vulnerable to state intervention—perhaps even if the attorneys have so far been able to obtain statutes to their specifications. Similarly, it is striking that although the law societies are authorized to make rules governing attorneys' conduct, these rules must receive the approval of the chief justice or, if the chief justice disapproves, of the State President. See Attorneys Act 53 of 1979, s. 74; Mellet, 'Attorneys' (cit. n. 297), 365. In addition, the conditions of attorneys' practice seem less insulated than those of advocates' work. Attorneys, after all, *do* deal directly with clients; no one provides attorneys with the insulation they may ensure for advocates. Attorneys are also not subject to, or protected by, a general 'cab rank' rule, see E. Lewis, *Legal*

many prominent individual exemplars of liberal opposition to government policies as advocates have enjoyed. Other political and cultural differences between the two sets of lawyers have probably also contributed.[320] None the less there have been anti-apartheid attorneys, as well as advocates, for many years,[321] and today their numbers have become quite significant.[322] No doubt these attorneys' anti-apartheid beliefs and efforts have many sources. The strength of the anti-apartheid bar, however, may have provided, and may still provide, inspiration and even some protection to anti-apartheid attorneys, whose immediate professional environment might not have encouraged or safeguarded independence so well. Ironically, the élitist nature of the bar—whose aura of superiority, and exclusive rights of audience in the Supreme Courts, can hardly fail to be grating to attorneys—may have indirectly helped to foster anti-apartheid efforts among attorneys as well as among advocates.[323]

An account of the structure of the legal profession would not be complete without some mention of money. If lawyers are surprisingly independent of the government, after all, most are not independent of the need to earn a living. Opponents of apartheid who are unlucky enough to be snared in the government's enforcement machinery are not likely to be able to afford a full-throttle legal defence. In this respect as in others, however, South Africa does not exist in a vacuum. South African lawyers have adapted models of public-interest law work developed elsewhere, and have looked abroad for much of the funding for their efforts as well. There are enough of these lawyers, and there is enough of this funding, to support a substantial volume of legal effort—though far, far less than what South Africa's black citizens could use. The government could block this money, of course, but that could have costs in terms of both domestic politics and international reaction. In the mean time, the substantial moral and financial support from abroad helps make anti-apartheid law viable and may also help anti-apartheid lawyers to feel less isolated and beleaguered than they otherwise would.

Ethics: A Guide to Professional Conduct for South African Attorneys (Cape Town: Juta, 1982), 49, 75. And attorneys are permitted to work in firms rather than in the enforced independence of solo practice.

[320] For example, Afrikaners may make up a greater proportion of attorneys' ranks than of advocates'. In addition, attorneys are not required to locate their offices in the major cities of the country, as members of the bar are, and so a greater number of attorneys may live in, and be influenced by, relatively rural and conservative communities.

[321] Perhaps the most famous is Nelson Mandela, who practised law together with his partner Oliver Tambo.

[322] This sketch of the position of attorneys in South Africa owes much to comments from Geoff Budlender.

[323] In making this argument, I do not mean to take a position on the intrinsic desirability of South Africa's maintaining a divided bar. My purpose, rather, is to explore the ways in which the institutional structures now in place have contributed to the flowering of anti-apartheid legal practice.

(c) The Tradition of Judicial Independence.

The third salient feature of the South African legal community is the independence of the Supreme Court judiciary. It is important not to overstate the general role of these judges, for the bulk of political trials are actually heard not by the judges but by magistrates,[324] whose independence is by no means assured.[325] At the same time it is a great mistake to consider the judges of the Supreme Court fundamentally irrelevant, just as it would be a great mistake to consider the judges of the federal judiciary in the United States irrelevant, despite the immense amount of legal decisionmaking done in less exalted tribunals. The Supreme Court judges in South Africa exercise appellate jurisdiction over the work of the magistrates; in addition, they have original jurisdiction over a range of matters, including, most importantly for our purposes, all of the cases we have considered in which the government's powers under the state of emergency have been challenged.

I will argue that the traditions and institutional position of the judiciary have contributed to the presence on the bench of a significant number of judges who are not readily disposed to embrace the supposed necessities of apartheid and of its defence. Their role is a morally difficult one, for they may feel constrained by fidelity to the law to enforce laws that are part and parcel of the injustice of apartheid.[326] But they are not always so constrained. The presence of these judges is significant not only because it helps ensure that claims against the state have some chance of prevailing (a meaningful chance, as the Corbett court's judgments demonstrate) but also because the potential for a receptive hearing encourages anti-apartheid lawyers to continue their efforts.

That there are people on the bench who are opposed to aspects, or even all, of apartheid is at first blush paradoxical. The government, after all, appoints every judge, and the National Party, the party of apartheid, has been in power

[324] J. Dugard, 'Tipping Scales of the Law', *Rand Daily Mail* 8 (29 Mar. 1985).

[325] Judge, now Judge of Appeal, Milne has commented quite bluntly on the conditions which call the independence of the magistrates into question. For example, they 'are appointed from within the personnel of the Department of Justice—usually from amongst the ranks of the prosecutors'—rather than from the independent bar. Milne, 'Speech' (cit. n. 292), 457. 'Moreover, while no doubt some magistrates can and do resist it, there is insidious pressure built into the promotion system to please those who promote one to higher status and salary.' Ibid. 458. Subsequently Milne and three other judges recommended that 30 out of the 46 Durban-area magistrates be barred from hearing political trials, after they attended confidential police briefings arranged for them at the request of Durban's chief magistrate. C. Rickard, 'Magistrates Too Political, Says Expert', *Weekly Mail* 9 (17–23 Jan. 1986). The work of anti-apartheid lawyers before the magistrates *can* bear fruit all the same, but the Supreme Court is a more independent forum.

[326] South Africans (and others from afar) have debated whether liberal judges ought to resign. See R. Wacks, 'Judges and Injustice', 101 *SALJ* 266 (1984); J. Dugard, 'Should Judges Resign? A Reply to Professor Wacks', 101 *SALJ* 286 (1984); R. Wacks, 'Judging Judges: A Brief Rejoinder to Professor Dugard', 101 *SALJ* 295 (1984). My concern at this particular point is primarily explanatory rather than prescriptive, but in the following chapter I will argue that lawyers have been right to pursue challenges against apartheid through the courts of South Africa, and, for broadly the same reasons, that liberal judges have been right not to resign.

since 1948! Yet by no means every judge can be relied on to vote with the government. In 1987 John Dugard commented that '[s]ome judges, probably not more than thirty'—or approximately a quarter of the full members of the Supreme Court at the time—are 'troubled by their office and seem to be determined to dissociate themselves from the executive or, at least, to maintain a decent distance from the executive'.[327] Whether because of political beliefs which they held before appointment to the bench or out of convictions they have formed since appointment, these judges are not the automatic allies of the executive.

Three institutional or traditional aspects of the judiciary help explain the presence and the work of these judges. The first is that almost every judge comes from among the senior counsel of the private bar.[328] Judges, in other words, are likely to be deeply imbued with the ethos of the bar, and the bar's spirit, as we have seen, is both independent and somewhat liberal. Moreover, the people appointed as judges are people who have already completed much of their professional career, and for whom this appointment is more of a capstone than a stepping-stone.[329] Supreme Court judges in South Africa no doubt aspire to elevation to the Appellate Division, but such promotions can come only to a small number of judges in any decade,[330] and so promotion is unlikely to be a compelling concern for most members of the Supreme Court bench. In civil law countries, on the other hand, the judiciary tends to be lifetime career, largely distinct from a career in legal advocacy.[331] Judges do not experience the immersion in the values of independent advocacy that South African, and some other common-law, judges do.[332] In civil-law systems, moreover, the initial appointment *is* a stepping-stone, and promotion a serious

[327] Dugard, 'Judiciary' (cit. n. 34, 247. Dugard in 1987 put the total complement of the court, including the Appellate Division, at 'some 120 judges' (of whom he noted 'all but one are men'). Ibid. 485. As of December 1990, the court's size is somewhat greater. See n. 330 below.

[328] Gretchen Carpenter refers to 'the practice of appointing them [judges] from the ranks of practising senior advocates'. See G. Carpenter, *Introduction to South African Constitutional Law* (Durban: Butterworths, 1987), 257. Although it is possible for advocates in the public service to become senior counsel and judges, almost all judges are appointed from the members of the societies of advocates. (Probably the most important exception was the 1951 appointment of L. C. Steyn. The Johannesburg bar (the society of advocates) decided on a three-week boycott of Steyn's court because he had not been a member of the bar. See A. van Blerk, *Judge and Be Judged* (Cape Town: Juta, 1988), 120–1. Steyn was elevated to the Appellate Division only four years later and to the post of chief justice in 1959.) One particularly striking result of the near-exclusion of state employees from the bench is that prosecutors are unlikely to receive judicial appointments. It seems reasonable to infer that the exclusion of prosecutors and other civil servants deprives the government of a group of appointees who—whatever their personal independence of mind—would be likely to sympathize with government positions.

[329] Otto Kirchheimer makes somewhat similar observations about the appointment of judges in the United States, *Political Justice* (cit. n. 45), 183–4.

[330] According to the *South African Law Reports* of Dec. 1990, there were 18 full members of the Appellate Division, and 3 acting judges (an unusually large total for the Appeal Court, at least since the beginning of the state of emergency); there were 120 other full members of the Supreme Court as a whole, and 21 other acting judges.

[331] See Abel, 'Civil Law World' (cit. n. 233), 8.

[332] See Kirchheimer, *Political Justice* (cit. n. 45), 181.

concern;[333] the Nazis wielded this incentive—more, it seems, than the cruder incentive of the menace of terror—in their co-optation of the German judiciary.[334]

Even so, the impact of the practice of selecting judges from among senior counsel in private practice should not be exaggerated, for politics may well affect the process of appointment in various ways.[335] Not every liberal senior counsel may be prepared to accept the potential moral compromises entailed in enforcing the present laws of South Africa, however benignly he or she might read them.[336] The government, for its part, can engineer a designation as senior counsel,[337] and can select less illustrious, but more conservative, senior counsel for elevation to the bench. During their first years in power, as we have seen, the Nationalists pursued a deliberate policy of appointing Afrikaners to the bench.[338] One prominent advocate, Sydney Kentridge, has forthrightly declared 'that over the past thirty years political factors have been placed above merit—not only in appointments to the Bench but in promotions to the Appeal Court. This has undoubtedly led in many cases to better qualified men being passed over in favour of others less worthy of appointment or

[333] So Kirchheimer indicated in 1961. Ibid. 181.

[334] Marsh believes that the explanation for 'German judicial subservience to the state' is not 'general acceptance of their [the Nazis'] peculiar theories of law'—he maintains that the Nazis did not achieve this—but rather 'the special forms of pressure which the State could bring to bear on the individual judge'. Among these forms of pressure, and 'more effective than the crude threat of the Gestapo, was the power to block the promotion of the comparatively ill-paid junior judge'. See Marsh, 'Some Aspects' (cit. n. 297), 373. (The Nazis also employed an illegal and 'elaborate system of administrative directions' to communicate the regime's wishes to the judges. Ibid. 373–4.) No doubt German judges sensed that the terror around them *could* be directed at them, but '[i]n fact, no judge in the [T]hird Reich was ever prosecuted within the German legal system for anything in connection with his jurisdiction.' Reifner, 'Bar in the Third Reich' (cit. n. 31), 101 n. 8. One small-town judge who 'reproached the official responsible for the policy [of putting feeble-minded people to death], Hermann Goering, for committing murder' suffered no more than a transfer to another court. Ibid. 103. Though the Nazis did eliminate security of tenure for judges, Müller, *Hitler's Justice* (cit. n. 28), 72, they did not in fact fire 'any high proportion' of them, except of course for Jews, Marsh, 'Some Aspects', 373.

[335] Kirchheimer points out that political factors influence appointment in England and America, while they affect promotion in Europe, Kirchheimer, *Political Justice* (cit. n. 45), 182.

[336] See Commission of Inquiry into the Structure and Functioning of the Courts, *Fifth and Final Report* (RP 78/1983), i, Part II, para. 1.3.11.2, pp. 68–9 (memorandum of Johannesburg Bar Council on reasons for advocates' reluctance to become judges). For some liberals, however, the motive for rejecting appointment may have been more financial than political. See 'The Judiciary: A New Liberal Era', *Financial Mail*, 59 (8 Aug. 1986).) It deserves special mention that, after decades during which the idea of a black judge would undoubtedly have been anathema to the government, the state now might well be pleased to make such an appointment—but there is strong feeling among blacks that black advocates should *not* accept appointments to the bench. See Higginbotham, 'Racism' (cit. n. 83), 503 n. 68. As of Dec. 1990 every judge of the Supreme Court was white (and only one was a woman).

[337] Mervis cites the cases of P. M. Cillie, who became a Queen's Counsel (the equivalent of senior counsel before South Africa became a republic) and then a judge within the same month, and of Fritz Steyn, who became a senior counsel in 1969 while serving as Ambassador to Belgium, at a time when 'he had not practised law for almost four years', and two months later became a judge. Mervis, 'How the Nats' (cit. n. 146).

[338] This period seems to have lasted from 1948 through perhaps 1962. See ibid.; 'The Judiciary' (cit. n. 336).

promotion.'[339] No doubt there have also been cases in which the government was able to choose senior counsel who were both talented *and* conservative.

Yet the very force of Kentridge's criticism suggests that the principle of appointment on merit retains considerable vitality.[340] Though there have been voices within the government urging the appointment of advocates employed in the civil service (who would normally not be members of the private bar),[341] the actual cases of such appointments have been very few. Beginning in the 1960s, it has been suggested, the government began to rely more on merit in its appointments, apparently because it felt it had sufficiently constrained the judiciary through changes in the statutory law. In 1986 John Dugard felt that most appointments were being made on merit.[342] Whether the reason is simply the sort of calculation Dugard infers, or a desire on the part of the executive to avoid criticism from the bar, or some adherence even on the part of the government to the bar's traditions,[343] the fact is that the government does appoint or promote judges whom it must expect to render distinctly liberal judgments.[344]

Second, these judges have virtual life tenure once they are appointed. They are subject to removal only by the State President in response to 'an address from each of the respective Houses of Parliament in the same session praying for such removal on the ground of misbehaviour or incapacity',[345] and no one has ever been removed in this way.[346] Though the government in 1959 drafted legislation that would have eased this process of removal, it abandoned the proposal.[347] As a result life tenure, in South Africa as in the United States,

[339] Kentridge, 'Telling the Truth' (cit. n. 74), 652; for a comparably blunt assessment reaching very similar conclusions, see Didcott, 'Didcott Memorandum' (cit. n. 260), 661–2.

[340] Indeed, Kentridge says that 'we are entitled to expect' that the executive will avoid purely political appointments: 'Telling the Truth' (cit. n. 74), 651.

[341] See Didcott, 'Didcott Memorandum' (cit. n. 260), 659–60.

[342] 'The Judiciary' (cit. n. 336); see also C. Rickard, 'The More Flexible Judiciary: A Retiring Judge Looks Back', *Weekly Mail* 4 (4 Sept. 1987).

[343] In 1980 Judge Didcott sharply attacked what he saw as 'a deliberate and determined strategy' by bureaucrats and 'politicians in league with them'—in essence, it appears, by the government—'[t]o harness' the Supreme Court, 'to control it as far as possible'. Didcott, 'Didcott Memorandum' (cit. n. 260), 657. Didcott's argument is a grim one, see ibid. 657–63, yet it may be that even within the government such disregard for the traditions of the courts had its limits, or that (as in the case of the government's attitudes towards a bill of rights) there has been some evolution during the 1980s.

[344] The relatively benign decisions of appellate judges in the *ante bellum* Southern United States may also have reflected a comparative insulation from politics. By the time of the Civil War these judges were chosen by elections and did not have life tenure (obviously a very different system from South Africa's), but Nash suggests that the voters focused on judges' 'personal and legal capacities rather than their party affiliation', and considered the judge 'a special species of politician'. Nash, 'A More Equitable Past?' (cit. n. 155), 237–8.

[345] Supreme Court Act No. 59 of 1959, s. 10(7).

[346] Milne, 'Speech' (cit. n. 292), 456. Milne notes (ibid.) that occasionally judges have chosen to resign rather than face the scandal of the removal process, but I know of no case in which the source of the threat of removal was the government's desire to silence an anti-apartheid judge.

[347] Mervis, 'How the Nats' (cit. n. 146).

gives judges the security to throw off, if they wish, whatever political entanglements might otherwise cloud their vision.

Third, the bench has its own tradition of independence, and its own insulation of prestige. '[A]mong South African élites, judges rank second only to Cabinet Ministers in terms of prestige.'[348] This lustre dates back to the Cape Colony when its court was headed by de Villiers, and even before.[349] It seems fair to say that this prestige exists not in spite, but because, of the courts' willingness on occasion to resist the calls of state authority; that is to say, the tradition of independence is intertwined with what I have called the human rights tradition of South African law. We have already seen that as early as the 1820s the courts began to play a role—albeit a limited one—as protectors of blacks' rights.[350] In colonial days, judges of the Cape Supreme Court 'frequently handed down rulings which embarrassed the administration or the police, and by so doing earned for themselves a reputation for independence and impartiality'.[351] In the 1930s Sir James Rose-Innes, a liberal and very respected chief justice of South Africa, declared 'that people of all races realise that when a man takes a seat on our Bench, he strips himself of all predilections and endeavours only to do right to all manner of men according to Law'.[352] Many black South Africans might have had trouble agreeing with this claim, but it is none the less a striking reflection of the judiciary's ideals.

In John Dugard's words the judiciary 'prides itself on its independence and professes allegiance to the legal traditions of the Western world'.[353] Despite this tradition, the courts have rendered many decisions that rejected the arguments of the victims of apartheid. Yet the tradition remains and, I believe, continues to offer a shield and even a guide to judges who must decide whether such arguments have merit. Clothed in this tradition, even judges who might agree with many aspects of government programmes have been prepared to hold particular elements of the government's policies unlawful.[354]

[348] Corder, *Judges at Work* (cit. n. 2), 232.

[349] See Sachs, *Justice* (cit. n. 52), 41 (early 19th-cent. Cape judges 'invested judicial office, if not always with a dignity, then with a sense of importance').

[350] Ibid. 36.

[351] Ibid. 66.

[352] 'A Memorial to Sir William Solomon', 1931 *SALJ* 150, 153 48/(1931) (address by Sir James Rose-Innes).

[353] Dugard, 'Judiciary in Crisis' (cit. n. 34), 487.

[354] One of the most prominent examples may be the decision by Chief Justice Rumpff in *Komani NO* v. *Bantu Affairs Administration Board, Peninsula Area*, 1980 (4) SA 448 (A), a case which rejected part of the government's system of 'influx control' over blacks' right to live in urban areas. As a trial judge, Rumpff had earlier joined in, and announced, a no less striking decision, the acquittal of all the remaining accused in the final phase of the massive 1950s treason trial. See T. Karis, 'The South African Treason Trial', 76 *Pol. Sci. Q.* 217, 239–40 (1961).

3. The Jurisprudence of Human Rights in South Africa

Even judges well prepared by background and conviction to vindicate human rights through law do not necessarily do so. What judges do will depend, as well, on what they are asked to do, what justifications they are offered for doing what is asked, and what authority they believe they have to comply with these requests. This is to say that what judges do depends, in part, on jurisprudence. Their actions certainly depend on much else besides, for the jurisprudential theories that judges adopt, and the applications of those theories that they embrace, are no doubt profoundly influenced by other beliefs, values, and desires dear to them. But there is no reason to assume that jurisprudential views are merely the *effect*, while other aspects of the judge's thoughts and needs are the *cause*. Judges' beliefs about the nature of their responsibilities and powers are part of the judges' concerns. Reflective judges will try to bring all of these concerns into harmony with each other; less self-conscious jurists will at least try to avoid collision with any of the potentially discordant beliefs that they hold. Lawyers who hope to prevail in court will have to take cognizance of the judges' jurisprudence, and in the manner that the lawyers present their claims they will reveal or adopt a jurisprudence of their own.

Hence it is important to assess the impact of positivism, the characteristic jurisprudence of South African law, on judges' acceptance or rejection of human rights claims. Precisely because positivist principles provide only one of many elements of the thinking of South African lawyers and judges, however, we should not expect to find that positivism has a uniform and unitary impact. I will suggest, in this light, that there is force to the argument that positivism has encouraged decisions favouring state power over human rights. But positivism in South Africa also helped preserve and make available the doctrinal tools for arguments, and decisions, that have vindicated human rights claims. Indeed, the framework of positivism in South Africa has proven to be, within limits, notably supple, and so may have made the course of human rights advocacy in South Africa's courts less difficult than it would have been had the legal foundations of oppression been nailed down more tightly.

The inimical effects of positivism on judicial thinking have been emphasized by John Dugard, who has repeatedly argued that positivism has played a part in leading judges to acquiesce in repressive interpretations of the law, interpretations which they need not have reached.[355] 'The result of this allegiance to the positivist creed', Dugard writes, 'is that statutory interpretation is seen as a mechanical operation in which value judgments play no

[355] See J. Dugard, 'The Judicial Process, Positivism and Civil Liberty', 88 *SALJ* 181 (1971); id., *Human Rights* (cit. n. 80), 366–402. Anthony Mathews has taken a similar position, 'The South African Judiciary and the Security System', 1 *SAJHR* 199, 207–8 (1985); id., *Freedom, State Security* (cit. n. 172), 296–302. However, by no means all critics of South African law agree that positivism, whether sophisticated or crude, is the cause of the courts' deficiency. See Forsyth, *In Danger* (cit. n. 3), 228–30; Wacks, 'Judges and Injustice' (cit. n. 326).

part.'[356] Viewing their role as the implementation of legislative commands, judges can 'apply the harshest of laws obediently with an easy conscience' and may also be led to 'a failure to realize the extent to which technical rules of interpretation may be invoked to moderate the laws' inequities'.[357] The brooding omnipresence of parliamentary supremacy may discourage, even when it does not intellectually refute, the most free-wheeling understandings of the scope of the courts' discretion.

Dugard may well be right that positivism in South Africa has contributed to executive-minded judicial decisons, by rationalizing and so encouraging a ready receptiveness to the perceived commands of the political branches of government. H. L. A. Hart argued in his famous debate with Lon Fuller that positivist principles do *not* dictate subservience to immoral laws,[358] but that in itself does not acquit positivism of all responsibility. Jurisprudential theories, as Mark Osiel has thoughtfully observed, may generate 'low' versions of themselves, with consequences quite different from those the pure formulation would portend,[359] and Dugard sees a 'popular, vulgar, positivist message' as guiding the thinking of the average lawyer in South Africa.[360] Moreover, for some judges this message no doubt fell on receptive ears, and functioned less as impetus than as facilitator for decisions to which the judges were favourably predisposed. Though positivism had been somewhat eclipsed in Nazi Germany by the Nazis' own emotionally charged legal views,[361] it may have had such facilitative effects there too, providing a pathway for decisions which some judges' political sentiments and career ambitions already supported and buttressing the distinction between law and morality for judges who might otherwise have been more troubled than they were.[362]

[356] Dugard, *Human Rights* (cit. n. 80), 374.

[357] Ibid. 373–4.

[358] H. Hart, 'Positivism and the Separation of Law and Morals', 71 *Harv. L. Rev.* 593, 615–21 (1958). For Fuller's views, see L. Fuller, 'Positivism and Fidelity to Law: A Reply to Professor Hart', 71 *Harv. L. Rev.* 630, 657–9 (1958).

[359] Osiel, 'Sources' (cit. n. 32), 17–26. Osiel analyses the genesis of 'deviant' versions of jurisprudential theories, and in particular of a positivism that divests courts of the power to scrutinize the morality of the law.

[360] J. Dugard, 'Some Realism about the Judicial Process and Positivism: A Reply', 98 *SALJ* 372, 376 (1981). Forsyth argues that there could not be many judges who 'in the depths of their hearts really believe that interpretation of difficult statutes is purely mechanical'. Forsyth, *In Danger* (cit. n. 3), 230. This may well be correct. But most judges, like most other people, probably do not regularly plumb the depths of their hearts. It should be no surprise that what they find when they do descend to these depths is not the same as what they ordinarily accept as guiding principles of their work. And even if judges were uniquely clear in their moral natures, Forsyth's formulation allows for the possibility that judges do believe that interpretation of not-so-difficult statutes is almost purely mechanical, and that belief would be sufficient to carry them a long way towards the decision of many cases.

[361] See text and notes at nn. 176–83, 333–4 above.

[362] Mathias Reimann suggests that positivism 'certainly facilitated the demise' of the rule of law under the Nazis. Reimann, 'National Socialist Jurisprudence' (cit. n. 39), 1658 n. 35. More generally, Reimann sees positivism as having played a role in generating a legal culture, predating and postdating the Nazis, in which the law was seen as separate from politics and morality. Ibid. 1657–8. But he also says that 'this heritage of positivism only allows, but does not demand, discounting political factors. These factors can, and often have been, considered

None the less I will argue that widespread adherence to positivist argumentation in South African courts has also made a contribution to the rise of more rights-minded decisions. It has done so by providing an agreed-upon framework for argument, within which a considerable range of human rights contentions can be presented as legitimate grounds for decision. And it has been able to offer this opportunity in good part because the central positivist dictate of South African law, the supremacy of Parliament, has proved to be a relatively unconfining doctrinal constraint—as we saw in Chapter 2, which examined the variety of interpretive rules available to South African judges for use to mitigate the rigours of statutory provisions. The result is that the South African judiciary does not have to fundamentally restructure its jurisprudence, with all the doctrinal and even moral strain that might entail, in order to render a range of decisions in favour of human rights.

It might not have been so. In the United States before its Civil War, Robert Cover has argued,[363] Northern judges of sometimes very strong anti-slavery conviction acquiesced in, and to some extent may even have expanded upon, a series of grim decisions under the hated fugitive slave laws.[364] The fugitive slave laws employed governmental power in the Northern states to return runaway slaves to their masters in the South, and these decisions gradually defeated the challenges brought by anti-slavery forces against these laws. The judges not only shrank from overtly using morality to rework the law, but also 'seemed very reluctant to resort to, and thus legitimate, substantial doctrinal innovations that might have made certain cases less a choice between law and morality and more a choice between alternative legal formulations'.[365] And yet these judges were, in the eyes of the people of the day, 'independent and high-minded'.[366] Indeed, on occasion they were the authors of anti-slavery judgments or dissents.[367]

The experience of these judges, as Cover recounts it, illuminates the role that positivism has played in South Africa. This is not because the issues these

when it is opportune, for example, against scholars critical of the usually conservative majority.' Ibid. 1659 n. 38. This is positivism more as rationalization than as principle.

[363] R. Cover, *Justice Accused: Antislavery and the Judicial Process* (New Haven, Conn.: Yale University Press, 1975).

[364] There were two such laws, the first passed in 1793, and the second in 1850: 'An Act respecting fugitives from justice, and persons escaping from the service of their masters', 1 Stat. 302 (1793); 'An Act to amend, and supplementary to, the Act entitled "An Act respecting Fugitives from Justice, and Persons escaping from the Service of their Masters," approved February twelfth, one thousand seven hundred and ninety-three', 9 Stat. 462 (1850) (the Fugitive Slave Act of 1850).

[365] Cover, *Justice Accused* (cit. n. 363), 199; see ibid. 208. For the most striking, but 'fleeting', exception to this pattern, see ibid. 185–8.

[366] Ibid. 178.

[367] Cover focuses in particular on four members of the group of anti-slavery judges: Story, Shaw, McLean, and Swan. As Cover shows, each of these judges rendered one or more anti-slavery decisions from the bench. See ibid. 238–56. For example, McLean wrote a vigorous dissent in *Dred Scott*, 60 US (19 How.) at 529–64. Shaw decided the important case of *Commonwealth* v. *Aves*, 35 Mass. (18 Pick.) 195 (1833), which held that a slave (other than a

American judges faced, or the social context in which they acted, were the same as those in South Africa in the 1980s—far from it. Nor is it because the South African judges, overall, proved more attentive to human rights than the Americans—this may or may not have been true. Rather, my focus is on the plight in which these anti-slavery judges found themselves when they addressed the particular area of fugitive slave cases. In this area, jurisprudential theory played a role in humane judges' deciding to reject arguments on behalf of slaves; in certain important respects, as we will see, the role of jurisprudential theory in South Africa has been quite different, and more benign.

Cover's account of these decisions suggests that they were in significant part the result of the constraints, or at any rate the influences, of jurisprudence. The judges of the day were fundamentally positivists.[368] Two great sources of positive law constrained them, the fugitive slave laws and the constitution, which in several euphemistic but clear ways embodied the framers' 'acknowledging the legitimate presence of slavery in American life'.[369] The fugitive slave clause itself placed the authority of the constitution behind the return of fugitive slaves to their masters, although it is far from plain exactly what governmental intervention in favour of the masters the clause meant to require.[370] The Northern judges whom Cover studies, however, were not by any means narrow positivists. These judges were fully capable of creatively reshaping pre-existing law—though they were much less able to offer a jurisprudential explanation for the judicial power they knew they had.[371]

fugitive) brought into Massachusetts to stay there temporarily, but not to acquire a domicile there, became entitled to freedom as a result.

368 See Cover, *Justice Accused* (cit. n. 363), 26–30, 125, 257–9.

369 This phrase is Fehrenbacher's, *Dred Scott Case* (cit. n. 208), 27. Fehrenbacher is at pains, however, to cast doubt on the claim of Southerners 'that the right to hold slaves as property was "distinctly and expressly affirmed in the Constitution"'. (Ibid.) He emphasises the constitution's delicate avoidance of the word 'slavery', and comments that '[i]t is as though the framers were half-consciously trying to frame two constitutions, one for their own time and the other for the ages, with slavery viewed bifocally—that is, plainly visible at their feet, but disappearing when they lifted their eyes.' Ibid. One of the provisions in question dealt with fugitive slaves and is quoted and discussed in n. 370 below. A second dealt with the extent to which slaves would count towards the slave states population total to determine their taxes and the number of Representatives they would have in Congress. US Const., art. I, s. 2 (providing for apportionment of Representatives in Congress, and of 'direct Taxes', based on figures 'determined by adding to the whole Number of free Persons, including those bound to Service for a Term of Years, and excluding Indians not taxed, *three fifths of all other Persons*': emphasis added). The third dealt with the slave-trade. Ibid. art. I, s. 9, cl. 1 (denying Congress the power to prohibit 'the Migration or Importation of such Persons as any of the States now existing shall think proper to admit' [i.e. slaves] until 1808).

370 US Const., art. IV, s. 2, provided in relevant part that: 'No Person held to Service or Labour in one State, under the Laws thereof, escaping into another, shall, in Consequence of any Law or Regulation therein, be discharged from such Service or Labour, but shall be delivered up on Claim of the Party to whom such Service or Labour may be due.' Fehrenbacher suggests that the clause may have been meant to prohibit state interference with masters' rights to their slaves, rather than to authorize federal legislation to compel fugitive slaves' return: *Dred Scott Case* (cit. n. 208), 25. As he says, however, 'both Congress and the Supreme Court eventually came to the opposite conclusion'. Ibid.

371 See Cover, *Justice Accused* (cit. n. 363), 131–48, 257–9.

Among these judges was one, Lemuel Shaw, who was 'one of the principal carriers of what Llewellyn called the grand style of common law jurisprudence'.[372] It remains to be explained, therefore, why these judges did not exploit the creative potentials of their jurisprudence in the fugitive slave cases, as they did elsewhere.

Although Cover is not entirely explicit on this score, his study suggests two main explanations. Cover's own answer appears to be that the gradual accumulation of precedents made anti-slavery decisionmaking in this field harder and harder to square with the dominant understanding of the judicial role,[373] an understanding which—despite the presence of the 'grand style'—tended to stress restrictive formulations of judicial responsibility.[374] As Cover puts it, '[a]ntebellum jurisprudence was positivist and preoccupied with refuting the Jacksonian myth of judicial lawmaking run amuck.'[375] Thus constrained by their perception of positivist principles, the judges of the day confronted what Cover calls the 'dialectical environment'.[376] The charged quality of this environment combined with the doctrinal setting to make the judges 'subject to intense psychological forces'.[377] Precisely because they were genuinely sensitive to this conflict, rather than ruthlessly indifferent to the moral claims of the anti-slavery forces, Cover argues, those judges who chose not to render anti-slavery decisions embraced modes of self-justification which they might otherwise have used less or not at all, such as assertions that their obedience to the dictates of the Fugitive Slave Act was essential to the very maintenance of society, 'retreat to a mechanistic formalism', and 'ascription of responsibility elsewhere'.[378]

This interpretation of the role of positivism portrays it as both constraint on and rationalization for the judges' fugitive slave decisions.[379] Some students of this period, however, have questioned Cover's characterization of the judges' decisions, and have argued that they were not the cramped performances Cover portrays. Instead, according to these critics, the judges of this period were deciding as 'grandly' in their fugitive slave cases as elsewhere; when they said that the preservation of the Union depended on the enforcement of the Fugitive Slave Act, they were not excusing themselves defensively but stating what they genuinely, and with good reason, believed.[380] Similar arguments

[372] Ibid. 251.

[373] See ibid. 208, 210.

[374] Ibid. 257–8.

[375] Ibid. 258. For a discussion of the efforts in the jurisprudence of the day to square judicial lawmaking with the impropriety of imposition of judicial will, see ibid. 132–48.

[376] See ibid. 211–25.

[377] Ibid. 225.

[378] Ibid. 226–38. Cover suggests that the psychological mechanism prompting these responses was the desire to avoid 'cognitive dissonance' between the judges' belief that slavery was wrong and their judgments enforcing the fugitive slave laws. See ibid. 229.

[379] Ronald Dworkin emphatically agrees that jurisprudence did constrain the judges of this period, although he analyses the judges' jurisprudential position somewhat differently than does Cover: 'The Law of the Slave-Catchers' (Book Review), *TLS* 1437 (5 Dec. 1975).

[380] A number of reviewers of Cover's book offered criticism on these lines. See E. Genovese,

can be made about positivism's role in South Africa; I have suggested that positivism did facilitate South African judgments that have denied human rights claims, but positivism was only one of the factors at work, in conjunction with such pressing concerns as the judges' perception of emergency and onslaught.

What distinguishes the contribution of jurisprudence in South Africa from its part in the cases Cover studies is suggested by a second, complementary explanation for the fugitive slave decisions, an explanation which focuses on the role of the dialectical environment. Cover seems to see the dialectical environment as affecting the way the judges justified their decisions; this second explanation submits (and perhaps Cover would have agreed) that this environment also affected the substance of the decisions themselves, by heightening the judges' sense that their jurisprudence forbade them to reach different results. Perhaps, as some of Cover's readers suggest, the judges' opinions did not exaggerate their convictions. Those convictions, however, were shaped by a range of influences, and among them would have been the arguments that were put to them, and the atmosphere in which they were offered, in the anti-slavery cases. This is not only because jurisprudential beliefs are likely as a general matter to be among the ideas which influence, as well as rationalize, judges' behaviour. It is also because of the particular jurisprudential positions which flourished in the anti-slavery movement before the Civil War.

Cover focuses on two lines of anti-slavery jurisprudence, both of which embodied such sharp challenges to the reigning principles of the day that they could not have been easy for judges to adopt.[381] What they had in common was that each theory starkly and aggressively intensified the moral dilemma in which these judges found themselves. One body of anti-slavery thought purported to be faithful to the fundamental American positivist rule of the

'Political Foundations of Justice', 85 *Yale LJ* 582, 587–88 (1976); M. Tushnet, 20 *Am. J. Leg. Hist.* 168, 169 (1976); J. Ely, 1975 *Wash. ULQ* 265, 270–3. See also W. Nelson, 'The Impact of the Antislavery Movement upon Styles of Judicial Reasoning in Nineteenth Century America', 87 *Harv. L. Rev.* 513, 538–47 (1974). Somewhat similarly, Redmond Barnett suggests that judges' repeated statements about the obligations the law imposed might have been attempts to persuade others rather than (solely) to cope with their own doubts. R. Barnett, 'Professionalism and the Chains of Slavery', 77 *Mich. L. Rev.* 655, 673–7 (1979). Derrick Bell raises the sad possibility that the judges' resolution of their moral–formal dilemma reflected the taint of racism rather than anxiety about the security of the country (or their principled understanding of the force of positivist obligations). D. Bell, Book Review, 76 *Colum. L. Rev.* 350, 356–61 (1976).

[381] As Derrick Bell points out, the abolitionists 'never commanded majority support in the North': Book Review (cit. n. 380), 358. Moreover, Cover indicates that there *were* lawyers who offered antislavery arguments that stayed within conventional doctrinal bounds. Cover, *Justice Accused* (cit. n. 363), 155–56. Cover's account suggests, however, that the judges were not easily able to dismiss the sharpest challenges from their minds. See ibid., 211–16. No doubt the most ardent abolitionists played a role in fugitive slave litigation vastly out of proportion to their numbers, and thus were well positioned to achieve what Genovese calls 'the growing transformation of the courts into a theatre for guerrilla politics'. Genovese, 'Political Foundations' (cit. n. 380), 587.

authoritativeness of the constitution—but only purported to be. This line of argument asserted that the constitution itself outlawed the slavery which it seemed so plainly to acknowledge as part of American society. Cover's judgment of the 'most complete' of these arguments is that it showed ingenuity, but only 'the haphazard ingenuity of rule and phrase manipulation ignoring the "method" of the judge in any real sense'.[382] In short, it had to be hard for any judge to swallow.

The second body of anti-slavery thought presented the judge with an even more difficult challenge. This line of argument, fiercely and steadily put forward by the Garrisonians, maintained that the constitution did bind the judges, and that it did enshrine slavery, and that therefore a moral judge had no choice but to resign.[383] None of these judges did resign; very few have done so in South Africa either. But it is easy to understand that once they had chosen not to resign they would have been driven by the sheer intensity of the attack upon them to insist all the more on the morality of the decisions they were handing down.

Reacting against patently fallacious interpretations on the one hand, and calls for their resignation on the other, the judges also may well have been driven to worse decisions than they would otherwise have rendered. It is hard, after all, to embrace a position whose surface attractiveness masks an underlying logic one considers unacceptable—and all the harder when the elements of this underlying logic are called to one's attention. Thus the judges may have been impelled to embrace a particularly relentless understanding of their duty of compliance with the rules of the system within which they acted.

The doctrinal environment was not only sharp but also heated, and this constituted, in a broad sense, a further jurisprudential challenge, a challenge to the ideal of detached and reasoned adjudication. The fugitive slave cases were hardly litigated in the calm, reflective atmosphere that this ideal at least welcomes, and perhaps requires. Lawyers were directly involved in creating a very different atmosphere instead. As Cover says, the judge 'could not control the public meetings, the demonstrations, and the ideological press. Nor could he easily ignore them when they were the principal news of the day.'[384] Before some judges and perhaps many juries, and before the people, anti-slavery advocates and lawyers explicitly urged that morality be placed ahead of law, and conveyed to the judge the threat of 'scorn and damnation for being a gutless sycophant'.[385] An ideological segment of the bar seemed increasingly indifferent to the legal merits of the claims they pressed, and '[s]ometimes their pursuit of the client's rights seemed to have no basis except the hope of a stroke of the lawless mob effecting a rescue.'[386] Counsel came to be identified

[382] Cover, *Justice Accused* (cit. n. 363), 156, 157.
[383] Ibid. 150–4.
[384] Ibid. 211.
[385] Ibid. 212.
[386] Ibid.

'with the militant appeal in the street',[387] and a lawyer might even chair a protest meeting at night after contending in court during the day.[388] This heated atmosphere could well have compounded the judges' adverse reaction to the jurisprudential theories with which abolitionists articulated their challenge to the judges.

South African lawyers human rights advocacy has, I believe, largely avoided this danger of polarizing potentially sympathetic judges, and done so even though a dominant theme of criticism of the courts has been that they should respond to the moral values at stake in the cases, and even though much of the academic commentary has urged the adoption of non-positivist forms of decisionmaking.[389] It has been possible to avoid such fundamental doctrinal confrontation, first, because the resources available within South African law for benign decisions can readily be fitted into a positivist framework.[390] Thus John Dugard, who had in earlier works explicitly called for judicial adoption of what he recognized was a startling jurisprudential guide-line, a combination of legal realism and natural law or values,[391] later justified benign judicial decisions in quite different terms. Responding to Raymond Wacks's Dworkinian argument that the true core of South African law, in light of which all legal questions should be answered, is repressive, Dugard argues that it is ironic but true that:

> our courts must still interpret and apply the law of apartheid in accordance with the common law. And here one refers not only to the values, traditions, principles and spirit of the common law, but also to rules of positive law. For many of the principles of equality and liberty immanent in Roman–Dutch law have been recognized as positive rules of law by our courts. Statutory presumptions in favour of equality, liberty and reasonableness, the principles of natural justice by which the lawfulness of administrative actions are judged, and the standards of reasonableness for testing subordinate legislation enunciated in *Kruse* v *Johnson* are rules of positive law to be applied before the judge enters the uncertain terrain of principles, policies and tradition.[392]

The judgments in the various emergency cases indicate quite clearly that the arguments which have been put to the judges in favour of human rights have

[387] M. Corbett, 'Speech to Johannesburg Bar', *Consultus* 73, 74 (Oct. 1989).

[388] For an example, see ibid. 210.

[389] See e.g. E. Mureinik, 'Security and Integrity', 1987 *Acta Juridica* 197; C. Hoexter, 'Judicial Policy in South Africa', 103 *SALJ* 436 (1986).

[390] Mark Osiel has addressed issues similar to those I discuss here, in his analysis of the Argentinian courts' use of realist and positivist jurisprudence to exercise some restraint over the actions of the military government: 'Sources' (cit. n. 32), 55–70. As he suggests (p. 68), the use of natural law principles to challenge that government might have implied a 'more root-and-branch' criticism, criticism that perhaps would have been less persuasive and surely would have been more dangerous to the critics.

[391] J. Dugard, 'The Judicial Process, Positivism and Civil Liberty', 88 *SALJ* 181, 199 (1971) ('realism-cum-natural-law'); id., *Human Rights* (cit. n. 80), 400 ('realist-cum-value-oriented approach').

[392] Dugard, 'Should Judges Resign?' (cit. n. 326), 289–90.

been couched, as Dugard's comment demonstrates they can be, within rather than without the normal parameters of South African legal argument.[393] Thus judges need not burst the bonds of their role to render many decisions in favour of human rights—and the state cannot, or at any rate does not, assert that the decisions the courts render are actually illegitimate, as American politicians so often do.[394]

In addition, these judges do not seem to have been subjected to the same level of personal pressure to challenge the fundamental contours of their role as American judges may have encountered. They have, to be sure, been criticized, and this criticism has often been severe[395]—even though for many years it may have been restrained to a degree by the fear of criminal prosecution, which had befallen one outspoken critic.[396] The new chief justice has urged critics to 'play the ball and not the man', and this advice may reflect his feeling that judges *are* being pushed too hard on a personal level.[397] But the import of this criticism has, I suggest, questioned the fundamental contours of the judge's role less than anti-slavery jurisprudence did. Where some anti-slavery lawyers sought to construct legal arguments which paid lip-service to conventional understanding but 'ignore[d] the "method" of the judge in any real sense', South African critics have had much to say that fitted well, or at least tolerably, into their country's conventional legal discourse. And although one South African academic, Raymond Wacks, did follow the Garrisonians in arguing that judges should resign,[398] there has been no sustained Garrisonian pressure for them to take this course.

The personal pressure on the judges is also alleviated by the battery of conventions which sustain the idea of adjudication as a neutral and objective process. There has been judicial suspicion towards lawyers,[399] and there has

[393] It is, of course, quite consistent with positivist theory to acknowledge the existence of a zone of uncertainty in the positive law, and to accept the propriety of judges' resolving uncertain cases in light of their beliefs about what the law *should* be. Hart, 'Positivism' (cit. n. 358), 606–15. It is also perfectly possible to argue that in important areas, such as the availability of *audi alteram partem* protections, the courts are not merely resolving uncertainties but rather—unless and until Parliament constrains them—are themselves the positivist lawmakers. Cf. C. Forsyth and J. Schiller, 'The Judicial Process, Positivism and Civil Liberty II', 98 *SALJ* 218, 221–2 (1981). Ironically enough, the conservative judgment of Hefer JA in *United Democratic Front* supports such an argument.

[394] Otto Kirchheimer noted 30 years ago the capacity of South African judges to use positivism to constrain the injustice of their government. See Kirchheimer, *Political Justice* (cit. n. 45), 210–11.

[395] For instances of such criticism, some of it very sharp indeed, see the articles collected in 'Focus on *Omar*', 3 *SAJHR* 337 (1987).

[396] See Dugard, *Human Rights* (cit. n. 80), 288–302.

[397] Corbett, 'Speech' (cit. n. 237), 75.

[398] Wacks, 'Judges and Injustice' (cit. n. 326).

[399] Rabie ACJ, for example, was not prepared to consider baseless the state's asserted anxieties about the security risks that might ensue from permitting detainees to have access to their lawyers as a matter of right. *Omar*, 1987 (3) SA 859 (A) at 895B–C, 897C–G. See also *S. v. Baleka and Others*, 1988 (4) SA 688 (T). A South African human rights lawyer has spoken to me of the atmosphere of distrust in the Rabie court, but also of the very different, much more receptive, atmosphere in the Corbett court.

been some organized political activity by lawyers as well.[400] Still, especially considering the level of political conflict in the country as a whole, the dialectical environment affecting South African judges could hardly be more removed from that of the pre-Civil-War United States. In South Africa, any commentary by anyone on pending cases is restrained by the threat of contempt of court,[401] and the advocates who argue the cases are particularly tightly bound.[402] In court, lawyers are restrained by strict rules of decorum. These rules do not prevent counsel from making their feelings known,[403] but they make a political trial in South Africa a vastly different affair than, say, the 1969–70 trial of the antiwar protesters known as the Chicago Eight in the United States.[404] Accused political activists, such as Nelson Mandela, have spoken plainly and eloquently for their cause in the course of their trials, but even these statements may generally have been notable for their sober dignity rather than their flouting of convention.[405] The rhetoric of judicial judgments and (to some extent) of academic commentary is also notably restrained, with disagreements often introduced with a reference to the 'learned judge' with whom the writer is about to take issue.[406] Dissents remain infrequent in

[400] One example of such activity is the fast which some lawyers undertook in solidarity with emergency detainees' efforts to win release from detention by going on hunger strikes. See 'Strikers Spark New Spirit in South Africa', 31 *Africa News* (No. 4) at 2 (20 Feb. 1989). The ranks of currently practising lawyers, perhaps especially of black lawyers, include politically prominent people, such as the black advocates Dikgang Moseneke (a deputy president of the Pan Africanist Congress) and Abdullah Omar (active in the United Democratic Front and now in the African National Congress).

[401] For a recent exercise of this power, see *S.* v. *Harber and Another; In re S.* v. *Baleka and Another*, 1986 (4) SA 214 (T).

[402] Among many other restrictions on the publicity that advocates are permitted are a prohibition on an advocate's issuing 'statements to the Press' in connection with cases in which he is involved, *Uniform Rules* (cit. n. 271), Rule 4.21.1; a prohibition on any appearance on television without seeking the prior permission of the Bar Council, Rule 4.20.7; and a requirement of prior consent from the Bar Council for the writing of any article on legal topics for 'the Press', Rule 4.18.3(a).

[403] For an example, see Sachs, *Justice* (cit. n. 66), 48, recounting an advocate's statement to a judge that a witness had mistakenly 'addressed me, my Lord, as "My Lord", my Lord, instead of my Lord, my Lord, as "My Lord", my Lord'.

[404] See P. Gabel and P. Harris, 'Building Power and Breaking Images: Critical Legal Theory and the Practice of Law', 11 *NYU Rev. L. and Soc. Ch.* 369, 380–1 (1982–3); D. Macdonald, 'Introduction', in M. Levine, G. McNamee, and D. Greenberg (eds.), *The Tales of Hoffman*, (New York: Bantam Books, 1970), xi. For a rare South African exception—but one in which only the accused, and not their counsel, breached the rules of decorum—see *S.* v. *Mange*, 1980 (4) SA 613 (A), discussed in the text at nn. 108–9 above.

[405] I have already referred to Nelson Mandela's careful presentation of his motion to recuse a magistrate because of the inherent racial bias of the South African legal system. See text at nn. 85, 89 above. His statement at the beginning of the 1964 trial which led to his life sentence (and could have led to his execution) is as restrained in style as it is firm in content. N. Mandela, '"I Am Prepared to Die," Second Court Statement, 1964', in Mandela, *The Struggle is My Life* (cit. n. 85), 155. The words of the Namibian Herman ja Toivo, before he was sentenced to 20 years of hard labour in the late 1960s, were similar in tone. See Carlson, *No Neutral Ground* (cit. n. 111), 120–2.

[406] Etienne Mureinik has recently explicitly defended the propriety of 'discourteous' criticism of judges—though the fact that this has required repeated defence is perhaps itself an indication of how measured much South African legal commentary is. See E. Mureinik, Reply to letter of

Appellate Division cases (though their frequency has been rising),[407] and when they come, even in such charged cases as the emergency decisions, they are free of the ferocious rhetoric now common in the United States Surpreme Court. Adjudication, as liberal South African legal scholars have repeatedly emphasized, is *not* a neutral and objective process, but the various accompaniments of the idea of such a process may well operate to make innovative arguments more palatable and less of an affront to the judges.

I do not mean to argue that the more confrontational legal positions taken by the anti-slavery movement were pointless, or that the more tempered South African arguments were intrinsically preferable. The uncompromising efforts of the abolitionists—efforts by no means confined to court cases—played a major role in generating the profound political struggle which would ultimately lead both to war and to the freeing of the slaves. But the abolitionists' stance weakened their legal hand in the fugitive slave cases. Perhaps the abolitionists hoped that the moral force of their position would more than fill any legal gaps the judges perceived, but the task of converting those whom one confronts—as a Gandhi might have[408]—is a delicate and difficult one, and the abolitionists do not seem to have managed it in the fugitive slave cases.

South African litigation has not generally been designed to prick, or slash, the judges' conscience in the abolitionist manner. Nor is it clear that a more confrontational anti-apartheid jurisprudence would have had the political impact of the abolitionist movement; it is quite possible that more avowedly radical strategies would have been dismissed as extremist rather than heeded, or at least weighed, as moral stricture.[409] Confrontation, moreover, tends to polarize as well as energize; even such carefully shaped movements as those of Gandhi and King may not have escaped this danger, and the abolitionists

J. R. du Plessis, in 'Correspondence', 5 *SAJHR* 510, 512–13 (1989); id., Reply to letter of M. J. D. Wallis, in 'Correspondence', 6 *SAJHR* 112–13 (1990). As Mureinik's defence of discourtesy forcefully argues, the practice of verbal restraint can have negative effects. (So, too, Christopher Forsyth has suggested that less restraint in an important constitutional case of the 1950s would have helped make space for judicial resistance in the years to come, *In Danger* (cit. n. 3), 66–76.) Like positivism, then, verbal restraint may both safeguard and undercut human rights arguments in the law.

[407] In 1988 there were dissents in about 15% of the Appellate Division's cases; in 1980 the figure had been only 1%. Cameron, Marcus, and van Zyl Smit, 'Administration of Justice' (cit. n. 100), 541.

[408] An example of the hard choices which Gandhi presented to the British colonial authorities is his statement to a court that: 'I am here ... to invite and submit cheerfully to the highest penalty that can be inflicted upon me for what, in law, is a deliberate crime and what appears to me to be the highest duty of a citizen. The only course open to you, the Judge and the Assessors, is either to resign your posts and thus dissociate yourselves from evil if you feel that the law you are called upon to administer is an evil and that in reality I am innocent, or to inflict on me the severest penalty if you believe that the system and the law you are assisting to administer are good for the people of this country, and that my activity is, therefore, injurious to the public weal.' R. Prasad, *At the Feet of Mahatma Gandhi* (Bombay: Hind Katabs, Ltd., 1955), 25.

[409] Cover mentions this possibility of 'the progressive "isolation" of extremist groups, which can then be suppressed'. Cover, *Justice Accused* (cit. n. 363), 221.

helped to trigger ferocious political enmity in the United States.[410] In any event, South African legal tactics and legal manners have not generally aimed in this direction in human rights cases; they have aimed instead, and aimed well, to win such courtroom victories as could be won.

Thus I suggest that this conventionalist legal strategy helped preserve the doctrinal space for human rights claims. But there were also other reasons why this doctrinal space proved so hard to erase in the field of emergency law, while in the fugitive slave cases it was gradually, if not completely, obscured. One part of the answer is surely that American politics were moving towards confrontation, while South African politics, though long seeming to be headed in this direction, had been groping towards reform and in 1989 began to turn decisively towards an effort at reconciliation. Had South African white society been blinded by nationalist fire, the choice of what legal strategies to adopt against apartheid—if any—would have been very different. Given the shift between the Rabie and Corbett courts, it seems clear that a second part of the answer must be that particular judges, such as Chief Justice Corbett, played a significant role in shaping the course of the law.

Doctrinally, however, the pliability of South African law reflects that the core positivist tenet of South African law, the principle of legislative supremacy, is a relatively loose one. This is not a logically inevitable feature of a system of legislative supremacy; instead, it is a product of South African history and tradition, and in particular of the intertwined traditions of concern for human rights and maintenance of judicial independence that we considered earlier in this chapter. In the light of this broader tradition, the rule of legislative supremacy, important as it has been, loses some of its force. Ironically, it may be that when, as in the case of fugitive slaves, the United States constitution's basic thrust seemed negative, the constitution's tremendous symbolic force[411] made it a greater obstacle to reformist argument than the principle of legislative supremacy has proved to be. A wholehearted, often expansive, enforcement of the constitution was surely an article of judicial faith in the early United States to a degree that an enthusiastic application of legislative supremacy in South Africa is not.[412] The jurisprudential tools for abridging or recasting the

[410] Don Fehrenbacher writes that the Garrisonians' 'inflammatory rhetorical style won some converts but made many enemies, in the North as well as the South. The effect was to intensify greatly the antagonism over slavery that had never been entirely absent from American life, to aggravate southern fear of slave revolt inspired by northern agitation, and to evoke a related phenomenon of transcendent importance that can perhaps best be labeled "southern rage"'. Fehrenbacher, *Dred Scott Case* (cit. n. 208), 118.

[411] See Cover, *Justice Accused* (cit. n. 363), 132–4.

[412] This article of faith is at the core of such lasting foundations of American constitutionalism as Chief Justice Marshall's judgment in *McCulloch* v. *Maryland*, 17 US (4 Wheat.) 316 (1819). Certainly there were important debates over the proper manner of interpreting and applying the constitution, and the Taney Supreme Court did not read the constitution identically to the Marshall court, its predecessor. Yet the degree of continuity between the two courts appears to have been substantial, see R. McCloskey, *The American Supreme Court* (Chicago: University of Chicago Press, 1960), 82–3; Fehrenbacher, *Dred Scott Case* (cit. n. 208), 228–30. Thus it should not be surprising, though for a modern reader it is painful, to see expansive rhetoric

seeming implications of the constitution—controversial even today—would have been considered even less legitimate in these years. And for those abolitionists who saw the slavery clauses of the constitution as a bargain with the devil, the sense of taint might have further discouraged any disposition to seek to manipulate the terms of that bargain.

Despite the malleability of the principle of legislative supremacy, we should not forget its negative potential either. Early in this section we considered the role of positivism, in some hands, as a facilitator and encourager of executive-minded decisions.[413] Despite all the devices of statutory interpretation, South Africa's Parliament can write statutes whose import is so unmistakable that it cannot easily be denied, and a system of legislative supremacy precludes the courts from striking down what cannot be interpreted away. In this light, it is worth emphasizing that a constitution that explicitly protected human rights in South Africa might well have promoted more vigorous human rights jurisprudence than South Africa has in fact enjoyed. Such a constitution would by no means have been a guarantee, for the rare cases in which the Appellate Division has decided such constitutional questions, under the constitution of Bophuthatswana and a quasi-constitutional proclamation governing what was then South-West Africa, have had mixed results. But in the first case in which the Appellate Division considered such an issue, it decided, on grounds that were clearly not doctrinally unavoidable, that provisions of Bophuthatswana's terrorism and sabotage laws, actually South African laws carried over to the newly 'independent' Bophuthatswana, were unconstitutional.[414] Emergency powers are almost by definition difficult to keep within constitutional confines—but while this task is difficult, it is not impossible. A number of international human rights documents offer instructive approaches to this

similar to *McCulloch*'s deployed by Justice Story (a holdover from the Marshall years) on behalf of the Taney court to uphold the constitutionality of the fugitive slave law in *Prigg* v. *Pennsylvania*, 41 US (16 Pet.) 539, 612, 618–20 (1842).

[413] See text at nn. 355–62 above.

[414] *S.* v. *Marwane*, 1982 (3) SA 716 (A). *Marwane* was a judgment of an 11-person bench, and thus gives considerable insight into the views of the full court at that time. (Whether the court would have been as vigilant had the case arisen in South Africa proper rather than in Bophuthatswana, however, cannot be known.) Some years later, however, in a quasi-constitutional case in South-West Africa, a 5-judge panel of the Appellate Division denied a human rights claim. The panel in this case, *Cabinet for the Territory of South West Africa* v. *Chikane and Another*, 1989 (1) SA 349 (A), included Rabie ACJ and Hefer JA as well as Jansen, Grosskopf, and van Heerden JJA (the latter being the sole dissenter), and denied relief under the bill of fundamental rights which had been proclaimed for what was then South-West Africa. In *Cabinet of the Transitional Government of South West Africa* v. *Eins*, 1988 (3) SA 369 (A), the same panel had decided, in this case unanimously, that a litigant lacked *locus standi* (standing) to test the validity, in light of the bill of fundamental rights, of a statute authorizing the government in certain circumstances to eject from South-West Africa people not born in South-West Africa or doing military service. The court indicated that no one had standing to challenge this law before the government exercised or intended to exercise its powers under it, and maintained that its decision was wholly consistent with, *inter alia*, United States standing law. Ibid. 395I–J.

task,[415] and the new Namibian constitution also provides a welcome example of the application of constitutional limits to emergency power.[416]

I do not mean to suggest that if such a constitutional provision had been in place (hard as that would have been to imagine) the jurisprudence of the Corbett court would have been altogether transformed. The decisions of this court, although a sharp improvement over those of the Rabie court, have been a mixed bag. The doctrinal changes the court has worked, I suggest, do reflect both the presence of the human rights tradition I have sought to identify in South African law, and the compatibility of this tradition with the reigning jurisprudence of the day. But the changes the court has *not* worked equally attest to the diversity of views on human rights matters, and no doubt on the boundaries of positivist judicial discretion, among the members of the Appellate Division. They remind us, in short, that the human rights tradition in South Africa, despite the substantial institutional and normative support that it has, is not the dominant feature of South African law. The court *is* a conservative institution, though as we have learnt from the Corbett years it is also an institution concerned about human rights and groping, like the nation as a whole, towards change.

Conclusion

South Africa's bitter passage through the states of emergency is, most obviously, a lesson in the lengths to which governments may choose to go, and in the lengths to which they may have to go, in the defence of an unjust social system. No one would wish these aspects of South African experience on anyone else. Moreover, the lessons of South African experience may not travel well, for the strategies that have proved of some value in South Africa may fit poorly in legal institutions and social climates very different from South Africa's. But because South Africa, at least for many Westerners, turns out to be unnervingly familiar rather than alien, I do not believe its experience is unique. Instead, it offers us a lesson in the ideological and institutional safeguards that can make the law a genuine constraint on power, even deeply unjust and autocratic power.

For law to have this effect, adherence to law must have taken root among those who wield authority. Otherwise, rulers might choose to act outside the law or they might choose to use law to their ends while disavowing any legal limits on their actions. It seems, however, that it is the rare tyrant who makes no use of the law. South African experience suggests that the image of rulers

[415] I have discussed the kinds of safeguards that should be included in a constitutional treatment of emergency powers, and made reference to several of these international instruments, in Ellmann, 'Constitution' (cit. n. 9).

[416] See Namibia Const., arts. 24, 26.

who use but are unruled by law is an unstable and often misleading one. Laws adopted to repress the powerless join laws enacted to regulate the interests of the powerful, and principles which the powerful insist on for their own protection may begin to creep into the law of the powerless. Rulers who enact laws in an effort to lend a veneer of legitimacy to injustice must then pay attention to the likely reactions of their audiences, and so must face the possibility that only some measure of justice can possibly win the approval or acquiescence that they seek. And, especially when the rulers are not some handful of plotters but a community of millions of people, as in South Africa, the rulers do not come on the scene shorn of traditions and values. Adherence to law has deep roots in South African culture, as it surely does in many other cultures, and the rulers themselves expect and want to live, in some fashion, by law. These considerations suggest that there are likely to be few societies in which adherence to law has no roots among the rulers, and that it is likely as well that in many unjust states law will have real force as a component of the rulers' values.[417]

Even with this wealth of factors prompting adherence, the law may still fail to exercise a check on oppression. Racist passion or nationalist idealism, and no doubt other similar commitments, can sway a people away from the law towards some 'higher' goal. South African experience illustrates this danger, for the jurisprudence of the Rabie court, and the sheer existence of the emergency team, may reflect the continued pull of such passions, relatively attenuated as they were by the late 1980s.

South African experience also suggests, however, that this danger is not entirely unlimited or illimitable. The passions that can support the most sweeping departures from the realm of law tend to burn out.[418] While South Africa's passions wore out in part because they faded but in part because they were frustrated and attacked, again and again, by the victims of apartheid. An effort to protect human rights that is unaccompanied by a direct challenge to those distorting passions, however adamantine they seem, cannot be expected to have great success.

And the law and legal institutions can provide firebreaks. South African experience points to this conclusion, from two quite different perspectives. On the one hand, the traditions of independence of lawyers and judges in South Africa may well have helped insulate the courts from the full distorting force of white political sentiment. On the other hand, where adherence to the law is under pressure, the impulse to exploit gaps in the legal structure may be irresistible. South Africa had such a gap, in its lack of express legal requirements for the drawing up of the roll of judges' case assignments. Had there been no

[417] For an intriguing study of the resilience of legal institutions and, so the authors contend, of legal values, in the Soviet Union, see Barry and Berman, 'Soviet Legal Profession' (cit. n. 222).

[418] Cf. M. Walzer, 'On "Failed Totalitarianism"', in I. Howe (ed.), *1984 Revisited: Totalitarianism in Our Century* (New York: Harper & Row, 1983), 102, 111–21.

gap, the emergency team might have been impossible to set up—and the course of South African emergency law might have changed. There may be good reasons for a discretionary system of case assignments, and so I do not suggest removing such discretion as a step for all societies. But in a country in need of firebreaks, the loss of flexibility does not seem too great a price for this constraint on manipulation.

South African events indicate that the law's endorsement of human rights is important as well. That endorsement requires more than words, however, to make it real. South Africa reminds us that the members of the legal profession, both lawyers and judges, can be an important source of support for these ideals. Moreover, South African experience teaches that the structural features of the legal profession can contribute to lawyers' capacity to play this role. Lawyers' assertions that their professional independence protects society's liberty should not be dismissed, and the nurturance of an independent legal profession and of an independent judiciary in South Africa may well have helped sustain the modest, but real, attention to human rights in South African law.

But here, too, the protection of liberty has a price. The spirit of independence of bench and bar in South Africa seems linked to a sense of membership in a prestigious élite, charged with the special duty, and seen as graced with the special ability, to stand somewhat apart from society. The creation of such an élite is a blow to egalitarian values. Perhaps it also undercuts aspirations towards a society more empathetic than atomistic. It will be important for future research to consider whether protections of human rights equal to or stronger than those the legal profession provided in South Africa can be obtained at a lesser price. This study, after all, has sought to show the contributions made by the institutions that South Africa now has; since we cannot experiment on human societies, we must look to comparative work for further evidence on whether other institutions, even in South Africa, might have served as well. No doubt we will learn, or confirm, that in some societies lawyers have worked for human rights without such emphatically élite status. We may also gather further evidence that many lawyers' assertions of the importance of their own professional independence have a decidedly self-serving quality. Yet we may also find that in other countries besides South Africa an élitist legal profession proves to be valuable when rights are most under siege. If we want to structure a legal profession for the worst of times—if we fear those times are not firmly behind us—then we may well need to grant some degree of inegalitarian status and authority to the legal profession.

Jurisprudence can also matter to whether the law does confine executive power. This is not because jurisprudential theories rigidly constrain judges' decisions, for those decisions are the result of many other influences as well. Nor, *a fortiori*, is it because some jurisprudential theories, such as positivism, necessarily breed decisions of specially pro-executive cast. But jurisprudential theories can make particular results easier or harder to sustain, and on this score, South Africa's positivist jurisprudence, built around the seemingly devastating principle of legislative supremacy, proves to be quite supple.

The jurisprudence of lawyers' arguments also affects the outcome of courtroom battles, and so the extent to which those battles result in victories for human rights claims. South African lawyers have chosen to speak in their courts in terms of the dominant jurisprudence, and to use respectful tones when they do so. Other, more confrontational strategies are possible, and they may have their uses. Such strategies, however, seem more likely to win their victories outside of court than inside. To win in court—to transform the judge while confronting him or her—is not necessarily an impossible task, but it may call for a Gandhian delicacy matched by a receptivity on the part of the judges that is not necessarily present in any given society. As studying South African decisions reminds us, judges are generally likely to achieve more when they are able to operate on doctrinal pathways that do not put a premium on overt and stark judicial creativity, than when they see the only route to human rights decisions as leading them on to unfamiliar and unprotected doctrinal ground. When courtroom victories seem possible and worth seeking, in short, South African experience suggests that lawyers' hoary strategy of staying within the shelter of established doctrine and precedent is a wise one.

Legal work in South Africa has not ended apartheid. Nor has it been the major force in undermining this system; political struggles rather than legal battles have played that role. This political struggle has been determined, brave, and radical, calling as it does for the overthrow of the South African racial order and the reconstruction or reorientation of all aspects of its society. In the context of this radical political challenge to oppression, incremental jurisprudence and élitist legal institutions may seem incongruous, and yet the implication of this study of South Africa is that legal incrementalism, a professional élite of lawyers, and political radicalism can be welcome companions. I will look closely at the political impact of emergency law practice in the final chapter; for now it is enough to say that in many circumstances there may be victories to be won in court and others to be won elsewhere, and a movement broad enough to encompass these two different styles of action may be ideally suited to win both sorts of victories. That this careful lawyering may seem much less radical than the politics it accompanies is, I believe, not an argument for quick adoption of a more radical lawyering. Instead, this contrast points up the degree to which the spheres of legal and political work, however overlapping, can fruitfully remain distinct,[419] and underlines the value of strategies which take advantage of the different contributions that each of these forms of struggle can make to building a more just society.

[419] Cf. S. Ellmann, 'Lawyering for Justice in a Flawed Democracy', 90 *Colum. L. Rev.* 116, 177–81 (1990), book review essay on D. Luban, *Lawyers and Justice: An Ethical Study* (Princeton NJ: Princeton University Press, 1988), (on distinction between moral responsibilities of political activists and those of lawyers).

7

Lawyers Against the Emergency

Perhaps some day we will remember this too with joy.[1]

Since 1985 many South African lawyers have devoted great effort and ingenuity to the practice of emergency law on behalf of the victims of the emergency. From the start, this work has had an ironic quality. Confronting a government armed with legal powers so vast as to call into question the legitimacy of the law itself, attorneys and advocates have none the less sought to fashion *legal* limits on the state's authority. The effort has been difficult, and those who have made the effort courageous. Yet it might be argued that this legal struggle has been to little avail, that the lawyers who have practised in this field have misdirected their energies, and that it would have been better either to adopt some harsher, more confrontational lawyering style or to reject such courtroom efforts altogether as a fruitless, and even counterproductive, response to apartheid. My purpose in this chapter is to demonstrate that in general the strategy South African lawyers adopted has been well-founded. In doing so, I will undoubtedly be urging a conclusion that many South African lawyers have long since reached. But this point has an importance extending beyond South Africa's borders, for lawyers in many other lands have faced, and will face again, the question of whether to try to protect human rights in the courts of an oppressive country.

This is a different question from the issue we have previously discussed, namely whether the lines of argument and the styles of advocacy used by South Africans on behalf of human rights claims were well calculated to win favourable attention from the courts. As I have said, I believe that South African human rights advocacy in the emergency cases was well aimed to win what could be won in court, and that the litigating posture which human rights lawyers have adopted in South Africa may help win such victories elsewhere. But the fact that lawyers litigated deftly does not necessarily mean that they were right to undertake these cases in the first place or, having undertaken them, to pursue them in the way that they did.

It may seem presumptuous for an American to offer a judgment on whether emergency-law practice in South Africa, and by implication in other countries, has been a worthwhile endeavour. The question, after all, ultimately calls for an assessment of the present state and future prospects of South African

[1] Vergil, *The Aeneid*, i. 203 (*Forsan et haec olim meminisse iuvabit*) (my trans.).

society; for a gauging of the strength of the various forces for and against change in that land; for an understanding of the relation between lawyers' efforts, in and out of court, and other challenges to apartheid, a relation that may prove complementary or conflicting; for an understanding of the alternatives open to those who might undertake emergency law cases; and for a grasp of what makes difficult and even frustrating work 'worth it' to an individual. Each of these subsidiary questions is immensely difficult and some may simply be unanswerable.

Yet the broad question does need to be asked, and answered. South African lawyers opposed to apartheid, and those of similar conviction who might become lawyers, have had no alternative but to address it. Those abroad who are concerned about lawyers' efforts in South Africa, I think, are equally without the option of ignoring this issue, since we must decide whether to support these and similar efforts, tangibly or morally. If such work is fruitless or even counterproductive, then we should not aid it; if it is valuable, perhaps we should aid it more. As individuals, as citizens of South Africa or of other nations, and in particular as lawyers we must offer the best answer we can, aware as we will be that our answer cannot resolve all the difficulties that the question presents.[2]

I will argue that anti-apartheid lawyers in South Africa had good reason to bring these cases and to pursue them as they did. This is not simply because clients, the victims of emergency power, wanted this representation, although that fact is important. Instead, I will maintain, first, that lawyers concerned about human rights cannot escape the necessity to decide, on broadly political or moral grounds, whether they will undertake such litigation. But I will contend, second, that the endorsement reflected in clients' requests for representation is a well-grounded one. Emergency-law work, as I will try to show, has been valuable, both for the benefits it has won for individual clients and for its broader political impact on South Africa. Now that South Africa is almost free of emergency rule and appears to be moving towards an end to apartheid itself, this conclusion may begin to seem obvious, but I will argue that the considerations which lead to it strongly suggest that this conclusion would have held true even before the Rabie court gave way to the Corbett court, and even before the shape of South African politics was so dramatically transformed. I will suggest, in short, that it is likely often to be worthwhile for lawyers in oppressive states to use what leverage they can obtain in the courts for the protection of human rights.

[2] Our answer to this broad question may also help us to address other issues, although I doubt that it will dictate their solution. If foreign companies doing business in South Africa provide donations that support anti-apartheid legal work, should calls for divestment be tempered? If South African lawyers doing such work can find intellectual stimulation and emotional support in university communities abroad, should such lawyers be welcomed to foreign law schools as graduate students or visiting professors, or should such contacts be proscribed as part of a cultural boycott of South Africa? Should anti-apartheid South African lawyers have been welcome in international fora while anti-apartheid South African athletes were banned from the Olympic Games? I will not address these subordinate questions here.

A. Lawyers' Moral Responsibility for Their Work

Perhaps we should say that so long as people opposed to apartheid choose to practise law, they should represent the victims of South African security powers if the victims want representation. It seems quite clear that the victims' position is almost always that they wish to have legal counsel. Exceptions to this generalization exist, but they are few and far between. Indeed, even when those accused of crimes refuse to participate in their trials as an expression of their rejection of the courts' authority to punish them, they may choose to continue to receive legal advice.[3] If the victims' wishes are dispositive, then clearly lawyers should pursue even such limited victories as this frustrating field of law may permit.

But *should* lawyers defer to their would-be clients' judgment? I do not mean to ask here whether lawyers have an obligation under South African rules of professional ethics to accept whoever comes to them as a client and is able to pay their fee. South African advocates do have such an obligation, though attorneys in general do not.[4] The cases that come to a lawyer, however, surely tend to be those in which the lawyer is expert and interested. This relationship is likely to be especially direct when the cases are as highly charged as emergency matters can be.[5] Even for those lawyers subject to the 'cab rank' principle, therefore, the question of whether to defer to potential emergency clients' desire for representation has been a live one—for these lawyers can structure their practices and careers either to discourage or to encourage such cases to arrive in the queue. Hence it is important for advocates and attorneys alike to consider whether the value of their efforts in the emergency-law field, or in the practice of law in general, is established by the fact that clients desire and value those efforts.

To raise this question is not to suggest that clients' wishes are unimportant to lawyers' obligations. On the contrary, I believe clients' wishes are very important. None the less, what clients want is not necessarily what lawyers must, or even may, do. Let us consider three respects in which clients' wishes are not altogether dispositive. First, clients may reasonably desire that their lawyers violate the rules of professional ethics so as to help the clients win their cases. Clients who deny the moral legitimacy of the state may find the notion that their cases should be circumscribed by that state's ethical prescriptions particularly implausible. Plainly, however, lawyers opposed to apartheid and ready to answer clients' calls for representation can be entirely unwilling to accede to requests for unethical conduct, and unwilling not merely

[3] See Ch. 6 n. 92 above, for an example of such a choice, in the 1989 case of *S.* v. *Masina and Others.*

[4] See *Uniform Rules of Professional Ethics of the General Council of the Bar, as Adopted by the Johannesburg Bar,* Rule 2.1, in *Rules of Professional Ethics of the Johannesburg Bar* (1986); E. Lewis, *Legal Ethics: A Guide to Professional Conduct for South African Attorneys* (Cape Town: Juta, 1982), 49, 75.

[5] See Ch. 6, text at n. 286 above.

for tactical but for moral reasons. Such lawyers have decided to offer their clients only vigorous representation within the law, and to limit their offer of aid in this way despite the clients' possible desire for assistance that the lawyers consider less scrupulous.[6] For any lawyer who adopts this position, clients' wishes are obviously not wholly determinative.

Second, client wishes—at least conscious, articulated client wishes—are not a necessary predicate for lawyers' engaging in some aspects of the practice of law with actual or potential clients. I think that this point holds true even for lawyers who accept fully the principle of client control.[7] Imagine a man in detention who tells his lawyer that he is not being properly fed. This is an important matter, and the client obviously wants something done about it. But perhaps the client assumes that nothing can be done about the sheer fact of his detention, and so makes no request that the lawyer try to free him from imprisonment. A lawyer who learns that the client has a valid basis for obtaining his freedom would not be serving her client well, however, if she failed to inform the client of this fact and ask him whether he wanted her to pursue this claim. So long as the client lacks this information, after all, he is effectively disabled from directing his lawyer.

Once we accept that acting in accordance with a client's unexpressed, inferred wishes is consistent with client self-determination, we must also consider the possibility that the wishes that clients do express are not those which they would endorse if they were properly counselled and fully informed about the implications of their stated desires.[8] For example, lawyers consulting with clients in detention might reasonably assume that many or most of their clients would not want to engage in court action if that action were likely to provide more benefit to the government of South Africa than to the clients themselves. On the basis of this assumption, such lawyers would not regard their clients' initial expression of a desire to go to court as dispositive. If the lawyers believed that emergency litigation was ultimately misguided, they could legitimately argue that it was proper, or even obligatory, for them to convey their view of the value of emergency litigation to their clients, so that

[6] Analysis of these reasons is a complex question in itself, and one which I will not explore here. In discussing the value of legal practice in this book, I mean to argue for the value of a legal practice that adheres to the normally applicable rules of professional ethics. If the argument set out here is correct then it would tend to show that the practice of emergency law and of other aspects of anti-apartheid law in South Africa is a worthwhile enterprise even if on occasion a case that might be won is lost because of the practitioners' adherence to principles of legal ethics.

[7] The role of expressed client wishes is naturally even less salient for lawyers who believe that the lawyer is *not* always bound by what the client desires. See W. Simon, 'Visions of Practice in Legal Thought', 36 *Stan. L. Rev.* 469, 484–9 (1984). For a critical assessment of the legitimacy of client manipulation as part of a 'political law practice', see S. Ellmann, 'Lawyering for Justice in a Flawed Democracy', 90 *Colum. L. Rev.* 116, 177–81 (1990), book review essay on D. Luban, *Lawyers and Justice: An Ethical Study* (Princeton, NJ: Princeton University Press, 1988).

[8] For insightful explorations of this problem, see Simon, 'Visions' (cit. n. 7), 475–84; G. Bellow and B. Moultón, *The Lawyering Process: Materials for Clinical Instruction in Advocacy* (Mineola, NY: Foundation Press, 1978), 232–5.

the clients could decide in light of this advice whether to proceed with litigation or not. A lawyer of this mind could firmly adhere to the principle that the client's ultimate, informed choice is controlling—yet just as firmly assert the propriety of urging the client not to undertake litigation that the client had initially stated a desire to undertake.[9] Such counselling, if carried out in a non-manipulative manner, can be part of a practice of law that truly serves client autonomy.[10]

Third, in at least one context, client wishes (even if these wishes are entirely lawful, and even if they are a *necessary* predicate for lawyers' action) cannot be a *sufficient* predicate for this work. If there are more potential clients than lawyers have time to represent, then lawyers have no alternative but to choose which cases they will take. This situation must exist, at least potentially, for any lawyer contemplating legal work on behalf of the victims of apartheid in South Africa. Lawyers may have to choose between deserving cases that arrive simultaneously in their office. Even more clearly, they must choose over time the sorts of deserving cases on which they will focus.

Even anti-apartheid lawyers, moreover, might choose not to take anti-apartheid litigation. Indeed lawyers might adopt this course while still agreeing that they should contribute to the struggle against apartheid through their work. It is no doubt true, in South Africa as in the United States, that lawyers can profoundly assist the cause of human rights in part-time efforts that are in a sense ancillary to a non-political career. Lawyers who practise in seemingly non-political fields such as corporate law may also find opportunities to counsel their powerful clients about those clients' broader political or moral obligations. Lawyers convinced of the injustice of apartheid may also think (mistakenly, if my arguments here are correct) that no good can be accomplished through their legal practice and that they should accordingly look on the law simply as a way to earn a living, while finding ways to express their convictions in other parts of their lives. Undoubtedly these lawyers could reasonably hope to have clients enough to fill their days. In addition, anti-apartheid lawyers are not forced to be lawyers; they might decide to forego the practice of law in favour of other forms of work such as community organizing, for which there surely is also considerable demand. The magnitude of the need, and the variety of possible professional responses to it, mean that lawyers in South Africa, and their supporters abroad, cannot escape the necessity of choice.

In the following evaluation of that choice, I will focus on the effects which

[9] Even a lawyer dealing with a client who initially expressed a desire precisely to sacrifice the greater good for his own personal needs would not be compelled by the principle of client control to accept the client's instructions without cavil. While still acknowledging the client's right to make the final decision, the lawyer might believe that it was entirely proper for her to try to persuade the client to become more altruistic. See C. Fried, 'The Lawyer as Friend: The Moral Foundations of the Lawyer–Client Relation', 85 *Yale LJ* 1060, 1088 (1976); S. Pepper, 'The Lawyer's Amoral Ethical Role: A Defense, A Problem, and Some Possibilities', 1986 *ABF Res. J.* 613, 630–2; Ellmann, 'Lawyering' (cit. n. 7), 147–8.

[10] See S. Ellmann, 'Lawyers and Clients', 34 *UCLA L. Rev.* 717, 774–8 (1987).

lawyers' work has on their clients, on others similarly situated, and on the course of political change as a whole. These are important factors indeed, but it would be a mistake to omit one other: the lawyer's own well-being. Human rights lawyering will certainly be stressful, although that is true enough of much of what lawyers do. It may also be dangerous: to reputation, to income, to liberty, even to life itself. South African lawyers have paid for their efforts in these terms, although fortunately the practice of anti-apartheid law has not *generally* become a lethal enterprise.[11] I do not wish to discount these costs at all, nor to suggest that lawyers act improperly if they take them into account in deciding how to shape their lives. The analysis that I offer does not try to factor these personal concerns into the lawyer's calculus; it explicates, instead, what *else* that calculus involves.[12]

B. The Value of Emergency Law Work

Lawyers might make the choice to reject their would-be clients' requests for assistance if they believed that the clients were being wrong-headed. They might reach this judgment on either of two grounds. First, lawyers might conclude that their clients were mistaken in believing that their particular cases would fare better with legal assistance than without. Second, lawyers might maintain that even though their presence would aid the particular individuals whom they represented, the ultimate effect of their efforts would be to undercut

[11] Whether anyone has died for anti-apartheid lawyering may not be certain, but it is certain that some anti-apartheid lawyers have been murdered. Members of an alleged police hit squad have confessed to the 1981 killing of one, Griffiths Mxenge, although the Harms Commission rejected these witnesses' evidence that such a thing as a police hit squad existed. See D. Ottaway, 'South African Judicial Inquiry Fails to Find Blame in Activists' Murders', *Washington Post*, A21, col. 1 (14 Nov. 1990). Mxenge's wife Victoria, also a lawyer, was murdered too, as was the Namibian lawyer Anton Lubowski. The Dec. 1989 death of a death penalty lawyer, Shucks Sefanyetso, has also prompted concerns about possible foul play. See G. Evans, 'Top Lawyer's Death: Inquiry into "Foul Play"', *Weekly Mail*, 3, col. 5 (20 Dec. 1990–10 Jan. 1991). These events are outrageous but not common; other forms of harassment through legal and extra-legal methods may be much more common. See R. Wilkins, 'The South African Legal System: Black Lawyers' Views', 7 *Transafrica Forum* (No. 3) 9, 30 n. 3 (Fall 1990).

[12] There are certainly other personal considerations, apart from risks of these sorts, that can lead people, even those who admit that apartheid is indeed an injustice, to deny any obligation to devote some part of their efforts to redressing that injustice. In a society tainted by only 'moderate' levels of injustice, consideration for the autonomy of human beings may lead to the conclusion that choices to stand entirely apart from the fray should be altogether beyond reproach. I think it is fair to say that, in a society so riven by injustice as South Africa's, decisions not to become meaningfully involved in the effort to correct that injustice are more troublesome than they would be in less anguished lands. Such decisions by lawyers, whose choice of career entails at least involvement in the world of affairs and arguably some special responsibility for the assurance of justice, seem particularly problematic. 'Meaningful involvement' can certainly be found in work that is by no means full-time—the South African legal profession offers notable examples of such part-time, yet intense, involvement—but at some point on the spectrum of disengagement a lawyer's abstention does become morally problematic.

the broader struggle against apartheid. I will argue that both of these positions would have been mistaken in the field of emergency law.

1. Have Emergency Lawyers Helped Their Clients?

Lawyers would have good reason to grow despairing about the practice of human rights law if they were unable to help their clients through this practice. Moreover, it is quite possible to imagine situations in which lawyers' intervention might fail to help, or might succeed in harming, their clients' interests. A lawyer who believes, for instance, that litigation about allegations of torture will not persuade the courts to grant relief, but may succeed in further antagonizing abusive law-enforcement officers, might well consider the entire enterprise misguided. Overall, however, the efforts of emergency lawyers have been far from fruitless.[13]

The results of emergency litigation before the Corbett court, needless to say, provide much better evidence for this conclusion than do the results of the cases decided by the Rabie court. The Corbett court's decisions express genuine concern for human rights, while the Rabie court's aims did not extend beyond keeping the emergency regime within a legal order, preserving the role of the courts, and remedying individual instances of clear-cut abuse. Indeed the Rabie court's decisions, as Etienne Mureinik wrote at the time, were leading '[m]any of our finest lawyers' to 'confess[] despondency', although Mureinik maintained even then that 'despair ... would be premature'.[14]

Even under the Rabie court, however, emergency work by lawyers remained valuable. This work had value in part because some of what lawyers do for their clients can be accomplished without explicit courtroom victories either in the provincial divisions or on appeal. We can see this even in the field of emergency detentions, one of the areas in which the state's emergency powers were at their zenith. As we noted in Chapter 3, the Appellate Division decided in *Omar*, perhaps the worst of its detention decisions, that the state had the power to deny detainees access to their counsel.[15] Yet detainees ordinarily,

[13] I do not mean to suggest that there were *no* fruitless cases in the emergency-law field. Rather, my point is that there were many fruitful ones. In the long run, lawyers can presumably structure their practices in accord with their views of which cases are fruitful. In the short run, however, the lawyer may face serious ethical difficulties, if she feels that what a would-be client wants her to do (and still wants her to do even after careful counselling) is unwise either for that client or for other people towards whom the lawyer feels a commitment. If the 'cab rank' rule applies, the lawyer may have no legal choice but to undertake the case. Even if the lawyer does not have a cab rank duty, she may recognize that her refusal to take the case is likely to make it impossible, as a practical matter, for the potential client to get 'his day in court'. Under those circumstances, her rejection of the case will be a blow to the autonomy of someone who, as a victim of apartheid, has probably already suffered many such blows. I would suggest that a lawyer should be deeply reluctant to mete out such blows, but that she may none the less properly decide to reject such a case in order to protect the interests of *other* victims of apartheid, or in extreme cases in order to protect the client's own needs.

[14] E. Mureinik, 'Pursuing Principle: The Appellate Division and Review under the State of Emergency', 5 *SAJHR* 60, 72 (1989).

[15] See Ch. 3, text at nn. 182–99, above.

perhaps almost always, were able to get permission to see their lawyers and at least some were permitted to see family members as well. These contacts were surely psychologically important in and of themselves.

Moreover, such contacts could lead to litigation. Despite the state's power under *Omar* to interfere with detainees' access to lawyers and so to the courts, cases *were* brought (and presumably others that were never brought were threatened) on behalf of detainees. Some of these cases did result in at least partial victories in court. Lower court decisions may have tempered the government's plans even where, some time later, the Appellate Division rejected the lower court initiative—and occasionally, as we saw in Chapter 4, victories were even won in the Appellate Division. Perhaps other cases to useful settlements out of court. Still others, by bringing judicial attention or even newspaper publicity to bear, may have helped constrain officials who were never subjected to an actual judgment or settlement binding them. All of them helped protect detainees from disappearance, and if emergency lawyering did no more than this, it still made the emergency regime better than it might have been.[16]

Even though by the end of the Rabie period the cases in which courts would grant relief must have been few, and even though the broad contours of the emergency system were resolutely upheld, emergency litigation also had potential value as the basis for a legal war of attrition to hold in check the worst possibilities of the states of emergency.[17] The continuing effort to combat capital punishment in the state and federal courts of the United States provides a vivid illustration of the impact that determined lawyers may have on the working of a legal system.[18] As of mid-December 1990, this effort has held the number of executions to less than 145 over the fourteen years that have passed since the Supreme Court ruled in 1976 that the death penalty was not *per se* unconstitutional. This success has been achieved despite the broad

[16] A grim paradox of emergency lawyering, and indeed of all internal security lawyering against the state, is that the more success lawyers had in court on behalf of the targets of the state's power, the more they gave some forces in or close to the state reason to resort to extra-legal methods. Whether this means that emergency lawyering contributed to the growth of the death squads is hard to say, however, since in the absence of such legal work the resulting looser constraints on official action might also have reinforced thoroughly lawless behaviour at or beyond the fringes of the state's structures. In any case, even if the presence of some limits on the state's lawful authority contributed to the rise of this illegal violence, abandoning the enforcement of those limits would have been a poor solution to the problem. What anti-apartheid activists and lawyers have done, instead, has been to try both to preserve the limits on official state action and to document, investigate, and publicize the unofficial conduct.

[17] In somewhat similar vein, Geoff Budlender has discussed the important contribution that lawyers' resistance to 'routinised processing' of cases by the state made to the prevention of the 'imminent destruction' of the Crossroads community. G. Budlender, 'Lawyers and Poverty: Beyond "Access to Justice"', in J. Hund (ed.), *Law and Justice in South Africa* (Johannesburg: Institute for Public Interest Law and Research, and Cape Town: Centre for Intergroup Studies, 1988), 1, 5–6.

[18] In South Africa, the efforts of Lawyers for Human Rights to ensure legal representation for people on death row have also had important results, not only in terms of protecting the rights of condemned prisoners, cf. text at n. 32 below, but also in contributing to the public revelation of evidence of death squads in South Africa's security forces.

popularity of capital punishment in the United States, despite the presence of *thousands* of convicted men and women on death rows around the nation, and despite Supreme Court decisions that have grown progressively more hostile to the legal arguments of those who face execution.

Emergency work in the Rabie period was also valuable for what it preserved of the doctrinal foundations for human rights arguments and decisions. As we saw in Chapter 4, what was preserved was actually quite substantial, however much it appeared at the time that benign doctrines were being honoured only in the breach. At the time, it might have been questioned whether any purpose was really being served by preserving those doctrines, but the use the Corbett court has made of such principles now attests to their value. As Arthur Chaskalson recently said:

> [D]espite all the paradoxes they [the judges] have somehow held to the infrastructure and have kept alive the principles of freedom and justice which permeate the common law. True, at times no more than lip service has been paid to these principles, and there have been landmark cases where opportunities to give substance to and uphold fundamental rights have been allowed to pass without even an expression of discomfort, let alone a vindication of the right. Yet the notion that freedom and fairness are inherent qualities of law lives on, and if not reflected in all the decisions, is nonetheless acknowledged and reinforced in numerous judments of the courts. That is an important legacy and one which deserves neither to be diminished nor squandered.[19]

Admittedly, such judgments have had the benefit of hindsight. In 1988 it was by no means certain that Corbett would become chief justice, or how much difference it would make if he did. Two thoughtful participants in this field of law argued that '[i]t is difficult to imagine how even a reconstituted Appellate Division could rescue our system of administrative law from the treatment it has received at the hands of the Rabie court—unless such a court were to be as creative in the face of recent precedent as the Rabie court has been in the face of older precedent.'[20] There *was* ground for pessimism, but there was also reason to hold on to the doctrinal resources that were available in the hope of being able to use them before a more sympathetic court.

The upshot of this analysis is that clients' apparent belief that their individual interests would be served by having legal representation has been correct. Their fates have been less grim if they have had the aid of lawyers. And this effect will not be confined to the particular clients alone, for the protections that lawyers established in any one case might shield other South Africans thereafter. Even so, it is possible to argue that these gains are outweighed

[19] A. Chaskalson, 'The Past Ten Years: A Balance Sheet and Some Indicators for the Future', 5 *SAJHR* 293, 295 (1989). Arthur Chaskalsan helped me to understand other aspects of the impact of human rights lawyering as well.

[20] N. Haysom and C. Plasket, 'The War against Law: Judicial Activism and the Appellate Division', 4 *SAJHR* 303, 305 (1988).

politically by losses generated through the very process of pursuing relief within the existing legal structures. Let us now consider this political attack on the value of lawyers' work.

2. Have Emergency Lawyers Undercut the Struggle against Apartheid?

It can be argued that the best way to undercut apartheid is to reject it at every turn. For those who encounter the system of apartheid through South Africa's courts, the correct response could be to refuse to participate in the system's legal forms. Opponents of apartheid would seek to manifest in their refusal to participate the illegitimate character of the power that oppressed them.

Until the freeing of Nelson Mandela and the beginning of movement towards negotiations, a broad principle of non-participation did guide much of black political life in South Africa,[21] and in some respects even those events have not deprived it of importance. When Africans chose not to vote in segregated municipal elections—the only occasions on which South Africa accords them a right to vote outside their 'homelands'—they were seeking to undermine a structure of apartheid, rather than risk lending it legitimacy by their very participation. When 'Coloured' and Indian South Africans boycotted parliamentary elections, they were doing the same thing. The price of such boycotts is that a modicum of power falls into the hands of those blacks who for ideological or personal reasons are prepared to play the game, but that is a price that other blacks have been prepared to pay. In a similar vein, it could be argued that blacks and whites would be wise to turn away from the use of the law and of litigation altogether (or at least in emergency cases), even at the risk of personal suffering as the immediate result, for the sake of longer-term objectives.

The practice of those subjected to emergency powers suggests their refusal to take this step, for many challenges to emergency authority have been pursued in the courts.[22] Perhaps, however, a sympathetic lawyer could have concluded that this refusal was a political mistake. Should a sympathetic lawyer have substituted her judgment for that of the would-be clients, by refusing to take their cases? There would be two reasons not to have adopted such a stance. The first would be a hesitation on the part of the lawyer to adopt the role of political activist or decisionmaker; the second would be a judgment that the decisions to seek legal representation that clients had made were justified on political as well as individual grounds. I will argue that anti-

[21] This theory by no means governed all of the fields of popular struggle in South Africa, as the rise of black labour unions (legal bodies which have made extensive use of the protections given them by statute) reflects.

[22] According to N. Haysom and S. Kahanovitz, '[e]mergency detentions were subjected to literally hundreds of challenges.... In September 1986 over 100 applications for emergency detainees were pending': 'Courts and the State of Emergency', in G. Moss and I. Obery (eds.), *South African Review 4* (Johannesburg: Ravan, 1987), 187, 193. These numbers probably fell as the applicable law grew less favourable during the Rabie years. For further discussion of the practice of black potential litigants, see Ch. 6, text at nn. 90–2, above.

apartheid lawyers do not have to be activists, but that even so they cannot avoid making some political choices. I will also suggest that lawyers' emergency work has been, on balance, politically valuable rather than damaging.

Should anti-apartheid lawyers be political activists first and foremost? A lawyer who has chosen to focus part or all of her professional life on attempting to limit the depredations of apartheid is not a person who has excluded political and moral judgments from her field of responsibility. Perhaps such lawyers should take their principles one step further, and assert that it is their responsibility, rather than anyone else's to decide which cases are so politically and morally productive that the lawyers should undertake them. Such lawyers might see themselves, and present themselves to the world, as activists first and lawyers second, the stance that the union leader Cyril Ramaphosa in 1988 urged lawyers to take up.[23]

This stance can be an admirable one. South Africa presents us with distinguished examples of lawyers who have indeed become 'activists first'—Nelson Mandela, Oliver Tambo, and Abram Fischer among them. But conscientious anti-apartheid lawyers are not, I submit, obliged to see themselves as activists. They might feel, for example, that their professional standing with their peers, on which their effectiveness as lawyers depends, rests on their being, visibly, 'lawyers first and activists second'. Or they might feel that their effectiveness with their clients depends on their retaining the capacity for objectivity that lawyers practise but activists may not prize. Or they might feel that by disclaiming the role of activist they are able to be better lawyers, or better people as lawyers, than they would be if they tried to play an activist part for which they are not well suited. On any of these grounds, and no doubt more, men and women can properly conclude that it is their responsibility to serve as lawyers rather than to become activists themselves.

I have already suggested, however, that every anti-apartheid lawyer potentially faces the responsibility for choosing which case, out of the many possible ones, to undertake. A lawyer indifferent to political matters might choose cases based on the fees they brought in, and as a practical matter even a lawyer committed to the struggle against apartheid cannot wholly ignore this criterion. (This reality underlines the importance of the political and moral criteria applied by those who assist in funding these lawyers.) Where money and other non-political concerns ('gaining experience', 'handling interesting matters', and the like) are not dispositive, however, I see no way for lawyers to make their decisions except by applying some political or moral standards. Perhaps lawyers can properly borrow these standards, for example by adhering to a principle of 'taking cases on behalf of representative popular organizations'.[24]

[23] G. Davis, 'Lawyers Group Calls for "Isolation" of Bar Councils', *Weekly Mail*, 8 (27 May–2 June 1988). I do not mean to suggest that Ramaphosa intended to support the particular conception of lawyers' responsibility that I have sketched in the text. A call for lawyers to be activists first can be interpreted in a wide variety of ways.

[24] This standard embodies a deference to popular decisionmaking that is welcome, and perhaps rare, in lawyers. It does, however, have a price, namely that the lawyer will no longer

But at the least, the lawyer must choose to do the borrowing, and needs a political or moral justification for this choice.

What if a lawyer did take the 'activist first' course? Lawyers who become activists first may conclude that they must make detailed judgments about their professional lives based on political principle. (Non-activists might reach the same conclusion.) Such lawyers might conclude as a matter of politics that participation in the legal system is a mistake, and that the contrary view of the majority of apartheid's victims does not bind them to join in that mistake. Many activists might still believe that so long as the people with whom they work hold on to the idea of legal representation, it is not the activists' place to deny them access to counsel. Presumably, though, activists who believe that lawyers' work ultimately does more harm than good will at least try to lead the people as a whole to share that view.

But *is* it a political mistake to participate in the legal system? We have already seen that such participation could somewhat lessen the impact of the state's emergency apparatus on its individual victims. But this immediate boon could have political value as well. The harder it is for the state to punish or coerce any given individual, after all, the easier it is for that individual to continue to play a role in political struggle. The broader these ripple effects become, the more lawyers' work serves not only to safeguard individual South Africans but also to help provide 'space' for the political movements of which these individuals may be a part.

Moreover, the targets of emergency law have not by any means been limited to individuals. When the state seeks to muzzle free reporting by the press, or to clamp down on the activities of an anti-apartheid organization, any successful challenges to the state's designs obviously may affect the broader course of change. To be sure, it would be a mistake to overstate the victories that could be won on these fronts. At the height of the emergency extensive media controls were imposed, and the closure of a radical newspaper under these powers was upheld by the Corbett court in the *Catholic Bishops* case. In that period, as well, many anti-apartheid organizations were deprived of their legal right to carry on any activities 'whatsoever'. Yet lawyers may have had some successes all the same, for example in impeding the state's efforts to close such newspapers, or in securing some legal room for events such as the Mandela birthday celebrations of 1988 or the mass integration of beaches in 1989.

Perhaps an example, not from emergency law but from nearby, will confirm this point. Late in 1988 five men were sentenced to lengthy prison terms at

be available for other deserving cases. Some standards might raise much more serious questions. For example, a standard of 'taking cases identified as important by representative popular organizations' could result in the denial of legal services to individuals who have valid, and deserving, legal claims which for one reason or another do not fit the priorities of a political grouping. For a discussion of the ethical problems posed by lawyers' efforts to represent the interests of groups while not ignoring the claims of individuals within those groups, see Ellmann, 'Lawyering' (cit. n. 7), 181–9.

the end of the 'Delmas' treason trial. In that case more than 400 days of trial were taken up with an examination of the actions of the twenty-two individuals actually facing charges in the case and of countless others not before the court—in a sense, the entire society. That only five of the accused were in the end sentenced to imprisonment[25] was a partial, bittersweet victory for the accused, and for their lawyers. This case became a clear triumph when the Appellate Division, in a judgment written by Corbett CJ, threw out all of the convictions on the ground of procedural irregularities, just before Christmas 1989.[26] Some of the former prisoners are now, once again, active political leaders.

But long before then the case may have contributed to another victory. The massive defence mounted on behalf of the twenty-two people charged in this case (and similar efforts in other recent treason cases) may have slowed the march of government repression of the national resistance that sprang up in the mid-1980s, for this work helped to deprive the government not only of convictions but also of the imprimatur for broader oppression which a quick and easy conviction of leading activists for treason could have provided. Denied this weapon for a time, the government found another device in early 1988 in the effective banning of the United Democratic Front under the emergency.[27] Yet some precious time had perhaps already been won, for organized opposition to apartheid might have been even more bluntly and thoroughly suppressed had it been easy, rather than difficult, for the state to run its opponents through the gauntlet of a treason trial.

Still, even as we recognize the individual and political value of emergency law work, we must also ask whether its costs might have outweighed its value. In making such an evaluation, lawyers (whether activists or not) might well hesitate to sacrifice relatively tangible benefits to clients and others in light of costs that might be less certain or less immediate. But we could hardly rule out a priori the possibility that some lawyers might find, perhaps correctly, that these costs were too much to pay.[28]

Let us consider two types of potential costs. First, a focus on legal protections might divert activists and potential activists from more fruitful forms of activity. After all, if it was clear—and even the Corbett court's decisions pointed to this conclusion—that the courts were unlikely to alter the fundamental contours of the state's system of emergency powers, then perhaps those who opposed that system should have looked for alternative means of challenging it. In one sense, this argument is overdrawn, for it suggests that legal work and political work are mutually exclusive alternatives. We have

[25] Six others were given suspended sentences.

[26] *S.* v. *Malindi*, 1990 (1) SA 962 (A).

[27] Order No. 334, *Government Gazette* 11157 (24 Feb. 1988).

[28] Whether those who speak for the oppressed, in political fora or in courts, have an obligation not to deprive their people of attainable benefits despite possible long-term costs is an issue beyond the scope of this discussion. See M. Walzer, *Obligations: Essays on Disobedience, War, and Citizenship* (Cambridge, Mass.: Harvard University Press, 1970), 46–70.

just seen one reason why this premiss is misleading: legal work may sustain and protect political efforts. It is not misleading, however, to recognize that legal work might come to enjoy a reputation for efficacy that it did not deserve. The work of lawyers might as a result attain a cachet that exalted its importance above that of the political campaigns it might seek to benefit, or even encouraged people to dispense with political organizing in favour of litigation.[29]

The significance of this possibility can only be measured empirically. An activist lawyer might ask whether there exist other means of aiding political struggle which promise greater success at this time—and might find, regretfully, that under a state of emergency the work of lawyers ranks quite highly, in terms of its effectiveness, among the courses of action available. An activist might also ask whether those who might undertake more political forms of protest in fact lapse into quiescence because of the availability of courtroom challenges. It may be that such misplaced dependence on the law can develop, and so should be a matter of concern in framing tactics in any particular situation. Lawyers may be able to minimize this danger without departing the field altogether, if they shape their relations with their clients in light of a recognition of this potential.[30] Broadly speaking, though, the history of the past decade is a history of mass mobilization as well as widespread litigation, and it is simply difficult to see in that history any evidence of a general tendency on the part of South Africa's oppressed majority to forego political challenge for judicial disquisition.

The view that legal work undercuts political work also seems to entail a relatively narrow definition of 'legal work'. Much of what lawyers do is of course in courts or similar professional settings, and thus could pose the risk of impairing mass mobilization discussed above. But not all that lawyers do is so narrowly confined. Consider, for example, the fast undertaken by lawyers for emergency detainees, in support of the detained hunger strikers.[31] It may seem odd to describe this fast as a form of lawyers' work. Even if the fast itself was not part of the practice of emergency law, however, the fact that those fasting were lawyers was part of what made the fast a noteworthy symbolic gesture, and so the lawyers' professional status directly supported this arguably extra-professional conduct.

In any case, less vivid forms of political work may more readily be recognized as within the sphere of lawyers' professional obligations. Lawyers as a profession, in the bar councils and law societies, can decry unjust laws and work for their reform. Two South African organizations, Lawyers for Human Rights and the Society for the Abolition of the Death Penalty in South Africa

[29] See D. Luban, *Lawyers and Justice: An Ethical Study* (Princeton, NJ: Princeton University Press, 1988), 387–91.

[30] For an insightful description and analysis of the efforts of a lawyer and a community organizer to avoid such unfortunate results, see L. White, 'To Learn and Teach: Lessons From Driefontein on Lawyering and Power', 1988 *Wisc. L. Rev.* 699.

[31] See 'Strikers Spark New Spirit in South Africa', 31 *Africa News* (No. 4) at 2 (20 Feb. 1989).

(at least some of whose members are lawyers), have recently pressed the case against South Africa's death penalty. Brian Currin, one of the leaders of this effort, has said that he is 'convinced that the lobbying in high places, our execution monitoring programme and the high profile campaigns have together contributed towards the realization in government circles that something needed to be done'.[32] The risk that lawyers' work will undermine political efforts declines the more lawyers' work is understood to include political efforts, although the choice to become overtly political is a delicate tactical decision, since it may jeopardize the success of lawyers' more conventional efforts in court. (The more lawyers undertake political struggle, moreover, the less it would seem that they can properly limit their responsibility for making political choices among the various, possibly conflicting, strategies to which they might lend their support.)

A second possible political cost of a focus on legal protections could be the legitimation of the courts, and by extension the government of which the courts are a part. The better lawyers do in their use of the rules of the game—the more useful they are to their individual clients—the more they may, according to this argument, tend to strengthen support for the current regime and to deflate opposition to it. We might take the fact that opponents of oppression in a wide range of countries have attempted to invoke the law as a sword or shield on their behalf as some evidence that those closest to these questions do not usually see the risk of legitimation as a dispositive one.[33] Even if this risk is usually not prohibitively severe, however, it might be so in South Africa. We have reason to be attentive to this possibility, because, as we saw in Chapter 6, it appears that a source of whites' adherence to the law in South Africa is their hope, or sense, that governing by law contributes to their society's legitimacy.[34]

It is especially challenging to assess the legitimating potential of emergency law practice now that the state itself has half-acknowledged that the existing order lacks enough legitimacy to continue. The government styles itself 'part of the anti-apartheid struggle', and its Minister of Constitutional Development says that '[w]e are in a hurry' to negotiate the basis for a new South Africa.[35] This does not mean that the legitimacy or lack thereof of the existing system has become completely irrelevant, for assessments of the institutions of the current South Africa will affect the shape of the South Africa to come. But if emergency work had provided legitimation for white rule, that effect would

[32] G. Evans, 'Turnabout Welcomed as Number of Hangings Declines', *Weekly Mail*, 3 (3–9 Mar. 1989).

[33] For arguments that such legitimation does occur, however, see R. Shamir, '"Landmark Cases" and the Reproduction of Legitimacy: The Case of Israel's High Court of Justice', 24 *Law and Soc. Rev.* 781 (1990) (Israel's occupied territories); F. Snyder, 'State of Siege and Rule of Law in Argentina: The Politics and Rhetoric of Vindication', 15 *Lawyer of the Americas* 503 (1984) (Argentina). For the possible legitimating effects of the criminal law in 18th-century England, see Ch. 6, n. 88, above.

[34] See Ch. 6, text at nn. 68–115, above.

[35] S. Johnson, 'We're in a Hurry to Sign, Says Viljoen', *Weekly Mail*, 1, col. 2 (22 June 1990).

have been especially disturbing when whites themselves showed far less disposition to yield some of their power. Let us look, as we did in Chapter 6, at three different audiences before whom these events have been played out. We will begin with the audience perhaps most easily persuaded of the legitimacy of South African institutions, South African whites, and then consider the audience outside South Africa, before looking closely at the possible impact on the largest audience in South Africa itself, South African blacks.

South Africa's whites, or at least many of them, appear to place real value on their society's adherence to law, but I do not think the legitimating effects of emergency-law work have been great so far as they are concerned. It may have been easier for whites to summon up the feeling that their society does live by the law if they saw that even the emergency was grist for lawyers' mill—and easier still if lawyers won an occasional victory. But this almost paradoxical result of lawyers' challenge to state conduct should not be of great concern to the lawyer weighing the political consequences of her work. Unfortunately, most whites are not profoundly opposed to the present order in South Africa, nor are they the primary engine of political pressure for change. As a result, confirming their support for the *status quo* probably does not sharply alter the political equation. Indeed, now that the current regime is more aggressively in favour of change than many of its erstwhile white supporters, it might even be argued that if emergency litigation has reinforced the government's legitimacy with its white electorate, it has thereby promoted the chances of a peaceful transition to a non-racial South Africa!

In any event it is not clear that that the existence of emergency law practice (or anti-apartheid practice generally) has greatly affected whites' views on whether their society is ruled by law. To be sure, the visible evidence of emergency practice (the reports of the progress and decision of court cases) received attention in the press, an attention probably magnified during most of the emergency by the fact that legally court proceedings could be reported more freely than many events 'on the street'. Developments in the courts, however, are only a small part of the political and social scene. Government statements, unrest reports, debates in Parliament, filtered through the media and whites' own predispositions: sources such as these probably form the bulk of the information that South African whites look to in their daily experience of their society. Over time, such insulation might be penetrated, but at least in the short run it seems quite possible that if there were *no* lawyers overtly using the law against apartheid, most whites would still be prone to believe that their society adhered to the law.

Moreover, emergency law work, like much anti-apartheid practice, had a distinct defect as a source of legitimation even in the eyes of whites, since such work was by definition focused (on the victims' part) on displaying and condemning the injustices of the existing order. Perhaps even many whites have found the reports of such litigation more disturbing than reassuring.

To gauge the effects of lawyers' work on the views of people outside South Africa necessarily entails considerable speculation. Undoubtedly some foreign observers sympathize deeply with South African whites, or hope for profit from business in South Africa, and might have been eager to count the existence of emergency law practice as a welcome confirmation of South Africa's adherence to Western legal values. But there has also been strong opposition to apartheid from outside South Africa, and it seems entirely plausible to suggest that the existence of the state of emergency helped fuel that opposition. If anything, the occasional news reports of court action in emergency cases may have functioned primarily to remind outsiders of the state of affairs in South Africa and thus to confirm their sense of the injustice of apartheid.

I suspect that for most foreign watchers the question is not whether the existing order is a legitimate one, but rather how to encourage it to change. For these observers the existence of emergency law practice may well have affected their assessment of strategies for bringing about such change—and an activist lawyer in South Africa might worry that outsiders would overestimate the utility of the courts—but their perception of the legitimacy, or rather illegitimacy, of most aspects of the system would not have been at issue.

The risk that outsiders may overestimate the utility of legal practice could be a serious concern, but I doubt that in fact it currently should be. The modest, and modestly reported, achievements of emergency litigation surely played no more than a limited role in shaping affected observers' attitudes on such broad strategic issues as the need for sanctions. Perhaps it is more likely that the results of emergency practice affected the judgements of those foreigners who concerned themselves with the narrower question of the value of legal tactics, as compared to other methods, in the struggle inside South Africa. Given the reality of limitations on the amount of foreign support available at all, however, it seems unlikely that the result of an overestimation of the value of this strategy will be an *absolute* 'over-funding' of this effort, in terms of financial or moral support.

This effort might still be overfunded *relative* to other deserving candidates for assistance, but it is not clear either that this is actually so or that, if it is, there is much that can be done about it. I doubt that a survey of foreign support for anti-apartheid efforts would actually show anything like a single-minded focus on the activities of lawyers (particularly in the wake of Nelson Mandela's foreign visits since his February 1990 release from prison). Even if legal work is receiving a disproportionate share of foreign support, a decline in support for this work might not translate into an equivalent increase in assistance to other activities. Funding could not simply be transferred, for example, if those who support the work of lawyers and those who support different strategies, such as union organizing, constitute relatively distinct and non-overlapping groups, whose members do not readily adopt new targets for their aid. In short, the possible misdirection of foreign support hardly seems a strong basis for sacrificing the various benefits of emergency litigation that we identified earlier.

To suggest, finally, that the effect of emergency law practice has been to legitimize the system in the eyes of South African blacks is simply implausible. South Africa today is not a state in which the black majority accepts the legitimacy of its white rulers' dominance. Blacks who reject apartheid may recognize and seek to utilize such protections as the law gives them, but surely remain well aware of the rights they are denied.[36] The state of emergency was a particularly open and sweeping abridgement of human rights, and it is wholly unlikely that the partial checks on that dominance that emergency litigation could achieve conferred an aura of virtue on the government as a whole. To borrow E. P. Thompson's words, 'people are not as stupid as this spectre of abject legitimation would suggest'.[37]

A narrower version of this argument, however, may be more credible. If people go to court and win some relief, is it not possible that they will conclude that the courts—the Supreme Courts, in particular—deserve more respect than the rest of the current system? Is it not possible that South African blacks might entertain the view that 'justice' is available, at least some of the time, in these courts?

This effect *is* possible, but it is hardly a certainty. We should not overstate the likelihood that emergency law work would have had such an effect, given its limited visibility, its focus on some of the worst features of the existing order and its decidedly modest level of success. We should also remember that lawyers' work broadly understood can include political gestures meant to counter the subliminal legitimation that conceivably is the result of even unsuccessful efforts in court. The fasting lawyers' declaration that the courts had failed their detainee clients is such a gesture.

The most important problem with this legitimation argument, however, is that it assumes that the particular kind of legitimation envisaged is undesirable from the point of view of opponents of apartheid. Let us grant that it is possible that blacks might conclude as a result of judicial victories that justice can sometimes be won in the courts. Then we might say that emergency law practice could have legitimized the courts in the eyes of blacks, to the extent that the courts were seen as providing fair results or, failing that, at least fair process. Whether South African blacks do give the courts a greater measure of legitimacy than they accord to other institutions of the government is not entirely clear, but let us assume for purposes of argument that they do and that emergency cases contributed to their doing so. Should opponents of apartheid seek to forestall this qualified form of legitimation?[38]

[36] I discussed black South Africans' attitudes towards the legal system in Ch. 6, text at nn. 83–96, above.

[37] E. Thompson, *Whigs and Hunters: The Origin of the Black Act* (New York: Pantheon, 1975), 262.

[38] I am grateful to Jenny Marcus for calling my attention to this issue.

If South Africa's Supreme Courts generally are institutions in which honest judges seek to act fairly, and are prepared on occasion to follow their convictions or the law's dictates even to the extent of opposing, in some measure, the worst excesses of the government, it would seem that these virtues should be recognized by blacks just as by all opponents of apartheid (although they should not be exaggerated). To say that they should not be recognized would be to say that people should remain ignorant of such bright spots as the South African system presents—a view that could be held but that does not reflect great respect for the judgment of those to be kept in ignorance. And to suggest that black South Africans who do see these modest virtues of the courts will abandon their struggle for liberation (particularly now, when victory may at last be at hand) is absurd.

There is, in addition, a political reason for holding that it is extremely important that the relative independence of the South African courts be widely seen, and by both blacks and whites. That reason is that the attitude of South Africa's people towards the courts now will influence their attitude towards courts in the future. It was possible for American colonists to hate the British monarchy and yet retain much of British law (albeit with some sharp controversy in the process).[39] Such an effort to meld continuity with change now seems to be under way in Namibia. It seems equally appropriate for South African citizens to hate the system of apartheid but retain in the future the beneficent principles of the common law that still inhere within the South African legal system, and the welcome tradition of judicial independence that also still holds meaning. Violations of human rights are not likely to cease permanently and absolutely with the end of apartheid, and the need for judicial resistance to them will not cease either—as the long Zimbabwean state of emergency, and the Zimbabwean courts' efforts to restrain governmental powers, attest.[40]

Considering the shape of things to come is not timely only now, when a new South Africa may be at hand. On the contrary, it was always appropriate for opponents of apartheid to try to nurture, even in the society they opposed, the seeds of a new nation. It is impossible to be certain, of course, what the impact of the past years' judicial decisions or of their public reception will be on the character of South Africa's government after apartheid. Yet it makes

[39] See L. Friedman, *A History of American Law* (New York: Touchstone, 1973), 93–8.

[40] See E. Dumbutshena, 'The Rule of Law in a Constitutional Democracy with Particular Reference to the Zimbabwean Experience', 5 *SAJHR* 311 (1989). Sydney Kentridge has emphasized that 'the Chief Justice [Dumbutshena] and his courts have not simply been followers of the Rhodesian tradition. They have created a new tradition of independence and impartiality which far transcends anything inherited from the controversial courts of the Rhodesia of the 1960s and 70s.' S. Kentridge, 'Concluding Remarks', 5 *SAJHR* 355, 357 (1989). Zimbabwe's state of emergency, which was declared in 1965 prior to the 'unilateral declaration of independence' by Ian Smith's white government, and was continued by Robert Mugabe's government after the 'coming of majority rule in 1980', J. Hatchard, 'The Implementation of Safeguards on the Use of Emergency Powers: A Zimbabwean Perspective', 9 *Oxford J. Leg. Stud.* 116, 117 (1989), was finally brought to an end in 1990.

sense to expect that the more reality lawyers have given to the highest aspirations of the law, the stronger the appeal of these ideas will be to the citizens of a future South Africa. In this respect, then, a qualified legitimation of the courts through emergency law work would have been, in political terms, a benefit rather than a cost of this enterprise.

To this political benefit we should add another that we have not yet assayed. It is possible that the courts will have a valuable political role to play along the road to a future South Africa as well as when the journey is complete. As central as the course of negotiations will hopefully be, it seems quite unlikely that those negotiations will be the only factors shaping the coming developments. In this context, an independent and sympathetic judiciary may play a part greater than the one the South African courts have performed in years past. The government may find it convenient to place responsibility for some changes largely in the hands of the courts; desegregation was left largely to the courts for some time in the United States. Conceivably the South African government's interest in the adoption of a bill of rights stems in part from such a strategy.

Moreover, the process of change may have a momentum that encourages courts to go considerably further than the government might desire. The more legitimate the popular struggle for democracy becomes, the more reluctant courts may be to approve the use of law for its suppression. The willingness of Van der Walt J. to 'tak[e] into account the conditions in Alexandra [a black, poor residential area near Johannesburg] ... [and] the amount of perceived provocation of the residents of Alexandra because of what they subjectively saw as unwarranted police action', in acquitting Moses Mayekiso and others of sedition, exemplifies this potential.[41] So did the recent response of the Appellate Division at the argument of a case involving the forced removal of a small community of blacks, the Bakwena ba Magopa, from their long-time homes. According to Allister Sparks's news report, 'In an unprecedented development that may reflect changing times in South Africa, a five-judge panel of the country's highest court ... intervened Friday in the little tribe's drawn-out struggle with apartheid's eviction laws to advise President Frederik W. de Klerk's government to negotiate a settlement with it.' The judge who intervened was Joubert ACJ, one of the members of the Rabie court's emergency team. '"Before we begin this case," Joubert said, "I want to ask what is at stake here? These events deal with the past, and I am looking to the future. Is there no prospect of finding a solution to this matter?".' Needless to say, lawyers for the Magopa were optimistic about the chances of settlement![42]

But to have an independent and sympathetic judiciary for this difficult but

[41] *S.* v. *Mayekiso and Others,* No. 115/89 (Witwatersrand, 5 May 1989), typed judgment at 55. The duty to hear the other side may already compel judges to hear much more extensive and vivid explanations of blacks' struggles than many whites encounter. The more legitimate this struggle becomes, the more judges may welcome such evidence even if they are not compelled to do so.

[42] A. Sparks, 'Home from the "Homeland"', *Washington Post,* A16, col. 1 (27 Aug. 1990).

welcome future argues today, and has argued throughout the emergency, for insisting on such a judiciary now. On this score, abandonment of the field, whether by lawyers or by judges or by academic commentators, would have been a political mistake—as well as a sacrifice of the modest human rights protections that the efforts of these people have secured. If lawyers in South Africa had not pressed for decent decisions, and had not struggled to sustain and expand the positive elements of South African law, that law might well have grown worse. If liberal judges in South Africa had resigned, there would have been, as Etienne Mureinik has pointed out, no sympathetic judges available to turn to.[43] If South African legal scholars had abandoned a criticism of their courts that asserted that the courts should do better than they do, it would be harder to make the case for positive judicial intervention today. The pressure of emergency litigation has been only a part of this insistence on justice, but it is a rather prominent part. In this respect too, therefore, the practice of emergency law may have been valuable to the broader political challenge to apartheid.

Conclusion

In short, the supposed political costs of emergency law practice, as we have examined them so far, did not call for the abandonment of this form of anti-apartheid work and of its benefits to individual clients and groups. On the contrary, the dangers either of defusing popular militancy or of lending legitimacy to an evil system seem to have been decidedly modest, and the potential political gain from the struggle to realize the rule of law of far-reaching importance. The benefits of this field of South African legal practice, with its generally incrementalist cast, *have* outweighed its costs. And if a comparable calculus applies to other fields of legal challenge to apartheid, then it follows that the notably incrementalist legal efforts on many different litigation fronts have also been valuable (and so I believe).

But this conclusion does not exclude the possibility that some other strategy, say of confrontation or of Gandhian non-participation, would have produced even better results; in that case we would have to add to the costs of the strategy that these lawyers chose the loss of these potential achievements. Because these alternative strategies have not set the tone for legal struggles in South Africa, it is difficult to assess their value definitively; they are, at least so far as courtroom events are concerned, the way not taken. None the less there are important reasons to doubt that lawyers' resort to such strategies as these would have served apartheid's victims as well as incremental lawyering has.

There is particularly strong reason to question whether an attempt to

[43] Mureinik's point is quoted in J. Dugard, 'Should Judges Resign? A Reply to Professor Wacks', 101 *SALJ* 286, 294 (1984).

import into South African courts the stern denunciations of the Garrisonian abolitionists, or the disruptions of the Chicago Eight trial, generally would have served the interests of apartheid's victims. Such approaches could have jeopardized the gains to be won by incremental lawyering, might have undercut the courts' potential to play a valuable role in the future, and might even have heightened the polarization of South African society and the risk of civil war—as indeed the abolitionists' campaigns in the United States may have.[44]

A Gandhian rejection of legalistic approaches in favour of a respectful, but profound, challenge to the conscience of the judges and of society might have been more promising.[45] By offering the judges moral example rather than condemnation, this stance might have won judicial sympathy that would have balanced the tactical loss entailed in foreswearing legal argumentation. This approach might also have mitigated the danger of polarization, for it would not have denied that there was virtue as well as weakness in the legal system and the society.

But there would have been three perhaps serious obstacles to the success of a thoroughgoing Gandhian project. The first would have been the legal community itself. Even for many anti-apartheid lawyers, the adoption of such tactics might have been wrenching, involving as it would have both a sharp rejection of the society around them and a departure from the familiar dimensions of legal advice and argument. As a result, it seems likely that many lawyers would have been reluctant to take such steps, and if only a few had actually turned with their clients to a Gandhian disclaimer of legal protections, their efforts would probably have been of little avail.[46] And unless a substantial number of lawyers had agreed on this strategy in advance,[47] any lawyer or client who thought it *could* win wide support would have had to test this possibility by experimenting with it; the fact that the particular clients who made the experiment could suffer for it would naturally have tended to discourage such ventures. Moreover, even if the strategy had been implemented and even if some judges had proved responsive to its moral

[44] See Ch. 6, text and notes at nn. 410–1, above.

[45] For an example of such an appeal, by Gandhi himself, see Ch. 6 n. 408 above.

[46] Cf. J. Dugard, 'Should Judges Resign?', (cit. n. 43) 293–4. (For Professor Raymond Wacks's argument that resignations by judges could have a substantial effect, see his: 'Judges and Injustice', 101 *SALJ* 266, 282–5 (1984.) If a long-term withdrawal by lawyers from the courts was beyond the realm of possibility, perhaps a boycott of particular courts or agencies for limited periods would have been more feasible. For examples of such precisely targeted boycotts, in Spain, Ghana, and the West Bank, see Ch. 6 nn. 220, 223, and 225 above. There is at least one, rather ironic, South African precedent for such action: the decision of the Johannesburg bar in 1951 to boycott the court of L. C. Steyn, a newly appointed judge, because he had been a civil servant rather than a privately practising advocate before his appointment! See Ch. 6 n. 328 above. But even a 'limited' boycott that sacrificed visibly attainable victories might have been a radical and unlikely step.

[47] Anti-apartheid lawyers might well be in a position to coordinate their actions, as Joan Hartman has suggested in comments on this book. But whether they would actually be in agreement on this strategic choice is less clear.

force, others might have been more obdurate, and many, perhaps most, anti-apartheid causes could have suffered in court as a result.

The second possible obstacle would have been the white community at large. The ultimate success of Gandhian tactics depends on the response of the challenged party as well as the commitment of the challenger, and in South Africa whites had proven strongly resistant to such tactics in the past. During the Defiance Campaign of the 1950s, '[t]he defiers went to prison, and the more they defied the tougher the laws became and the longer their prison terms.'[48] Perhaps whites would have responded differently in the 1980s—but perhaps not.

The third obstacle would have been the client community. It is quite uncertain whether Gandhian courtroom tactics, however abstractly desirable, would have won the support of apartheid's victims. 'The African National Congress had been founded under the strong influence of Gandhi's philosophy of non-violence',[49] but the government's response to non-violent efforts was unbending. The era of non-violence in a sense culminated in the state's massacre of sixty-nine people at Sharpeville in 1960. In the aftermath, the African National Congress turned, albeit with notable restraint, to the 'armed struggle'.[50] Clients of similar, or more militant, mind might not have accepted the value of Gandhian persuasion through self-sacrifice—even if their lawyers had tried to urge this course upon them. Courts, moreover, as well as the white public might have found Gandhian appeals less persuasive from litigants who were accused of being part of a 'total onslaught' rather than from a non-violent moral witness.

For these reasons, a broad Gandhian legal programme, despite its potential virtues, might not have been feasible in South Africa during the emergency. It deserves mention, too, that the central advantage of such a course—its vivid call to the holders of power to recognize the injustice of their ways—was not necessarily sacrificed in the strategy of incrementalism. Powerful challenges to the morality of apartheid have been voiced in many sectors of South African life, and have been reiterated in court. When Van der Walt J., in the *Mayekiso* trial, took 'into account the conditions in Alexandra ... [and] the amount of perceived provocation of the residents in Alexandra because of what they subjectively saw as unwarranted police action',[51] he was apparently responding to such a plain indictment of the existing order, an indictment made in the

[48] A. Sparks, *The Mind of South Africa* (New York: Knopf, 1990), 238. One part of the state's response was the imposition of special penalties for any crime 'proved to have been committed by way of protest against any law'—a provision that remains on the books. Internal Security Act 74 of 1982, s. 58. See J. Dugard, *Human Rights and the South African Legal Order* (Princeton, NJ: Princeton University Press, 1978), 175.

[49] Sparks, *Mind* (cit. n. 48), 236.

[50] For an account of these events, see ibid. 233–49. For Sparks's critical appraisal of the ANC's rejection of non-violence, see ibid. 269–77.

[51] See text at n. 41 above.

course of what appears to have been a full-scale legal defence.[52] Legal doctrine and legal tradition, it appears, are capacious enough to offer space for such arguments. Indeed, there is even a tradition, the fruit of the conflicts between English-speaking and Afrikaner whites, of some judicial leniency for armed rebellion.[53]

Significant as these considerations could be, I do not mean to dismiss a Gandhian approach altogether. There is in fact a striking example of such tactics being used to challenge a core element of emergency power—the detainees' hunger strikes which began in January of 1989 and led within months to the release of hundreds of emergency detainees (a great many of them under severe restriction orders).[54] Moreover, lawyer's sympathy fasting in support of the hunger strikers could be seen as an instance of their concurrence in Gandhian strategy. But the hunger strike is also a special case. For both lawyers and clients, there was little to lose in the courts; such cases as *Omar* and *Dempsey* had seen to that.[55] In this sense, the years of courtroom efforts on behalf of these detainees were a helpful, if not necessary, predicate for the hunger strike. Yet even so the hunger strikes might not have succeeded, if the detainees had not been prepared to raise the stakes so high and if the politics of the government had not been beginning to change.

Thus the hunger strike does not demonstrate the feasibility of a general Gandhian response to the law. If anything, these events seem to point more to the possibility of complementing a sustained incrementalist legal campaign with the special clarity of a Gandhian effort. The hunger strike also highlights the importance of client attitudes, and may thus confirm that a central reason for the absence of a more sustained Gandhian approach to the courts was, as I have inferred, the clients' reluctance—except in the most extreme circumstances—to forego such legal defences as they had. Perhaps lawyers could fruitfully have explored further the possibility of a much more widespread

[52] One indication of the character of the defence in this case is *S.* v. *Mayekiso and Others*, 1988 (4) SA 738 (W), a mid-trial decision in which the court considered and rejected the accused's motion to dismiss the charges, a motion offered not on the basis of the evidence but on the ground that the state's papers failed to allege an assertedly essential element of the offence. See ibid. 739F–G. The legalistic flavour of this argument is reflected in the authorities on which counsel for the accused relied, authorities which included venerable sourcebooks of Roman–Dutch law.

[53] Counsel invoked this tradition in *S.* v. *Mange*, 1980 (4) SA 613 (A) at 614. Rumpff CJ agreed that there was a South African tradition of sparing the lives of people convicted of high treason, but argued that this tradition had evolved mostly in 'situations in which military forces were openly engaged against persons who could be called rebels'. Ibid. 619D–E. Contrasting these cases to the terrorist attacks which he saw as 'the present type of high treason', he warned that 'a complete change now ... would not be surprising, nor, in the circumstances, be unjustified'. Ibid. 619F.

[54] See Human Rights Commission, 2 *Human Rights Update* (No. 1) 49–51 (Oct. 1988–Mar 1989). The decision of ANC guerrillas in *S.* v. *Masina and Others* to forego representation by counsel also reflects a strategy of self-sacrifice akin to a Gandhian approach. See Ch. 6 n. 92 above.

[55] Detainees from Johannesburg Prison emphasized in a press statement that '[t]he regime ... closed up whatever existing legal channel there was to secure our release'. Ibid. 54.

Gandhian stance. But given the significant obstacles to a successful Gandhian strategy (as well as the pitfalls of a confrontational approach) on the one hand and the potential of more traditional legal work on the other, I suggest that in general South African lawyers have been right to concentrate on more traditional lawyering.[56]

Even if lawyers opposed to apartheid can fruitfully express their opposition to apartheid in their legal practice, it does not automatically follow that they should have done so in the particular field of the emergency. After all, the courts have probably been less receptive to emergency law claims than to the claims that South Africa's oppressed people have brought in a variety of other contexts. While the courts' unresponsiveness may mean that any risk of lending legitimacy to South Africa's institutions was also reduced, it is easy to understand why lawyers might wish to practise in fields where more could be achieved.

I can offer no criterion by which to judge the exact balance of emergency law and other forms of work that would have been ideal. Even if I thought it possible to argue convincingly that greater emphasis on emergency cases at any particular moment might have been appropriate, I would not want to suggest that lawyers practising anti-apartheid law—a group facing difficulties enough as it is—should discount the sense of satisfaction that other areas of this practice may give them.

I do want to argue, however, that it was important that emergency law work continued even though other fields of law might have offered more frequent victories.[57] I doubt that this proposition is a controversial one, but it is worth stating none the less. One reason for maintaining this practice was a moral proposition: such profound breaches of human rights should not be left unopposed. Were lawyers' efforts against them wholly ineffective, the need to express opposition to such injustice would have remained. But there was also a much more practical reason. The emergency was the cutting edge of the South African government's effort to control by law the rise of effective black opposition to apartheid. Even now this edge could be unsheathed again. The direct victims of the emergency were likely to be those individuals and those organizations in the forefront of the effort to bring change to South Africa. Protecting the people who have taken up such roles is important morally; preserving space for them and the organizations of which they are a part is important to the course of political events as well. That course has often been bleak and hard to predict, but could hardly be abandoned.

[56] If incremental litigation has been worth bringing, sympathetic judges have also been needed. (See text and note at n. 43 above.) While judges in theory might have made their own Gandhian point, independently of lawyers or clients, by resigning, John Dugard is surely right that widespread judicial resignations are extremely unlikely: 'Should Judges Resign?' (cit. n. 43), 292. Even so, there might have been moments where judges could have sounded each other on this possibility; Dugard writes that 'the sad truth is that judges have missed the boat'. Ibid. With that qualification, I conclude that judges opposed to apartheid have been right to remain on the bench to hear the cases that anti-apartheid lawyers and clients brought before them.

[57] Comments by Geoff Budlender were important to my understanding of this issue.

The lesson of this analysis for lawyers in other countries suffering under oppression is not prescriptive, but it is suggestive. In other countries, as in South Africa, lawyers committed to challenging the injustice in their states cannot generally decide whether to undertake a particular case, or any cases at all, simply on the basis of whether there are potential clients who want them to do so. They must, in some measure, undertake the kind of weighing of the benefits and costs of litigation that I have outlined here.

When they do, I suspect they will very often choose, and choose rightly, to pursue litigation analogous to South Africa's emergency cases (and its other challenges to the laws of apartheid). Indeed the prevalence of human rights lawyering around the world suggests that lawyers in many countries have long since reached such conclusions. I do not suggest that the calculus of the value of human rights work, and of emergency law work specifically, will always call for the same conclusion as in South Africa. But we can expect to see such similarity often. No doubt the victories that incrementalist lawyering like South Africa's can win will usually be modest ones, although the more widely human rights law is practised and the more attentively it is supported from abroad the greater its chances of success—and modest victories count, as South Africa's experience shows. The costs, moreover, will often be limited (provided, that is, that zealous representation is not itself an official or unofficial offence for which the lawyer may suffer greatly). In particular, at least in countries where popular political organization has some strength, it should be possible to shape lawyers' work so as to narrow the risk of diversion and blunting of political mobilization. Moreover, the greater the oppression in a country, the more implausible the fear of 'legitimation by litigation' becomes. And there will always remain, as in South Africa, the hope of influencing the future. Though other strategies, abolitionist or Gandhian, may provide valuable complements to or substitutes for incrementalist legal work, the incrementalist effort to use the tools available within the system on behalf of the system's victims will often be a key element in the struggle against injustice.

In any event, South African lawyers *have* pursued the claims of the oppressed, both those in detention and those suffering only the injustices of normal South African life. Often this work must have been deeply frustrating—perhaps even more frustrating than the efforts of the lawyers involved in the first steps of the struggle against racial segregation in the United States, decades before *Brown* v. *Board of Education*.[58] But the decades of legal work and popular struggle leading up to *Brown* did bear fruit. Looking back, we can say that the potential—not the guarantee, but the potential—for that victory was always present in the little-heeded constitutional mandate of 'equal protection of the laws'.[59] The tasks ahead of South Africa are by no means the same as those still challenging the United States almost four decades after *Brown*. As we have seen in this book, however, South African law too

[58] *Brown* v. *Board of Education*, 347 US 483 (1954).
[59] US Const., amend. XIV, s. 1.

contains potential support for human rights, even though it still is without an authoritative declarations of constitutional rights. With this perspective in mind, we can similarly value the intellectual and moral potential still inherent in South African law, and the prizes to be won by pressing, at the bar, on the bench, in the academy, and in the dock, for that potential to be realized.

INDEX

Lightning Source UK Ltd.
Milton Keynes UK
UKHW022304251118
332870UK00004B/554/P

9 780198 256663